PREACHING
ON THE WORDS
OF JESUS

252.07
C4672p

PREACHING ON THE WORDS OF JESUS

4 Books in 1

Clovis G. Chappell

Contains the complete text of
The Sermon on the Mount
Sermons from the Miracles
Questions Jesus Asked
The Seven Words

BakerBooks

A Division of Baker Book House Co.
Grand Rapids, Michigan 49516

To
Mr. and Mrs. R. D. Hart
with affectionate appreciation

To
Polly,
latest and littlest
of our dear grandbabies

To
my two brothers
who were ministers,
Edwin and Ashley,
with tender and grateful memories

CONTENTS

PUBLISHER'S PREFACE

He was first of all a preacher. "Dr. Clovis Chappell was every where acknowledged as one of the outstanding American preachers of his day," wrote Bishop Roy H. Short in 1978. "For forty years he filled some of the strongest pulpits of the Methodist denomination, among them Mount Vernon Place Church in the national capital, and a number of great downtown churches in the South and Southwest."[1]

Clovis Gillham Chappell (1882–1972) was also an author, whose 37 books appeared over a span of 52 years (see fig. 1). These volumes consisted of his sermons, and a representative from his publisher said in 1962 that he had more than 8.5 million sermons in print.

In his *History of Preaching,* Ralph G. Turnbull selects three men to represent the best of Southern preaching during the first half of the twentieth century: two Baptists, George W. Truett and Robert G. Lee, and Methodist Clovis G. Chappell.

"Wherever he served," writes Turnbull of Chappell, "he preached to full churches as people waited upon his word with eagerness. He stood in the mainstream of

Fig. 1
Chappell's Publications

1	1921	*"The Village Tragedy" and Other Sermons*	Williams & Wilkins
2	1922	*Sermons on Biblical Characters*	Doran
3	1923	*The Modern Dance*	Methodist Episcopal Church South
4	1923	*More Sermons on Biblical Characters*	Doran
5	1924	*Sermons on New Testament Characters*	Doran
6	1925	*Sermons on Old Testament Characters*	Doran
7	1926	*Home Folks*	Cokesbury
8	1927	*Familiar Failures*	Doran
9	1928	*Christ and the New Woman*	Cokesbury
10	1929	*Men That Count*	Doubleday, Doran
11	1930	*The Sermon on the Mount*	Cokesbury
12	1931	*Sermons from the Psalms*	Cokesbury
13	1933	*Sermons from the Parables*	Cokesbury
14	1934	*Sermons on the Lord's Prayer*	Cokesbury
15	1936	*Chappell's Special Day Sermons*	Cokesbury
16	1937	*Sermons from the Miracles*	Cokesbury
17	1938	*Ten Rules for Living*	Cokesbury
18	1939	*Values That Last*	Cokesbury
19	1940	*The Road to Certainty*	Cokesbury
20	1941	*Faces about the Cross*	Abingdon-Cokesbury
21	1942	*Feminine Faces*	Abingdon-Cokesbury
22	1943	*Sermons from Revelation*	Abingdon-Cokesbury
23	1944	*Living Zestfully*	Abingdon-Cokesbury
24	1945	*If I Were Young*	Abingdon-Cokesbury
25	1946	*And the Prophets*	Abingdon-Cokesbury
26	1948	*Questions Jesus Asked*	Abingdon-Cokesbury
27	1950	*When the Church Was Young*	Abingdon-Cokesbury
28	1951	*Anointed to Preach*	Abingdon-Cokesbury
29	1952	*The Seven Words*	Abingdon-Cokesbury
30	1953	*In Parables*	Abingdon-Cokesbury
31	1956	*Meet These Men*	Abingdon
32	1957	*Sermons from Job*	Abingdon
33	1959	*Sermons on Simon Peter*	Abingdon
34	1960	*The Cross before Calvary*	Abingdon
35	1962	*Living with Royalty*	Abingdon
36	1967	*Surprises in the Bible*	Abingdon
37	1973	*Evangelistic Sermons of Clovis G. Chappell*	Abingdon

the Methodist tradition and while loyal to that background he proclaimed the gospel to hungry people with the zeal of his heritage."[2]

During his forty-one years in the pastorate, Chappell served churches in Texas, Oklahoma, Tennessee, Alabama, Mississippi, and North Carolina. He occupied major pulpits in such cities as Dallas, Washington D.C., Memphis, Houston, and Birmingham. His nephew and biographer, Wallace D. Chappell, writes that "he served more downtown churches than any minister with whom I have been familiar."[3]

After his retirement in 1962, he was an itinerant minister, which had him preaching annually an average of 250 to 300 sermons! By one estimate, he preached 5,000 times during these years.

Obviously Chappell loved to preach. When giving a series of lectures to students, faculty, and visiting ministers at Emory University's Candler School of Theology, Chappell made this clear: "I have so loved my vocation that it has been without a rival. While I honor other callings, they have been as starlight to sunlight in comparison with preaching the unsearchable riches of Christ."[4] These lectures were published in 1951 as *Anointed to Preach*.

Chappell's first book had appeared thirty years earlier when two laymen of Mount Vernon Place Church obtained their pastor's permission to publish, at their own expense, a selection of his sermons. "This kind of manuscript clicked almost immediately," writes Wallace Chappell, "and within a very few years his sermons were being widely read across America."[5]

His first real publisher was George H. Doran, who got his start in publishing at Fleming H. Revell Company (now a division of Baker Book House) before beginning his own company. Doran, a general publisher with a strong line of religious titles, released Chappell's second book, *Sermons on Biblical Characters,* in 1922. Five more books followed, but not before Chappell established a relationship with his denomination's publishing arm.

The Methodists organized Cokesbury Press in 1923, and three years later *Home Folks* appeared, Chappell's first book to bear this imprint. Many more followed. In all, 29 of Chappell's books bore the Cokesbury, Abingdon-Cokesbury, or Abingdon imprints, and of these volumes the company sold about 600,000 copies.

What made his books so popular? "His themes were primarily biblical, but he made large use of human experiences, his own and those of others; and [he] used many references from literature," writes Walter Newton Vernon Jr. "He impressed his readers with his sincerity, earnestness, and humility. He made effective use of stories and of humor."[6]

The four books that comprise *Preaching on the Words of Jesus* were originally published during the Depression and the post-War years: *The Sermon on the Mount* in 1930, *Sermons from the Miracles* in 1937, *Questions Jesus Asked* in 1948, and *The Seven Words* in 1952.

PUBLISHER'S PREFACE

Baker Book House Company first reprinted these titles in the 1960s and 1970s and is pleased to offer them now in a single binding. This four-books-in-one edition is released with the hope that many readers will discover Clovis G. Chappell for the first time.

Wallace Chappell described his uncle as "a great man whose message was timely and timeless and whose ministry lives on in the lives of countless ministers and laymen."[7] May *Preaching on the Words of Jesus* extend Clovis Chappell's ministry well into the twenty-first century!

1. Wallace D. Chappell, *Preacher of the Word* (Nashville: Broadman, 1978), 3.

2. Ralph G. Turnbull, *A History of Preaching*, vol. 3, *From the Close of the Nineteenth Century to the Middle of the Twentieth Century* . . . (Grand Rapids: Baker, 1974), 219.

3. Chappell, *Preacher of the Word*, 27.

4. Clovis G. Chappell, *Anointed to Preach* (New York: Abingdon-Cokesbury, 1951), 28–29.

5. Chappell, *Preacher of the Word*, 59.

6. Walter Newton Vernon Jr., *The United Methodist Publishing House: A History*, vol. 2, *1870–1988* (Nashville: Abingdon, 1989), 270.

7. Chappell, *Preacher of the Word*, 6.

BOOK 1

THE SERMON
ON THE MOUNT

CONTENTS

I

POVERTY THAT MAKES RICH

Matthew 5: 3

"Blessed are the poor in spirit: for theirs is the kingdom of heaven."

WHAT an audience this is that faces the Master!
The inner circle is made up of his special friends.
Beyond them stretch acres of human faces. It is a
vast throng. It is made up of all kinds and conditions of men. It is a cross-section of humanity.
There are the successful and the failures. There
are those who have conquered and those who have
been defeated. There are the rich and the poor.
There are the literate and the illiterate. They are,
doubtless, of varied races and varied religious
creeds. In fact, as Jesus speaks to this multitude
he is speaking to a miniature world.

But as he looks into their faces, as he looks beyond their faces into their hearts, he sees that they
are all out on the same quest. They are all seeking
for the same thing. Most of them are seeking
blunderingly. They have been disappointed and
are doomed to further and deeper disappointment.
The pathos of their blind gropings lays hold on the
Master's heart. It suggests to him a theme for the
sermon of the hour. "Every heart here," he says
to himself, "is in search of happiness. But they

have missed the way, most of them. I can do nothing better than point out the way that they have missed." Therefore he said: "Blessed are the poor in spirit: for theirs is the kingdom of heaven."

The audience that Jesus faced in that long ago is very close akin to the audience he would face were he to come to our city this morning. The heart of humanity remains unchanged through the years. Were he to stand in Court Square to-day and speak, he would still be moved with compassion as he looked upon the multitude. He would still see them scattered and harassed as sheep without a shepherd. He would still find folks doing a thousand different things in order to be truly happy. He would only find a few who had laid hold on the open secret that is so often hid from the wise and prudent and revealed unto babes. He would take little account of our scientific discoveries and inventions. He would tell us that the roadway to happiness is the same to-day that it was nineteen centuries ago. He would have no better direction to give than that given in our text.

And Jesus can speak with authority about happiness, because it was his constant possession. I am not forgetting that he was a man of sorrows and acquainted with grief. But in spite of that his was the gladdest heart that ever beat in a human bosom. His was the sunniest face that ever looked out on this world. And those who share his poverty of spirit share his happiness. Sorrow may come, but it will only be temporary. "Joy cometh with the

10

morning." It is happiness that abides. It is sorrow and sighing that flee away

1

Who are the blessed folks? Who are those that find real happiness?

Jesus makes it plain at once that our happiness is not born of any outward conditions or circumstances. This is a truth that lies right on the surface. It is one that has been established by the experiences of countless millions, yet it seems that every man has to learn it for himself. We still have a feeling that the happy man is the one who achieves outward success. Blessed is the man who makes a fortune. Blessed is he who can write a check in seven figures. Happy is the man who has a palace in the city and a summer palace by the sea or in the mountains. Blessed is the man that has won the applause of his fellows. Blessed is the woman who has become the darling of society. But Jesus says that happiness is not born of what we have.

No more is it born of what we fail to have. When Luke reports this sermon he says: "Blessed are the poor." But poverty is not in itself a blessing. Since it tends to give one a sense of need, it may more readily become a roadway to real happiness than riches. Riches tend to give a false independence. But no man is necessarily blessed simply because he is poor. Nor is any man necessarily unblessed because he is rich. Dives blundered out into the dark. Lazarus found a place in Abraham's

11

bosom. But Dives was not condemned because he was rich, any more than Lazarus was saved because he was poor. One may be just as poor as Lazarus and yet be greedy and grasping and wretched, while another may be as rich as Dives and yet be truly blessed.

When I was a boy there was a rather notorious character in our community who pretended to farm. In reality, however, with the coming of spring the song of Buffalo River cast its spell upon him, and he went fishing practically every day. Now and then, on Saturday afternoons, some farmer who had caught up with his work would go fishing and get Uncle Zeke's fishing place. This gentleman would return from his noon meal to find himself crowded out. Then he would say piously: "You can stay here and fish if you like; I have a family to support." With that he would turn on his heels, go out to the little village, borrow a chew of tobacco, and sit in front of the store and talk theology. And this is what he would say: "Well, I'd rather be a poor man and go to heaven than be a rich man and go to hell." But nobody ever believed that Uncle Zeke was absolutely sure of entrance into the pearly gates simply because he was miserably poor.

Happiness depends not upon what we have, nor upon what we do, but upon what we are. If we seek happiness on the outside, we shall miss it forever. Happiness, if it ever comes, must come from within. It does not depend upon the kind of house in which we live; it depends upon the kind of man that lives in the house. It does not depend upon the kind of garments in which we dress; it depends upon the kind of individual that is dressed. The kind of man that is happy, said Jesus, is the man that is poor in spirit. He arrives, and he alone.

How utterly ridiculous this must have sounded to some who were listening! How absurd was such a declaration to that Roman, for instance, whose nation had its foot on the neck of the world! How absurd it must have sounded to the Jews who were even more proud than the Roman! It still sounds unbelievable enough even to us. There were those that heard it that day who glanced at each other knowingly, shrugged their shoulders, and swaggered off down the mountain side saying that the Preacher was mad and that there was nothing of real worth in what he was saying. We try to be a little more respectful, yet there are millions to-day who are just as far from believing this statement as the audience to which it was first spoken.

"Blessed are the poor in spirit." "Maybe so," you reply, "yet I cannot work up any enthusiasm for such poverty." But even if you are only half convinced that the poor in spirit are blessed, of one thing you may be sure—that the proud in spirit are unblessed. Here is a truth that not many will deny: Wretched are the proud in spirit. Did you ever see one afflicted with proud flesh? Proud flesh is about the most sensitive something that I know. There is only one thing that is more sensitive and that is a proud spirit. You may be proud of your pride, but

13

of this you may be sure—it is a certain road to wretchedness. Miserable are the proud in spirit. Happy are the poor in spirit.

II

But what does Jesus mean by poverty of spirit? Maybe our lack of enthusiasm for this treasure grows out of our misunderstanding. To be poor in spirit does not mean self-contempt. Jesus never tells us to despise ourselves. He never asks any man to crawl and cringe and grovel. He discovered to us the worth of the individual. He believed that the meanest human soul had immeasurable possibilities, might realize a glorious destiny. To be poor in spirit, therefore, is not to despise yourself. It is not to look upon yourself with contempt. It is to be humble, childlike, teachable, ready to lean upon a higher power.

In order to really understand poverty of spirit it is necessary to see it become incarnate in a personality; otherwise it tends to remain a mere abstraction. The same is true even of so familiar a something as love. I asked a group of little folks sometime ago, "What is love?" and they were utterly silent. I then asked: "Did you ever see any love?" At once every hand went up. They could not define love according to the International Dictionary. Even if they could have done so they would have been little the wiser. But they knew love, none the less. They had seen love become human life. This they had done as they had looked into mother's face

14

and had felt the kiss of mother's lips and experienced the tender ministry of mother's hands.

Where, then, shall we look for poverty of spirit? Maybe the ten spies will serve as an illustration. They went into Canaan to spy out the land. They came back with a sense of their utter littleness and worthlessness. They declared whimperingly: "We saw the giants that live over there, and we were in our own eyes as grasshoppers. There is no use to undertake to go forward with the enterprise. We can never succeed. God has done nothing more than play a grim joke on us. The whole enterprise is no more than madness." But these men were not poor in spirit; they were poor spirited, and nothing more.

Then we might try the man with one talent. One day he came from his master's presence with a treasure in his hand. That treasure indicated that he was trusted. It showed that his master had confidence in him. He gripped it proudly and thought of the many high adventures that he was going to have with it on the marts of trade. But as he was going to make his first venture he met a friend who had two talents. That dampened his ardor somewhat. Then he met another who had five. After that his zest and ardor went ice cold. He said: "This one little talent is nothing in comparison with what these others have. I will stand no chance at all." So he crept away back home, slunk out into the garden as the shadows gathered, and hid his talent in the earth. But he was not poor in

15

spirit; he was full of pride and fuller still of cowardice.

Where, then, shall we go? Answer: to Jesus himself. These beatitudes are descriptions of the character of our Lord. It is to him, therefore, that we go to find one who in the deepest and fullest sense was poor in spirit. He was so poor in spirit that he said: "I can of mine own self do nothing." He was so poor in spirit that he one day girt himself with a towel and washed the feet of a little handful of men, fishermen and taxgatherers and such like. What a menial task! It was far too mean for any of the disciples. Had I been host that day I might have said to Peter: "Simon, the servants are all out. There is no one here to wash the feet of my guests. You are the leader among them. Suppose you do it." Simon was an excellent man, but he would have bristled and said: "Are you talking to me? You think I am going to wash the feet of Judas and Thomas, of James and John? They are always arguing with me that they are going to be greater than I in the kingdom. If their feet don't get washed till I do it, they will go unwashed forever. Are you trying to insult me?" "No," I might have answered, "I am trying to crown you."

But what none other would do Jesus did. Why? Because he had no respect for himself? No, that was not the reason. Look at the state of his mind as he did this. "Knowing that he was come from God and went to God." That is, when he was conscious of his divine origin, when he was conscious

16

that he was going to sit down at the right hand of his Father to receive a name that is above every name, then he girt himself with the towel. Here is true poverty of spirit. Here also is manhood at its best.

III

Why is it that poverty of spirit leads to happiness?

1. It is through poverty of spirit that we come into possession of the kingdom of God. Not that the kingdom is given to us as reward. There is nothing arbitrary about it. "Blessed are the poor in spirit: for theirs is the kingdom of heaven." Such enter naturally, and the door is closed to all others. One day when the disciples were having one of their oft-recurring disputes as to who should be greatest they brought the matter to Jesus. In answer to their question Jesus took a little child and set him in the midst of them and said that the most childlike should be the greatest. Not only so, but that without childlikeness, which is none other than humility or poverty of spirit, it is impossible to enter the kingdom at all. "Except ye be converted, and become as little children, ye shall not enter into the kingdom of heaven."

Jesus told a story of two brothers. The older brother was a steady, hard-working chap who seemed altogether dependable. He kept constantly at home and gave himself with diligence to his duties. But his brother was a waster. He ran

17

away and squandered the wealth his father had given him in riotous living. But though this elder son remained at home and worked, there was never a feast given in his honor. He himself said he had never had so much as a kid with which to make merry with his friends. But one day, as he was returning from the field, he was greeted by the sound of music. He came a little nearer, and the whole household was astir with wildest revelry and joy. Naturally he was concerned to know what was going on. Therefore he called a servant and asked what it meant, and the servant said: "Your brother has come home, and your father has killed for him the fatted calf."

Little wonder that this steady worker was a bit indignant at the turn things had taken! Why did the father show such seeming partiality? It was not that he cared nothing for hard work, but rather set a premium on dissipation. The difference in the treatment of these two sons grew out of what they were in themselves. The elder son reveals himself thoroughly. "Lo, these many years do I serve thee, neither transgressed I at any time thy commandment." That is, he insists that he had never sinned; he had always been perfectly upright. He was, therefore, in no sense poor in spirit. The younger son, on the other hand, had nothing better to say for himself than, "I have sinned against heaven, and before thee, and am no more worthy to be called thy son." The doors of the feast opened before him automatically, because he was poor in spirit.

2. Then, it is only through poverty of spirit that we remain in the kingdom. Pride certainly goes before destruction, and a haughty spirit before a fall. There is a deal of truth in that classic story of the frog that decided to seek a warmer climate. At first he could think of no fit conveyance in which to go. At last he hit upon this happy contrivance. There were two wild geese that were friends of his. He found a string and asked each one of the geese to take an end. As they did so, he seized the string in the middle. These geese rose into the air, and the frog found himself hurrying toward the land of his dreams. But a spectator from far below, looking up, saw the strange sight and shouted: "Who invented that?" The frog's pride would not allow him to keep silent. He shouted back: "I invented that." But in so doing he let go of the string, and his questioner a moment later was looking upon a bit of minced frog. As in the case of a vast multitude, his pride had been his ruin.

Jesus had a friend who was devoted to him. But this friend was at times a bit proud in spirit. Jesus saw that this was going to undo him, so he undertook to warn him. "All ye shall be offended because of me this night." And Peter took it as personal and denied it flatly. He said: "I cannot speak for these others, James and John and Andrew and the rest. They may fail you, but you can certainly count on me. Though I should die with thee, yet will I not deny thee." And Peter went out in the strength of this confidence to utterly fail. No wonder when he had wept his way back to God he urged his friends to clothe themselves with humility as with a garment. "God resisteth the proud, but gives grace to the humble."

3. Then, poverty of spirit leads to blessedness because it fits us to serve in the kingdom. When the wise man names the six things that God hates, one of them is a proud look. In that we are exactly like him. No one offends us more deeply than the individual who undertakes to lord it over us. It is the man who identifies himself with us, the man of poverty of spirit whose ministry we welcome and find helpful. "Brethren, if a man be overtaken in a fault, ye who are spiritual restore such an one in the spirit of meekness." It is the only way we can restore them. If we go in the spirit of pride, in the spirit of self-sufficiency, we shall repel rather than restore.

F. B. Meyer tells this story: On one occasion he was stopping at a hotel in Norway where there was a little girl who was very fond of playing the piano. But she played only one tune, and played this with just one finger. Naturally she became a bit of a nuisance. When the guests were awakened by her each morning, they would endure it as long as possible, then make their escape as best they could. Now, it so happened that one of the greatest pianists of Norway came that way. He was awakened the next morning along with other guests by this tuneless pecking on the piano. He hurriedly dressed and went down into the parlor that the little girl had all to herself. He made himself acquainted with her, told her that he knew the song that she was playing, and asked that he might play it with her. She consented, for she was poor in spirit. He, therefore, took her upon his lap and drowned her discord with his own marvelous melody. And so it may be for ourselves. If in true humility we give first place to the Supreme Master, he will surely touch our heart harp and change its blundering discord into the exquisite music of abiding blessedness.

II

BLESSED MOURNERS

Matthew 5: 4

"Blessed are they that mourn: for they shall be comforted."

WHAT a strange paradox! How flatly it contradicts the accepted views of our day and of every day! Who thinks of congratulating a man because his face is wet with tears? Who thinks of congratulating him because he carries a heavy burden and an aching heart? We pity such. We should no more think of envying a man with tear-blinded eyes than we should think of writing a letter of condolence to some son of good fortune who was managing to get through life without ever receiving a wound or ever struggling under a heavy load. "Blessed are they that mourn," says Jesus. But we cannot agree, so we mark it out and write: "Blessed are the tearless."

But our Lord persists in pronouncing a blessing on the mourners. To his mind the supreme tragedy is that of the tearless eye and the heart without tenderness. You remember how Father Damien went as a missionary to the lepers of far-off Molokai. For thirteen years he shared their Gethsemane. For thirteen years he was their teacher and companion and friend. At last the dread disease laid hold of him. At first he was not aware of it, but one morning he chanced to spill some boiling water on his foot. "How painful!" you say. No, there was not the slightest pain. It was this that told him of his doom. His loss of sensitiveness informed him in language not to be mistaken that death was creeping on him from out the dark.

But there is a far sadder loss than that of physical sensitiveness, even though that loss be the messenger of death. That is the loss of our spiritual sensitiveness. In one of his epistles Paul makes use of a most startling and arresting word. He speaks of certain individuals as being "past feeling." Their sensory nerves had atrophied. They were as incapable of suffering, as completely invulnerable, as the dead. Such loss of feeling indicates something far worse than the death of the body. It indicates the death of the soul. And, mark you, this frightful tragedy was not confined to Paul's day. It has its victims among us who are of the living present.

Yesterday, for instance, you committed a certain sin. But your conscience did not pain you. It did not stuff thorns in your pillow last night when you tried to sleep. That sin had been so persistently repeated that it could now be committed without any pang at all. Recently you heard a sermon that once would have broken your heart. Once such an appeal would have made your very soul leap within you with hope and longing. But to-day it leaves you as unmoved and undisturbed as the pew upon which you sit. Once you could not have passed

23

one who was wounded by the wayside. His suffering would have touched you. You would have bled through his wounds, you would have suffered in his anguish, even though that anguish was of the spirit rather than of the flesh. But now you can look upon the most desperate spiritual need with an indifferent eye.

Some years ago I knew a father of beautiful character and deep devotion. He had a wayward and worthless son. I saw him go to that boy one day and make such an appeal as I have seldom heard. He spilt his hot words of tenderness along with his hot tears upon that son. But the boy seemed neither to hear the words nor feel the tears. He felt the burning yearning and anguish of his father no more than the heroic missionary felt the boiling water upon his foot. But the loss suffered by the wayward boy was infinitely greater than that suffered by the missionary.

"Blessed are they that mourn." Of course Jesus does not mean that every mourner is necessarily blessed. Tears are not good in and of themselves. There are tears, thank God, that seem to wash bright the eyes and spread beauty on the cheeks as they flow. They seem to water the gardens of the heart and set the fields of the soul to flowering. But there are other tears that leave the eyes smarting and blinded. They fret channels upon the cheeks and scorch and wither the verdure of the heart. There are, then, mourners whose mourning brings them no comfort. There are others whose

24

mourning is the open roadway to heavenly consolation.

I

Among those mourners whose mourning leaves them without comfort we may mention the following:

1. The deliberate pessimist. There are those who are veritable gluttons for wretchedness. They search for despair as bees search for honey. They are never so happy as when they feel that they have a perfect right to be miserable. They are never so miserable as when they feel duty bound to be happy. They make Paul's beautiful words read like this: "Finally, brethren, whatsoever things are false, whatsoever things are dishonest, whatsoever things are unjust, whatsoever things are impure, whatsoever things are unlovely, whatsoever things are of evil report, if there be any vice, and if there be any condemnation, think on these things." So they think, and so thinking mourn, but their mourning brings no comfort.

2. Neither is one necessarily blessed for mourning over some selfish loss or thwarted ambition. I knew a man years ago who seemed to have a veritable passion for popularity. He was keenly ambitious to lead. But his plans went awry, and I cannot but think of him to-day as a most unhappy man. But his mourning brings him no consolation. It would be hard to find a more tragic mourner than Napoleon in his lonely exile. His crown had been

snatched from his brow, his scepter wrenched from his hands. But his mourning was not the pathway to blessedness. What a mourner was Dean Swift! "It is awful," says Thackeray, "to think of the great suffering of this great man. . . . As fierce a beak and talon as ever struck, . . . as strong a wing as ever beat belonged to Swift. I am glad, for one, that fate wrested the prey out of his claws, and cut his wings and chained him. One can gaze, not without awe and pity, at the lonely eagle chained behind the bars." A pathetic mourner, indeed, but one without comfort.

3. Not even are those necessarily blessed who have suffered the loss of some loved one. Of course such loss has been the roadway to comfort for multitudes. Elisha was never the same after he had seen Elijah go home. You have not been the same since your baby died. You have had a different feeling about God, about the reality of the unseen, since you kneeled by the coffin of your mother. But even this kind of loss does not always bring blessed results. I recall a mother who belonged to my church in another city. This mother lost her boy. But she was not made soft and tender by her sorrow. She was made hard and bitter and rebellious. If I were out searching for one of the most miserable beings in all the world, I should certainly knock at her door.

4. Nor are those blessed whose mourning is born of remorse. There are many sinners who mourn, but their mourning is not always born of any hatred

26

of sin. They do not hate evil, they hate its effects. Our jails and penitentiaries are full of people who mourn, but their mourning does not always bring them comfort. Jesus tells us that hell is full of mourners, people who weep and wail; but their tears bring no blessing, and their sorrow is without consolation. Therefore it is possible to mourn, and mourn deeply, and yet find no benediction.

II

Who, then, are those whose mourning ends in comfort?

Speaking broadly, this is true of every one whose mourning leads to Jesus Christ. Whatever your sorrow, whatever your burden, whatever your heartache, if it turns your blundering steps toward him, you are sure to find consolation and comfort. How many could testify to the truth of this! Some of you could stand in your places even now and tell how the blackest days of your lives became, through the riches of his grace, roadways into the brightest of mornings. The very thing that you thought would work your ruin has been your remaking. The rough path of yesterday that seemed all thorns and jagged rocks has become strangely smooth under your weary feet. You would not now exchange your bitterest sorrow for the world's rarest joy. This is true because it was through that desperate night of agony that you were led to seek and to find Jesus.

But the mourning that the Master especially has

27

in mind is mourning over sin. This beatitude follows naturally upon the heels of the one preceding. "Blessed are the poor in spirit," Jesus said in the first. Blessed is the man who is conscious that he is not what he should be. Blessed is the man with a sense of need, the man who realizes that he can of himself do nothing. But our beatitude goes further. Blessed is the man who is not only conscious of his failure, but who grieves over it, who takes it to heart. Blessed is the man who is so grieved over his moral and spiritual lack that he turns his face toward Him who is able to supply his need.

The knowledge of our spiritual poverty would be of little worth unless it led to mourning. It would avail little for the prodigal to realize that he was away in the far country by the swine trough should such realization bring him no grief. It would count for nothing for him to be conscious of his hunger if he should content himself with the husks that the swine did eat. The tragedy of his plight must strike home to his heart. He must be so tortured by it that he will loathe the thing that he is. He must be so tortured that he will resolve to rise and go to his father. So often our poverty is without a pang. So often our very confessions of sin are cold and formal. They do not burst from us hot with shame and wet with tears. Too few care enough to mourn. Therefore we do not find the consolation and the strength promised in our text.

Not only are those blessed who mourn for their

own sins, but there is blessing and comfort for those who mourn over the sins of others. Jesus was this kind of mourner. Let us remember that these beatitudes, while partially describing the children of the kingdom, far more accurately describe the character of the Master himself. "Himself took our infirmities, and bare our sorrows." Blessed, therefore, is the man that shares with Jesus the pain and anguish of a world gone wrong. Blessed is the man who enters into the fellowship of his suffering. Blessed is he that fills up that which is lacking of the suffering of Christ in his own body. Blessed is he who struggles under the weight of another's woe, who cries: "I will gladly spend and be spent for you; though the more I love, the less I be loved."

III

What is the natural outcome of such mourning? Those who so mourn are comforted. They are strengthened and consoled.

1. That is true of those who mourn because of their own sin. The outcome of such mourning is reconciliation with God. It ends in pardon and peace that passeth all understanding. Here, for instance, is a young man in great anguish. "Woe is me," he cries desperately, "for I am undone. I am a man of unclean lips." The careless world looks on with amazement and pity. "Why does he take things so hard? Why does he not throw it off and forget about it?" But do not pity him. He is on the threshold of a great discovery. He is entering

29

upon a new day. For a live coal is laid upon his lips, and a voice whispers: "Lo, this has touched thy lips, and thine iniquity is taken away, and thy sin purged." His mourning was the gateway to comfort.

Here is another miserable creature whose agony is utterly amazing. He is not a weak man; he is one of the world's strong men. Yet the tragic cry that is wrung from him by his pain makes us shudder after all these centuries. "O wretched man that I am! who shall deliver me?" "Poor fellow," one says, "he is too sensitive." But again I say, dare not pity him. He is on the point of entering upon a new world. "Who shall deliver me?" He cries desperately: "God will and does. He does it through Jesus Christ. 'There is therefore now no condemnation to them that are in Christ Jesus.'"

But, mark you, this mourning must be mourning for sin and not simply for its consequences. There are two outstanding sinners in the Old Testament whose paths cross. One is Saul, the other is David. Saul sinned and sinned deeply, though not so deeply as David. Saul confessed his sin, too. He confessed more often than any other man in the Bible. Saul was a mourner. But he never mourned except for the evil plight into which his sin brought him. He never learned to hate sin itself. He never confessed his sin except when he was in a tight corner and there seemed no other way of escape except through confession. Therefore he died uncomforted and unblessed.

But with David it was different. What a desperate sinner he was, and how he suffered! His moisture was turned into drought of summer. The garden of his heart became a burning desert. At last he burst into God's presence and threw himself at his feet and prayed: "Have mercy upon me, O God, according to thy loving-kindness: according to the multitude of thy tender mercies blot out my transgressions." "Create in me a clean heart, O God. Deliver me from bloodguiltiness." His heart is broken over his sin. And what is the outcome? His sobbing is changed into song. "Blessed is he whose transgression is forgiven, whose sin is covered."

There are also two outstanding sinners in the New Testament whose paths cross. They are Peter and Judas. Peter through cowardice committed a sin close akin to that of Judas. But when Peter realized the wound that he had inflicted upon the Master whom he loved and who loved him, it broke his heart. He wept his way back to the cross. Jesus could hardly wait till he had got the door of his tomb open before he gave Peter a private interview. After that he trusted him with the delicate task of feeding his lambs and being the shepherd of his sheep. Judas also mourned. But there was no grief for wounded love in his tears. Therefore his mourning brought him nothing better than a hangman's noose and a grave in the potter's field.

Then there is comfort and consolation for those who mourn over the sins of others. This is the case,

31

not because such mourning is cheap; it is very costly. The tears of Jesus were not shallow tears. He beheld the city and wept over it, but he did more than weep. He went down to cleanse its temple. He went down to plead with its crowds. He went down to die for its heedless and hating multitudes. And if we mourn as Jesus our grief must not be the shallow grief of the votary of the movies who wipes his eyes that have grown wet over some imaginary sorrow that he forgets as soon as the show is over. It must be a grief that sends us out to share with Jesus in his efforts to save the world.

Paul was a mourner after this fashion. What burdens he carried, and how gladly he carried them! He speaks again and again of his tears. He tells us that he has suffered the loss of all things. He knew the inside of numerous Roman prisons. There was scarcely a square inch of his body that did not bear a scar. He was always giving himself eagerly, gladly. His life was a daily dying. He writes out "of much affliction and anguish of heart." In his solicitude for others he has "great heaviness and continual sorrow." He has a passion to save that will give him no rest.

But, so burdened, is he not miserable? No, strange to say, he is the most joyful of men. The lilt of his song rings with amazing sweetness and gladness through prison cells. Though he is writing in great anguish of heart and with tears, even in the midst of these tears he cannot repress a shout of genuine gladness. "Blessed be God, even the

Father of our Lord Jesus Christ, the Father of mercies, and the God of all comfort; who comforteth us in all our tribulation. . . . For as the sufferings of Christ abound in us, so our consolation also aboundeth by Christ." "The greater the mourning," says Paul, "the greater the comfort." It is perfectly natural that it should be so. The more we mourn after this fashion, the more dead we become to self. The more dead we become to self, the more alive we become to God. It is when self dies under the stroke of the cross that we can truly sing:

"Only the sorrows of others
Cast a shadow over me."

It is then that we enter most fully into the comfort which Jesus promises in our text.

Those who enter into the fellowship of Christ's suffering do find comfort. They find it not only by and by, but here and now. They find it in all circumstances, in all situations. Here, for instance, is a man clinging to a bit of wreckage in an icy sea. The Titanic upon which he was a passenger has just gone down. His freezing fingers can with difficulty keep their grip upon all that holds him from death amidst the creeping things at the bottom of the ocean. But there is no panic. He is strangely at leisure from himself. Therefore, when another bit of wreckage floats by in the dim twilight of the early morning, he thinks only of the needs of the man he sees clinging to it. He calls to him: "Young

man, are you saved?" "No," comes the answer.
"Believe on the Lord Jesus Christ, and thou shalt
be saved." And the young man then and there believed. He lived to tell the story. But the man
that flung open the door of life to him lost his hold
a moment later and was seen no more. But surely
he knew through his own experience in that testing
hour that God does give comfort to those who
mourn. There was a Presence with him more real
than death, a Presence that made the unstable
waters to become the very Rock of Ages under his
feet, that made the bit of wreckage to which he
clung the threshold of his Father's house.

III

THE MEEK

Matthew 5: 5

"Blessed are the meek: for they shall inherit the earth."

I

THIS beatitude is by no means popular. To the man of the world it makes the least possible appeal. In truth, I think it safe to say that it makes no appeal at all. This is true for at least two reasons. 1. Meekness is not looked upon by him as an asset. He regards it rather as a liability. He is by no means convinced that the meek are really blessed. He is not at all sure that they are to be congratulated. He thinks it possible that they are to be despised. He feels at times that they might well be looked on with contempt. Occasionally they are to be pitied. But surely they are not to be looked upon as having come into possession of a truly worthful treasure. Who really desires to be meek? Most of us would be ashamed of such a virtue. We regard meekness as little better than a synonym for weakness. A newspaper spoke recently of a certain man who had assisted his dominant paramour in the killing of her husband as "a meek little murderer."

2. Then, the man of the world objects to this text because he does not believe it true that the meek

shall inherit the earth. In fact, he feels that there is no group that is less likely to inherit the earth than the meek. He is ready enough to believe that they will go to heaven when they die; but as for inheriting the earth in the life that now is, nothing could be farther from the truth. He believes in the survival of the fittest. He believes the most fit to survive in a world like ours is the aggressive, heavy-handed, hard-fisted, self-assertive man. What chance has the meek in a world where it seems so evident that the race is always to the swift, and the battle to the strong?

Now, there is no shutting our eyes to the fact that this position seems quite sane. It seems shot through with an abundance of good common sense. "Blessed are the meek; for they shall inherit the earth." How ridiculous that would look if it were framed and hung as a motto in many a business office! How out of place it would sound to many, if heard amidst the busy rush of our city streets or the loud hum of our factories. Yet it would certainly sound no more ridiculous to us than it did to those to whom it was first spoken. It seemed little less than madness then. Yet Jesus believed in the truthfulness of it and said so with conviction. Were he to come amidst the hustle and push of our modern life, he would still say with calm and quiet confidence: "Blessed are the meek: for they shall inherit the earth." And we, sad to say, would be almost as far from believing him as was the multitude on the mountain side. There are still all too few who look upon this beatitude with appreciation and confidence.

II

But if meekness seems small and worthless to many of ourselves, there is no shutting our eyes to the fact that this was not the case with those saints whom we meet upon the pages of the Bible. It is especially not the case with the writers of the New Testament. Take Paul for example. No cowardly weakling was he. He was one of the most dauntless of men. He admired those virtues that are virile and masterly. He declared proudly: "We Christians are not cowards." He rejoiced that God has not given us a spirit of fearfulness, but of power and of love and of a sound mind. No one would have been further than he from urging his friends to seek a cheap and flimsy virtue. But one day he wrote a letter to Timothy, his own son in the faith. Timothy, you remember, was a young man who really never succeeded in growing up. He was sickly. He was timid and retiring. Yet Paul urges this timid youth to "follow after meekness." He is to pursue it. He is never to rest satisfied till he had enriched his spiritual life by the possession of this priceless virtue.

On another occasion this same author is writing to his converts at Colosse. He is telling them how to dress in a fashion becoming the sons and daughters of the King. He is instructing them how they are to clothe themselves so as to vastly enhance their

37

charm and usefulness. Therefore he writes this wise word: "Put on . . . meekness." It was his conviction that one garbed in this fine fashion would be equipped both for the life that now is and for that which is to come.

Again, in his letter to the Galatians Paul is telling us of some of the rare and winsome flowers that the Heavenly Gardener plants in the garden of the soul when he is allowed to have his way. "The fruit of the Spirit is love, joy, peace, long-suffering, gentleness, goodness, faithfulness, meekness." Meekness, then, is a fruit of the Spirit. It is a virtue so priceless, so altogether winsome that we cannot attain it in the energy of the flesh. It must come to us, if at all, through the power of the Spirit. It is, therefore, very evident that this aggressive, clear-thinking, and Christlike saint was convinced that meekness is not a liability, but a most worthful and beautiful asset.

A glance at the letters of Peter indicates that he was of the same opinion. In his first epistle he says: "Whose adorning let it not be outward, . . . but let it be the hidden man of the heart, . . . even the ornament of a meek and quiet spirit, which is in the sight of God of great price." He is aware of the fact that meekness often fails to look well in the eyes of men. He knows that we have a tendency to despise it, to regard it as utterly worthless. But it is not so looked upon by Him who sees things clearly and sees them whole. We often mistake the worthful for the worthless, and the worthless for the worthful. Often we mistake tinsel for fine gold, and gold for tinsel. We count of high value what God despises, and despises what He sees to be of abiding worth.

Years ago, we are told, there was a peddler who pushed a cart about the back streets of Paris earning a meager living by selling cheap jewelry and trifling gewgaws. Among his commonplace wares there was a bit of stone tagged with a dirty little card that bore this inscription; "Rock crystal, price twenty-four francs." It seemed for a long time that nobody wanted this piece of rock crystal. Of course the price was rather high for an object of such seemingly small value. But one day a man chanced to pass that way who had a seeing eye. He had ability to distinguish the worthless from the worthful, the best from the second best. He saw value in this bit of rock crystal that other eyes failed to see. In fact, he saw that it was not rock crystal at all, but genuine diamond. So he bought it, and that rare gem is now said to be among the royal jewels of a great nation. In the same fashion many tend to pass by the rare gem of meekness, while only the few realize its value and seek to possess it.

Then, when we ask what men of the Bible are the most conspicuous for their meekness, what do we find? For instance, who is the outstanding example of meekness in the Old Testament? He is not some despised weakling, he is not some nameless craven. The supreme example of meekness in the Old Testament is Moses. And what a superb man he is! He is a lawgiver of the highest order. He is a prophet. He is the builder of a nation. In fact, he is one of the genuinely great men of all time.

When we turn to the New Testament we find that the supreme example of meekness is none other than Jesus himself. When the evangelists tell of his entrance into Jerusalem, it is his meekness that they emphasize. Paul, writing to the Corinthians, beseeches them by the gentleness and meekness of Jesus. Even Jesus himself calls our attention to his possession of this fine virtue. "Learn of me," he says. And when he makes this appeal he does not base it upon his possession of wisdom, though in him are hidden all the treasures of wisdom and knowledge. But he says, rather: "Learn of me; for I am meek and lowly of heart." Meekness is his outstanding characteristic. It is the one virtue in himself to which he calls our attention. It is that which he seems most to desire us to imitate. Therefore we are safe in concluding that meekness is a virtue of real worth. Whatever makes us more like Moses, especially whatever makes us more like Jesus, will not impoverish, but will surely enrich us.

III

What is meekness? It is a word that is a bit difficult to define. One reason for this is that it has largely gone out of use. We do not employ it very often in our ordinary conversation. To some, therefore, it has almost no meaning at all, while to others it has a meaning that is inadequate, if not altogether erroneous. There are those, for instance, who think of the meek man as a rather spineless creature, gifted by nature with a sweet temper and a quick readiness to bow before every breeze. He is, therefore, to be tolerated only because he never takes a stand on any question, nor ever dares to get in anybody's way. But nothing could be further from the truth. What a hot-tempered man is Moses when we first meet him! He could strike a fellow being dead in his blazing anger without the slightest compunction. Yet he became the meekest of men. Meekness is, therefore, something far different from being merely good natured. It is far different from weakness. It is strength grown tender. It is might with a caress in its brawny hands. There is a word that is used in connection with meekness more than once. That word is "gentle." "The servant of the Lord must not strive, but be gentle, patient, apt to teach, in meekness instructing those that oppose themselves." Again: "Put them in mind, . . . that they be no brawlers, but gentle, showing all meekness to all men." That is, the meek folks are the gentle folks; the meek man is Christ's real gentleman.

Now, what are some of the characteristics of this Christian gentleman? Mark you, I am not describing what the world calls a gentleman. I am not undertaking to give the characteristics of the man who is commonly styled a gentleman in the social sense. I am not talking about him who is a gentleman by accident of gentle birth. I am talking about the man who is a gentleman by spiritual birth, the man who has come to possess, in some measure, the meekness and gentleness of Jesus. I am, therefore, talking about the highest type of gentleman.

> "Kind hearts are more than coronets,
> And simple faith than Norman blood."

1. This Christian gentleman is considerate of others. He does not insist upon having the best for himself. He does not elbow women and children out of the way in order to get on a street car first. He does not turn two seats together on the train while a woman with a crying baby in her arms is compelled to stand. He does not seek to push others to the rear of the procession in the rush of life. He is thoughtful of others. He is genuinely courteous. He never inflicts a needless wound. He lightens his brother's burden when he has opportunity. He gives to all men something of the fine consideration that was accorded by Jesus himself.

2. This gentleman has a sweet temper. He does not give himself the luxury of flying into a rage and speaking his mind. Now, I am aware of the fact that bad temper is not generally looked upon with very great disapproval. In fact, there are those who rather pride themselves on being quick to blaze and to let themselves go. But I think that Drummond was probably right in saying that bad temper causes more real suffering than almost any other one sin. This Christian gentleman refrains from anger, not because he has no temper, but because he controls his temper by the grace of God.

3. This gentleman is humble-minded. He does not swagger. He does not boast over his possessions or over his achievements. He does not see fit to be everlastingly informing the world about how good he is, or how much he has suffered, or how many crosses he bears for others. He has the child heart. He is teachable. He is ready to take the lowest place. He is so thoughtful of others that he forgets himself. He is Christlike in his humility.

4. This gentleman is courageous. He has the highest type of courage. He dares a terror before which many of the most lion-hearted quail. What do men fear most? It is not pain, nor death, nor sin. There is nothing of which the average man is more horribly afraid than of being thought a coward. We are ready to face almost any danger rather than that dread foe. But the meek man is so courageous that he dares look that terrible enemy in the face with quiet eyes. This he does because he longs, above all else, to be like Him who, "when he was reviled, reviled not again."

5. Christ's gentleman is strong. The gentle things are ever the strong things. Gravitation does not make any great noise, but how mighty it is! When Elijah stood in the mouth of his cave an earthquake shook the mountain. That suited the temper of the prophet. That was his idea of what God ought to do for the sinful of the world. But he discovered that God was not in the earthquake. He discovered, further, that he was neither in the roaring tempest, nor in the raging fire. He was rather in the voice

small and still. There are people yet who fancy that the power is in the thunder rather than in the lightning. But noise is not necessarily strong. It may be very weak. More than once have I heard loud talking and loud swearing made into a kind of smoke screen behind which some coward was seeking to hide his weakness. It is gentleness that is strong.

How did it come about that those money changers in the temple ran so readily at the approach of Jesus? Why did they not resist him? Why did they not hold their ground and defy him? Why did they not challenge his authority and demand that he show his credentials? They were not all cowards. Besides, their interests were at stake. To have their tables overturned and their business interfered with was both annoying and costly. Yet they fled wildly without counting the cost. Why was this the case? It would never have happened if Jesus had been no more than a mere dictatorial blusterer. That which made his anger so terrible was that it was the anger of the meek. That which made his wrath so irresistible was that it was "the wrath of the Lamb."

IV

Now, the text tells us that the blessing promised to the meek is that they shall inherit the earth. This, you know, is a quotation from the thirty-seventh Psalm. Jesus did not originate this word, but he read it and memorized it and believed it with all his heart. He believed it because it is true.

1. It is true literally. If we believe our Bibles, we believe that there is coming a day when Jesus is going to reign "from the rivers to the ends of the earth." We believe that the glory of God is one day going to cover the earth as the waters cover the sea. We believe that in spite of the seeming eternity and prosperity of wrong it is righteousness that is going to abide and to be finally triumphant. We believe that when Jesus taught us to pray, "Thy kingdom come," he was not teaching us to dream dreams that could never come true. He was teaching us to pray for that which is one day sure to be realized. And when that day comes there will not be a man in all the world who is not meek. When that day comes every man will be a gentleman.

2. Then, the meek are already entering upon their inheritance. They are coming more and more to possess the earth with the passing of the centuries. We recognize this fact among the lower orders of life. There certainly ought to be more eagles and hawks and owls than sparrows and doves and catbirds. What chance have these latter little creatures against the fierce beak and talons of the birds of prey? But, strange to say, it is the birds of prey that are being slowly exterminated, while those that are defenseless continue to multiply. The lion and the tiger certainly ought to have a better chance in a world like ours than the lamb. Yet for every lion and for every tiger there are millions of

lambs. Among the lower orders of life it is the meek that are inheriting the earth.

The same is true among the nations. It certainly seems that the warlike nations ought to be counted on to inherit the earth. But history flatly contradicts this assumption. There have been all too many nations in the past that were little more than beasts of prey. They ground the weak beneath their heels and grew rich and mighty through the shedding of blood. But where are they now? They have passed into the graveyard of buried nations. They died of their own conquests. They got themselves exterminated, committed actual suicide, in a mad and futile effort to possess the earth. The nation in any age that seeks by force to inherit the earth is certainly doomed. This is as true of the self-seeking nation of to-day, if it continues its course, as it is of those dead nations whose dust already litters up the roadways of the centuries.

3. The meek inherit the earth in the finest and truest sense in the here and now. For, to inherit the earth, it is not necessary that one literally possess it. Those inherit it who find in it the richest and fullest and freest life. The selfish man cannot inherit the earth. The small bit of the earth that he wins rather possesses him and makes him, in some measure, its slave, while the wealth that is not his tends to make him restless by exciting his desire or his envy. But with the meek it is different. I have an old friend who recently spent a day sight-seing in New York City. He had a delightful time. But

when he returned to his hotel, he bowed reverently before God and said: "Lord, I just want to thank thee that I haven't seen a thing to-day that I want." This man is inheriting the earth. He can admire without coveting, and enjoy without owning.

Then, the meek live the fullest and richest life because they are the most capable of giving. Paul was wise when he told Timothy to use meekness in his instruction. We enjoy being instructed by the meek, but if the proud and boastful swaggerer seeks to instruct us we resent it. He was wise in instructing that we restore the erring in the spirit of meekness. The true Christian gentleman can so rebuke as to soften and win us back to God. But the man who is proud and arrogant embitters and alienates. Therefore, in the here and now, the meek, in the fullest and finest sense, are inheriting the earth.

"We live in deeds, not years; in thoughts, not breaths;
In feelings, not in figures on a dial.
We should count time by heart throbs when they beat
For God, for man, for duty.
He most lives who thinks most, feels the noblest, acts the best."

IV

A GOOD APPETITE

Matthew 5: 6

"Blessed are they which do hunger and thirst after righteousness: for they shall be filled."

I

EVERYBODY recognizes the fact that a good appetite is a bit of a treasure. That is, everybody with the possible exception of some one who has never lost his appetite. If you have always gone eagerly and gladly to three square meals a day, if you have always been able to eat whatever you wished and whenever you wished it, then, possibly, your appreciation will be small. But, on the other hand, if you have known what it is to lose your appetite, if you have passed through long, lean, gray months when the very odor of food was repellent and the taste of the most palatable of dishes nauseated, then you know at least in some measure how to appreciate a good appetite and are ready to agree that those who hunger and thirst, even in the realm of the physical, are to be congratulated. A good appetite is a blessing for the following reasons:

1. It is a mark of life. Living things hunger and thirst. That tree out yonder is hungering and thirsting every moment. This is true for the simple

48

reason that it is alive. An ordinary beech tree will drink sixty-five gallons on a hot summer day. An oak tree will drink far more. Some of this water must be carried to a height of more than one hundred feet. How this is done, nobody knows. But the tree lifts it in some way because it is so thirsty. When a tree ceases to hunger and thirst it will die. Or, to speak more correctly, it is already dead. The living hunger. Only the dead are absolutely without appetite. I officiated sometime ago at the funeral of a Chinaman. When the services were over a friend of the deceased came forward and put a bottle of water and a bit of bread into the casket. This was to serve the departed on his journey into the unknown. But the gift was received without the slightest appreciation. The dead man showed no gratitude whatsoever. He had ceased altogether to hunger and thirst.

2. Not only is a good appetite a mark of life, but it is a mark of normal and vigorous and healthful life. Hunger and thirst are perfectly normal. The other day you went to see your physician. You were below par for some reason. So you consulted an expert in the matter of health. The doctor questioned you about your symptoms. Among the questions that he asked was this: "How is your appetite?" He knew that if you did not hunger and thirst something was wrong with you. Loss of appetite is the red flag that nature hangs out to tell us that there is danger ahead. Happy, therefore, is the man who has a good appetite.

49

3. Then, a good appetite is a roadway to growth. That little baby in the cradle is a bundle of hungers and thirsts. He does not know for what he is hungering and thirsting, but he knows when he gets it. Not only so, but he compels the whole household to know if he does not get it. That is as it should be. Just so long as he keeps a good appetite will he grow, but if he ceases to hunger and thirst he will cease to grow. He will fail to reach his highest physical possibilities. If one has already reached maturity, hunger and thirst are needful in order to keep the body in repair. Our cars can no more run without gasoline than our bodies without food and drink. There is a sense in which we die daily. This death must be constantly repaired by wholesome eating and drinking, or our physical machinery will become mere wreckage.

4. Then, incidentally, a good appetite is a blessing because it is a source of genuine enjoyment. We are fond of speaking of the bread that mother used to make. Excellent bread it must have been, but I am not at all sure that it was any better than the bread we have to-day. We only had better appetites then. A good appetite is certainly the most essential factor in the enjoyment of a dinner. It is a delight to eat when one is genuinely hungry. It is a delight to feed a hungry man, as every housewife will testify. But it is next to impossible to feed one that is not hungry. More than one faithful wife has grown gray before her time in an effort

to coax the lagging appetite of some dyspeptic husband whose every meal was a bore.

II

But there are other hungers than the hunger for bread. Man must have bread. He cannot live without it. But while bread is essential, it is not enough. "Man shall not live by bread alone." His hunger for bread is very real. This hunger he shares along with the lower orders of life. In addition, however, to this hunger he has higher hungers that are the badge of his superiority. When I was a boy on the farm I owned a faithful dog named Jack. Jack and I were the best and most intimate of friends. I have never loved any other dog as I loved him. Many a meal have I shared with him. I would give him of my bread and meat ungrudgingly. At times I would even give him a bit of cake, if I could spare it. Having eaten together, we often went together and drank out of the same gurgling spring. His appetite was quite as keen as mine. His enjoyment of his eating and drinking seemed quite as great as mine. But having left the dinner table, we parted company. I had hungers and thirsts to which he was an absolute stranger.

For instance, I would sometimes look at the range of majestic hills that encircled our farm and wonder what lay beyond. "What a wonderful world that must be over there!" I would say to myself. "Some day I am going to see that world. I

am going to mix with it and become a part of it."
As other normal boys, I would now and then feel

"The wild pulsation that we feel before the strife,
　When we hear our days before us and the tumult of our
　life."

But Jack never shared my dreams. He knew nothing of my eagerness to see the big world that lay beyond the hills. I early learned to love some of the musical passages in the King James Version of the Bible. But, when I quoted the twenty-third Psalm or the fourteenth chapter of St. John, Jack was not even mildly interested. I liked songful poetry, even when I did not understand it. But the reading of the most tender and tuneful songs failed utterly to win his interest. Sometimes in sorrow for sin, or under the spell of a longing to be better, I would pray. But all this was beyond the comprehension of my dog. He never thrilled at the splendor of a sunrise, never paused to listen to the song of a mocking bird. We could share a piece of bread with mutual enjoyment, but the music that thrilled and delighted me only made him howl.

Now, these higher hungers belong in a larger or lesser degree to every one of us. They are a badge, I repeat, of our superiority. They are a mark of our greatness. They are the secret of our progress, intellectually and spiritually. Take the hunger to know, for example. How much we owe to the men who have possessed an insatiable hunger for knowledge! How much we are indebted to those who determined

A GOOD APPETITE

"To follow knowledge like a sinking star,
Beyond the utmost bounds of human thought!"

These have been the teachers of the race. They
have brought to us all our inventions. They have
been the great explorers and discoverers. Their
hands have mapped the continents. They have also
mapped the heavens as well. Blessed is he of the
hungry mind. Blessed is he who longs to know.
He shall find in some measure for himself and, possibly in finding, become a teacher of others.

But man has not been and cannot be content
with the knowledge of things. He has not been
satisfied with the exploring of the little world on
which he lives, nor even with his partial exploration of the universe. He is hungry to know Him
who is the Creator of it all. He is thirsty for the
knowledge of him

"Whose dwelling is the light of setting suns,
And the round ocean, and the living air,
And the blue sky, and in the mind of man."

God has placed in every one of us an insatiable
hunger for himself. Therefore when the Psalmist
says,

"As the hart panteth after the water brooks,
So panteth my soul after thee, O God,"

he is speaking a universal language. When Philip
says, "Lord, show us the Father, and it is enough,"
he is voicing a longing that is as old as man, and
that is the very mother of religion.

But while the hunger for God is a universal hun-

53

ger, the tragedy is that so often we misunderstand our own longings. We do not know that for which we hunger. Hence we pursue many false trails. We attain many vain goals that, when attained, leave the lips still parched and the heart still unsatisfied. The secret of a great part of the fret and restlessness and fitful feverishness of our world today grows out of the fact that it is a hungry world and is failing to find that for which it hungers. In our desperation we often so persistently cultivate an appetite for the second best, or even for the worst, that we allow our higher hungers to become dormant and, for all practical purposes, utterly dead.

As a proof of this, consider the vast number of people who frankly have no taste for the spiritual. The most inspiring service ever held would scarcely awaken their interest. The best sermon ever preached would bore them. The very thought of worship is repellent. The Bible, throbbing with "thoughts that breathe and words that burn," is to them the deadest of dead books. The great hymns of the Church, that for centuries have thrilled the hungry hearts of devout men and women and have served as stairways by which they have climbed into the presence of God, leave them dull and listless and uninterested. The man who has lost all appetite for his daily bread is to be pitied, but how infinitely greater is the tragedy when we lose all desire for the Bread of Life! It is by no means difficult to find those who have so long and so persistently fed upon the leeks and garlic of Egypt that they seem to have lost all taste for the heavenly manna.

I was reading not long ago of a certain man who took a street car in an effort to attend a Sunday baseball game. In some way he got on the wrong car. He found himself, to his utter consternation, surrounded by a group of pious people who were on their way to a revival meeting. There was much spiritual fervor among them. They that feared the Lord were speaking one with another, and this gentleman found himself rubbing elbows with two old saints who were telling what the Lord had done for them. He knew at once he was in the wrong pew. He was embarrassed and distressed. He rang the bell and hastened to get off at the next corner. Having made his escape, he sought the right car and at last found himself among companions more congenial. He told them about the distressing predicament from which he had just extricated himself. He described it in these fitting words: "I found myself between two old prayer meeting saints, and I was certainly in one hell of a fix." There you have it. What was heaven to the saints was hell to him. He had no taste for such things.

Such was the case of the man with the muck rake of whom Bunyan tells. He was a very busy man. His eyes were fixed upon the earth where he was diligently raking up some muck and sticks and straw. Meanwhile an angel was poised above his head with a crown waiting to crown him if he would only look up. But he had no interest in the higher things. Such was the case with the crane that was picking up snails on the muddy bank of a muddy pond. A swan lighted at his side. "Where are you from?" asked the crane. "From heaven," was the answer. And the swan began to describe the glories of that heavenly home. But the crane was not interested. He broke in for one question: "Are there any snails there?" When the swan answered in the negative, the crane would not listen for a moment longer. He simply had no taste for the beauties of which the swan spoke. Even so we lose our appetite for those higher values that outlast the ages.

III

But there are some who have not suffered this sad loss. Blessed, therefore, is he who hungers and thirsts after righteousness.

What is this righteousness that we are to desire? It is more than justice. It is more than fair play. It is goodness. Good is not a thrilling word in our day. It leaves us rather pulseless. Yet, when it becomes flesh and blood and walks among us, it is about the most gripping and winsome something that I know. Luke says of Barnabas that he was a good man. If we, therefore, get acquainted with Barnabas, we shall have some idea of goodness. What manner of man was Barnabas? Was he a man that one can truly admire? Was he a man that one would be glad to have as a friend? Was he one whose presence would be a delight? Would he be a genuine inspiration and benediction to any circle in which he might move?

When we come to know him we must confess that such was the case.

1. He was beautifully generous. He was always ready to believe the best. When Paul, who had recently been the scourge of the Church, came to Jerusalem claiming to have been converted, nobody believed him. Yes, there was one radiant exception, and that was this good man Barnabas. He stood by him and stood for him and saved him to the Church. When John Mark turned coward and deserted and went home, Paul refused to give him a second chance. But Barnabas was different. He could not give him up, even though he had failed and failed miserably. He clung to him till Paul acknowledged the victory of his generosity and wrote, "Bring Mark, for he is profitable unto me for the ministry." He looked for the best, not simply among his own people, but among others as well. When he came down to Antioch, where some who were not Jews were being won to Christianity, he was quick to recognize them as fellow Christians. He thanked God for them and entered heartily with them into the work. He was generous in his judgments, and equally so in the use of his wealth. He laid all that he possessed upon the altar of his Lord.

Then, he was a source of consolation. He was incarnate encouragement. He knew how to put heart into people who had lost hope. He had skill to fling a sunrise into the life that had grown dark and

57

black with night. Despair fled at the sound of his footstep, and despondency simply could not endure the sight of him. He was a good man, and, being good, he was generous in his judgments, generous in the use of his substance. He was so good that he won a new name, the Son of Consolation. In fact, he was so good that we cannot fail to see a family resemblance between him and Jesus Christ, whose goodness was goodness in perfection.

Blessed, therefore, is the man who really longs to be good. He is longing for the best. This is true because he is in quest of something that he can never know apart from God. To hunger and thirst after righteousness is, therefore, to hunger and thirst after Jesus Christ himself. Blessed is the man who has a conscious hunger after God. Blessed is he who not only possesses this hunger in regard to himself, but in regard to others as well. Blessed is the man who yearns with passionate longing that he himself and all men come into possession of vital goodness. Blessed is he who longs that he himself and the whole world shall become Christlike.

And, mark you, this longing is intense. Hunger is not a lukewarm something. It soon becomes a gnawing pain. It soon becomes an agony so intense that a crust of bread would be of more value than any jewel that glitters on the finger of wealth. Thirst is more painful still. A soldier, returned from the front, said that he lay for long hours in the trenches without water. "I became thirsty," he declared. "I became so thirsty that I would gladly

58

have given my right arm for one drink of water. I became so thirsty that I would have given both my arms for one drink of water. I became so thirsty that I would have given my life for one drink of water." Jacob was thirsty when he cried desperately: "I will not let thee go, except thou bless me." John Knox was thirsty when he cried: "Give me Scotland, or I die." And Jesus Christ says: "Blessed are they that hunger and thirst after righteousness, that long intensely for goodness; for they shall be filled."

IV

Why are such blessed?

1. They are blessed in that such hungering and thirsting denotes that they are already in some measure the possessors of that for which they hunger and thirst. To really yearn to be good and to have others so is impossible for one who is not in some measure good already. God takes the will for the deed. When David longed to build the temple he was forbidden. But the temple was really his, after all. God said: "Whereas it was in thine heart to build me an house unto my name, thou didst well that it was in thine heart." "It is not what man does," said Browning, "but what man would do that exalts him." Certainly there is real exaltation in this hungering and thirsting after righteousness.

2. Such hungering and thirsting lead with absolute certainty to a fuller possession and a richer, more abiding satisfaction. They lead also to larger

59

usefulness. The one that so hungers and thirsts will seek and, seeking, will find. He will come to know from actual experience the truth of what Jesus said when he cried: "He that cometh to me shall never hunger, and he that believeth on me shall never thirst." He shall also experience the truth of that other great word: "If any man thirst, let him come to me and drink. . . . He that believeth on me as the Scripture hath said, out of his inner life shall flow rivers of living water." That is, he will find satisfaction for himself and be a means of bringing satisfaction to others.

This does not mean, of course, that when we have come to Jesus he meets our needs once and for all, so that we never need come any more. It rather means that we shall ever go on hungering and thirsting as those do who are in normal health, but that for every hunger and every thirst there shall be abiding satisfaction. It means that we shall consistently be saying with the governor of the feast: "Thou hast kept the good wine until now." This we shall say the first time we kiss the brimming draft. This we shall say as we get deeper into the years and deeper into the knowledge of Jesus. This we shall say as we come to the end of the journey, as we push our weary feet into the shadows. This we shall say when we wake in his likeness on the other side. Surely, "Blessed are they which do hunger and thirst after righteousness: for they shall be satisfied." They shall be satisfied in the here and now and satisfied in the eternal yonder.

V

THE MERCIFUL

Matthew 5: 7

"Blessed are the merciful: for they shall obtain mercy."

SPEAKING out of my own experience, I find this the most arresting of all the beatitudes. There is not one of them that, taken to heart, does not bring conviction. There is not one that does not tend to drive us to our knees in pentinence and prayer. But this, I think, is the most searching. It brings to mind our hasty judgments, our sharp criticisms, our callousness in the presence of heartache and pain. As we listen to it we feel that this prayer is the most fitting that we can pray: "God be merciful unto me a sinner."

I

Now, to be merciful is far more than to be possessed of a facility for shedding tears. Of course the merciful sometimes weep In the presence of the grief of Martha and Mary over the death of their brother, Jesus could not restrain his tears. In another place we read that he beheld the city and wept over it. There must have been something tremendously startling about the weeping of this strong and sunny man. Doubtless those who saw his face wet with tears were profoundly impressed. And how meaningful were his tears! They were born of emotions that were tremendously dynamic. But those emotions did not exhaust themselves in a mere flood of tears. "Jesus wept." But he did far more than weep: he gave himself even unto death to serving and saving of those over whom he wept.

But there are those who weep easily and copiously, whose tears are without any meaning or worth. There is no driving power in them. They only bring an added weakness. I am told that there was once a steamboat that after every whistle had to stop and get up steam again. Its driving power exhausted itself in one trumpet blast. There is often a like result from weeping of certain emotional folks. Through their tears all the driving power of their emotions escapes. Such often feel themselves very pious and very merciful because of their facility for weeping. But their tears are vain and futile because they lead to no helpful crusade. In fact, they lead to no activity at all except the use of a pocket handkerchief or the application of a powder puff.

To be merciful is to do something more than give and serve. Mercifulness is more than passing out sandwiches and hot coffee to down-and-outs. It is more than subscribing to the Community Fund or driving an ambulance. Not that a merciful man will not do all these when necessity requires. He will do them gladly. But it is possible to do them all and yet not be merciful. Rome fed and amused her populace to their undoing. But she did not for that reason show herself merciful. When Sir Launfal set out on his search for the Holy Grail, he saw a repulsive beggar crouched by his gate who asked him for alms. The knight did not refuse, nor did he give him a cheap and worthless gift. He gave him real gold. But he gave it with loathing and totally without any mercy in his heart. Therefore, hungry though the beggar was, he could not accept this loveless gift.

> "The beggar left the coin in the dust;
> Better to me the poor man's crust,
> Though he turn me empty from his door."

Thackeray, in his lecture on Swift, gives us a picture of the Dean's activities in the interest of others. He gave himself rather freely to the service of his fellows, but he was not a merciful man. Thackeray says that he insulted while he served, and that, therefore, he would rather have had a potato and a kind word from Goldsmith than to have been beholden to the great Dean for a guinea and a dinner.

What, then, is to be merciful? Mercifulness is primarily a thing of the inner life. It is a disposition of the soul. It is to be possessed of a forgiving spirit. It is to have a heart of pity and compassion. It is to have Christ's way of looking at men. It is to feel toward our friends and our foes somewhat as Christ felt toward his. It is to have Christ's attitude toward the sinful and the suffering. It is to feel somewhat as he felt toward those who were outcasts and toward those who had gone hopelessly wrong. It is to have a heart made warm with the springtime of genuine brotherliness.

II

Now, of course, if this springtime of brotherliness is in the heart, it will give an account of itself in outward conduct. Even if springtime comes to this wintry and seemingly dead world of ours it cannot keep the fact a secret. It will tell the story of its coming in a thousand voices. It will tell it through the bursting buds of the trees. It will tell it in the song of the catbird among the apple blossoms. It will tell it in the blush of the rose. Even the listless dirt beneath our feet will proclaim it.

> "Every clod feels the stir of might,
>   An instinct within it that reaches and towers,
> And groping blindly above it for light,
>   Climbs to a soul and the grass and the flowers."

Even so, if the springtime of mercy is in our hearts it will make itself known in a multitude of ways. We mention only a very few of these.

1. If we are merciful, we are going to be kindly in our judgments. We are going to search for the best in our fellows instead of for the worst. We are going to seek extenuating circumstances rather than those that incriminate and prove guilt. We are going to be slow to condemn and quick to commend. And this we shall do not simply from a sense of duty. Mercy is not merely a thing of duty.

> "The quality of mercy is not strained;
>   It droppeth as the gentle rain from heaven
> Upon the place beneath."

It is spontaneous expression of a loving heart. It we are merciful, we shall naturally think and say the best possible of our erring brother.

> "When on the fair fame of friend or foe
>   The shadow of disgrace shall fall, instead
> Of words of blame, or proof of thus and so,
>   Let something good be said.
>
> Forget not that no fellow being yet
>   May fall so low but love may lift his head:
> Even the cheek of shame with tears is wet,
>   If something good be said.
>
> And so I charge you, by the thorny crown,
>   And by the cross on which the Saviour bled,
> And by your own soul's hope of fair renown,
>   Let something good be said."

2. The merciful man gives and serves. "A certain man went down from Jerusalem to Jericho, and fell among thieves, which stripped him of his raiment, and wounded him, and departed, leaving him half dead. And by chance there came down a certain priest that way: and when he saw him, he passed by on the other side. And likewise a Levite, when he was at the place, came and looked on him, and passed by on the other side. But a certain Samaritan, as he journeyed, came where he was: and when he saw him, he had compassion on him. And went to him, and bound up his wounds, pouring in oil and wine, and set him on his own beast, and brought him to an inn, and took care of him." And the world has remembered this nameless Samaritan through all the centuries. It will remember him to the end of time.

This it will do, not because he was rich, not because he was a genius, not because he was a great physician, but solely because he was merciful. And, being merciful, he could not withhold his services from one who was in need.

The priest and Levite, on the other hand, share with each other an immortality of shame. This is the case not because they assisted in the robbery. They did not steal the few shreds of clothing that the brigands might have left him. They did not inflict other wounds in addition to those from which the half-dead man was already suffering. They only passed by without doing anything. Thus they showed themselves to be without mercy. Had the officers of the city of Jerusalem set out to arrest those responsible for this crime, they would have confined their search to the fastnesses of the mountains. They would have looked only for certain red-handed highwaymen. They would have never thought of disturbing the complacent priest and the self-satisfied Levite. But Christ dares to set these two in the prisoners' dock along with the robbers. They were all alike in this, that they were lacking in mercy.

Of course the merciful man does not confine his ministry to the giving of his material substance. There are times when our fellows need such help and need it desperately, and when sure need arises it is certainly our duty to meet it. This kind of service we are rendering just now better than ever before. I am sure there was never a time when men gave such help so freely as to-day. But there are other needs that we must meet. There may be those in our city who are actually hungry for physical bread. But for every one of these there are thousands that are in need of the Bread of Life. There may be those who are shivering with cold from lack of adequate clothing or for want of a fire to keep them warm. But for every one of these there are thousands who are shivering in their souls for lack of sympathy or encouragement or the handclasp of a brother. The merciful man does more than say, "I am sorry"; he comes to our relief and gets under our load with us.

3. Finally, the merciful man is forgiving. He refuses to nurse a grudge. He flings hate out of his heart as a thing that is deadly and damning. He loves his enemies. He blesses those that curse him and prays for those that despitefully use and persecute him. And in so doing he shows himself big with something of the bigness of Christ.

When William E. Gladstone was Chancellor of the Exchequer he sent down to the Treasury for certain statistics upon which he was to base his budget proposals. The statistician made a mistake. But Gladstone was so sure of this man's accuracy that he did not take time to verify his figures. He went before the House of Commons and made his speech, basing his appeal on the incorrect figures that had been given him. His speech was no sooner published than the newspapers exposed its glaring inaccuracies. Gladstone was naturally overwhelmed with embarrassment. He went to his office and sent at once for the statistician who was responsible for his humiliating situation. The man came, full of fear and shame, certain that he was going to lose his position. But, instead, Mr. Gladstone said: "I know how much you must be disturbed over what has happened, and I have sent for you to put you at your ease. For a long time you have been engaged in handling the intricacies of the national accounts, and this is the first mistake that you have made. I want to congratulate you and express to you my keen appreciation." It took a big man to do that, big with the bigness of the truly merciful.

III

Now, if we are eager to become merciful we might begin by remembering our own need of mercy. "Brethren, if a man be overtaken in a fault, ye which are spiritual restore such an one in the spirit of meekness, considering thyself." If we do seriously consider ourselves, we are likely to realize that the faults that we most sharply condemn in others are often those of which we ourselves are guilty. If we are at all acquainted with our own sinful hearts, we cannot but realize that it is only of the amazing mercy of God that we are any better than the chief of sinners. Therefore, since we have so much for which we must be forgiven, we ought to be ready to forgive. That was a wise and just word that John Wesley spoke to Governor Oglethorpe. The Governor was berating a servant who had just drunk all his favorite wine. "I will be avenged," he cried. "I never forgive." "In that case," said Mr. Wesley, "I hope you never sin." It is a fitting word for every one of us.

Then, we need to consider how imperfectly we often know those whom we condemn. If we knew all, we might find it easier to forgive all. There is a story of a certain preacher who was one day having his shoes shined. He was in a bit of a hurry. When he thought it was about time for the task to be finished, he looked down only to find his shoes in worse condition than they were at the beginning. He spoke sharply to the little bootblack. It was then that the little fellow looked up and showed a face that was wet with tears. "I am sorry, sir," he said. "But my mother died this morning, and I am trying to make a little money to buy some flowers to put on her coffin." And the preacher saw that it was his tears falling on his shoes that was making it impossible for him to shine them. Of course all condemnation died in his heart. "Since that experience," he declared, "I have gone about my ministry with a new outlook. I feel now as if I were walking over a battle field after the battle, caring for the wounded and the dying."

But there is no being merciful in the deepest sense without the help of Christ. "He delighteth in mercy." If we come to share his nature, if he walks with us, if he dwells within us through the Holy Spirit, then we shall share in his tender-heartedness and his willingness to forgive. We shall look upon needy men everywhere with eyes full of pity and compassion. True mercifulness is a gift. Apart from Jesus Christ we can never attain it. But he makes it possible even for the most callous and self-centered.

IV

The blessing promised to the merciful is that they shall obtain mercy. This does not mean, of course, that our Lord is hiring us to be merciful. It does not mean that if we show an ounce of mercy that same amount shall be exactly weighed out to us. Christ is not a merchant who sells; he is a Saviour who gives. The merciful receive mercy because they are capable of receiving it. To be wanting in mercy is to make the receiving of mercy an impossibility.

That the merciful obtain mercy is true in some measure in our everyday relationships. The attitude of men toward ourselves depends largely upon our attitude toward them. If folks are not friendly with you, the chances are that it is because you are not friendly with them. If nobody ever does you a kindness, it is exceedingly likely that you yourself never do a kindness. If the back of every man's hand is toward you, that is pretty good evidence that the back of your hand is toward every man. This I say, not forgetting that the most merciful Man that ever lived was hung on a cross.

Then the merciful always and everywhere obtain mercy from God, while the unforgiving make the receiving of mercy impossible. How strikingly Jesus emphasizes this truth in his story of that unforgiving debtor. He owed an enormous sum. It was in the millions. When he could not pay, his creditor ordered that he be cast into prison and that his wife and children be sold into slavery, so that as much as possible might be realized. But the debtor's heart was broken and he flung himself in an abandon of grief at the feet of his lord and said: "Have patience with me, and I will pay thee all." Of course he could never have paid, but the creditor's heart was touched. He was a merciful man. He then and there forgave him all the debt.

But that forgiven man went out and met one of his fellows who owed him a sum that was a mere trifle. When he demanded payment, his debtor fell at his feet and prayed the same prayer that had been on his own lips a short while before. But he flatly refused to hear. Instead he had the man thrown into prison. And what was the outcome? This unforgiving creditor had his pardon canceled, and he himself was arrested and cast into prison. "So likewise," Jesus concludes, "shall my Heavenly Father do also unto you, if ye from your hearts forgive not every one his brother their trespasses." God can no more forgive the unforgiving than he can make twice two eight. This is true because when God forgives he creates within us a new heart of love. But a new heart of love is impossible so long as we cling to the old heart of hate. Therefore to refuse to show mercy is to shut the door of mercy in our own faces.

71

But whenever we show mercy or even a real willingness to be merciful, then we surely obtain mercy.

In one of my pastorates there was a mother whose daughter went wrong. That mother was an upright woman, but she was as cold as ice and hard as a nail. When she heard the wretched news, instead of going to her wayward daughter and putting her arms around her and trying to help her, she vowed that never again would she allow that unfortunate daughter to cross the threshold of her home and never again would she look into her face. And the tragedy of it was that she meant it. So the girl was sent away to a rescue home in the city.

But as her time drew near, the poor thing became desperately heartsick and homesick. She ran away from the rescue home and came to knock on the door of her mother's home, but it was shut in her face. Then she went across the field to where one of her father's tenants lived, and there in the most delicate and trying moment that ever comes to a woman's soul she was in large measure alone. When the little laddie was three weeks of age a friend came to me with this question: "Did you know that the folks that took Mary in are going to turn her out?" "No," I answered. "But has she any other place to go?" "No," was the reply. "Will not her mother take her back?" I continued. Again my friend answered in the negative. "You see," he said, "her mother has forbidden Mary's name to be mentioned in her presence. Besides, she has heart failure, and everybody believes that if her name should be mentioned it would throw her into such a rage that it would be the death of her."

With this information I went to my study. After a season of prayer I rose from my knees to go to see this woman, highly resolved to kill her, provided that should be the result of my speaking to her about her daughter. I found her unbelievably bitter. She went deadly white as I told her why I had come. And as I spoke to her, using great plainness of speech, she burst into tears, partly, I think, from grief and fear and partly from anger. Then I made my final plea. I asked her to let me go for her daughter. I told her that I would be glad to go and bring her home. But she only answered: "I can't let you." At last she said: "But I will do this, I will ask God to help me." With that I went away, fearing that I had accomplished nothing.

That evening another friend met me on the street and said: "Did you know that Mary had gone home?" "No," I said, "but I am going to see." I hurried to the parsonage. Our houses stood back to back. I ran through my back yard and garden and through the garden and back yard of this mother. As I stood there in the rain, I heard the rocking of a straight-back chair and the cracked voice of a grandmother singing a lullaby. The last service I performed before leaving the little village, as I did in a few days, was to go at the invitation of this grandmother and baptize the little fellow that had come into the world branded by shame in the eyes of society, but with the sanctifying kiss of his

Heavenly Father upon his lips and with a right to a chance. And the most wonderful part of it all was the change that had taken place in the face of that grandmother. The hardness and coldness and frozen hate had passed away, and the peace of heaven looked out from her kindly eyes. She had become merciful, and in so doing she had obtained mercy.

VI

THE VISION SPLENDID

Matthew 5: 8

"Blessed are the pure in heart: for they shall see God."

I

THIS is the most familiar of the beatitudes and the best loved. It is not difficult to see why this is the case. It speaks of the promise and possibility of our seeing God.

1. This possibility is a badge of our greatness. It lifts us to immeasurable heights above all other creatures of the earth. There are those who are very fond of telling us how close akin the embryonic man is to the embryonic monkey. They are so nearly alike that one cannot tell them apart. Yet they are traveling roadways that separate them by distances infinitely wider apart than the spaces between the stars. The one is traveling toward a life that is, in the very nature of things, of the earth earthy. The other is headed toward amazing possibilities. He is traveling toward a capacity for a clear vision of God. That is the pledge of his vast superiority. Surely the Psalmist was right in the light of this fact when he said: "Thou hast made him a little lower than God, and hast crowned him with glory and honor."

2. Not only does this beatitude tell of man's highest possibilities, it also tells of his deepest longings. The desire to see God is characteristic of the race. When Philip said, "Lord, show us the Father, and it is enough," he was voicing a longing that was uttered long before Abraham left Ur of the Chaldees to journey into the unknown. It was uttered long before the towers of Babylon ever lifted their tall heads to gaze down upon the smiling waters of the Euphrates. It is a cry that is older than civilization. It is older than human history. It is as old as man. Throughout all the centuries man has cried either articulately or inarticulately: "O that I knew where I might find Him! that I might come even to his seat!"

3. Then, this beatitude not only speaks home to our deepest longings, but also to our supreme need. As I am speaking to you, I cannot but be conscious of the fact that you have come together at this hour with many different burdens and with many pressing needs. Some have come from beside graves so distressingly new. Some have come from separations more tragic than the separations caused by death. Some of you are the slaves of habits from which you cannot break away. You have resolved and re-resolved only to become worse entangled. You have cursed yourself for a fool only to have the shackles tightened about your wrists. Some are spending life for a poor second best, getting very little when you might get so much. What is the one big need of every one of us? It is just this: a clear

and satisfying vision of God. Those of you who are seeing him who is invisible know that your deepest needs have been met. You know that every iron gate opens of its own accord as you approach it in his fellowship. No wonder, therefore, that we love this beatitude. It is a pledge of our greatness. It offers the satisfaction of our most intense hungers and of our deepest needs.

II

What is it to see God? Of course to see God is not to look upon him with our natural eye. The truth is that the one who sees only what meets the eye sees very little. There was a poet once who declared that he could see in the meanest flower that blows thoughts that lay too deep for tears. That is what made him a poet. There were multitudes that looked upon Jesus and saw nothing of winsomeness in him. To them he was as a root out of dry ground, utterly without form or comeliness. They looked upon him and trudged on their weary and monotonous ways as totally unhelped as if they had looked upon the face of a mummy.

But there were others who saw him with different eyes. As they looked into his face they became conscious of God. As they fellowshiped with him they said: "Thou art the Christ, the Son of the living God." And when he had gone home to heaven they still saw him. They still realized him as one "closer than breathing, and nearer than hands and feet." Paul, who had never looked on his face in the flesh, said: "Have I not seen Jesus Christ our Lord? . . . I know whom I have believed, and am persuaded that he is able to keep that which I have committed unto him against that day."

To see God, then, is to realize him, to be sure of him. It is to have life made radiant by the most blessed of all certainties, the certainty of God. And, mark you, this is an experience that takes place in the here and now. So often we read this beatitude and postpone its rich promise to some far-off to-morrow. "Blessed are the pure in heart, for they shall see God," when they wake in his likeness on the other side. That is true, certainly; but the pure in heart do not have to wait until then. They see him in the here and now. They enter into his fellowship in the life that now is. The truth is that if we do not see him in the here and now we have no promise of seeing him at all. If we do not get acquainted with him in this present to-day, we have no slightest guarantee of enjoying his fellowship in that distant to-morrow. To see God, therefore, is to be sure of him, to realize him amidst all the laughter and tears of the life that now is.

III

What are some of the blessings that come as a result of this vision splendid?

1. To see God is to see one's self. Job was a character of unusual worth and beauty. He was tragically afflicted in his body. One fancies, at times, that he was even more afflicted through his

78

friends. They came to tell him, as pain tortured him, that the whole tragedy was the result of his sin. Job denied it with hot indignation, and we cannot help siding with him. We applaud him as he maintains his integrity. But by and by a vision of God bursts upon him. Then all Job's self-sufficiency is gone, his knees go weak, and in deep humility he cries: "I have heard of thee by the hearing of the ear: but now mine eye seeth thee: wherefore I abhor myself, and repent in dust and ashes."

Here is another man, certainly one of the cleanest and most upright of his day. He is telling us of the personal experience that made him the man that he became. "In the year that King Uzziah died, I saw the Lord." And what was the outcome of the vision? In the brightness of that light he also saw himself. And what he saw caused him to put his lips to the dust and cry: "I am a man of unclean lips, and I dwell in the midst of a people of unclean lips." Similar was the effect upon the repentant robber. His companion in crime could see the visible Christ as well as himself. But seeing only that, he joined with the mob in their howls of abuse. But this greater robber saw more deeply. He penetrated the disguise of weakness. He penetrated the dusky disguise of death itself and saw the real Christ, and that vision smote him with a conviction of his own deep guilt. "Dost thou not fear God, seeing thou art in the same condemnation? And we indeed justly; for we receive the due reward of our deeds; but this man hath done nothing amiss."

79

His vision of Christ brought him, as it always does, a vision of self.

2. To see God is to be transformed. For when we see him we are always convicted of sin. Whenever there is a sense of God, there is always a sense of sin. And the opposite is also true, absolutely and always. Whenever there is no sense of sin, there is no sense of God. We are told that certain Africans never realized that they were black till they looked on the white face of David Livingstone. Then they could not help but realize it. And whenever we see ourselves in the light of the divine countenance, we never fail to come to a realization of our guilt. To see God is always to cry with the prophet: "Unclean, unclean!"

But the vision does more for us than simply show us our own sinfulness. It also brings us cleansing from sin. Was it not so in the case of Isaiah? No sooner had he confessed his sin than he became conscious of cleansing by the power of God. Was it not so in the case of the dying robber? Having confessed his own guilt, he dares to pray the most amazing prayer ever uttered, I think: "Lord, remember me when thou comest into thy kingdom." "I know this is not the end," he seems to say. "When you have passed through this black tunnel of death, when you have come out under the clear skies of your kingdom, don't forget the needy, sin-stained robber at whose side you died." And Jesus gave an answer that made the robber forgetful of the pangs of the cross: "To-day thou shalt be with me in paradise."

How strikingly the transforming power of God is illustrated in the life of Jacob! In his earlier years Jacob is exceedingly disappointing. You could not love him if you wanted to. He is a creature of shifts and trickery. He delights to live by his wits. Laban is no paragon of honesty himself, but he is no match for his wily nephew. Jacob knows all the tricks of the trade. Had he been in the dry goods business instead of handling live stock, I am confident that he would have had no less than a half dozen successful fires during his sojourn with Uncle Laban. As it is, he disappears over the plains one day driving the better part of what had been his uncle's herds before him. He has been successful. He has succeeded in a most dangerous fashion, by trickery. He is going now to possess his inheritance with a feeling that he has made sin to pay. But in that awful night by the ford something happens to him. From a spiritual pauper he becomes a prince. As he limped away next morning, the sun that looked over the eastern hills was not so bright as the light that shone in his heart. And when they asked him how the marvelous change had been wrought, he answered: "I have seen God face to face."

3. To see God is to come into possession of a new and steadfast courage. That is a bracing word that the writer to the Hebrews uses in his story of Moses. "He endured," he tells us. There was much opposition from the authorities of Egypt, but he en-

dured. There was much opposition among his own people, but he endured. His hopes were long deferred, but he endured. There was persistent whining, there was a distressing lack of patience, but he endured. They threw mud at him instead of flowers, but he endured. How steadfast he was, how courageous, how dauntless! What is the secret of it all? "He endured as seeing Him who is invisible." There is a courage, a steadfastness, a gallant staunchness that belong to those that see God that cannot be won except through such high vision.

4. Then, to see God is to become in the highest sense useful. This is true, in the first place, because it is the man who has seen God who is the most eager to serve. To see him is to be gripped with a holy passion to share your vision with others. How strikingly this is illustrated throughout the Scriptures and throughout the history of the Church! No sooner does God call for volunteers than Isaiah replies eagerly: "Here am I; send me." How bent on giving were those who had been with the Lord Jesus! The world did not think that it wanted their story. It paid them with ostracism, with stones and dungeons and wild beasts and forests of crosses. But it could not destroy their passion for giving. They continued to declare by word and deed: "We cannot but speak the things that we have seen and heard."

Then, it is the man who has seen God who is the most capable of giving. There is absolutely no service that one human being can render another that is quite so high and helpful as the giving of a sense of God. Our first conviction of the reality of God often comes to us through some friend or loved one. Listen to Ruth, for instance, as she makes about the most beautiful confession of love and faith ever uttered: "Entreat me not to leave thee, or to return from following after thee: for whither thou goest, I will go; and where thou lodgest, I will lodge; thy people shall by my people, and thy God my God: . . . the Lord do so to me, and more also, if aught but death part thee and me." How did Ruth come to turn her back on the gods of her people and give herself to the God of Israel? It was through the vision of God that she had had in the life of Naomi. As she looked into that sweet face, as she read that tender heart, she said: "If God is like you, then he shall have me and mine forever."

To be able to give a sense of God, I repeat, is the highest of all services. Blessed are the children that are able to see in the beautiful and radiant lives of their parents something that can only be accounted for in terms of God. Blessed are those who by the sweet and heavenly atmosphere of the home are made to feel "surely God is in this place." Blessed the Sunday school teacher that can bring to the class Sunday by Sunday a sense of God. Such a teacher may be very limited in knowledge, very limited in a thousand ways; but in spite of all limitations, such an one will leave a blessing behind that none but God can fully estimate. Blessed is the preacher that can so speak as to make his hearers look past him into that Face that is "altogether lovely and the fairest of ten thousand." God pity him if those that hear him sympathetically must say, as a very cultured and hungry-hearted gentleman said recently of a certain minister that he had heard: "He interested me, instructed me, even fascinated me, but he left me with no sense of God." Surely, of all people that enrich us, of all those to whom we owe unpayable debts, there is none to whom we are quite so indebted as to him who brings to us a sense of God. And the only man who can do this is the man who has himself seen God.

IV

Now, how shall we see God? What roadway can we take with the assurance of the coming into possession of this vision splendid?

Let us begin with the sure conviction that to see God is a possibility that is within reach of every one of us. It is not simply for some aged saint who is nearing the sunset and evening star. It is not simply for the minister. It is not simply for some choice soul here and there. Here is a prize of supreme worth that is within reach of every heart that is willing to lay hold of it. Let us grip that truth and refuse to let it go. Say to your own needy heart: "This blessing is for me. It is my privilege to see God, to realize him. It is my privilege to live in the realm of radiant certainty."

Having become convinced that the blessing is for yourself, the next step is to meet the conditions.

"Blessed are the pure in heart: for they shall see God." What is it to be pure in heart? On the surface it sounds forbidding. It suggests the impossible. But to be pure in heart does not mean sinlessness. Jesus is not saying: "Blessed are the perfect: for they shall see God." To be pure in heart is to be simple, sincere, whole-hearted. Jesus was uttering the same truth in different words when he said: "If any man is willing to do his will, he shall know of the doctrine." Blessed is the fully surrendered man, for he shall know, he shall see God.

This is the clear teaching of the New Testament. It is also the teaching of experience. Its truth has been demonstrated in countless millions of lives. E. Stanley Jones tells us that while he was visiting Gandhi a Sadhu came eight hundred miles to ask Gandhi two questions. The questions were these: "How can I get rid of sin, and how can I find God?" Having asked Gandhi, the seeker after God came to ask Jones the same questions. He said to the inquirer: "Before I answer you, would you mind telling me what Gandhi told you?" "No, I don't mind telling you," he answered. "He told me to sit down in one place and not roam about as the Sadhus do, but stay in one place till I had conquered my senses and my passions and worn them out, then I might find release." "Was there no offer of immediate relief?" Jones asked. "O, no," was the reply. "He said it would take a long, long time." And then he turned to Jones and said: "Now what do you say?" And this radiant missionary told

85

him what had happened to himself. He said: "My yearning was exactly your yearning. I needed to know how to get rid of sin, and I needed to know God. But I did not need to stay in one place till I had worn out my passions; I simply turned over a bankrupt soul to Jesus Christ, and, lo, as I gave my all he gave me his all. It did not take ages, it took surrender. It did not take time, it took me."

That is a clear path that all human feet can travel. And, regardless of the starting point, he who travels it finds God. In England years ago there was a man, a pessimist and a cynic, who had become bankrupt in faith and joy and hope. One desperate night he wrote on a piece of paper something like this: "If there is a Being above who takes thought of the needs of man, if that Being will reveal his will to me, it will be my highest joy to do that will wherever it may take me and whatever it may involve." And what was the outcome? That man spent forty years in the enervating climate of India as a medical missionary without ever a vacation. He was willing to do His will, therefore he came to know. He was pure in heart, therefore he saw God. The same may happen to every man, for this is forever true: "Blessed are the pure in heart; for they shall see God."

VII

THE PEACEMAKERS

Matthew 5: 9

"Blessed are the peacemakers: for they shall be called the children of God."

"BLESSED are the peacemakers." For nineteen centuries this great word has been knocking at the shut doors of men's hearts, largely in vain. We have said "Yes" with our lips, but by our lives we have said: "Blessed are the sowers of discord. Blessed are the fomenters of strife. Blessed are the war makers." But Christ in loving patience still proclaims that it is the peacemakers who are blessed.

I

Now, to make peace is to do far more than merely abolish strife. To make peace is to do more than cause men or nations to be peaceable. We may keep the peace without having peace. We may bring about a cessation of strife without in any real sense being peacemakers. The Roman Empire brought about peace within her borders, but she was not a peacemaker according to the meaning of Jesus. Her subjects had not lost the will to fight. They kept peace through fear. They were not at war solely because the dread of Rome forced them to swallow their hate and to submit with sullen rage to their fortune.

When I was a boy we owned two magnificent dogs. These dogs were of different breed. They had a natural antipathy to each other. Now and then, they would come to open war. When they did so they fought to utter exhaustion. Having reached this state, they would cease to tear at each other, but they would still glare at each other in such a fashion as to indicate that the only reason they were not fighting was because they could not. And that was the impression that one received as he traveled among the nations of Europe just after the World War. One could not but feel that the only reason they were not at each other's throats was because they had already fought to complete exhaustion. They had been bled white. Therefore the peace that existed was a peace born, not of good will, but of weakness. It was a purely negative peace.

Then, there may be peace that is the outcome of mere indifference. Rip Van Winkle and his wife were accustomed to have some very stormy sessions in their humble little home. But by and by these domestic wars ceased. The noise of conflict was no longer heard. How had this peace come about? It had not come because husband and wife had arrived at a better understanding. It had not come because they had agreed, out of mutual love, to be more forbearing. There was peace because one day Rip took his musket upon his shoulder and strolled off into the mountains for a twenty-year nap. I read some months ago where two deadly enemies met and shot each other to death. As they lay side by side they were at peace, but it was the peace of indifference, it was the peace of death. Therefore it was a purely negative something.

But the peacemaker of whom Jesus speaks does a positive work. He puts an end to strife by the bringing in of its opposite. He does not pull up the noxious weeds of discord and enmity and hate one by one and leave the garden bare. He rather sows and cultivates such a luxuriant crop of the flowers of the Spirit—love, joy, peace, long-suffering—that the disturbing weeds are all crowded out. He drives out suspicion by confidence, enmity and misunderstanding by understanding and good will. He puts brotherliness in the place of unbrotherliness. He puts love in the place of hate. Through his ministry men not only cease to fear each other and to fight each other, but they come to love and to trust each other. He does more than take the sword and break it into fragments. He does more than blunt the spear and burn its shaft. He beats the sword into a plowshare, and the spear into a pruning hook. He converts the implements of war and waste into implements of peace and prosperity. He overcomes evil with good.

II

Now, that peacemakers are needed in our world no one will deny. The peacemaker is a benefactor. I take it that he is the supreme benefactor.

89

1. We need peacemakers because there is such a widespread lack of peace. Strife and discord, hate and misunderstanding are on every hand. This I say not minimizing the marvelous advancements that have been made. No man can look upon our world with open eyes and fail to recognize that there has been encouraging progress. The fact that the Prime Minister of England has recently crossed the Atlantic to talk with our President in the interest of world peace is surely the prophecy of a better day. But there still remains much land to be possessed. In spite of all that has been done, our peace is not yet like a river. We are still far from a "parliament of man and a federation of the world."

Think, first, of the strife between man and his Maker. This strife is as old as human history. In the Eden story, man after his sin no sooner heard the voice of God walking in the garden than he hid himself. He had come to fear the One that he should have loved best. Instead of seeking God, instead of crying in his need, "O my God, where art Thou?" God had to do the seeking and cry, "Adam, where art thou?" This is an old story, I know. You may no longer believe it. But surely you believe the more modern story of your own life. Account for it how you may, some of you are keenly conscious of the fact that there is a quarrel between you and God. There are many, thank God, for whom this quarrel has been healed. But there are vast multitudes for whom it has not been healed. The supreme tragedy of their hour is that there are so many in our world that are not on friendly terms with God.

With the loss of peace between man and God there comes also the loss of peace between man and his better self. That has always been the case. To be at war with God is to have civil war within your own soul. "There is no peace, saith my God, to the wicked." If I could take my soul into my own two hands and utterly erase the image of God from it, I might have a certain kind of peace apart from God. But this I cannot do. It has been well said that no man can be as bad as he wants to be. The hogs may be content within the pigsty of the far country. But for the prodigal, contentment is impossible. He was made for something better. He is persistently tormented by memories of his father. He is made miserable and restless by dreams of his finer possibilities.

"My soul cleaveth unto the dust" is the cry of the Psalmist. Then why does he not lay hold on the dust and be content? Because he cannot. The cleaving is all very real, but that is only half the story. "My soul cleaveth unto the dust; quicken thou me according to thy word." That is the other half. While he cleaves to the dust, he also aspires to the heights. While with one hand he fingers the mud, with the other he reaches after the stars. Why does not the sea lie down within its far-flung shores and be at rest? Because the heights will not let it alone. When it is minded to become content with the earth, the voices of cloudland call it.

Therefore it is always tossing and restless. And man is forever like that troubled sea till he finds rest in God.

Then there is widespread discord and strife between man and man. Men glare at each other individually. Group looks askance at group. Racial prejudices and racial hates abound. Nation glares at nation, and each proclaims itself *the people*. Many Americans still say, "America first"; Many British, "England first;" Germans, "Germany first." We are still far from seeing in every man a brother for whom Christ died. We are still far from a brotherhood of nations.

2. Then we need peacemakers because strife and enmity and hate are so costly. It is certainly true that the most expensive something in all the world is hate. Think of its cost to the individual. Enmity between God and man is the fountain source of all wretchedness. It was when Paul looked to the heights and went toward the depths that he cried, "O wretched man that I am!" Such hostility makes for ineffectiveness. This it does because it makes for a divided personality. "Unite my heart to fear thy name" is the wisest of prayers. It is the only way that we can come to the fullness o four powers. A divided personality means at once the loss of happiness and the loss of our highest effectiveness. A unified personality, on the other hand, means the attainment of both peace and power.

How costly is hate between man and man! I know of nothing that is so deadly as hating somebody. What havoc it sometimes works to the one who is hated! What havoc it always works to the hater! How many an organization has been disrupted by it? How many a church has had its usefulness impaired and the thews of its spiritual strength clipped by it! When given right of way it changes our homes into hells and puts within our hearts that which bites like a serpent and stings like an adder.

How all but infinite has been the cost of hate between section and section, nation and nation! War has certainly been a supreme curse of the world. It is the most deadly foe of mankind. It kills men's bodies, and too often their souls as well. Every war brings in its wake an aftermath of blighted ideals and lowered moral standards. Think of the cost of the World War. Its cost in material wealth was incredibly great. But that was as nothing in comparison with its cost in other directions. It is estimated that its total casualties up to the present time are more than thirty millions of human lives. And so many of them were our choicest and our best.

> "Where are you going, Young Fellow, My Lad,
>   On this glittering morn of May?
> I am going to join the colors, Dad,
>   They are wanting men, they say.
> But you are only a boy, Young Fellow, My Lad,
>   You are not obliged to go.
> I'm seventeen and a quarter, Dad,
>   And ever so strong, you know.

So you are off to France, Young Fellow, My Lad?
  And you are looking so fit and bright.
I'm dreadfully sorry to leave you, Dad,
  But I feel that I am doing right.
God bless you and keep you, Young Fellow, My Lad,
  For you are all my life, you know.
Don't worry, I'll soon be back, dear Dad,
  And I'm awfully proud to go.

What is the matter, Young Fellow, My Lad?
  No letter again to-day?
And why did the postman look so sad
  And sigh as he turned away?
I hear them say that we've gained new ground,
  But a terrible price we've paid.
God grant, my boy, that you are safe and sound,
  But O, I'm afraid, afraid!

They've told me the truth, Young Fellow, My Lad,
  And you'll never come home again.
O God, the dreams and the dreams I've had
  And the hopes I've nursed in vain!
For you passed in the night, Young Fellow, My Lad,
  But you proved in that terrible test,
Of the bursting shell and the battle hell,
  That my boy was one of the best."

War is always taking the best, and, taking them, it squanders their lives, so often for nothing and worse than nothing.

3. Finally, we need peacemakers because peace will never come of itself. Peace must be made. We may drift into war. We may drowse and trifle our way into confusion and conflict. But if peace is ever realized it must be through conscious, persistent, sacrificial effort. We must do more than dream of peace; we must make it. And that we can do.

Every soul may become a peacemaker. It is impossible for all of us to make fortunes. We cannot all make a great noise in the world. We cannot all make great names. But we can do something far better: we can all make peace, and in so doing invest ourselves for the attaining of the highest possible good.

III

Now, if we are to make peace, how are we to go about it? How is peace to be made? It is not going to be made through hate. That sounds obvious to the point of utter triteness, I know. But, as you turn the pages of history, you will see that it has not been at all obvious, even to the nations that are nominally Christian. Of course we have abandoned to some extent the idea that the way for one neighbor to get along with another is for each to carry a six-shooter. For me to mount a machine gun upon the front porch of the parsonage to defend myself against my neighbors would not be regarded as Christian. That, of course, everybody will recognize.

But somehow we are not so quick to recognize the fact that it is equally unchristian to depend on standing armies and battle ships to keep peace between nation and nation. We readily agree that one Christian cannot hate another, but we are by no means quick in our agreement that Christian nations cannot hate each other. How slow we are in learning that we cannot be Christian individually

95

and pagans nationally! How slow we are in recognizing the obvious truth that we cannot be good Samaritans as individuals and highwaymen and priests and Levites as a nation! We cannot bring about peace between nation and nation by killing each other any more than we can bring it about between man and man.

This, I know, sounds so evident as to seem almost puerile, yet we cannot forget that it has not been long since many of our statesmen and some of our preachers were encouraging us in our fighting by saying that we were waging a war that was to end war. There are multitudes that were honestly convinced that such was the case. They had persuaded themselves that somehow love could be born out of hate and discord, and strife could be the mother of peace. But "do men gather grapes of thorns, or figs of thistles?" "Who can bring a clean thing out of an unclean?" That which is born of love is love, and that which is born of hate is hate. War is an evil, a deadly evil. Hate is an evil. The antidote for this evil is not more evil. Hate is never killed by hate. It is only increased by it. The only successful foe of evil is good.

> "For heathen heart that puts her trust
>   In reeking tube and iron shard;
> All valiant dust that builds on dust,
>   And guarding calls not thee to guard:
> For frantic boast and foolish word,
> Thy mercy on thy people, Lord!"

How, then, I repeat, are we to become peacemakers? Our first step is putting ourselves into right relations with Jesus Christ. He is the supreme Peacemaker. He is the Prince of Peace. He came to teach us to say, "Our Father," and in so saying to see in every man a brother. He came "to gather together into one the sons of God that are scattered abroad." His last earthly prayer was that we all might be one. He declares that his one great task in the world is the gathering together of men into a brotherhood. "He that is not for me is against me, and he that gathereth not with me scattereth abroad."

What a startling declaration! Jesus here divides men into two groups. There are those who are for him and those who are against him. There are these two classes and these two only. "Some men," he declares, "enter my service. They make my plans and purposes their plans and purposes. My work becomes their work. They are with me. They struggle to make my dreams into realities. But there are others who oppose me. There are others who fight against me, who antagonize me, who add to the weight of my cross. There are those who by their opposition postpone the coming of that good day when the kingdoms of the world shall become the kingdom of the Lord and his Christ."

In this word also Jesus states with bold emphasis what is the acid test of our loyalty to himself. He declares that all those who make for strife and for discord are arrayed against him. Whoever cherishes hate in his heart, whoever makes it easier for men

97

and women to suspect each other, to mistrust each other, that man, regardless of what his profession may be, is fighting against Christ. Whoever is hard to live with in the home, whoever is a promoter of strife between man and man, whoever makes for discord and misunderstanding within the Church, whoever preaches a patriotism of selfishness, whoever fosters sectional or national or racial prejudices —that man is surely the foe of Jesus Christ. This is true regardless of his claim to loyalty or of his professed orthodoxy. Jesus is come to break down all dividing walls. He is come to abolish unbrotherliness and hate everywhere. If your life and mine are making for the opposite, then we have arrayed ourselves against him whom we claim to serve.

On the other hand, if we are peacemakers, if by what we are and by what we do we preach a gospel of reconciliation, if we make for peace in the home, peace in the social circle, peace between nation and nation and between race and race, then we are making common cause with Jesus Christ. Then we are fighting under his banner. This is true whatever our denomination or lack of it. John brought some great news to Jesus on one occasion. "Master, we saw one casting out demons in thy name." How the heart of Jesus must have leaped for joy! But John had not finished his story. "We forbade him because he followed not with us." What a calamity! "Forbid him not," said Jesus emphatically. "He that is not against us is on our part." Whoever is making for peace in the hearts of men and for peace

98

in the world is a friend and servant of Jesus, and to him we give the right hand of fellowship.

Now, it is through the friends of Jesus that peace is to be made. It is said that a gentleman of saintly life stood one day in a great art gallery before a picture of Jesus. As he looked into the face of him who is the fairest of ten thousand and the one altogether lovely, his heart became strangely warmed and strangely glad. "Bless him, I love him," he said softly to himself. It so happened that there was a man at his side from another nation who overheard his exclamation. "Bless him, I love him too," this man replied. Then there was another and another, till by and by a little group stood reverently about the picture. These represented different nationalities and different races, but they were brought together in the bonds of a sweet and tender brotherhood by their mutual love for Jesus Christ. And one day nation is going to say to nation: "Bless him, we love him." One day the Occident is going to say to the Orient, and the Orient to the Occident: "Bless him, we love him." Then, and not till then, will men beat their swords into plowshares, and their spears into pruning hooks, and learn war no more. Then, and not till then, will the glory of God cover the earth as the waters cover the sea.

What, then, is our first and supreme duty as individuals? If we are to become peacemakers, our first duty is to accept the peace of Christ for ourselves. "He is our peace," Paul tells us. He brings peace between God and man. He brings peace within. That is the first step toward the realization of the great dream of world-wide peace. Have you accepted his peace for yourself? "Peace I leave with you, my peace I give unto you." Let us accept it. If in faith we really receive this peace, we shall come to feel, with the poet:

> "God hath given me birth,
> To brother all the sons of earth."

We shall go forth to a ministry of reconciliation. Our appeal will be that of Paul: "Now we are ambassadors for Christ, as though God did beseech you by us; we pray you in Christ's stead, be ye reconciled to God."

VIII

THE PERSECUTED

Matthew 5: 10-12

"Blessed are they which are persecuted for righteousness' sake: for theirs is the kingdom of heaven. Blessed
are ye, when men shall revile you, and persecute you,
and shall say all manner of evil against you falsely,
for my sake. Rejoice, and be exceeding glad: for great
is your reward in heaven: for so persecuted they the
prophets which were before you."

I

THIS is the last of the beatitudes. Up to this time
Jesus has been describing the Christlike character.
In this last beatitude he tells us the reception that
this genuine Christian is to meet at the hands of the
world. And what he says tends to fill us with amazement. One would certainly think that a character
such as Jesus has described would meet with universal acclaim; that every man's heart would be open
to him. But such, says Jesus, is not the case. On
the contrary, the vital Christian is sure to meet with
some form of opposition or persecution.

Now, the fact that the genuine Christian provokes opposition does not mean that this opposition
is to be universal. Every real Christian will make
friends. Every real Christian will surely win the
loyal love of at least a few. I am not forgetting that

101

Jesus said; "Woe unto you when all men shall speak well of you." But he did not mean by that for us to pride ourselves on being universally hated. If it is a tragedy to have all men speak well of us, I am sure that a yet greater tragedy would be for all men to speak evil of us. What Jesus is here asserting is not that a real Christian is universally unpopular; He is emphasizing the fact that vital goodness provokes opposition.

This fact is clearly and emphatically demonstrated in his own life. Jesus not only spoke these beatitudes; he lived them to the point of perfection. He was meek, he was a peacemaker, his was the tenderest heart that ever beat. No man ever gave himself so freely to the service of others. But in spite of this he did not meet with universal acclaim. There were those who loved him with passionate devotion, but there were those who hated him with hellish hatred. There was nothing too harsh and cruel for them to say about him. They called him a gluttonous man and a winebibber. They said that he was a blasphemer, that he was crazy, that he was in league with the devil. At last they crowned him with thorns and hung him on a cross. He was done to death, not for any evil that was in him, but because of his vital goodness.

Paul also lived these beatitudes in an amazingly beautiful fashion. What a peacemaker he was! How compassionate! He felt himself in debt to all men. He was willing to spend and be spent for them; though the more he loved them, the less he

102

was loved by them. But all men did not give him welcome. All did not approve. He stirred the most strenuous opposition. He was chased from one city to another. He had intimate acquaintance with the whipping post. Again and again he was thrust into prison. There was a day when he stood among flying stones till he could stand no longer. At last he died a martyr's death. And this is the word that he shouts across the centuries to you and me: "All that will live godly in Christ Jesus shall suffer persecution."

III

Why is it that real goodness provokes opposition? That such is the case is the plain teaching both of the New Testament and of history as well. This was the case in the days of Jesus. It will be the case till the kingdom of God is fully come. Of course this opposition will be less widespread and less intense the more the will of God is done and the more fully the kingdom of God is set up in the hearts of men. We are more tolerant and less bitter now than were the people who lived in the days of Jesus. This is the case because the kingdom is coming. We are accustomed to bewail the fact, and rightly so, that the Church of to-day is so much like the world. But there is this heartening fact, that the world is becoming more and more like the Church. Therefore persecution is not so bitter now as in other days. But it is still true that real goodness provokes opposition, and will continue, in some measure, to do

103

so, till God fully has his way with us and the kingdoms of the world shall have become the kingdom of our Lord and his Christ.

1. A genuine Christian provokes opposition because he is different. If our Christianity has not made us different, then it is spurious. A certain little Indian girl rightly described the Christians that she knew as the folks that were different. To fail as a Christian, it is not necessary to be worse than the man of the world; it is only necessary to be like him. When Samson's temptress was seeking to know the secret of his strength, he informed her that if his vow should be broken he would then become weak and be like any other man not weaker than any other man, not worse than any other man, but only like him. The Christian is different, and, being different, he arouses opposition.

This is not saying that there are not those who will approve. We love and admire the man who dares to be unique. Yet we often resent him, too. We approve those who share our prejudices, who conform to our customs, who look at things through our eyes. Society constantly seeks to rob us of our individuality. Those daring saints who insist on accepting Christ's way of life are sure to be resented. They are certain to meet those who will dismiss them with a shrug of contempt, saying: "They are so peculiar." "If ye were of the world, the world would love its own: but because ye are not of the world, but I have chosen you out of the world, therefore the world hateth you."

2. Then, the vital Christian arouses opposition because he is a constant rebuke to our selfishness and our sin. Every man who in the power of Christ lives out these beatitudes becomes an incarnate conscience. He makes the self-centered, the worthless feel uncomfortable. Some of them he wins. Others he worries and offends. Elijah, so far as we know, had not said a word to the widow about her ungodly life. But he rebuked her by being what he was. "Art thou come unto me to call my sin to remembrance?" she asked. The vital Christian rebukes the sinful both by what he is and by what he says and does. Therefore he arouses opposition.

3. Finally, the truly Christlike man stirs opposition because he interferes. In a sense, as the world would put it, he meddles with our affairs. He rebukes our prejudices. He reminds us that God is the Father of all mankind and expects all men, regardless of race or creed or color, to live as brothers. He interferes with some of our pleasures. While telling us that no pleasure is sinful except sinful pleasure, he asserts that our sinful pleasure must be put away. If Jesus were to come to our city today he would possibly escape crucifixion, but he would certainly not be universally popular. In many so-called Christian homes he would not be welcome. His presence would change the cheap and vulgar laughter that often abounds there into embarrassed silence. And while showing him over our city, there are certain sections that we should carefully avoid.

105

Then, the vital Christian sometimes even dares to interfere with our business. There were those long ago who counted up their losses with hot rage just after Jesus had driven them out of the temple. Paul had his clothing torn from him and was publicly whipped and cast into prison because he interfered in the business of certain slave owners in the city of Philippi. And that mob that was aroused in Ephesus would gladly have torn him limb from limb had they been able to lay their hands upon him. And why should they not do so? He was ruining their business. They were making a most decent and respectable living by selling images of Diana. But by his preaching he was threatening to reduce them to poverty. No wonder they opposed him.

It has not been many years since slavery was looked upon as an institution that was altogether consistent with the teachings of Jesus. When men arose who declared to the contrary, they aroused the most bitter and intense opposition. They were interfering with vested interests. They seemed bent on robbing their fortunate fellows of their personal property. Even more recently the vast majority of our citizens thought it perfectly right and proper for this nation to engage in the liquor business. When those came forward who said that as a nation we had no right to sell that which tends only to blight and blast and damn, they, too, aroused bitter opposition. Nor does this opposition belong to a distant past. When the liquor question was dragged into national politics recently, how the party whip was popped over our heads and how almost every newspaper and politician sought to scourge the preachers into silence! The Church has yet a disturbing and provoking word to say about the industrial situation, and in saying it she is going to provoke opposition. Christianity is bound to be a disturbing factor in a social order that is largely unchristian.

III

Now, the nature of this opposition is somewhat different to-day from what it was in the days of Jesus. Persecution then usually had its culmination in physical violence. Christians were thrown into prison. They were burned at the stake. They were fed to wild beasts. They were hung upon forests of crosses. In Christian America we no longer employ such crude methods. And yet there are still Christians that have to face forms of persecution that, while more refined, require as genuine courage as that required of the Christians of the first century.

But there were at least two modes of persecution employed nineteen hundred years ago that are still in vogue. And we are often capable of using them quite as effectively as did they of the long ago. "Blessed are ye," said Jesus, "when men shall revile you, and . . . shall say all manner of evil against you falsely, for my sake." We can still revile, or reproach. We can still call people narrow and fanatical. We can still shrug our shoulders and laugh at them as cranks. The young man and the young woman who would dare go into the so-called

107

best society of our city, taking their ideals with them, would be put to tests almost as sharp as those met by the Christians of the long ago. There are positions in the business and industrial world that, if filled in accordance with the principles of Jesus, would require a courage almost as stanch as that possessed by the martyrs.

And there is still another weapon that the world knows how to use; that is slander. When Jesus made himself the dauntless foe of evil, those who were its friends slandered him. They tried to destroy his good name. They said all manner of evil against him falsely. And such has been the lot of the choicest sons and daughters of God through the centuries. It is not always easy to suffer slander. Some have allowed their hearts to be broken by it. But it is a form of persecution that every great servant of mankind has had to endure. This has been true from Socrates and beyond, down to Woodrow Wilson.

IV

Now, since vital goodness certainly provokes opposition, since a genuine Christian is sure to have to face persecution, what are we to do about it? Suppose as a Christian I look up into the face of my Lord and say, "Jesus, Master, I am having a hard fight, I am meeting with strenuous opposition, I am face to face with persecution," what answer does our Lord give? He does not say, "I am sorry for you." He does not say, "How I pity you!" He rather says, "Let me congratulate you." "Rejoice and be exceeding glad: for so persecuted they the prophets which were before you." That is, persecution for righteousness' sake is not something to whine about. It is something over which to rejoice. This is true, not because persecution is good in itself; it is true because of what such persecution indicates and the ends to which it leads if rightly borne.

1. Persecution for righteousness' sake indicates that the one so persecuted is a child of the kingdom. Mark you, the Master does not say that every man who is persecuted belongs to the kingdom. He says that that is true only of those who are persecuted for righteousness' sake. There are those who are persecuted, not because they are righteous, but because they are the opposite. They are persecuted, not because they are meek, but because they are pushful and self-assertive; not because they are merciful, but because they are harsh and cruel; not because they are peacemakers, but because they are trouble makers.

For instance, I have in mind two preachers. You could never guess who they are, therefore I can speak of them with safety. One is an extreme fundamentalist, the other is an equally extreme modernist. The fundamentalist consistently assigns all those who differ from him to the bottomless pit. The modernist would do the same, only he is too scholarly to believe in any such a crude place or to indulge in such crude language. Both are rabid and contentious. Both are gluttons for martyrdom. Seeking persecution with such diligence, they both find it. But somehow it is not easy for me to believe that they enter into the blessing that is pronounced by Jesus upon those who are persecuted for righteousness' sake.

But to be persecuted for righteousness' sake, I repeat, is an indication that the one so persecuted is a child of the King. It indicates that such a one has become a menace to the kingdom of evil. The devil is far too shrewd to turn his guns upon a foe who is spineless and who carries no threat. If you will read the second and third chapters of Revelation, you will find that every Church there mentioned that was counting for anything for the kingdom was being persecuted. It is only the dead or lukewarm Churches that are being let alone. If you are persecuted, that means that you are in great company. You are fighting shoulder to shoulder with the prophets who were before you. You are being opposed because, like them, you are counting in the good fight of faith.

2. Christ congratulates the persecuted because persecution is a pathway to spiritual growth. It is not by difficulties dodged, but by difficulties met and overcome that we become strong. A lotus land is a good place to sleep, but it is a poor place to develop rugged, Christlike character. Then, opposition rightly borne makes for spiritual growth because it drives the persecuted to their Lord. "My grace is sufficient for thee." When the situation is

especially hard, when the opposition is too great for our petty strength, then we may expect great grace, for there is always enough. John G. Paton tells of the bitter opposition that he met in the far-off Hebrides. During a season of persecution he spent one night in a tree. He could hear the savages beating the bushes beneath him, carefully searching for him in an effort to take his life. But he declared that he would gladly pass through another such experience of peril to be privileged to enjoy the assuring and comforting presence of Jesus as he did on that night.

This is one reason that the Church has always experienced its greatest power in times of persecution. By it she was brought into intimate relationship with her suffering Saviour. Then, persecution renders another important service. It not only makes for a more Christlike Church by bringing her into a closer fellowship with Jesus, but it also serves to drive away the triflers and the cowards. It repels those who are not willing to pay the price. The writer of the Acts says in one place: "And of the rest durst no man join himself to them." That is, this persecuted Church had a repelling power as well as an attracting power. It appealed to those of heroic heart, but it frightened the rest away. There was a real gain in that. It would be a real gain in our own day.

3. Then, persecution is a roadway to a larger usefulness. That is true because, as stated above, it brings a larger purity and a closer intimacy with

111

God. The surest way to do more is to be more. The great awakenings of the past have not been begun by the gathering in of the many, but by the deeper consecration of the few.

Then, persecution makes for usefulness because it is one of the most effective methods of broadcasting the truth. When I was a small boy my brother and I set fire to an old dry stump that stood in the center of a grassy field. Father did not want this grass burned. But, by and by, a spark blew out and set it on fire. We organized ourselves into a fire department and began to fight the blaze. Each of us had the branch of a tree, and we fought with great zeal. We put out the fire at the spot we were fighting it, but every time we raised our weapons above our heads we scattered it to other parts of the field. The result was that all the grass was burned, to say nothing of the fence that shut it in. "Behold, how great a matter a little fire kindleth!"

Once in the city of Jerusalem there was a handful of saints who by the grace of God were incarnating these beatitudes. Suddenly persecution swept down upon them. The Jewish hierarchy, backed by the power of Rome, sent them flying from the city. "But they that were scattered abroad went everywhere preaching the Word." Instead of putting out the little blaze that had been started in Jerusalem by their persecution, they only helped them to set the world on fire. And that conflagration is burning to this good hour.

112

This, then, is the appeal of Jesus. He calls upon us to share his nature, to be like himself. He does not base his appeal on promises of exemption from battle. He is finely frank with us. He will allow no man to follow him without giving that man to understand something of the difficulties involved. He tells us openly that to be a Christian is to meet opposition. But if we dare face the opposition our reward will be great. It will be great in this present world. It will bring us deeper spiritual life and richer usefulness. It will enable us to rejoice with those of old because, for his sake, we, too, are counted worthy to suffer shame. By and by it will enable us to feel at home among those "who have come up out of great tribulation, and washed their robes, and made them white in the blood of the lamb."

> 'The Son of God goes forth to war,
>   A kingly crown to gain:
> His blood-red banner streams afar;
>   Who follows in his train?
> Who best can drink his cup of woe,
>   Triumphant over pain,
> Who patient bears his cross below,
>   He follows in his train.
>
> The martyr first, whose eagle eye
>   Could pierce beyond the grave,
> Who saw his Master in the sky,
>   And called on him to save:
> Like him, with pardon on his tongue,
>   In midst of mortal pain,
> He prayed for them that did the wrong:
>   Who follows in his train?

113

THE SERMON ON THE MOUNT

A glorious band, the chosen few
  On whom the Spirit came,
Twelve valiant saints, their hope they knew,
  And mocked the cross and flame;
They climbed the steep ascent of heaven
  Through peril, toil, and pain:
O God, to us may grace be given
  To follow in their train."

IX

"SALT"

Matthew 5: 13

"Ye are the salt of the earth: but if the salt have lost its savour, wherewith shall it be salted? It is thenceforth good for nothing, but to be cast out, and to be trodden under the foot of men."

I

JESUS is speaking primarily to his own disciples. He is speaking to those who have left all to follow him. Those who are the salt of the earth are the men and women who through poverty of spirit have entered into the kingdom. They are the meek and the merciful. They are the peacemakers, and those who through purity of heart have come into possession of a redeeming and transforming vision of God. But since Christ's invitation is to every man, since every man may enter the kingdom if he is willing, Christ is also speaking to the multitude. He is telling them that they, too, if they are willing, may become the salt of the earth.

"Ye are the salt of the earth." If this is taken as a declaration of our privileges, it flings a bow of hope athwart our skies beautiful and alluring beyond our dreams. If it is taken as a declaration of our obligations and responsibilities, it becomes an

115

epitome of all the commandments and a summing up of the whole duty of man. If it is taken as a statement of fact, as it surely is, it becomes the highest of all compliments. We so recognize it to this hour. In every community there are certain characters of outstanding worth. When we want to describe such a character we say: "He is the salt of the earth." That is the highest compliment we can give. No finer could be given even by Jesus himself.

II

"Ye are the salt of the earth." Jesus is here telling us of the influence that the type of personality described by these beatitudes is to have upon the world. He is indicating the high vocation of those who possess Christlike character. He says that they are to be the salt of the earth. What does he mean by this?

1. He means that Christian character is a positive force in the world. Salt is something that cannot be ignored. It is a positive quantity. If it is present, one must recognize it. If it is absent, it is certain to be missed. It is the antithesis of the negative and the neutral. It is the sworn antagonist of the insipid. When it comes to town, folks are sure to find it out. When it leaves, they are certain to miss it. Sometimes its presence is exceedingly welcome. At other times it is keenly resented, but always it must be recognized.

Some months ago I was invited to dine in a very

lovely home. The dinner was a great success till we came to the dessert. There we came face to face with calamity. The waiter brought in some most delicious-looking, homemade ice cream. It required great self-restraint to wait till all the guests were served before tasting it. At last we were ready. The hostess began, but her brows were at once puckered into a frown. "I am so sorry," she said at once, "but you cannot eat your cream. It is full of salt." But why, I wonder, did she not keep the matter a secret? Why did she not say to herself, "A little salt will not hurt my guests; therefore I will not spoil the feast by telling them that something is wrong"? She knew that that salt would speak for itself. And so it did. It literally shrieked. She could no more quiet it than she could quiet her small boy.

Now, Jesus tells us, Christians are, in a measure, like that. They are not mere moral minus signs. They are not harmless nonentities. They are not uninteresting creatures who are "faultily faultless, icily regular, splendidly null." They are positive, pungent, strengthful folks. You may like them or dislike them, you may love them or hate them, you may fight with them or fight against them, but you cannot ignore them. Jesus was like that. Wherever he went dullness took to its heels and stagnation fled in deadly fear. Some loved him with a love that nothing could kill. Others hated him with a hatred that would not endure his being on the earth.

117

But wherever he went he divided men into excited groups. He simply could not be ignored.

2. Now, since salt is a positive something, it gives taste to whatever it touches. It gives piquancy to all of our feasts. Any dinner would be a most insipid affair without salt. Salt is a luxury. But it is far more than that. For civilized men it is a positive necessity. We can, if we must, get on without beautiful carpets on our floors. We can get on without lovely pictures on our walls. We can manage somehow without high-powered cars. We can, in case of absolute necessity, get on without the movies. In fact, should the worst come to the worst, we might find life very livable without a great many commodities that we now feel that we just must have. But there is one commonplace something that we cannot get on without. That something is salt. It is at once a luxury and a necessity.

And Jesus ranks himself and those who are like him among the necessities of life. Christlike character may be regarded by some as a luxury. But it is more; it is a necessity. Without it the feast of life loses its tang. How dull and stale the world had grown when Jesus came!

> "On that hard pagan world disgust
> And secret loathing fell,
> Deep weariness and sated lust
> Made human life a hell."

Life always grows stale and dead without him and
118

those who are like him. It has no richness, no depth of meaning. It becomes a mere

> "tale told by an idiot,
> Full of sound and fury,
> Signifying nothing."

Jesus must break in upon us in order for life to thrill with lofty meaning and sing with deathless hopes. Those who regard Christians as mere incarnate insipidities that take the joy out of life are the farthest possible from the truth. On the contrary, they are the ones without whose presence the anchor soon drags, and life inevitably loses its tang.

3. Then salt is a preventive. It is the open enemy of decay. It is the foe of impurity. It is the avowed antagonist of rottenness and disintegration. It stands in the presence of the corruption, of the impurity, of the decay that so persistently lay siege to all things here and say: "They shall not pass." It purifies and sweetens and keeps sound all with which it comes in contact.

"And Christians are like that," says Jesus proudly. Without the presence of those who are Christlike, civilization does not climb upward, but goes downward. Society does not become more and more pure, but tends rather toward moral rottenness and decay. The presence of Christlike character in the world is an absolute essential if the world is to be kept from disintegration. No nation is made safe by its natural re-

119

sources, its geographical position, its standing army, or by its navy. It is only made safe by the character of its people.

That is what Elisha meant when he shouted that rather startling word after Elijah. You remember how those two prophets did that last mile together before they reached the little station where God sent his own private chariot to meet Elijah. At last they have come to the parting of the ways. Elijah is being carried up into heaven. Elisha looks after him and shouts: "My father, my father, the horsemen of Israel, and the chariots thereof." What did he mean? He meant to say: "Yonder goes the defender of this nation. Yonder goes the one who, above all others, has stood between Israel and ruin." Some had been blind enough to believe that Israel's safety was in her diplomacy, in her army, in her war chariots. But her real standing army wore a prophet's mantle and tramped about the country calling men back to God. And it is my conviction at this hour that one man of Christlike character is worth more in the real defense of the world than any battleship that was ever built, or all of them together.

Saintly character is the supreme safeguard of the world. Every great disaster that has come to our race has come because there was a lack of this saving salt. There was a preacher of righteousness once who had something to say about a coming flood. But Noah did not preach the flood as inevitable. He declared that it was inevitable if men did not repent; therefore he called to his fellows to bring to bear the saving salt of saintly lives upon a world that was rotting down. They refused to hear; therefore disintegration continued to the point of final disaster. But the real tragedy of the flood was not that a certain generation ceased to live. It was, rather, the fact that that generation had ceased to be fit to live.

I have no doubt that Sodom was quite a busy and thriving city. It was buying and selling and boasting and rotting, all at the same time. Had one gone to the Chamber of Commerce and suggested that they try to induce a few men like Abraham to move down into the city to save it from moral corruption, he would doubtless have been laughed at for his pains. But that was by far the most pressing need of the city. We are informed beyond the shadow of a doubt that ten good men could have so salted the city as to have saved it. But these were not to be found. Therefore its destruction was inevitable.

Before the outbreak of the French Revolution, France became very short on the saving salt of saintly lives. Many laughed and quaffed and said: "After us the deluge." And the deluge came. It was a deluge of blood and tears. Certain historians tell us that England was on the verge of a like revolution. But somehow the tragedy was averted. Somehow this great nation did not slip into that awful abyss. Why not? It was not saved by its army and navy. It was not saved by its diplomats.

There was a man who had his heart strangely warmed in a little service in Aldersgate Street, London. That man came out from that service to bring to bear the saving salt of his transformed personality upon the masses of England, and the nation was not only saved from revolution, but it was reborn to a new moral and spiritual life.

III

Notice next the sphere of our activities. If we are salt, where are we to unloose our preventive and purifying powers?

The Master does not say that we are to salt heaven. No doubt there will be great tasks for us to do over there, but that is not the matter of which Jesus is speaking here. Nor are we to salt some far-off yesterday. There are those who exercised all their preserving and purifying powers years ago. We were genuine salt in the old home Church, but, sad to say, we are doing nothing now. Nor are we to salt some ideal situation in some to-morrow that never comes. "Ye are the salt of the earth." That is, we are to exercise our sweetening and preserving and purifying powers in the here and now. It is not an ideal sphere, maybe, but it is the only one so far as we are concerned. It gives us our one privilege for serving and lays upon us our one big responsibility.

It is our business to serve as salt in our community. It is our business, as far as in us lies, to see that our city is a clean city. We are to see to it that its atmosphere is such as will give the boys and girls the best possible chance to grow up into clean and wholesome manhood and womanhood. We are to see to it that it is as free as possible from those temptations that blight and damn. To this end we are to be ourselves Christian citizens. To this end we are to give our moral and political support to such men as stand for decency and law enforcement. We are to be relentless foes, politically, of those who violate the law or make it easy for others to do so.

We are to serve as saving salt in our own Church. This is a day in which it is especially fashionable to stone the Church. Her critics are numerous, and their voices are loud and full of clamor for attention. Nor can anyone claim that the Church is altogether blameless. It is not perfect, because it is made up of imperfect people. Yet it is doing more to salt down our present civilization and to keep it from rotting than any other institution in the world. It is doing more to safeguard those fundamental integrities on which civilization rests than all other institutions combined. Many a man who has his own life and the lives of those he loves safeguarded by it makes no better returns than that of cheap and sometimes ignorant criticism. Kipling's rebuke to those who ridiculed England's peace-time army seems to fit in here:

> "Making fun of uniforms
>   That guard you while you sleep,
> Is cheaper than them uniforms,
>   And that's starvation cheap."

123

Nor is it fair to judge the Church solely by its positive accomplishments, though, judged according to that measure, its benefits are incalculable. Every other institution that I know that is exercising the lifting power of an ounce receives its inspiration from the Church. But we need to judge the Church also in the light of what it prevents. Our city is not what it ought to be, but how much worse would it be without the Church! We ourselves are not all that we ought to be, but how much worse would we likely be without the influence of the Church! A young chap presented me with a check some years ago, saying that he had forged it. His comment was this: "I did not cash that check this morning because I heard you preach last night." Sometimes there are services that seem very meager in positive results. But we can never really know what was accomplished. We can certainly never know how many were fortified and strengthened and kept from falling.

But granting that the Church is not what it should be, what is your remedy? Do you expect to cure it by letting it alone? Do you expect to cure it by ignoring it? Do you expect to cure it by throwing stones at it? Or, do you propose to bring to its languishing life that saving salt of a Christlike personality? Years ago I went to serve a Church that was torn to shreds by internal strife. "The devil has this Church," a man said one day. But a certain old saint overheard the remark and answered: "He hasn't got my seat yet. I am in it myself every service, and I am going to see to it that he does not get it." And that man became a rallying point round which God wrought a great victory.

Then, we are to salt our own homes. That is the surest way to salt the Church. That is the surest way to salt the world. If we really bring to bear the saving salt of saintly character in our own homes we shall thereby help to salt our nation. We shall thereby sooner or later help to salt every nation in the wide world. And the world will never be salted any other way. A man may be born again when he is old, but, comparatively, it is a rare miracle. The longer I live, the more I come to realize that the only sure way to have Christians is to raise them. If we bring to bear the saving salt of Christlikeness upon our children in their young and tender years, we shall not only save them for heaven, but we shall save them for this world as well. How many have been brought back from lives of sin by the memory of a godly father and mother! How far many more have been prevented from going into sin by these same precious memories! "I could not do it," said a certain young chap as he faced a sordid temptation, "because I remembered my mother." How often is it so!

> "Her voice is heard through roaring drums
> That beat to battle where he stands:
> Her face across his fancy comes,
> And gives the battle to his hands."

IV

Then, if we are to salt the earth, how is it to be

done? What is the method that Jesus here suggests? Two words give the answer. We are to salt through character and contact.

1. We are the salt of the earth by being Christ-like. Jesus did not say: "You are to scatter salt." He said: "Ye are salt." If we are to save the world, it must be through the compelling power of saintly character. It is important to do, but to be is of supreme and fundamental importance. I cannot help to salt the earth unless I have salt in myself. If the Christian loses his enthusiasm, if he loses his tang, if he becomes insipid, then he becomes utterly useless. He is fit for nothing but to be thrown away.

We can easily understand why this is true. Moffatt makes the author of the one hundred and nineteenth Psalm say: "I hate men that are half and half." With that sentiment we all agree. With that sentiment Christ agrees. There is no type of character that he finds quite so repellent as the half-hearted. That was the trouble with the Church at Laodicea. It had lost its zeal. It had lost its glow. Its enthusiasms were dead. It had become dull, listless, insipid, mere savorless salt. No wonder Jesus said: "I would thou wert cold or hot. So then because thou art lukewarm, and neither cold nor hot, I will spew thee out of my mouth." If we hope to salt the world, we must shun insipidity as we shun the very pangs of hell.

Then, if we are to salt the earth we must come into contact with those whom we are to salt. When we used to kill our meat on the farm, I often assisted at the salting. We did not salt meat by putting the salt in one barrel and the meat in another. The two had to be brought into contact. Not only was the salt given to the meat, but that salt lost itself in a sense by that giving. It passed out of sight altogether. It saved the meat at the expense of itself. It could not possibly save in any other way.

And the same law holds good for you and me. If we are to bring to bear the saving salt of a saintly life upon the world, it is going to be costly. It was so for Jesus. When he set out to save the world, he did not undertake the task while keeping himself at a distance. He came into contact with men in the most intimate fashion possible. He knew no cheaper way than the laying down of his life. "The Son of Man came not to be ministered unto, but to minister, and to give his life a ransom for many." And it is enough for the servant that he be as his Lord. We can serve in no other way. To be unwilling to bleed is to be incapacitated to bless. "Except a corn of wheat fall into the ground and die, it abideth alone; but if it die, it bringeth forth much fruit."

X

LIGHT

Matthew 5: 14-16

"Ye are the light of the world. A city thát is set on a
hill cannot be hid. Neither do men light a candle, and
put it under a bushel, but on a candlestick; and it
giveth light unto all that are in the house. Let your
light so shine before men, that they may see your good
works, and glorify your Father which is in heaven."

I

"Ye are the light of the world." Here again our
Lord is giving us his conception of the Christian
life. To be a Christian is to be a light-bringer.
What a thrilling and breath-taking word! Last
Sunday we said that when Jesus called us salt he
paid us the highest possible compliment. But it is
certainly no higher than this. In fact, in saying,
"Ye are the light of the world," he couples our
names with his own in a way that is perfectly
amazing. For he who said, "Ye are the light of the
world," is the One who said: "I am the Light of the
world."

Of course there is this vast difference between his
light and ours. Our Lord is light in himself. When
the prophets dreamed of him they saw him as the
bringer of a new day. He was to rise on a darkened
world as the Sun of Righteousness with healing in

128

his wings. He is the true light that, coming into the world, lighteth every man. We shine only as we are touched and transformed by himself. If he dwells with us, we shine through him. But apart from him we can do nothing. The moment we lose contact the light goes out.

It was Paul who said: "For me to live is Christ." He might have said with equal truth: "For me to shine is Christ." So we also may say. That distant planet that keeps eternal lids apart in the night sky says: "For me to shine is the sun." Not that all the light of the sun is centered in that one star, but all the light it has and gives comes from the sun. Buffalo, N. Y., is lighted by the power that comes from Niagara Falls. Every light that blazes in that city says: "For me to shine is Niagara." Not that all the power of that thundering cataract is expended on that one light, but whatever power it has comes from Niagara. Apart from that power it could not shine. Apart from Christ we cannot shine.

II

But if we know Jesus, if we are possessors of the kingdom, we are light. Being light, we can shine. That is our business. That is what we are lighted for. Of course Christ has a purpose in our salvation that reaches beyond ourselves. He wants every man to know him because of the transforming power of that knowledge and the joy it brings to the man himself. But no man is saved simply and solely for himself. No lamp is ever lighted just for its own benefit. It is lighted in order to give light. That is true of ourselves. Since it is true, how are we to shine?

1. We are to shine naturally. That is what any real light will do. How did this rose become so red? What rouge does it use? It uses none at all. Its nature is to be red. Why does the ocean sprawl so broad and wide between the continents? Why does it boom its perpetual cannonade along all shores? It does so naturally. Why does that mountain climb so high that it has to wrap a mantel of shimmering whiteness around its shoulders even during the hottest days of summer? It is not standing on tiptoe. It is naturally tall. Why does that bird sing as if the whole world were listening? It is not putting on a show; it is the nature of that bird to sing.

And if we are light in the Lord, we are going to shine naturally. There is going to be a beautiful spontaneity about our radiance. There was once a gifted and fascinating young man who was being mobbed. The stones were flying thick about him. But the stones could not banish the light that shone upon his face. "They saw his face as it had been the face of an angel." He did not make his face bright of set purpose. His fellowship with God made that brightness natural to him. Looking unto him, he became radiant with a radiance that those who beheld him could not fail to recognize. Paul saw it, and it haunted him till it brought him to Christ.

Peter and John were arrested one day. The court

that tried them gave them very strict orders. They were not to speak any more nor teach in the name of Jesus. But what was their answer? It was very clear and emphatic. "We cannot but speak the things we have seen and heard." "What you command," they say, "is utterly impossible. We are light, and, being light, we cannot but shine. We have a story that is far too good to keep. Were we resolved to do so, the Word would be as a burning fire shut up in our bones. Being light, we cannot but give light to those that sit in darkness."

2. Not only are we to shine naturally, but we are to shine willingly and of set purpose. We are to shine sacrificially. Shining is natural for light, but it is always costly. Wherever you see a light you may know that something is being burned up. You may know that energy is being expended. As the candle burns, it grows shorter and shorter. As the lamp burns, it consumes not only the oil, but the wick as well. And even though it is electricity that is burning in that globe, by and by we shall have to throw the globe away because it will be burned out. When Jesus came as the Light of the world, his shining was infinitely costly. The disciples received a hint of the price he was paying when they looked into his tired, spent face. The very weariness they recognized brought them the interpretation of a text they had not understood before. They said: "The zeal for God's house is burning him up." Jesus said of John that he was a burning and a shining light. So he was. But if you will take a glance

into that gloomy prison cell, if you will look at that severed head that is now glutting the vengeance of that hard-faced woman, you will realize something of the price he paid. Shining is expensive even when God supplies the power, for the wick must burn with the oil.

3. Then, we are to shine openly. We are to shine before men. That is not always easy. There are some who are not friendly to light. Jesus knew such in his day. "Some men," he tells us, "love darkness rather than light, because their deeds are evil." When a criminal sets out to do a crime, he does not welcome the light. He desires that the shadows be as black as possible. Lady Macbeth did not look for the light as she purposed and planned the murder of Duncan. She rather said:

> 'Come, thick night,
> And pall thee in the dunnest smoke of hell,
> That my keen knife see not the wound it makes,
> Nor heaven peep through the blanket of the dark
> To cry, 'Hold, hold!'"

When the Bastille was stormed, those engaged in the task came to one dark cell where the light had not shone for long years. They battered down the door, let in a flood of sunshine, and invited the prisoner to come out to freedom. But he shrank back and covered his eyes and begged them to shut the door to keep out the light. So long had he lived in the dark that light had become painful to him. Did you ever turn over a rotting log in the forest and see the creatures of the dark that were hidden under

132

it? How the light troubled and frightened them! If you could have heard them, I think they would have been saying; "Put out the light." And there are those in every age that shrink from the light that flashes from the face of Christ or from the life of one illuminated by the light of Christ.

But we are not for this reason to leave off our shining. We are not for this reason to put our lights under a bushel. We are not to be afraid to be openly Christian We are not to be afraid to be ourselves. Dr. Sockman spoke recently of "The New Hypocrisy." He declared that there was a day when the Church was strong and dominant in the life of the people; that, in that day, to win popularity men often sought to appear better than they were. That was the old hypocrisy. To-day, when the Church does not loom so large in the public eye, there are those who seek to appear worse than they are. That is the new hypocrisy.

And this new hypocrisy is altogether too common. How many are afraid to appear as good as they actually are! They are ashamed of the convictions that they possess. They are ashamed to acknowledge the faith that is very dear to them. They are ashamed of the ideals that are the very glory of their manhood and womanhood. This same speaker referred to a conversation that he overheard in the smoking room on a train. A group of fairly clean-faced men were talking. From their conversation one would have thought that every one of the group had his private bootlegger and that every one spent all his leisure time in the lowest night clubs of New York. If we have been lighted by the power of God, let us not hide our light under the bushel of cowardice.

Then we must avoid hiding our light under the bushel of inconsistency or positive sin. I once had a most earnest worker in my Church. There was scarcely any task that she was not willing to undertake. I have seen her serve sacrificially for hours and even days, till her light was shining with beautiful radiance. Then she would turn down a bushel of temper over it and put it almost absolutely out. In the little church that I attended as a boy the brother who led the singing at night used to hold a lamp in his hand with which to beat time and, incidentally, to help him to see. But too often he would tilt the lamp to such an angle that the chimney was soon so blackened that the light was dimmed. A lamp to shine its best must stand upright. The same is true of ourselves. We cannot shine before men if we are not morally and spiritually erect.

4. Then, we must shine where we are. This is one glory of light, that it is democratic. When the sun rose this morning it illuminated the pigsty with the same radiance that it spilled upon the flower garden. It shone upon the clean and the unclean with equal brightness. A candle will shine just as beautifully in a poor man's cottage as in a rich man's palace. It will shine just as brightly in the most obscure corner of the earth as upon the steps of a throne. And if we

are going to light the world we must do so by shining where we are. There is not much poetry, but plenty of excellent sense, in that popular song, "Brighten the Corner Where You Are." If you do not shine where you are, then you will not shine at all. I don't know what your candlestick is. It may be some conspicuous place. It may be a high social position. It may be a prominent place in the business world. It may be the platform of a popular pulpit. Or it may be a very obscure place. It may be a humble home. It may even be no larger than a sick bed. But whatever it is, and wherever it is, there you are to shine. It is your one chance.

It is by our thus shining where we are that the world's night is to be banished. For it is as we shine individually that we are to add to the sum total of the world's light. It is by each individual shining that the Church comes to be as a city set upon a hill. That city upon the hill that cannot be hid is not made up of just one individual. It is composed of many. In the pioneer days when the saints set out for the night service, each carried a candle. One candle did very little toward making the house bright. But all the candles brought the needed light and made the service possible. So as each shines in his own place the shadows are to flee away, and the new day is to come.

III

Now, if we thus shine, Jesus has no slightest doubt as to the beneficent results that will follow.

He says that such shining will be victorious, that such shining will conquer the night. He says that such shining will result not in applause for ourselves; that is not what we are seeking if we are Christians. It will result in the salvation of men and in their giving glory to God. The reasons for this are very obvious. Such results are but the natural outcome of light. This is true for the following reasons:

1. Light is a positive something. Wherever light shines it is going to be seen. That is absolutely sure. If nobody sees our light, it is certainly for one of two reasons. It is because we have no light, or because we have hidden it away under some kind of bushel. Light, just as salt, is something that cannot be ignored. Black night might say: "I am not going to pay a bit of attention to the sun. I am not going to give an inch." But in spite of its boasting when the sun comes it takes to its heels. Light is positive, and the positive forces win.

2. Then, light is cheering and comforting. There is something depressing about darkness. It is the symbol of the sorrowful and the mysterious. There is something frightening about it. In the dark one can see anything that a fevered imagination suggests. The most familiar object can easily become a distorted monstrosity. It is not to be wondered at that when John dreamed of heaven he thought of it as a land of light and said: "There shall be no night there." I think I have never been much given to fear, but when I hear things about the house in the

late hours of the night, I love the light. There is something cheering and consoling about it.

And how cheering and consoling is this light that flashes from the face of Christ! "Be of good cheer" is a word that was on his lips again and again. He said it in the presence of the fury of nature. He said it in the presence of the ravages of sin. He said it in the presence of the mystery and tragedy of death. These glooms are about us still. We all need the light to shine into our darkness. We need to be delivered from the fear of yesterday and the fear of to-morrow. We need to see life illuminated by the light of God. We need to see death, not as a blind alley that leads to oblivion, but as a wide-open roadway into our Father's house.

3. Light awakens. A few hours ago the world was asleep. The sheep and the cattle were lying down in the pastures. The birds had their heads tucked under their wings, except here and there an enthusiastic mocker who, having to sing all the songs in the birds' hymn book, must needs turn night into day. But now all our world is awake. How did it come about? Did God turn loose a million alarm clocks? Did he shake the birds out of the trees? No. He just lifted the sun above the eastern hills, and the multitudinous life of the world awakened and began a new day.

When Christianity was born, it was night. Almost the whole world was in the grip of a common religion, the religion of polytheism, which was a religion of shadows. But the preaching of these

137

early disciples awakened the world and brought in a new day. When the Church forgot her high task and hid her lamp under a bushel, then came the Dark Ages. There were a thousand years of night. Then Martin Luther came into vital contact with the Light of the World. Through the light that blazed from his hot heart and radiant face there came a great awakening. Through the centuries Christian character has been an awakening power.

4. Light makes for health. It is at once a preventive and a cure. It tends to shut the door in the face of invading disease, or to cast it out if it has already entered. It makes incessant war against the friends of sickness and gives help to the friends of health. A house physician in a London hospital declared that it took a simple fracture from seven to fourteen days longer to heal in a certain dark ward of the hospital than in another that was well lighted. Unsunned places are ever the abodes of weakness, sickness, and degeneracy. It is our high task as Christians so to shine as to help bring light to all that sit in darkness. In so doing we shall do our part toward bringing health and healing to our sick and disordered world.

5. Finally, light reveals. Light enables us to see. A face of beauty is no fairer than one of ugliness if we have no light. It is in the radiance of the light of Christ that we see ourselves. It is in the radiance of this light that we see our possibilities. Old Born Drunk, in "Twice-Born Men," had never known a sober day. He had been made drunk at his mother's

breast. Few, indeed, imagined that he could ever be different. But one day he looked into the face of Joe, who had once been almost as low as himself, but who had been wonderfully transformed. At once he began to dream that there was hope for himself. "All at once," he declared, "it came home to me that I might be like Joe." From that hour Old Born Drunk began to walk in newness of life. From that hour he became a shining light in his sordid world.

It is by the light of Christian character that we get a vision of the face of God. That is why Jesus came as the Light of the world. He came to show us God. He revealed to us God's infinite loveliness as the world had never seen it before. He showed us that God was our Father. The Psalmists had come close to him, but they had never come close enough to discover that fact. And what higher vocation can you and I possibly dream of than just this, to live such lives day by day that those who come in contact with us will see in the radiance of our lives something of the loveliness of God, that they will discover that God is our Father and theirs? Making this discovery, they will surely glorify our Father who is in heaven.

XI

FULFILLING THE LAW

Matthew 5: 17-48

By the time the Young Prophet had reached this part of his sermon his audience was on tiptoe of expectation. They were wondering whether he was a radical or a conservative. Had he broken with the old religion as, in a measure, John the Baptist had done, John who never went to the temple and never offered sacrifices? Or was he still loyal to the faith of his fathers? Each group was listening eagerly for an answer to these questions just as a present-day audience might listen for some catchword that would indicate whether the speaker was a fundamentalist or a modernist.

Jesus soon made his position clear. "Think not that I am come to destroy the law and the prophets." He disclaimed at once the rôle of an iconoclast. He is no mere destructionist. Naturally not. No man was ever sent of God to do nothing but destroy. To tear down, to wreck, requires little either of heart or of brains. An idiot can destroy more in an hour than a great artist could build in a score of years. Jesus, therefore, is not here as a mere destroyer. What is essential in the law is going to abide. "One jot or one tittle shall in no wise pass till all be fulfilled."

What, then, is to be his attitude to the law? He is here to fulfill it, to perfect it, to bring it to completion. When a youth passes from high school to college, he does not do so to destroy what he has learned in his earlier years. He is undertaking to carry the knowledge already acquired further toward completion. When the soil and the sunshine and the rain lay hold of an acorn, they do not destroy it. They bring it to its completion in the giant oak. Thus Jesus fulfills the law. The old law was good, but it was not perfect. It was of value, but it was not complete. Had it been so, we should not have needed the work of Jesus.

And with what a kingly stride he goes about the task, with what superb assurance, with what majestic audacity! "Ye have heard that it was said by them of old time, . . . but I say unto you." This he repeats again and again. Who are these who spoke of old time? They are the prophets. They are men who spoke as they were moved of the Spirit. They are men, therefore, of great authority. They begin their messages, and rightly, with this big declaration: "Thus saith the Lord." But this Young Prophet appeals to no authority other than himself. He speaks in his own name. "But I say unto you." Thus he speaks as only he has a right to speak in whom are hidden all the treasures of wisdom and knowledge. He speaks as one who can say: "He that hath seen me hath seen the Father."

How, then, does Jesus fulfill the law?

1. He fulfills the law in his own person. That is not the point emphasized in this sermon, but it is true none the less. It became him to fulfill all righteousness. The law found its complete fulfillment in him.

2. He fulfills the law by giving it a greater inwardness. Before his coming the law had to do largely with the outside of life. It concerned itself with conduct. Its attention was fixed on the flying wheels of action. Jesus takes us down into the power house. He takes us into the engine room. He shows us the dynamo. He takes us into the hidden chambers of the heart. He knows that one is not always known by his actions. To really know a man we must visit the inner chambers of thought and imagination. We must hear him dream and see him think. For, "as a man thinketh in his heart, so is he."

3. Jesus gave to the law a new positiveness. He made it constructive. Before his coming it consisted largely of prohibitions. Its predominant word was: "Thou shalt not." There were so many things that one was not allowed to do that there was little time for positive doing. Jesus changed the emphasis. He said: "Except your goodness exceeds the goodness of the scribes and Pharisees, ye shall in no case enter into the kingdom of heaven." He focused our attention, not upon what we are not

142

to be, but what we are to be. He emphasized, not what we are forbidden to do, but what we are to do. Every parable of judgment that he uttered was against those guilty of failure in duty rather than against those who had violated some definite law. Goodness, according to Jesus, is not an absence of faults, but the presence of positive virtues.

II

The remainder of this chapter is taken up with illustrations of how Christ fulfills the law. I am not going to take these illustrations in their order.

1. Look at the seventh commandment. "Ye have heard that it was said by them of old time, Thou shalt not commit adultery." Nothing was forbidden but the act of sin. "But I say unto you, Whosoever looketh on a woman to lust after her hath committed adultery with her already in his heart." The word translated "to" here means in order to. The one condemned is the one who has a deliberate purpose to sin. His intentions are all in that direction. He only fails to carry out those intentions because of fear or because he cannot. His intention, his will being toward the wrong, the man himself is wrong. The intention is taken for the deed.

Now, what is true of the seventh commandment is true of every other. Sin homes in the will. The man who wills to come to Christ is a Christian. The man who wills to sin is a sinner, whether the thought and purpose of his heart are ever translated into act or not. The man who refuses to steal simply because

143

he fears detection is a thief. The man who is honest simply because honesty is the best policy is really not honest at all. "Thou shalt not commit adultery," said the law. "Thou shalt be clean in thy thoughts and in thy purposes," said Jesus.

2. "It hath been said, Whosoever shall put away his wife, let him give her a writing of divorcement." This was the law. It was some protection for the divorced woman. But it was very incomplete. It was exceedingly imperfect. About all a husband had to do who wanted to be rid of his wife was to give her a statement saying, "Whereas this woman was once my wife, she is now mine no more." He could then send her on away and still be fully within the law.

But how vastly Jesus deepened and widened this law, and how much of purity and of decency and of moral uplift the world owes to that fact! He said: "For this cause shall a man leave father and mother and shall cleave unto his wife, and they twain shall be one flesh. What, therefore, God hath joined together, let not man put asunder." That is, marriage is a divine institution. It is for life. There is but one valid reason for divorce, and that is adultery. This is a hard saying to some, I know, but the seriously regarding and obeying of it is necessary in order to keep civilization from disintegrating.

3. "Thou shalt not forswear thyself, but shall perform unto the Lord thine oaths." So spoke the law. Jesus said: "Swear not at all, . . . but let your communication be, Yea, yea; Nay, nay: for whatso-

ever is more than these cometh of evil." Now, what Jesus is forbidding here is not the taking of a legal oath. He himself accepted a legal oath on one occasion, as we see in Matthew 26. He is commanding us to tell the plain, unvarnished truth, to be genuinely sincere. Thus he is laying down a law so wide and deep that an oath becomes superfluous. It becomes utterly unnecessary. "Tell the truth. Be truly honest, and you will have no need to swear."

Now, it is a fact that a genuinely honest man does not need an oath in order to make him truthful. If a man is truly sincere in the inner deeps of his soul, he will speak the truth without any oath. In fact, I am convinced that the man who will lie when not under oath will also lie if he is under oath. The taking of an oath becomes a positive evil when it leads one to believe that lying is less hurtful and less wrong when no oath is taken.

This was the horrible situation into which the habit of swearing had plunged the people to whom Jesus was speaking. They did not believe the obligation to tell the truth was binding at all except under oath. They did not believe that all oaths were binding. One might swear by heaven or by earth or by his head and get away with it. Thus lying had become a veritable plague among them. They had the greatest number of oaths and were about the most prolific liars in the world. And lying hurts the liar. It is also a menace to the social order. No wonder, therefore, that Jesus did not say, "Do not violate your oath," but passed on to the higher ground and said: "Tell the truth and make oath-taking absolutely unnecessary."

4. Then there are three striking illustrations that have to do with the treatment of our fellows. They have especially to do with the treatment of those with whom for one reason or another we are tempted to be at enmity.

(1) There was the law against killing. "Thou shalt not kill." To keep this law one had only to refrain from striking his brother dead. His attitude toward him was not taken into consideration at all. Jesus pushed the law back into those depths where murder is born. He forbade us to be angry with our brother without cause. There is a question as to whether or not "without cause" belongs in the text. Personally, I think it has a right there. I think so because there are times when anger is altogether just and right. We must believe this or discredit our Master.

For instance, one day Jesus went into the temple, where he found a man with a withered hand. This man had a heavy handicap. He was not playing his part in the world of men as he might have played it. But there were certain religious leaders present who were far more concerned about their petty regulations than they were about the man's cure. And we read that Jesus looked round about upon them with anger. It was an anger that scorched and blistered and burned. But it was not born of any injury that these religionists had done to Jesus himself. It was not selfish, as ours so often is. It was born of love.

146

And such anger becomes at times not only a right, but a positive duty.

But what Jesus is forbidding here is selfish and vindictive anger. And this is the type of anger with which we are tragically familiar. We meet it in ourselves and others. Such anger is wrong. It is incipient murder. The difference between the selfishly angry man who does not strike and him who actually kills is in degree rather than kind. Therefore to be thus angry is to be guilty. To allow that anger to lead to words of contempt, as "Raca, you common fellow," is to be more guilty still. To allow it to lead to terms of abuse, as "Thou fool," is to be in danger of the very severest punishment.

But not only are we forbidden to be angry and contemptuous and abusive. These are merely negative. We are to do our best to make up with our brother, to get on good terms with him. This is of supreme importance. It even comes before worship, for without it real worship is impossible. "Therefore, if thou bring thy gift to the altar, and there rememberest that thy brother hath aught against thee; leave there thy gift before the altar, and go thy way; first be reconciled to thy brother, and then come and offer thy gift." Our singing, our giving, our praying—these will all come to little if we have an unbrotherly attitude toward any human soul.

Then, the Master gives us an extreme case. He says, if you are on your way to the court and meet your adversary, do your best to come to terms of friendship with him, try to settle the matter out of court. If you do not, he may turn you over to the judge, and the judge to the officer, and you be cast into prison. This does not mean a literal prison, but the prison of your own anger, of your own hostility, of your own hate. I have known many in such prisons. There may be some present who are locked in the gloomy dungeon of their own malice. If such is the case, let me remind you that you are in about the most wretched and ruinous prison in the world.

(2) Next, Jesus tells us how to treat those who have done us an injury or who would appeal to us for help. "Ye have heard that it was said by them of old time, An eye for an eye, and a tooth for a tooth." This was not the best possible law, but it was best for the time when it was enacted. Under this law, if you should knock my eye out, I would have the right to knock yours out. That would be justice, and no more. Without such a law, if you had knocked my eye out, I might have knocked both of yours out. If you had broken my arm, I might have broken both of yours. So this law was good, but it was not good enough. Therefore Jesus said: "But I say unto you, that you resist not evil: but whosoever shall smite thee on thy right cheek, turn to him the other also."

An arresting word, surely. Nor does it become easier as we proceed. "And if a man will sue thee at the law, and take away thy coat, let him have thy cloak also. And whosoever shall compel thee to go a mile, go with him twain. Give to him that asketh

148

thee, and from him that would borrow of thee, turn not thou away." Certainly this is one of the most startling utterances that ever fell from the lips of Jesus. If we interpret it in a crass and wooden and literal fashion, it brings us into a situation that is nothing short of impossible. And it is well to remember that our Lord never calls us to throw dust in the eyes of reason nor spit in the face of sanctified common sense.

Just what, then, does Jesus mean? I do not take his meaning to be that we are to give to every one who asks a gift, regardless of who the individual is or how he intends to use what we give. There are times when such giving would rob both him that gives and him that takes. I do not take it that it is never right to resist an evildoer. To fail to do so would often hurt the evildoer, his victim, and society as a whole. There was one occasion when Jesus resorted to measures that look very much like physical force. When the temple was being desecrated by a crowd of irreverent tricksters, he took a scourge of small cords and drove the whole herd out, pell-mell, and overturned their money tables.

But while there are times when resistance may be both a right and a duty, those cases are certainly exceptions. Therefore, while we are not to interpret this passage with bald literalness, we must remember that Jesus means something by it. He means something high and exacting, and he means that something most intensely. We must remember also that he was no dreamer. He was no spinner of idle and worthless theories. In taking him seriously we are sure to find the best way of life both for ourselves and for others. This is Jesus's way of treating those who did him wrong. He means for us to go and do likewise.

What is our attitude toward those who insult us? What is our attitude toward those who slap our faces, if not with their hands, then in some other fashion equally hard to bear? If one slaps my face, it is suggested that I can take either one of three courses. I can hit back. In that case the most skillful boxer wins. But nothing is decided save who is the stronger man physically. That is about all that has been decided by the wars that have billowed the continents with graves through the long centuries. Another thing I can do is to run. In that case I may save myself temporarily from personal harm, but I also encourage my antagonist in his evil ways. Again, I can refuse either to run or to fight. I can stand my ground and take his insult. I can thus demonstrate that I had rather suffer wrong than to do wrong.

This is the method of Jesus. It is one that we have tried out all too little, either individually or nationally. But it is the only one in which there is any real hope. I know a man who some years ago in the heat of discussion on a conference floor got his face slapped. He refused to hit back. There was not the slightest retaliation in any fashion. But every man knew which of the two was really courageous The aggressor on that occasion has slipped into utter oblivion. The other is one of the most influential forces for moral uplift in America to-day. The way of Jesus is not an easy way. It outrages our human nature. It requires a bigness of soul and a grandeur of courage that are truly Christlike. "When he was reviled, he reviled not again." But it is infinitely the best way both for the individual and for society.

(3) The climax is reached when Jesus commands us to love all men, whether friends or foes. What said the old law? "Thou shalt love thy neighbor." Hate for an enemy was not commanded, but it was permitted and that was enough. Therefore Jesus said: "Ye have heard that it was said, Thou shalt love thy neighbor, and hate thine enemy. But I say unto you, Love your enemies, bless them that curse you, do good to them that hate you, and pray for them which despitefully use you, and persecute you." In other words he says: "Treat your enemies as God treats his."

Now, that is just where we fail. We take publicans and pagans rather than our Lord for our example. Pagans love their own friends. They love those that are kind to them and appreciate them. We must do far more than that if we show ourselves kinfolks with God. He is not only kind to his friends, but to his enemies as well. He maketh the sun to shine upon the evil and upon the good. When the sun rose this morning it illuminated that Christian home where pious hands were folded in prayer. It also shone just as brightly upon that stenchful

151

brothel where depraved men and women were wakening from a night of debauch. It shone upon the wheat field of the consecrated widow. It shone also upon the fields of the scoffer who denies and despises the God in whose hands his breath is and in whose are all his ways.

You see, our Lord does not retaliate. He is not spiteful. He is never after getting even with a foe. He never takes a dare. When he hung on the cross they dared him to come down. "If thou be the Son of God, save thyself." But he did not take the dare. And when a few months ago a poor misguided author took out his watch and dared him to strike him dead, he was infinitely too big to pay any attention to the poor egotist. And we are to take him as our example. We are to meet the world, not our friends only, but our foes as well, with a dauntless friendliness like that of Jesus Christ himself.

It is a high standard. It is so high that we cannot attain in our own strength. The Sermon on the Mount is said to be purely ethical. But it implies a gospel of redemption. More, it demands one. It makes the new birth an absolute necessity. These commands are even beyond the reach of us unless we become partakers of the divine nature. We cannot love according to the Sermon on the Mount except we are empowered by him whose "nature and whose name is love."

XII

DRASTIC OPERATIONS

Matthew 5: 29, 30

"If thy right eye offend thee, pluck it out. . . . .
If thy right hand offend thee, cut it off."

THESE are bold and startling words. They seem
to have a decided flavor of the extreme. I wonder
just what they would mean to the average man of
the world were he to read them. I wonder what
they actually mean to the average member of the
Church. What lesson did Christ intend to teach
when he spoke of the plucking out of the right eye
and the cutting off of the right hand? It is very
plain language. Any child can understand it.
These words were easily comprehended when they
were first uttered. It is even more easy to understand them, at least superficially, to-day, because
surgery is now far more common than it was in the
days of Christ. And these words smack of the
operating room. As we hear them there comes to
us the odor of ether or of gas. We catch a glimpse
of the faces of the attendant physicians. We hear
the soft voice of the nurse. We look into the anxious
eyes of loved ones and friends. We catch the faint
perfume of flowers. We shrink again at the cutting
pain. We turn restlessly with a torturing nervous-

153

ness and struggle with annoying nausea. All of us know either from our own experience or from that of some loved one, what it is to undergo an operation.

I

Why are operations performed?

One would almost think that their purpose was to give us a new topic of conversation. Irvin Cobb declares that since his hospital experience, whenever he meets a friend, though the subject has not even been hinted at, he opens the conversation by saying: "Speaking of operations." "Then," says he, "I am off." He proceeds to entertain his audience with his early symptoms, with the doctor's diagnosis, and he reaches a grand climax in telling of his actually going under the operation. And, truly, it is a great subject for conversation. I confess that some of the most impatient moments of my life have been spent in listening to some friend tell how he felt as he was coming from under the anæsthetic. Not that the story was not interesting, but I was eager for him to get through so I could tell how I felt when I was coming from under the anæsthetic.

But this is not the real purpose of operations. Nor are they performed solely for the entertainment of the physician and the attendant nurses. One would almost fancy at times that this is the case. Mr. Cobb said that he thought his was going to be a kind of private affair, but that he discovered

154

that the physician had invited all his friends, and that the patient had no more privacy than a gold fish. Neither do we undergo operations for our own pleasure or amusement. Possibly there were some pleasurable moments connected with your sojourn in the hospital, but the experience is not one that you would like to repeat. Most of us who have undergone operations of any degree of seriousness cannot think of the possibility of another without a dread that is often akin to terror. We think of the restless days and the sleepless nights. We recall how pain nagged at us as if it were taking a fiendish delight in our suffering. Undergoing an operation is no picnic. We should never enter upon such an experience just for the fun of it.

But why, I repeat, do we suffer operations? Sometimes we undergo an operation in order to improve our health. Our physician informs us that while our trouble might never prove fatal, yet we can never get entirely well without resorting to the knife. Therefore, in order to save ourselves from an annoying handicap, in order to avoid permanently lessening our efficiency, we consent to undergo an operation. Such operations are not matters of life and death. We suffer them because we believe that by so doing we shall be of more worth both to others and to ourselves.

Then there are times when the situation is more serious still. A man told me sometime ago of a certain gentleman who, while walking along the streets of one of our cities, seemingly in perfect health, suddenly fell to the pavement as if he had been struck by a rifle bullet. He was taken up unconscious and hurried to the hospital. An X-ray indicated that a little piece of bone was resting upon a certain very delicate part of the brain. The man might doubtless have lived for some time without the removal of that bone. But he would have lived with health impaired. He would have lived with sanity gone and, therefore, with all usefulness gone. He would have lived as a burden upon those who loved him rather than as a help. But with the removal of this bone he was restored to health.

Then there are times when an operation is essential for the saving of life. I have a friend who is one of the best specialists in America. He is a pioneer in his field. His discoveries have cost him much. His hands are horribly burned. Last year a blister came in the palm of one of his hands. The inflammation spread. At last the doctor told him that the only way to save his life was to remove that offending hand. And though the loss was a serious one, yet he underwent the operation. He threw his good hand away because he saw that if he kept it, it would mean the loss of his whole body. The purpose of operations, therefore, **is the improving** of health and the saving of life.

II

But when Jesus speaks the strong words of the text is he suggesting physical surgery as a preventative or as a cure for sin?

Does he mean that if my eyes tend to look to the impure and to the unclean the remedy is for me to pluck them out? Does he mean that if this tongue of mine is given to slander and to criticism and to profane swearing the remedy is for me to have my tongue taken out?. When the very talkative old lady told the new preacher that her one objection to him was that his coat was too long and that she would like to cut off a foot of it, was his answer wise when he suggested that her tongue was too long and that he would like to cut off a bit of that? If my hand tends to slip into the other fellow's pocket, or if it tends to knot itself into a fist to strike the other man's face, is the cure for this that I shall have my right hand cut off? I do not think so.

1. Such a remedy would be altogether ineffective. It would deal with the outside rather than with the inside. It would fail utterly in reaching the cause of the evil. When our organ gets out of tune, we do not cure the evil by polishing the pipes. When your watch ceases to keep good time, you will not cure it by treating the hands. When your well is found to be full of typhoid germs, you will not remedy the evil by painting the curb. When your car fails to run, you will not help matters by dusting the fenders or polishing the hood. No more can any operation performed on the body serve as a remedy for sin.

If this right hand of mine is constantly doing the wrong thing, the fault is not with the hand; it is with the will that backs the hand and sets it to the doing of its evil task. If these eyes of mine tend constantly to gaze into the mud rather than into the heights, if they are constantly seeking the unclean rather than the clean, it is not the fault of the eyes; it is the fault of the heart that is back of the eyes. If this tongue of mine is forever saying the unkind and the cutting and the discouraging word, the fault is not with the tongue; it is with the man that wields the tongue. When that man was killed the other day, it was not the gun that was tried for its life; it was the man who wielded the gun.

2. Not only did Jesus not suggest surgery as a remedy because such a remedy is inadequate and ineffective, but because, even were it effective, it would be purely negative. Even supposing that the cutting off of my right hand would prevent my ever stealing again, if I were a thief, that would be a very poor salvation. For, if I could never reach forth my hand again to take what was not my own, neither could I reach it forth to give. If I could not use it again for the despoiling of my brother, neither could I ever use it to lift him upon his feet. If the putting out of my eyes would prevent me from seeing what I ought not to see, it would just as surely prevent me from seeing what I ought to see. If the cutting off of my tongue would keep me from saying the unkind word, it would also keep me from saying that which was kind and helpful. The religion of surgery, therefore, could do nothing better than bring a purely negative gain. Since this is the case, it could not bring any gain at all. For no amount of "don'ts" can ever make a worthful man.

Add a column of ciphers as high as from here to Mars, and you still have absolutely nothing. Maim yourself, therefore, till you are as harmless as a corpse, and you will be just as useless as you are harmless.

3. We are sure, last of all, that Jesus did not suggest surgery as a remedy, because this would be contrary to all that he teaches elsewhere. A complete cure for sin is offered in himself. "They shall call his name Jesus, for he shall save his people from their sins." That means that he will save them at once from the penalty of sin and from the power of sin. "He was wounded for our transgressions; he was bruised for our iniquities. The chastisement of our peace was upon him, and with his stripes we are healed." There is a full and complete cure for sin in Jesus Christ if we are willing to accept it. He is our sufficiency, and there is none other. "For there is none other name under heaven given among men whereby we must be saved."

What, then, does Jesus mean by these strange words? He is seeking to bring home to our hearts a sense of the awfulness of sin. Sin causes the disorganization of our whole moral nature. It brings about sickness of soul. The words "holiness" and "health" come from the same Anglo-Saxon root. It would be as correct to speak of a holy body and a healthy soul as it is to speak of a healthy body and a holy soul. Lack of holiness means the lack of spiritual health. And how many of us are suffering from spiritual sickness! How many in the Church

159

are confirmed spiritual invalids! And some of these are even on the official board. They are so sick that they are seldom found in the Sunday services. They are so sick that they are never found at the prayer meeting. They are so sick that they are seldom seen even at the business meetings of the Church. They are confirmed invalids, poor souls! The only place in the Church that they fill worthily is the hospital ward.

Then there are those who, while not positive invalids, have their spiritual health seriously impaired. They are still able to sit up. They are even able to come out at times on Sunday morning if the day is warm and bright with sunshine. But they are exceedingly delicate. They are very easily tired. A sermon five minutes too long tears their nerves to pieces. The effort required to get their hands into their pocketbooks makes them sleepless for half the following week. They try to work after a fashion. But they go about their religious duties with leaden feet. There is no sparkle in their eyes and no elasticity in their step. They are enjoying very wretched spiritual health.

Now, this spiritual sickness is the worst possible. This is true both as regards ourselves and others. There are many whose bodies are racked with pain who in their hearts rejoice with a joy unspeakable and full of glory. Sick in body, they are yet strong and vigorous in soul. Not only have they joy for themselves, but they are a means of blessing to others. Some of the most helpful people in the

160

world are the knights of the sick room, the heroes of the bed of pain.

Not long ago a certain preacher in the course of his pastoral duties went to see two women in very different circumstances. One of them was a little seamstress who had been left with a large family of younger brothers and sisters on her hands. She had poured her life into the task of rearing and educating them. And now she was dying of tuberculosis. But when the preacher spoke to her to encourage her, she smiled into his face and said: "O, I have rest and peace, peace and rest." While her body was slowly wasting away, her soul was enjoying the vigorous life of a spiritual athlete. The other woman was a great actress. She decked her couch with a nation's praise. The preacher congratulated her on her success. But she answered in a voice dull with weariness and disgust: "O, I am sick of it all! What I want is rest and peace, peace and rest." What she needed was to learn the secret of the little seamstress.

Not only does sin mean sickness, but it is a kind of sickness that will prove fatal unless it is thoroughly cured. For sin is like a cancer in that it is constantly spreading. If you have been persisting in some certain sin for the last ten years, that sin has a far greater hold on you now than it had at the beginning. And unless you get rid of it, it is going to mean the ruin of you. For the sickness of sin is a deadly sickness. There is nothing more sure than this: "The soul that sinneth, it shall die." Sin in

161

the beginning may seem even to bring you a larger freedom and a larger life, but "sin, when it is finished, bringeth forth death." "For the wages of sin is death."

Sin, therefore, the Master tells us, is a thing so weakening, so deadening and damning that no price is too great to pay to be rid of it. No price is too great for Jesus Christ himself to pay, and no price is too great to be paid by you and me. Any sacrifice is to be counted as a mere trifle if it helps us toward being delivered from the terrible power of sin. According to our thinking, there are many calamities, there are many tragedies. But, according to Jesus, there is only one calamity, there is only one supreme tragedy, and that is the tragedy of sin, the tragedy of the quarrel of the soul with God. Sin must be given up even though the surrender seem more costly than the plucking out of the eye or the cutting off of the hand.

III

If our Lord does not propose to resort to surgery, how, then, does he propose to bring health to our souls? I think we might say for answer that he does it somewhat in the same way as the most skilled physician would go about restoring health to a diseased patient. There are times we recognize when an operation is necessary. In that case the patient is asked to trust his doctor. The faith expected of him is by no means a mean and meager faith. It is one great enough to make him willing to lie down upon the operating table and be as completely in the power of his doctor as the clay is in the hands of the potter.

Such a faith many of us have exercised. Such a faith I have exercised. And this I have done with the consciousness that the cure the physician was going to work was not going to be an altogether full and adequate cure. For instance, when I had appendicitis I did not expect him to give me a sound appendix for one that was diseased. My highest hope was that he leave me with none at all. Such a cure you will recognize is, in the nature of things, negative. A complete cure would be the substitution of a healthful organ for one that was diseased.

But the greatest cures are those wrought without the use of the knife. It is that surgery that is performed naturally by a strong, healthy body. There was a time when the physician gave most of his attention to the killing of the disease. Now he gives the greater part of his attention to the building up of the body. If he can build up a strong body, then that strong body will kill the disease by itself.

In some kindred way does Christ cure. He invites us to put ourselves completely into his hands. This we should do with perfect confidence; for he never enters our lives to maim us. He never enters to subtract. He does not propose to rob us of one single one of our members or to impair one single faculty of mind or of heart. He comes, rather, to bring these to the fullness of their powers. He comes to bring them to their highest usefulness.

163

The hand that has been used for wrongdoing he does not propose to cut off, but to put to right uses. The eye that has been trained to see the unclean, he does not propose to smite with blindness. He rather enables it to see those things that it ought to see.

Our failure to appreciate this fact, I think, accounts for the weakness and the faultiness of so many of our lives. Much of our Christianity is little better than Pharisaism. We concern ourselves altogether too much with the negative side of life. Of course we do not attach too much importance to refusing to do the wrong. But we certainly attach altogether too little to the positive and aggressive doing of the right. Such a program is doomed to certain failure. You cannot slay your sins one at a time. You cannot pull up the noxious weeds in the garden of your soul one by one. The only remedy is to put yourself in the hands of Christ and let him plant your garden so full of flowers that there will not be room for the weeds. Your only chance to keep from doing the positive wrong is to be so busy doing the positive right that there is no inclination for anything else.

The little schoolhouse that I attended years ago was surrounded by a great grove of scrubby black oak. These trees had a wonderful way of clinging to their leaves. When the frost killed other leaves and cut them from the boughs of the trees, these oak leaves still clung, though they were as sear as any that lay on the ground. Then came the sharp winds of winter, but even they were powerless to break the hold of these dead leaves. Still later came the snow and the sleet and the ice, but their efforts were equally futile. But one day a wonderful surgeon clipped off all those leaves of death. Who was that surgeon? His name was Spring. Springtime got into the heart of those oaks, and the sap rose up, and new leaves pushed out and said to the old dead leaves: "This is my place." And thus Christ will save us. Therefore, "This I say, Walk in the Spirit, and you shall not fulfill the lust of the flesh."

XIII

THE MOTIVE TEST

Matthew 6: 1-18

"Take heed that ye do not your alms before men, to be seen of them: otherwise ye have no reward of your Father which is in heaven."

THE text is a word of warning. Jesus is pointing out a real danger. He is telling us of a foe that is lurking in our path. "Take heed," he says with emphatic earnestness. And since he is no nervous alarmist, since he never warns of perils that are imaginary, we should do well to listen reverently and attentively that we may avoid the danger of which he speaks.

I

What is the danger of which Jesus is giving us warning?

It is not idleness. Of course idleness is deadly. But out Lord assumes here that every one who is making any serious effort to be his follower will be a worker. He takes our good deeds for granted. He seems to count it as flatly impossible that we should claim to be disciples of his and yet pamper ourselves by living idle and useless lives. He regarded it as unthinkable that we should enter his service and yet

166

through cowardice or sheer laziness avoid all contact with the cross.

"Take heed that you do not your good deeds." That we are going to do good is assumed, you see, as a certainty. He recognizes, and expects us to do the same, that vital Christianity is impossible without sacrificial service. He told the story of a man who lost both himself and his talent, not because he had grossly misused his talent, but because he had not used it at all. He tells of a heart cleansed of evil that became sevenfold worse than it had ever been before, not because of any violent rush into sin, but because of sheer emptiness. Even a fig tree that bore nothing but leaves was blasted. It is, therefore, taken for granted that every Christian will be a worker. Idleness is a deadly evil, but it is not the object of the warning of Jesus here.

Nor is he warning, as might appear to some, against open and aggressive discipleship. When he urges secret prayer, he does not for that reason condemn public prayer. When he urges giving in so hidden and quiet a fashion that the left hand shall not know what the right hand is doing, he does not hereby condemn giving that is done in the eyes of the world. Our Lord never sets his sanction upon secret discipleship. He rather commands us to let our light so shine before men that they may see our good works and glorify our Father who is in heaven.

There are in every community certain very decent and respectable people who do good in a quiet way and yet who never openly identify themselves with

Christ and his Church. These are often held up as being better than the average Church member. And their virtues are further emphasized by the fact that they make no profession. But in their failure to do so they are hurting both themselves and others. For it is not a question of how good or useful they are without the Church; it is a question of how much better they might be and do if they would only acknowledge the One who is the source of whatever of real goodness there is in them. Now, our Lord is not smiling upon this rather pleasing type of paganism that through cowardice or mistaken modesty refuses to take an open stand for righteousness.

Against what, then, is he warning? The answer is in the text. "Take heed that ye do not your alms before men, to be seen of them." He is warning against a wrong motive. He is warning against that subtle temptation that comes to all of us who are trying to follow him, of looking to men for their approval rather than keeping our eyes and our hearts fixed on him. He recognizes the fact that the moral quality of a deed is determined by the motive that gives it birth; that, therefore, not only the evil, but the very good we do, may have no merit at all. The best of deeds may be poisoned and vitiated by a bad motive.

II

Jesus then proceeds to bring the motive test to bear upon the whole realm of our religious activities.

He brings it to bear on those obligations that look especially toward ourselves and that are summed up in fasting. Next, upon these obligations that look toward our brother and that are summed up in giving. Finally, he brings this test to bear on the obligations that look especially toward God and which are summed up in praying Let us look at them for a moment in the order in which they are here named.

1. Fasting is by no means prominent in the religious life of to-day. It has, however, the sanction of the greatest of the saints. It was certainly practiced by the early Christians. Paul made use of it. It was one of the weapons that he used to buffet his body and bring it under subjection. It was prominent at one time in our Church. Its purpose was the subduing of self. It was to make more complete the mastery of the spirit over the body. And I am not at all sure that we have not lost in so nearly casting aside what other saints have found helpful.

But fasting in the days of Jesus had come to have little religious value. So often those who were fasting were too eager to advertise the fact. Having decided to fast, they looked as mournful and woebegone as possible. They wanted all whom they met to read wretchedness in every line of their faces. The fact that they looked like incarnate pain was their way of proclaiming that they were subduing the physical, that they were very religious, and, therefore, entitled to the applause of men. They had their reward, said Jesus. They had it in the

169

region in which they sought it—that is, the approval and recognition of their fellows. They looked to men for their reward and received in some measure that for which they looked.

2. "When you give," said Jesus, "or when you serve in any way, do not sound a trumpet before you as the hypocrites do in the synagogue." Our Lord does not mean that these gentlemen actually blew a blast when they gave a gift. He does mean that they gave for display, that they were ostentatious in their giving. They gave with their eyes fixed on the faces of men. Whatever they did, they did, not for the divine approval, but for the praise and applause they might win from their fellows. Thus giving and serving, their reward was of the earth earthy.

3. "When you pray," said Jesus, "do not pray to men, pray to God." To make this possible Jesus urges that we enter into the closet and shut the door. This we are to do that we may shut ourselves in with him. This we are to do that we may become the more conscious of the Divine Presence. This does not, of course, require a literal closet. We may thus retire even in the presence of the crowd. But those who have mastered this secret of being alone with God amidst the crowd have usually learned it in the hush and quiet of their own closets. They have also usually been at no small pains to learn it, for it is not easy to pray to God rather than to men. It is extremely difficult for many of us in the offering of our public prayers. The consciousness of the presence of men so often crowds out the consciousness of

170

God. We find ourselves praying a prayer perhaps quite as eloquent as that famous one that was declared to be the most eloquent ever addressed to a Boston audience, but also quite as futile. Such a prayer is heard only by the same kind of ears that heard the one in Boston, and brings no higher reward.

Then, our Lord gives further directions for praying, that while not concerned with motive, yet are exceedingly pertinent and greatly in need of emphasis. He warns against vain repetition, that fatal fluency in prayer that leads to the pouring out a mere deluge of words. Prayer, he tells us, is not judged by its quantity, but by its quality. It is easy to say endless words if we want nothing, but when the load is heavy and the sword has really pierced through our hearts, we come to the point very quickly and cry out with Peter: "Lord, save me."

Then, we are not to pray for the sake of informing God. I heard a prayer not long since that reminded me of *Pathe's Weekly*. The brother seemed trying to give the Lord a résumé of the world's history up to the present time. "Remember," says Jesus, "your Father knows what you have need of." You are not praying to inform him. You are praying to give him a chance to meet your needs. Prayer is a means of opening the door to the Christ, who, with all-sufficient grace, is already knocking and who will enter the moment you fling open the door.

171

III

What is the danger of thus giving away to wrong motives?

1. It poisons the very fount of life. It marks us as wrong at the heart and center of our being.

2. Since the fountain is wrong, the stream that flows out from it must of necessity also be wrong. Remember that the motive determines the moral quality of the deed. No service can be really good that is done from a base and sordid motive. We realize this in our dealings one with another. We appreciate only that which is done for Love's sake and not for the selfish interest of the one who serves us.

This is true regardless of how seemingly beautiful the deed may be. What a beautiful something was the kiss of Judas if one did not know the motive that lay back of it! Suppose Judas had been loyal and sincere. Suppose he had truly said in his heart: "My Master is in danger. They are going to arrest him. Possibly they will put him to death. His friends may forsake him. But whatever others may do, I, for one, am going to stand by him, and in token of my loyalty and love I give him this kiss." If the kiss of Judas had been sincere, his story would have been one of the sweetest ever told. But the fact that he took the most beautiful caress of love to make it an instrument of treachery has made his story about the blackest ever told.

No deed done from a wrong motive has any merit,

even though it may be greatly useful. In truth, many thoroughly selfish deeds are useful. Many a prayer has been blessed to the edification of some saint when it had no merit at all for him that offered it. Many a gift has been highly useful that was given sordidly and selfishly. Many a sermon has been used to the salvation of souls when the preacher had absolutely nothing to his credit in the eyes of Him "who sees things clearly and sees them whole." I doubt if anything better could have happened to Joseph than to have been sold into slavery. He was gifted. He was a dreamer of great dreams. But he was a spoiled son of a doting father. He was a bit of a self-centered prig. His trying education in the hard school through which he passed made a man of him. It made it possible for him to pass from a nomad's tent to a palace on the Nile without having his head turned. It made it possible for him to save countless lives. But for all that, no credit was due to his selfish and cruel brothers. Joseph recognized that. "Ye meant it unto me for evil, but God meant it unto good." Through the grace of God, what was intended for a curse became a blessing. But no credit was due to those who intended it to be a curse.

3. A wrong motive makes impossible any God-given reward. No reward is given, because none is deserved. There are those who have run past the morality of the New Testament and object to any offer of reward at all. But Jesus did not hesitate to speak again and again of rewards. He implies here,

and the New Testament implies emphatically elsewhere, that there is a reward for those who serve for love's sake. There is the reward of a growing likeness to Christ. There is also the reward of usefulness. Then there is the reward of the Saviour's "Well done." But the selfish servant can have no reward of our Father who is in heaven.

IV

How are we to take heed? How are we to rid ourselves of these wrong motives that so tend to vitiate even the best and noblest of our deeds? We are not going to do so by continually questioning our motives. We are not going to do so by constantly keeping our fingers upon our spiritual pulse. We are not going to do so by persistently looking at our tongues and morbidly subjecting ourselves to examination. It is possible to push self-scrutiny too far. I think I have known more than one to become physical invalids by keeping too close tab on themselves. And it is altogether possible for us to become spiritual invalids in the same way.

But, having said that, I must add that it is well now and then to face the facts about ourselves. How about our motives? Suppose we make this test. It is one that a wise man has suggested. Do we give over our good deeds when men fail to applaud? Do we work so long as we are chairman of the committee and quit when another takes our place? Do we attend church so long as we are greeted warmly and folks seem glad to see us, and do we quit if they pass us by for a service or two? If such is the case, we had better beware. Our eyes are likely to be upon men more than upon God.

But, having faced the evil, what is its cure? Here, as often elsewhere, this sermon demands a gospel that will regenerate. How do we drive out the darkness? We cannot do so with a club. The darkness goes when the light comes in. How are we to get rid of our wrong motives? We cannot pull them up by the roots and throw them away one at a time. We can only destroy them by bringing in of right motives. And right motives come when Jesus Christ comes. "Without me," he tells us frankly, "you can do nothing." "You need not be surprised that you fail, not only in service, but even in the motives for service, if you attempt to go it alone. I am the one absolute essential. You must have me; for, if you have me, you have love."

And love is enough. For, just as no deed, however seemingly great, is of any merit without love, so the very least is of abiding merit if love is its motive. "Though I bestow all my goods to feed the poor, and though I give my body to be burned, and have not love, it profiteth me nothing. But if I give even so much as a cup of cold water for love's sake, I am forever enriched. For it is love that God wants. He says: "Son, give me thine heart." And we are kinsfolk with God. It is love that the human heart wants. Love is the cure for every evil. It is the fulfilling of the law. Everything without love leaves

175

us paupers. If we have love and nothing else, we are unspeakably rich.

> "If all the ships I have at sea
> Should come a-sailing home to me,
> Weighed down with gems and wealth untold,
> With glory, honor, riches, gold,
> Ah, well! the harbor would not hold
> So many ships as there would be,
> If all my ships should come to me.
>
> If half the ships I have at sea
> Should come a-sailing home to me,
> Ah, well! I should have the wealth as great
> As any king that sits in state,
> So rich the treasures there would be
> In half the ships I have at sea.
>
> If just one ship I have at sea
> Should come a-sailing home to me,
> Ah, well! the storm clouds then might frown,
> For if the others all went down,
> Still rich and proud and glad I'd be
> If that one ship came home to me.
>
> If that one ship were lost at sea,
> And all the others came to me,
> Weighed down with gems and silks untold,
> With glory, honor, riches, gold,
> The poorest soul on earth I'd be
> If that one ship came not to me.
>
> Ah, skies be clear! Ah, winds be free!
> Bring all my ships safe home to me.
> But if thou sendest some a-wrack,
> To nevermore come sailing back,
> Send any, all, that skim the sea,
> But bring my love ship home to me."

That is the cry of the human heart. That is the cry also of the heart of our Lord. Therefore, "Take heed that ye do not your alms before men, to be seen of them: otherwise ye have no reward of your Father which is in heaven."

XIV

A WISE INVESTMENT

Matthew 6: 19, 20

"Lay not up for yourselves treasures upon earth, where moth and rust doth corrupt, and where thieves break through and steal: but lay up for yourselves treasures in heaven, where neither moth nor rust doth corrupt, and where thieves do not break through and steal."

I

The text deals with a matter of vital importance to every one of us. Jesus is instructing us as to where to invest. He is telling us where to desposit our treasure. "Treasure," you answer sadly, or, maybe resentfully; "I have no treasure. I am having the hardest kind of fight to keep the wolf from the door. I am having to skimp and save and cut corners constantly to make ends meet. I cannot deposit a penny anywhere. Preach to the money magnates. Preach to the misers. I hear that two hundred and ten men control two-thirds of the wealth of the whole world. Preach to them, if you have anything to say about treasure, but do not waste your time and my own as well by talking to me about where to lay up my treasure, because I have none."

But in saying this you are altogether mistaken. Everybody is the possessor of some kind of treasure.

Of course it does not always consist of silver and gold. It may not consist of stocks and bonds, of houses and lands. Our treasure is that something that we love the best. It is that which we most yearn to possess, if it is not ours. It is that which we most fear to lose, if we already possess it. It is that something to which our affections, our wills, our whole being clings. Your treasure may be entirely different from mine. And mine may be entirely different from that of my neighbor. But every man has a treasure, and every man is investing his treasure somewhere.

II

Now, not only are we all investing our treasure, but we are putting it into one of two places. We are either laying up treasure upon the earth, or we are laying it up in heaven. Our choice is strictly limited to these two places. There is no third place where we may invest.

What is it to lay up treasure upon the earth? It is to put the world first in our thoughts, our plans, our affections. Jesus gives us a striking example of what it means to invest our all in this world in the story of the unjust steward. This man received notice that he is soon to lose his position. What is his reaction? He does not consider first how he is to hold fast his integrity. His first and supreme consideration is how he is to have bread to eat and a roof over his head, after he has been retired, without the pains of working or the shame of begging. "I

179

cannot dig, and to beg I am ashamed." To gain this end he plays the rascal and induces his lord's creditors to play the rascal with him. Now, he may have cared for honesty and truth and uprightness, but, if he did, these were certainly secondary. His supreme care was for things. He was a man whose treasure was deposited in the bank of this world.

To lay up treasure in heaven is to take the opposite course. The first step in this direction is to accept Jesus Christ as our Lord and Master. It is to seek first the kingdom of God and his righteousness. Whoever enthrones Christ in his life lays up treasure in heaven. Jesus makes this fact clear in his dealings with the rich young ruler. This young man, spurred by a conscious lack, came and kneeled before the Master. "What lack I?" is his question. "You have made a wrong investment," our Lord seems to answer. "Go sell whatsoever thou hast, and give to the poor, and thou shalt have treasure in heaven: and come, take up thy cross, and follow me." The first and supreme essential, therefore, in the laying up of our treasure in heaven is to make a personal choice of Jesus Christ as our Saviour and Lord.

Then, having made this personal choice, we lay up treasure in heaven by living in loving and loyal obedience to Christ. For long centuries men sought how they might turn baser metals into gold, but they sought in vain. Through Jesus Christ we learn a far more priceless secret. We learn how to transmute the commonplace services that we may render in our everyday lives into wealth that will outlast the ages. Every deed that we do for love's sake becomes an eternal investment. Even one who renders so small a service as the giving of a cup of cold water in His name will be drawing dividends when this world of ours has become a wreck.

Is not this clearly taught in the parable to which we referred a moment ago? The first aim of this steward was to provide for his material welfare. This he did by making a shrewd use of his master's goods. And Jesus urges a like wisdom upon us who claim to be the children of light. He urges that we so use our possessions, our wealth, our talents, our opportunities to serve, that we may provide for our eternal future. "Make to yourselves friends of the mammon of unrighteousness; that, when ye fail, they may receive you into everlasting habitations." That is, we are to so love and give and serve here as to lay up for ourselves treasures in heaven.

Not only are we laying up treasure upon the earth or in heaven, but we are doing so exclusively. That is, we are putting all our treasure in heaven, or we are putting all our treasure upon the earth. Wise business men like to scatter their investments. They fear to venture their all in one single enterprise. If their investments are scattered, a loss may be compensated by a gain. If, on the other hand, all is invested in one place, then a loss means bankruptcy. Just so there are those who seek to scatter their investments by undertaking to lay up treasure both in earth and heaven. But this, Jesus tells us emphati-

181

cally, is utterly impossible. Look at the Pharisees, for example. They were a serious-minded and zealous people. They fasted, they prayed, they gave. They were at pains in the performance of their religious duties. Nor are we to assume for a moment that they had absolutely no care for the Divine approval. They desired to please God in all that they did. But their supreme desire was to please men. They received their reward, Jesus tells us. Men did approve, but God did not. Therefore all their treasure went to one place, and that place was the world.

This does not mean, of course, that men cannot act from mixed motives. They can and very often do. But there is always one motive that is supreme. "No man can serve two masters: for either he will hate the one and love the other; or else he will hold to the one and despise the other. Ye cannot serve God and mammon." When we come to the last rub, when we are pushed into the final corner, it is either love of the material or love of the spiritual that dominates us. We either put self first or we put Christ first. To put the world first is to shut out the love of God. That is what John meant when he said: "Love not the world, neither the things that are in the world. If any man love the world, the love of the Father is not in him."

III

Now since we are all investors, and since every man must invest in one of two places, it becomes us

182

to examine wisely and well these two opportunities that are offered. If we make a foolish financial investment, we may recover. Many a man has lost a fortune only to make a larger. But if we go wrong in this vital matter of which our Lord is speaking, there is no promise of a second chance. The loss is an eternal loss. "For what shall it profit a man, if he shall gain the whole world, and lose his own soul? Or what shall a man give in exchange for his soul?"

1. Look, first, at the opportunities offered by the world. This present world certainly has something to say for itself. There is the appeal of the multitude, for instance. "Commit your treasure to me," says the world, "and you will find yourself a part of a great crowd. My clients are many. My banking house is thronged by a vast multitude of eager and enthusiastic investors. Some of them are noted for their business sagacity. They are famous for their shrewdness and foresight. Some of them have grown so powerful that they fairly make the windows of Wall Street and Lombard Street to tremble whenever they pass by. Many of them declare boastingly: 'Everything I touch turns to gold.' My patrons are indeed an impressive multitude."

Then the world has this further appeal. It speaks ro the man who prides himself on the fact that he is practical. It says to such a one: "Treasure in heaven may be good enough for one who is very old, or for one upon whose brow the death dews are gathering. But when one is well and strong it seems little better than 'such stuff as dreams are made on.'

As a practical man, therefore, you want something more substantial. You want something that you can see, something that you can hold in your hand, can put into your pocket, or deposit in a safety vault. You are too shrewd by far to be satisfied by an unseen wealth. You have the good sense to 'take the cash and let the credit go.' I know there was once an old man who was foolish enough to say, 'The things that are seen are temporal, but the things that are not seen are eternal.' But according to his own testimony he had suffered the loss of all things, and died at last without even a cloak to keep him warm. He had nothing, in fact, except abiding peace, the handclasp of Christ, and the hope of eternity."

But since I am to invest and since I cannot afford to lose my treasure, I feel that I must ask one or two questions. The first is a question that cannot fail to occur at once to every intelligent investor. "World, suppose I invest with you, can you guarantee me against loss? You see I invested in a company once that went broke. Therefore, I am a bit timid. I must be sure. I acknowledge that your investors are numerous. I confess that many of them seem very wise and very prudent. But I am still not absolutely sure that the investment you offer is safe. Now, if I deposit with you, can you say with confidence, with absolute certainty, in fact, that my investment will be forever safe? Can I count on it? or is there a dark possibility that, in spite of all your parading of prominent names, I might lose all that I possess?"

What answer does the world give? What answer can it give? Only one. This is the answer: "If you deposit with me, I cannot say with positive assurance that your investment will be forever safe. But I can say with absolute certainty that you will be perfectly sure to lose it. Nothing under heaven can possibly be more sure than that." And to that fact, every one, regardless of where he invests, must agree. Every penny, every ounce of treasure, that we invest in this world we are absolutely sure to lose.

This is true regardless of the nature of our treasure. If it is in money, we shall lose that. When, I do not know. It may be to-day, it may be to-morrow, but certainly we shall lose it some time. How we shall lose, I cannot say. The possibilities for such disaster are numerous. If we lose by no other process, then Highwayman Death will at last wrench it from our fingers and fling us empty-handed and poverty-stricken out into the night. Very often the loss comes before death. A few years ago a man was carrying water in a certain city for ten cents per hour. Yet, that man owned a mausoleum that cost him two hundred thousand dollars. He had builded it in the days of his prosperity, but reverses had come. Now he had nothing left but a resting place for his dead body.

Then we just as inevitably lose our higher forms of worldly wealth. Your treasure may be physical

185

beauty. You may be as fair as an artist's dream. But one thing is sure, you will not always be so. The thieving years will rob you of your charm. You may have an intellect that flashes like a meteor. But one day your brilliant brain will cease to function. Dean Swift sat looking at a book that he had written in the heyday of his power. "My God," he said, "what a genius I had when I wrote that book!" He was speaking truth. He was surely one of the most brilliant writers of prose that ever set pen to paper. But he was confessing the fact that he was not a genius any more. Of all certainties, therefore, nothing is more certain than this, if our treasure is invested in this world we are one day going to lose it.

Then there is a second question I ask this world: "You have been honest with me thus far. You tell me that though my deposit may be safe with you for a while, I am sure to lose it in the end. What about the peace and the joy it will give me while it lasts? I would like a few moments of solid satisfaction even if they are brief. If I invest with you, can you guarantee to me such satisfaction before the final crash comes?" "I cannot," is the answer. "What you deposit with me is sure to be lost in the end, and it will fail absolutely to bring you abiding peace while you possess it.

To the truth of that statement every man whose treasure is in this present world must agree. It is no matter of wonder that the man of the world is full of care. He is so open to attack. He is capable of being wounded at so many points. The disaster that must come some day, may come any day.

"In sooth, I know not why I am so sad,"

says Antonio in the "Merchant of Venice." But it is easy for his companions to guess the reason.

"Your mind is tossing on the ocean,"

his friend tells him.

"Believe me, sir, had I such venture forth,
. . . . . . I should be still
Plucking the grass, to know where sits the wind;
. . . . . My wind, cooling my broth
Would blow me to an ague, when I thought
What harm a wind too great might do at sea."

These, then, are the facts we are to face: However great the claims of the world, it can offer nothing better than certain loss in the end and restlessness and worry while we possess.

2. Let us look next at our other opportunity. We may lay up treasure in heaven. This is what Jesus is urging us to do. "Lay up for yourselves treasure in heaven." Is his admonition sound? Has he solid reason for giving such command? Suppose we put to him the same questions that we put to the world. Can he give a satisfactory answer? Jesus leaves us in no doubt in this matter. Where the world fails he claims to be entirely adequate.

First, if we deposit with him we have a positive guarantee against all possibility of loss. The treasure that we lay up in heaven is surely safe forevermore. Moths cannot devour it, rust cannot corrupt it, thieves cannot wrench it from our hands. This is true because to lay up treasure in heaven is to have wealth not only in that house not made with hands, it is to have wealth within our own hearts in the life that now is. To make Christ our banker is to be rich in faith and hope and love in the here and now. It is to be rich in that most worthful of all treasure, Christlike character. Such wealth the world is powerless to give and is equally powerless to take away.

Years ago there lived near my old home a man who was a thorough-going miser. He worked hard and spent little and gave nothing. In this manner he managed to accumulate some five thousand dollars in gold. He would not deposit this money in a bank. He hid it in a secret place known only to himself. But one night a highwayman paid him a visit. He stuck the muzzle of an angry-looking gun close up against the man's face and asked him for a donation. The miser consented. He gave him every dollar, though it broke his heart. "Why did you not argue the question with him?" an old friend asked the next day. "Why did you not refuse?" "Hell was too close," was the simple answer. All this man's treasure was on the outside of him. None was in his heart.

But I read this story of another man, a college professor. He was rather a frail chap physically, but he had a clear mind and a clean heart. He was in love with a girl of great vigor and charm. He had a rival who was an athletic fellow, magnetic and attractive. This rival seemed to have everything that could appeal. Therefore, nobody was surprised when he became engaged to the girl of their choice. But he was lacking in character. In his eagerness for easy money, he stole certain trust funds that were committed to his care. The circumstances were such that it became the duty of the professor to witness against him. And it was through this testimony that he was convicted and sent to serve a term in the penitentiary.

One dark night years later, when the rain was falling in torrents, the professor was alone in his library. Suddenly he felt a breath of cold wind. He looked up from his work, and there before him stood his rival in the garb of a convict with a revolver in his hand. "I have dreamed of this meeting for a long time," said the intruder bitterly. "You have ruined my life and now I am going to make you pay." "I did not ruin your life," the little professor answered quietly. "You ruined it yourself when you became a thief. Nobody can ruin one's live but one's self." "How I have suffered," the convict continued. "And how I have longed to make you suffer as I have suffered!" "But that you cannot do," the professor replied. "You can kill me, of course, but you are entirely powerless to make me suffer as you have suffered. If you kill me, my suffering will be physical only, and doubtless very brief. Death will be for me the gateway into a fuller life. Therefore, you cannot make me suffer as you have suffered." This man possessed a wealth that thieves cannot break through and steal. No wonder the convict stood awed in his presence. His foe had that which is proof against any weapon that man can wield.

Not only is the investment that we make with Jesus safe, not only will it meet our needs through all eternity, but it will satisfy us in the here and now. "Godliness is profitable unto all things, having promise of the life that now is, and of that which is to come." If we lay up our treasure in heaven, it is our privilege to live the care-free life. Worry ought to be an utter impossibility for one who has made God his banker. This is certainly the conviction of Jesus. Three times over he says, "Be not anxious." We are not to worry about things. We are not to worry about to-morrow. He who keeps our treasure safe to-day will keep it safe forever. "I know whom I have believed, and am persuaded that he is able to keep that which I have committed unto him against that day." Therefore,

"Build a fence of trust around each day and therein stay;
Look not through the sheltering bars upon to-morrow,
For God will help thee bear whate'er there is of joy or sorrow."

XV

"ASK—SEEK—KNOCK"

Matthew 7: 7, 8

"Ask, and it shall be given you; seek, and ye shall
find; knock, and it shall be opened unto you: for every
one that asketh receiveth; and he that seeketh findeth;
and to him that knocketh it shall be opened."

WHAT a tremendous declaration! What a staggering promise! Jesus was a continuous source of
amazement to those who companied with him.
He was the most thrilling personality that this world
has ever seen. Over and over again we are told that
they were astonished at him. He was constantly
making men gasp. He was persistently filling them
with boundless amazement. Those who knew him
best had their otherwise ordinary and commonplace days changed by him into days of winsome and
unbelievable surprises. But, judging by the record,
there was nothing that Jesus did that so stirred the
wonder and longing of his disciples as what he
taught, expecially by example, about prayer.

Of course they were constantly amazed at him as
a wonder worker. But never once, so far as we
know, did they come to him and say wistfully:
"Lord, teach us to work wonders." They marveled
at his preaching. How fascinating he was! How he
put his hands on the commonplace things that lay

191

all about, salt and light, bread and water, and set them to uttering "thoughts that breathe and words that burn." Yet they never asked him to teach them to preach. But one day they came upon him at his prayers. They were as garrulous as a bunch of schoolboys, perhaps. Maybe they were disputing as to who should be greatest. But suddenly they heard his voice in prayer. They got a view of his upturned face. A holy hush fell over them. A deep reverence filled their hearts. Here, they felt, was real prayer. Here was something vital. Here was One who was having first-hand dealings with God. And though they had been accustomed to hearing prayers all their lives, though they themselves had been men of prayer, they felt that they had never witnessed real prayer before. And when the Master had ended they came to him with wistful hearts and said: "Lord, teach us to pray."

What a privilege to be taught by one who knows. And Jesus is certainly the supreme expert in the high art of prayer. Never was there another who used this matchless instrument of peace and power so constantly and so well. He knows from his own experience the worth of prayer. He knows its possibilities. He speaks as one having authority. And this is what he has to say: "Ask, and it shall be given you; seek, and ye shall find; knock, and it shall be opened unto you: for every one that asketh receiveth; and he that seeketh findeth; and to him that knocketh it shall be opened." A stupendous promise, surely! One that is wonderful in its richness. But even then the wealth of it is little more amazing than the treatment that it receives at the hands of many professing Christians.

I

How do we who claim to be followers of Christ treat this promise? How do we treat the privilege and responsibility of prayer?

1. There are those who make practically nothing of prayer. They face a rich promise like this with listless and lack-luster eyes and leave it unappreciated and untouched. I do not think I am in any sense a pessimist. I am certain that I am not an unsympathetic critic of the Church of to-day. But I am driven to this conviction: the modern Church is not a praying Church. The vast majority of the membership of our various denominations make very little of prayer. They believe in it after a fashion. They believe that for certain saints of their acquaintance it may be of value; but as for themselves, they give it but little effort, little thought, and little time.

For instance, take ourselves. How much do we pray? "Enter into thy closet and shut the door, and pray to thy Father which is in secret, and thy Father which seeth in secret shall reward thee openly." Have you tried this out? Do you have a secret place of prayer? Is it the habit of your life to meet God alone each day? How about this morning? Did you pray before coming to church? Did you ask God to prepare you for the service? Did you pray his blessing on the teachers of the Sunday

193

school? Did you pray that the minister might come into the pulpit in the fullness of the blessing of the gospel of Christ? We are decent, respectable people, who love the Church after a fashion, but most of us are not people of prayer.

2. Then there are those who have taken this promise more seriously, but have fumbled it. They have blundered in the use of it. Somehow, for them at least, it has failed to work. "Every one that asketh receiveth." "No, no," they say, "that is not true. I have asked, and I have not received. I have sought, at times desperately, and I have not found. I have knocked with bruised fists and broken heart, but the door has not been flung open to me." And the truth of this cannot be denied. There are those who do ask and fail to receive. There are those who seek, after a fashion, and do not find. Some of these become discouraged and indifferent. Others become rebellious and embittered. A woman of this type came into my office sometime ago. She looked at me with eyes red with weeping and said bitterly: "I prayed for my boy, God knows I did, but my prayer was not answered. God simply did nothing at all, and I will never pray again as long as I live."

3. Then there are others who have found that prayer really works. When I read this gracious promise, "Ask, and ye shall receive; seek, and ye shall find; knock, and it shall be opened," there were those who said a whole-hearted "amen." They have found prayer a source of comfort and power. They have found it a means of enrichment both to

themselves and to those for whom they have prayed. "I sought the Lord, and he heard me, and delivered me from all my fears." This Psalmist had found that God really does give good things to them that ask him. I do not know just what his fears were. He may have been afraid of the sins of his youth. He may have been afraid of the temptations of to-morrow. He may have been afraid of some deadly disease. He may have been afraid of loneliness or of the home-going of one dearer than life. But, what-ever his fears, as he prayed, they vanished, and he found himself enjoying the security of the Everlast-ing Arms. So multitudes have claimed something of the measureless wealth offered by this promise.

II

How did they succeed? How may we?

1. We must ask. Now, asking carries certain im-plications that we cannot neglect.

(1) To ask implies a sense of need. No one ever really prays without a felt need. The Pharisee can strike a pose in the eyes of men. He can compli-ment himself, he can criticize his brother, he can congratulate the Lord on having such a paragon of a servant as himself. But he cannot pray. There is another man present who has nothing to his credit. He is not half so decent as the Pharisee. He is an outcast, a publican. But he does all the praying that is done on that occasion. This is the case because, staggering under a load of guilt that he feels he cannot carry, he cries out of the depths of a

great need: "God be merciful unto me, a sinner."
And the asking that has reality in it is always born of
a sense of need.

(2) To ask is to apply to a person. Therefore the
asking of the text implies contact with a Personality.
It implies contact with the supreme Personality,
even God himself. But such contact can be made
only by one who has a faith that leads to obedience.
Our Lord is infinitely approachable. To the most
stained and hopeless he gives a welcome. But there
is one for whom prayer is impossible. That is the
one who will not surrender. Did you ever try to
pray when you knew you were clinging to something
that was hateful to God? Did you ever try to pray
when you were determined on a course of action that
you knew was contrary to the will of God? If you
have, then you know what I mean. Praying under
such circumstances is an utter impossibility. You
cannot make contact, you cannot ask God. You
may ask space, you may ask the black shadows that
encircle you, but you cannot make contact with
God. "If I regard iniquity in my heart, the Lord
will not hear me."

It is the unsurrendered will that accounts for
many an unanswered prayer. When you take the
business of praying seriously, when you seem on the
point of winning your way into the secret place of
the Most High, what is that something that inter-
venes and makes a vital approach impossible?
When you are praying for your children, does the
need of a family altar slip into your mind? Do you

196

see that as your duty and privilege, and yet tell God that it is impossible? Does the face of a friend to whom you owe an apology intervene? Does a practice that is questionable and that you know you ought to give up blur your vision and make your petition seem a sheer futility? It need not be so. There is a way of victory. John found that way, and he gives this joyful testimony; "Whatsoever we ask, we receive of him, because we keep his commandments, and do those things that are pleasing in his sight."

(3) Then, the asking of which Jesus speaks is asking according to the will of God. There are numerous times, of course, when we know what the will of God is, when we have a definite promise to plead. When this is the case, we can pray unconditionally for an answer. But there are other times when the will of God is not known. In such cases we are to pray in submission to his will. Surely we do not desire that he do for us contrary to his own will, for that could not be best. "That is the confidence that we have in him, that, if we ask anything according to his will, he heareth us: and if we know that he hear us, whatsoever we ask, we know that we have the petitions that we desired of him." For our own sakes, God cannot answer our prayers when we ask for that which is contrary to his will. He has not promised to do so. He has promised the opposite.

But, in spite of this, we are prone to misunderstand. Some years ago it was my privilege to know

197

two women who were exceptionally beautiful in their religious lives. They had a brother who was slowly weakening under the ravages of tuberculosis. They set themselves to pray for his recovery. They went to God with great confidence and determination and asked unconditionally that he restore that brother to health. They persuaded themselves that they had received the desired answer. Therefore, when the doctor said that the patient was dying, they would not believe it. They declared that it simply could not be true; that God would not fail them. But he died, nevertheless. And with his death, gloom settled down upon those two good women, and they came very near plunging into utter atheism.

But God had not failed them. They had simply misunderstood his promise. God knows what is best for us. He knows the end from the beginning. Therefore in his mercy he will not allow us to ruin ourselves by our sometimes foolish prayers. Jesus emphasizes the reasonableness of this by appealing to ourselves. "You, too," he says, "are accustomed to hear prayers and answer them according to your wisdom. If a son ask bread of any of you that is a father, will he give him a stone? Or if he ask a fish, will he give him a serpent? If ye then, being evil, know how to give good gifts unto your children, how much more shall your Father which is in heaven give good things to them which ask him?" It is not the willingness of God that is here emphasized; it is his wisdom in giving. We, in spite of our

198

limitations, know, in some measure, how to answer the prayers of our children. How much more may we rely upon the wisdom of God in this matter?

Now, there are times when we who are parents answer prayers on the part of our children that are at once foolish and hurtful. Our wisdom cannot always be trusted. There are times, also, when we answer prayers, not because we think it wise to do so, but because it is the easiest way out. Many a father has wrecked his boy by answering his foolish prayers. If my boy were to ask me for something that I knew would do him nothing but harm, I should refuse him. And the more I loved him, the more emphatic would be my refusal. A prominent man in our city went a few weeks ago to bring his son home. That son had been shot in an under-world brawl. He had turned criminal. How did his own father account for the tragedy? In these words: "I gave him too much money and allowed him to have his own way." We often make this mistake. We often hurt our children by answering their foolish prayers. But God never does. He is perfect in wisdom as well as in love.

Because this is true, if you look back over your yesterdays you will find it in your heart to thank God, not only for prayers answered, but also for requests not granted. The mother of St. Augustine prayed with desperate earnestness that her son might not go to Italy. He was already dissolute and wayward. She felt that Italy would be the ruin of him. But to Italy he went in spite of all her prayers,

199

and it was in Italy that he found Jesus Christ. Paul prayed with desperate confidence that God would remove his thorn. But God did not grant his request. He desired that his servant have the best. The removal of the thorn would have been only second best. Jesus asked in Gethsemane that the cup might pass from him. But God did not grant his request. Jesus did not desire him to grant it unless it was in accordance with his will. It was through this rejection of his prayer that Jesus "shall see of the travail of his soul and be satisfied."

2. Then, we must not only ask, we must seek. Seeking means asking plus effort. That is, there are times when we must help God in the answering of our prayers. We recognize the truth of this in the realm of the material. Jesus taught us to pray: "Give us this day our daily bread." But, having prayed that prayer, we do not betake ourselves to lives of idleness. My father was a farmer. He was also a man of prayer. But when he asked God to prosper his farming he did not sit down and leave the whole matter with him. He did not tell the Lord to sow wheat in one field and oats in another and plant corn in another. Had he done so, he would have starved. It is wise to pray for the blessings of God on our business. But our prayers go for nothing if we do not work.

The same is true in the realm of the spiritual. If I pray to God for spiritual health, in order for my prayers to be effective I must obey the laws of health. How foolish it would be for me to ask God to make me strong physically and then eat nothing at all! How foolish it would be to ask him for physical health and then gormandize upon food that I knew did not agree with me! Yet there are many of us praying for growth in grace, praying to be made more saintly, yet we are leaving off the food by which the soul grows. Or we do things every day that do not agree with us.

Take the amusement question, for instance. There are many decent and respectable folks who spend much time in the ballroom and more time at the card table. They do not seem to be greatly harmed by it. But how about you? Do these things agree with you? A young lady of rosy cheeks and vigorous health told me sometime ago that she drank nine cups of coffee a day. But one cup is too much for me. It is not a question of the effect of this or that practice on another, but how does it affect you? Does it hinder your growth in grace? If it hinders, give it up, or praying will come to nothing. It is useless to say, "Thy will be done," unless you set yourself resolutely to the task of doing the will of God as he gives you to see it.

The same holds true in our efforts to help others. We are taught to pray, "Thy kingdom come." But we must do more than pray for it. We must work for it. It is well to pray for our children, but we must do more. It is fine to pray for our Church, but we must do more. Sometime ago I heard one crying aloud in an almost empty church: "O Lord, go out into the highways and hedges and compel them to come in!" But that is just what the Lord told us to do. The sin of the priest and the Levite was not the fact that they did not pray for the man that was wounded by the wayside. In all probability they did so. The tragedy was that they did nothing else. We must coöperate with God in the answering of our prayers.

3. Finally, we must knock. Knocking is asking plus effort plus persistence. Jesus makes plain, in the story of the man who had a guest at midnight, what he means by knocking. This host, when he found that his larder was empty, went and knocked on the door of the house of his friend. At first his request was refused, but he persisted until the door was opened and the request was granted. Therefore do you go and do likewise is the teaching of Jesus. Ask, seek, knock. Persist in your asking and seeking until you get an answer.

It is necessary to persist because the answer to prayer is sometimes delayed. Of course this delay is often the fault of ourselves. At other times there is delay because our request is of such a nature that it cannot be answered at once. Christ prayed that his people might be one. That prayer has not been fully answered yet. But the answer is on the way. If, therefore, your prayer is not answered at once, do not give up. Jesus knows that you will be sorely tempted to do so. That is the reason he gave such marked emphasis to the necessity of persistence. "He spake a parable to this end, that men ought always to pray, and not to faint." It is so easy to give over the struggle. But to do so means that we lose the victory. We are to persist, not in order to make God hear us; we are to do so because God surely will hear us. Therefore, "if the vision tarry, wait for it." Do not faint; remember that "everyone that asketh receiveth; and he that seeketh findeth; and to him that knocketh it shall be opened."

XVI

THE WAY OF LIFE

Matthew 7: 13, 14

"Enter ye in at the strait gate: for wide is the gate, and broad is the way, that leadeth to destruction, and many there be which go in thereat: because strait is the gate, and narrow is the way, which leadeth unto life, and few there be that find it."

I

"ENTER by the narrow gate." This text is at once a command and an invitation. It has a certain appeal to the high and the heroic within us. But it has also that which tends to shock and to repel. This is true, first, because here, again, the Master is dividing men into two classes, and we do not altogether like that. As he speaks he sees before him a vast multitude. In the bosom of the centuries he sees multitudes infinitely more vast. These multitudes are made up of all sorts and conditions of men. They belong to all kindreds and tribes and tongues. He sees the wise and the foolish, the cultured and the unlearned, the hopeful and the despondent, the young and the old, the rich and the poor. But as he looks upon this vast and mixed throng he sees them arrange themselves into two great processions. He sees them traveling by just two roads. One of these is a broad road; the other is narrow. And

204

there is no third road in between. That is, every man is a pilgrim, and is traveling either by the broad way or by the narrow.

Then, the text is forbidding, in the second place, because it commends the narrow way. Now, "narrow" is an offensive word. Frankly, we do not like it. It connotes that which repels. It suggests the unpleasant. It smacks of the distasteful. When we hear it we think of the dwarfed mind; we think of the stunted soul; we think of the blurred vision and the contracted view. We are reminded of the provincial whose interests and whose sympathies are bounded by his own yard fence. We think of the sectarian who has a corner on the Infinite, and the greater part of whose religious joy grows out of his conviction that his brother is wrong rather than that he himself is right. We do not admire narrow folks. We do not wish to be narrow ourselves. Yet in the face of this we hear Jesus saying: "Enter by the narrow gate."

II

Why are we to enter by the narrow gate? It is surely not because it is easier to travel the narrow way than it is to travel the broad. Even if such were the case, it is well to remember that Jesus never once appealed to our love of ease in his efforts to win our loyalty. He frankly calls upon us to face the fact that to be a follower of him involves difficulties. He tells us that to walk with him is expensive, that it costs to enter in at the strait gate and to

205

follow the narrow way. This is true because, the gate being narrow, we cannot enter it so easily as we can the wide gate. We can enter the wide gate and carry with us all our sins, all our selfishness, all our prejudices and hates and lusts. But to enter the narrow gate is exacting. To enter it, much must be left behind.

We must leave all our sins. We must renounce every wrong attitude. We must be ready to give up, not only every known wrong, but every practice that is questionable. We must renounce our very selves. "For if any man will come after me, let him deny himself." Then, too, if we enter by this gate we must load ourselves with certain very definite obligations. We must become a bearer of burdens. We must become our brother's keeper. Our right to do as we please must be utterly renounced. We must take our place among those whose lives have certain limitations. Ours must be lives that are fenced in with such fences as "I ought" and "I must."

If we are to enter by the narrow gate and walk the narrow road, we must renounce the privilege of walking with the majority. That is not easy for most of us. We love the crowd. We love to feel that the multitude is on our side. But Jesus very openly declares that those who travel the narrow way walk with the few, not with the many. This was surely overwhelmingly true when Jesus was here. It is true even to this day, though those who walk the narrow road have vastly increased. But, even yet, he who chooses the narrow way must be willing to travel with the few. We must even be willing, if the need arises, to walk alone.

Why, then, are we urged to choose a road that is narrow and difficult? We are so urged because it leads to a worth-while goal. The first concern of every traveler is his destination. It is surely not enough to make speed. Rapid progress is worse than nothing unless it be in the right direction. The home of my boyhood was a most inaccessible place. But, when I was away at school, and the session was over, I did not go to the railroad station and ask for a ticket on the most popular train leaving the city. I asked for a ticket on the train that went toward my home. When I had gone as far as possible on the train, I had to travel over a horrible dirt road. But I faced all the difficulties involved simply because the road, in spite of its hindrances, led home. I was willing to travel the road, not because it was easy, but because it brought me to the goal of my desires.

"Enter ye in at the strait gate." Why? "Because strait is the gate, and narrow is the way, which leadeth unto life." It is worth while to travel the narrow road because by so doing one finds life. And by life here Jesus does not mean mere existence, but right existence, existence in fellowship with himself. And by destruction, which he tells us is the goal of the broad road, he does not mean extinction. He means rather the ruin that of necessity overtakes the soul that is separated from God. The narrow road leads to life, and it is the only road that does. Therefore with wisdom he urges all of us to make it our choice.

III

But why is the road to life narrow? In a God-ordered world we should expect that it would be the opposite. We feel that the way to death should be a narrow and difficult road, but that the road to life should be broad and easy. Why is not this the case? Why, at least, is not the way of life as broad as the way of death? In seeking an answer to these questions we may at least be sure of this: The way of life is certainly not narrow because God arbitrarily decreed that it should be so. It is true that Jesus declares that the way is narrow. But his saying so does not make it narrow. But knowing it to be narrow, he, in his mercy, tells us the truth about it. I used to have an arithmetic that declared emphatically that three times three is nine. But the fact that this book made such a declaration did not cause such result. Three times three is nine whether any book says so or not. And the way to life is narrow whether the fact is ever put into words or not. It is narrow in the nature of things. In fact, the road to every goal is a narrow road.

Did you ever go bird-hunting? If so, I guarantee that your first experience was a bit after this fashion: The dog found a covey of quails and flushed them. Your friend picked out a single bird and brought it down. You fired at the whole covey and killed nothing. This kept up till your friend said: "Don't shoot at the whole twenty; shoot at one." And what did he mean by this? If one is to hunt birds, narrow is the way. There are ten thousand ways that a hunter may miss the mark. There is only one way that he can hit it.

There is a magnificent skyscaper being built in our city. Do you suppose that the architect who planned this building went about the task in a careless and slipshod manner? Did he draw all sorts of pictures and make numerous blue prints just as the mood of the moment led him, without any regard to whether they were accurate or not? No, he found the way exceedingly narrow. His drawings and his calculations could not be made at random. They could not be only approximately correct, they had to be exactly correct. And the contractor who is undertaking to make the dream of the architect into a reality is also having to travel a narrow road. He cannot follow any set of blue prints that chances to fall into his hands. He is shut up to only one. No more can he presume to change those drawn by the architect according as the whim strikes him. He must build exactly as planned. Truly, "narrow is the way."

Every evening a train leaves our city for New York. Under what conditions can that train hope to make a successful journey? What instructions shall we give? Just this: "Narrow is the way." If that train will not follow the narrow way, it becomes a wreck. A ship is leaving New York for Europe.

What shall we say to this great vessel? "Narrow is the way." For it does not sail for the whole continent of Europe; it sails for one little speck upon the map. If it fails to do so, if it will not follow the narrow way, it becomes derelict.

And what shall we say to the man who would be a scientist? This same forbidding word: "Narrow is the way." Certainly this was the experience of Charles Darwin. He found the road of the scientist most narrow. It was so narrow that he lost his taste for music. It was so narrow that he lost his taste for poetry. It was so narrow that his mind became a mere machine, as he himself says, for grinding out general laws from certain known facts. Edison has also found the way narrow. He has found it so narrow that, in spite of his vast ability, he has missed, I fear, the very finest that life has to offer.

The same is true in the realm of literature, of art, and of music. The writer of great prose must walk a narrow way. The writer of great poetry must travel one that is more narrow still. The painter cannot handle his brush carelessly and sleepily and stupidly. If he ever succeeds in splashing a great dream upon the canvas, he must travel a narrow road. And the great musician also finds himself shut up to the same necessity. For all these, "Narrow is the way." The broad road is always at hand with its greater throngs and its easier travel, but it fails to lead to the desired goal.

Here is a young couple that has decided to share

210

life with each other in the marriage relationship. It is a high adventure, full of possible romance and poetry. How may they hope to succeed? How may they find the fullest and deepest joy? How shall we instruct them? We must tell them that narrow is the way. "John, wilt thou have Mary to thy wedded wife, to live together after God's ordinance in the holy estate of matrimony? Wilt thou love her, comfort her, honor and keep her, in sickness and in health; and forsaking all other, keep thee only unto her, so long as ye both shall live?" "It is a narrow way, indeed!" you say. "Yes, but it is the only way that leads to a successful wedded life. All other roads end in tragic failure."

Therefore we need not be surprised nor resentful when Jesus tells us that the way that leads to life is narrow. He himself found it so. He is speaking out of his own experience. He gave himself to one insignificant country at the back side of civilization. He never passed beyond its boundaries into the really great nations of the world. He gave himself mainly to one little handful of men, not one of whom counted for much until he found him. He was shut in by tremendous convictions. There were certain things that he felt he must do. He had a work to accomplish from which he could not turn aside. His way was so narrow that when it ran up against a cross there was not room for him to pass round that cross. He had to hang upon it. Truly his was a narrow road, and invites you and me to follow in his steps.

211

IV

But while the way to life is narrow and the way to death is broad, we are not to overestimate either the narrowness of the one or the breadth of the other. The way of life is narrow, yet it is broad enough to meet all our needs.

1. It is wide enough to accommodate all who are willing to travel it. In spite of the narrowness of the gate, everybody may pass through that gate who is willing to pay the price. When Jesus was dying, a highwayman hung at his side. There was blood on this man's hands. He had an evil and ugly past. But in his hour of death he turned to the dying Christ at his side and said: "Lord, remember me when thou comest into thy kingdom." And the narrow gate proved to be amply wide for him to enter, and he found himself traveling the road that leads to life.

When the prodigal came back, he had no good word to say for himself. He knew he had no right to come. He only hoped that by being very humble and very penitent he might find a place in the servants' quarters. He would at least go and knock at the door and ask for an interview. And what was the result? Did the father look down from some upper window and ask what he had done with his money, where and how he had squandered his moral and spiritual wealth? Did he say, "O yes, I knew you would come trekking home when you had spent your all and had nowhere else to go"? No, his father rather ran to meet him and gave him a welcome home. For, though the gate is narrow, it is yet wide enough, I repeat, to admit any who is willing to enter.

2. This road is wide enough for us to walk arm in arm with Christ. Such a road may be narrow, but it is none too narrow. The broad road, with all its breadth, is not wide enough for that. It is said of the prodigal that he gathered all together and took his journey into a far country. But there were some treasures that he did not take with him. There were many priceless things that he was compelled to leave behind. He could not take his old home with him. He could not take his father. He could not take his faith. He could not take God. The road to death is broad, but it is not broad enough for one to walk it in the fellowship of Jesus Christ.

3. Then, this narrow road is wide enough to permit all of us to come to our best and to realize our highest possibilities. For the fact that the way is narrow does not mean that those who walk it must themselves be narrow. The opposite is true. It is as we travel the narrow way that we ourselves become broad. Real Christians are never narrow. They cannot be. This is true because they share in the nature of Christ. And how broad is he! The breadth of Jesus is the breadth of the Infinite.

To walk with Christ in the narrow way is to become broad in our sympathies. How boundless was the sympathy of Christ! It bridged all chasms. It broke through all sundering barriers. It went out

213

to good and bad, to far and near, to wise and foolish, to those who loved him and to those who hated him. It took in the whole world. And a kindred breadth of sympathy he gives to those who know him. How narrow was John when Jesus found him! How narrow he was even during the early days of his discipleship! He was eager to burn down a little Samaritan village that had refused his Master hospitality. He pridefully sought to prevent a servant of God from doing good because he did not serve in just the same manner as himself. But how big he became as he traveled with Jesus in the narrow way! Of Christ's fullness he received. Therefore, before he reached the end of his journey, he had the weight of a world's need upon his heart.

As we walk the narrow way we become broad in our purposes. Here is Jesus at prayer. And what a narrow prayer he is offering! "I pray not for the world, but for them whom thou hast given me." Then he broadens out a bit: "Neither pray I for these alone, but for them also who shall believe on me through their word." That is better. It was then that he called your name and mine, if we are believers. But we feel that the prayer is still too narrow till we come to this thrilling word: "That the world may know that thou hast sent me." The purposes of Jesus take in the whole world. He is seeking to establish his reign over all the earth. He never will and never can be satisfied with anything less than the complete conquest of the world. And those who walk with him in the narrow way are privileged to share his vast dreams and work with him in his great enterprise. The followers of the narrow way are, therefore, broad in their purposes.

Those who walk the narrow way are broad in their hopes. All who journey by the broad road have hopes that are of necessity very small and very limited. They can stretch but a little way into the future. They bring but little joy while they last and are soon blighted by the biting frosts of death. All of them are bounded by the grave. But our hopes stretch away into the infinite eternities. They are so big and broad that they enable us to face all life's tragedies with steady eyes and quiet hearts. They enable us to laugh at death and the grave in the full assurance that these can work us no harm, since we are the sons of God and are on our way to be like him when we shall see him as he is.

Now, because the narrow road leads to life abundant in this present world, and because it leads to an ever fuller life in the eternal to-morrow, I have great boldness in inviting you to enter by the narrow gate. Remember, you are going to travel one way or the other. You cannot in the nature of the case walk both roads. As you came to church to-night, you came either by the broad road or by the narrow. As you go home, I do not know what street you will travel, but I do know that you will go either by the broad road or by the narrow. I know also that the road you travel determines your goal.

215

As there are only two roads, so there are only two goals, only two destinations. One is Life, the other is Death. Therefore, on the authority of my Lord, I am placing before you at this moment Life and Death. May we all have the wisdom and the courage to make choice of Life!

XVII

THE TWO BUILDERS

Matthew 7: 24-27

"Therefore whosoever heareth these sayings of mine, and doeth them, I will liken him unto a wise man which built his house upon a rock: and the rain descended, and the floods came, and the winds blew, and beat upon that house; and it fell not: for it was founded upon a rock. And every one that heareth these sayings of mine, and doeth them not, shall be likened unto a foolish man, which built his house upon the sand: and the rain descended, and the floods came, and the winds blew, and beat upon that house; and it fell: and great was the fall of it."

THIS parable marks the close of Matthew's version of the Sermon on the Mount. Jesus has been preaching to a vast and interested multitude. They have listened to him with mingled amazement and gladness. In conclusion he tells them, as he tells us, that it is not enough to listen, even though we listen with reverent approval. It is not enough to listen, even though we listen with keen appreciation and with emotions deeply stirred. If our listening is to be of any worth, it must lead to action. We must not only hear, we must obey. It was to enforce this truth that Jesus told the story of the two builders whose buildings were tested by the storm.

I

The first fact that Jesus brings home to our hearts in this story is that all who hear are builders. Of course we build, whether we hear or not; but it is to the hearers that he is confining himself in this parable. All who hear, he tells us, are builders. These builders he divides into two classes. There are the wise builders, and there are the foolish. Jesus, as we have noticed before, is constantly dividing folks into two groups. There are those who have the wedding garment, and those who do not. There are those who travel the broad way, and those who travel the narrow. There are those who are spiritually alive, and those who are spiritually dead. We of to-day do not relish such divisions. But the fact remains that Jesus makes them, and makes them constantly.

Now, the wise man is a builder. He is constructing something. He is building his own character. He is building his soul-home. He is building the temple in which he is to spend eternity. The same is equally true of the foolish man. He, too, is building. He, too, is constructing the temple or the hovel or the sty in which he is to spend eternity. Both alike are builders.

This is true of all of us. We are building all the time, whether wisely or foolishly. We are building by everything that we do. We are building by every thought that we think. We are building by every word that we speak, every dream that we

218

dream, every picture that we hang upon the walls of our imagination, every ambition that we cherish. All these go to make up the material that enters into the structure that we are building for the ages.

Some of us are putting some shoddy stuff into our buildings. We are putting material that cannot stand the test of the storm. That oath that you swore, that thoughtless blasphemy that you flung from your lips, that was poor material. That foul story that you told, that unclean thing that you did, that, too, was shoddy. That time that you ran with the multitude to do evil out of sheer cowardice; that time when you remained silent when you should have spoken—that, too, was poor stuff to put into your soul temple. That time you clutched your money in the presence of a pressing need; that time you passed by on the other side when a wounded life was calling to you—that also was shoddy. The fact that you are standing to-day, though a member of the Church, with your membership hidden away in the country or buried in your trunk, trying to play the neutral when God is needing soldiers—that means that you are putting some very flimsy stuff into your building.

Then some are building stanchly and beautifully. That was fine material that the widow put into her building when she threw in her two mites for love's sake. That was fine material that Daniel put into his soul palace when he purposed in his heart that he would not defile himself. That was rugged and substantial stuff that Joseph used when he fled his temptation, even though his escape cost him the horrors of a dungeon. That is fine material you are using as you walk life's common ways in loving loyalty to your duty as God gives you to see your duty.

But whether we are building wisely or foolishly, we are all building. Nor are our lives fragmentary things. They are not so much brick and lumber and mortar and nails flung down in confusion. Every life is a whole, with certain definite moral characteristics. For instance, when the Old Testament tells us that a certain king did evil in the sight of the Lord, that does not mean that every act of his life was necessarily wicked. It means only that the man was inwardly evil and that, therefore, the prevailing tone of his life was of the same character. Likewise, when it says of another that he did that which was right in the sight of the Lord, this does not mean that every act of his life was perfect, but that its prevailing tone, its moral characteristic was upright and pure. But whether wisely or foolishly, we are all building.

II

The second fact that our Lord brings to our attention is this, that the buildings that we are constructing, the characters we are making are going to be tested. For this reason we are not to build for fair weather only. We must build with a view to hours of crises. We must build with a view to times of tempest. For, sooner or later, to all the testing comes. Upon you, and you, and you some day the storm will surely break.

This is the case whether we build wisely or foolishly. The building of the foolish man is going to be tested, but the building of the wise man is going to be tested too. God does not coddle his saints. He does not protect them from the stress and strain of life. He never promises them exemption from conflict. Our Lord prays for us, but he never prays that we may dodge the storm and have an easy time. "I pray not that thou shouldest take them out of the world, but that thou shouldest keep them from the evil." He means for us not to flee the tempest, but to face it and defy it. For to all the storm must come.

We realize the fact of the coming storm in the making of our material structures. We do not want a garment that will spot and fade the moment a drop of water touches it. We seek to have those that will retain their shape and color. When I was a boy, seersucker suits were sometimes worn in summer. But woe unto the man that was overtaken by a rain! By the time he got dry his sleeves were to his elbows and his trousers to his knees. The ship that is constructed to sail only upon a glassy sea and under blue skies will not do for oceans like ours, where the heavens so often become black and where the seas are so often whipped by the tempest. Our bridges must be able to sustain more than their own weight. They must stand heavy tests. They must be built

221

with a view to a city's traffic. In the building of our houses, whether private or public, we must take the tempest into consideration. To fail to do so would mean disaster.

While I was pastor in Washington a few years ago there came a terrific snowstorm. For more than thirty-six hours the snow fell till it lay deep on the earth and upon the roofs of the houses. There was a theater in that city that was a thing of beauty, but the architect had only sunny days in his eye when he planned it. He foolishly built without due regard to the coming storm. Therefore, when the snow lay some thirty inches deep upon it, the strain was too great. The roof crashed, and more than one hundred lives were lost in the disaster.

Now, Christ tells us frankly that the test is coming to ourselves. Upon some here present heavy storms have already broken. You are in God's house even now having by his grace come bravely through more than one trying tempest. Others of you have seen your lives crash in ruins. For, while there are some who have storm-proof religion, there are others whose religion is a plaything of the winds. The rude fists of the tempest dash it ruthlessly aside. But to all the storm comes. Just when it is coming we do not know. It may be to-day; it may be to-morrow. Just how it is coming we do not know. It does not come to all alike.

1. Sometimes the storm breaks upon us in the guise of a great temptation. We are brought suddenly face to face with an inducement to evil that

222

we feel, if we accept, must line our pathway with roses. If we refuse, life will become a desert. A successful young banker said to me the other day, very seriously and very earnestly: "The most persistent petition in my prayer is this: 'Lead us not into temptation.'" It is a wise prayer. We need to pray it, every one of us; for any hour our crisis may be upon us. Any hour we may be overwhelmed if He does not help us weather the gale.

2. The storm may come in the guise of some bitter personal loss. One day out of the blue the news may come that you have lost every penny that you possessed; that from plenty you have been reduced to poverty; that the wolf is now howling at your very door. Or, worse still, it may be some bitter personal loss, the slipping out of your home of a loved one dearer to you than life. It may mean the sundering of ties most tender and binding. I wonder, when the storm comes, if you will be able to say with the stanch faith of Job: "The Lord gave, and the Lord hath taken away: blessed be the name of the Lord."

Or, what is even harder to bear, if we read Job's record aright, there may come to you the complete loss of health. There may come the persistent gnawing of physical pain. Sentence of death may be passed upon you weary months before its execution. You may be called on to suffer and to suffer long. Torture may sit astride your chest and clutch at your throat and lay its burning hands so heavily upon your lips that at times you cannot pray. When that terrible storm comes, I wonder if you can stand up against it bravely enough to say: "Though he slay me, yet will I trust him."

3. Then the storm may be of a different character. Instead of blowing away your treasure, it may bring it in larger abundance. When the Israelites were in the wilderness, there came to them a time of storm. But it blew nothing away. It brought them wealth. They were half buried in delicious quails. But those days of luxury were by no means their best days. They became days of pestilence and plague. These people could not endure prosperity. The place of their enrichment became a graveyard. The name of it signifies the "graves of lust." They were made to realize the tragic fact that there is a destruction that wasteth at noonday.

It is such a tempest that constitutes one of the chief dangers of our land to-day. Our spiritual progress lags so far behind our material progress. We are rich in things, but often deadly poor in the wealth that outlasts the ages. It is hard to face a tempest of adversity. It is harder still to stand against an avalanche of prosperity. As the Roman girl who promised to lead an invading army into her city if each soldier would give her the bracelet from his own arm was crushed under the weight of her own wealth, so many a one is crushed to-day. Happy is the man who lives in the consciousness of the fact that his life consisteth not in the abundance of the things that he possesseth.

4. Finally, to every one of us is coming the test of the judgment. This is true of those who build

wisely. It is true of those who build foolishly.
Every one of us is on the road to the hour of testing.
That is as certain as the fact of life. It is as certain as
the fact of death. It is as certain as the fact of God.
"Every man must give an account of himself to
God. . . . For we must all stand before the judg-
ment seat of Christ. . . . For it is appointed unto
man once to die, but after this the judgment."

How supremely important, therefore, that we
should build wisely and well, for every man's building is going to be tested!

> "Build thee more stately mansions, O my soul,
> As the swift seasons roll.
> Leave thy low-vaulted past,
> Let each new temple, nobler than the last,
> Shut thee from heaven with a dome more vast,
> Till thou at length art free,
> Leaving thine outgrown shell by life's unresting sea."

III

The final fact that our Lord brings before us is
that the issues of the testing are not going to be the
same for all.

1. Some are not going to be able to stand the test.
This is true of all whose lives are not founded on
Himself and his teaching. What a bold and daring
declaration! Yet he makes it, and makes it without
the slightest flinching. He makes it without the
least modification. "If you do not build on me,"
he says frankly, "your house will not stand. One
day the tempest will swoop down upon it and tear it

225

to fragments. One day there will be a crash, then shreds of wreckage upon the raging waters, and the ruin will be complete." "For other foundation can no man lay than that is laid, which is Jesus Christ."

2. But there are those, thank God, that are going to pass through the testing without loss. There are those that are going to outride all storms. There are those that are going to weather all gales. This is true of all who have builded their lives upon Jesus Christ. For such a life it is going to be written in time, and it is going to be written in eternity: "It fell not." "He shall be like a tree planted by rivers of water." He remains steadfast. He is unhurt amidst the crash of tempests and the wreck of worlds. "For the world passeth away, and the lust thereof; but he that doeth the will of God abideth forever." Such are the stupendous claims of Jesus, and these high claims have been vindicated countless millions of times. Lives builded on him really do stand the test.

A few years ago a mission worker who was a beautiful saint went to comfort a friend who had lost a wife. If this friend was a Christian at all, he was only nominally so. The minister spoke to him of the consolations of the gospel. But the bereaved man turned on him bitterly and said: "Have you ever lost your wife?" The preacher answered in the negative. "Well," said the other impatiently, "you don't know what you are talking about. Wait till you have a sorrow like mine and see if your Christ can meet the test."

226

The preacher went away with a sense of failure. But the testing time was closer to him, too, than he dreamed. Suddenly, without the slightest warning, the news came that his brilliant and gifted wife had been killed in a railroad accident. The remains were brought to the city and taken to the mission hall. This grief-stricken husband stood by the coffin of his wife to speak. He said: "Some six months ago I tried to comfort a bereaved husband, but I failed. He said I did not know what I was talking about. Is he here?" And the man stood up. The preacher then continued: "My friend, I know to-day. I am in the midst of a sorrow like your sorrow, and I want to tell you that, while my heart is bleeding and broken, I find His grace sufficient. I find that his hand holds me and steadies me. I find that my skies are as bright as the promises of God, and that underneath are the Everlasting Arms." May you find your foundation so secure when you come to your testing! If you do, you must build upon the Rock of Ages.

BOOK 2

SERMONS
FROM THE MIRACLES

CONTENTS

5

I

HIS RADIANT MINISTRY

"God anointed Jesus of Nazareth with the Holy Spirit and with power: who went about doing good, and healing all that were oppressed of the devil; for God was with him."

ACTS 10: 38

THIS IS A PART OF PETER'S SERMON IN THE HOUSE of Cornelius. We are told that this Centurion had been praying, and that God had answered his prayer by telling him where he might obtain a preacher. "Immediately therefore," says Cornelius, "I sent unto thee; and thou hast well done that thou art come. Now therefore are we all here present in the sight of God, to hear all things that are commanded thee of God." Then the Apostle Peter, who had responded to this invitation, under the leadership of the Spirit, delivered his message. At the heart and center of his sermon is our text. It is the very summary of the life of Jesus. It is as beautiful and impressive as it is brief: "God anointed Jesus of Nazareth with the

7

Holy Spirit and with power: who went about doing good, and healing all that were oppressed of the devil."

I

The first fact that Peter brings before us is the high use that Jesus made of life. What did he do with the privilege of living? He did not use it selfishly, but unselfishly. He went about doing good. He was utterly free from self-seeking. When James and John came to him, asking for special privileges, he declared that he was swayed by no such motives; but, on the contrary, that he had come not to be ministered unto, but to minister. On another occasion he affirmed that it was more blessed to give than to receive. This great truth he had discovered, not by close thinking, but by unselfish living. When we live in any other fashion life loses its tang, its springtime gives place to gloomy winter.

Back in the hill country, where I used to live, there was a standard answer concerning any sick body who was not improving. "How is Mr. Smith this morning?" one neighbor would ask another. "He is not doing any good," would be the sad response. That meant that there were no indications of returning health. Now, those who are not doing any good are always sick. They are missing the gleam to take the gloom. I read of one such not long ago. Living to no purpose, he soured on life. At last, in sheer boredom he decided to end it all. So he made his way to the pier and flung himself into the sea. But he had a friend. That friend had become suspicious, and was watching. So, when he flung himself into the sea, this friend sprang in after him. Now, it so happened that while this would-be suicide was an excellent swimmer, his friend could not swim a stroke. Therefore, when this poor wretch, who was fed up, saw his friend drowning for his sake, he had to help. After a hard struggle, he managed to save him. This experience proved such a thrill that he decided to live. And little by little his boredom vanished through the joy of an effort to do some good in the world.

Now, the fact that Jesus went about doing good indicates not only that he cared, but that he believed that good needed to be done. That is, Jesus recognizes the presence of evil in the world. He was no shallow optimist. He never once ignored the grim tragedy of sin, sickness, and death. He saw with clearer eyes than any other the terrible sufferings of men, their wounds, their bewilderments, their desperation. He saw behind these grim tragedies the deeper tragedy of alienation from God. Jesus faced with clear eyes the grim fact of sin, and all the wretched evils that result from it.

Not only did Jesus face the fact that good needed to be done, but he was convinced that good could be done. That is, he looked on sin as a usurper in God's world. He did not believe it to be a permanent part of the divine plan. Since sin itself was a usurper,

9

so were its tragic consequences. Therefore, Jesus believed that the evils of the world could be cured by getting rid of their cause. It was this faith that made him such a dauntless optimist. The Bible view of sin is often regarded as pessimistic. But it is the only view that offers one ray of hope. For, if sin and its consequences are parts of the natural order of things, then there is nothing to be done about it. But if Christ's view is correct, then we may pray and work in confidence for the coming of the Kingdom. We can look toward the day when the Kingdoms of the world shall become the Kingdoms of our Lord and his Christ.

Now it was in this faith that Jesus went about doing good. He believed in the reality of evil. He believed that man was lost, but he believed that he could be saved. But he believed this was only possible through man's co-operation with God. He never expected either the individual or society to drift into salvation. He believed that if a better world was ever to be made, man was to work with God in the making of it. Gripped by that conviction, he turned his back on his carpenter shop one day to go about doing good, never giving over till they nailed him to the cross. And the way he used his life is the way you and I are to use ours.

II

But, what good did Jesus do? Of course a full answer to this question is impossible. He showed men God. This he did by the life he lived, by the words he spoke, by the deeds he did. It is of his deeds that Peter is especially thinking in our text. He is thinking of the miracles of Jesus, particularly his miracles of healing. The mighty deeds of Jesus were one of the thrilling joys of the early saints. They gloried in them. They saw in them unmistakable evidences that the life of heaven was already beginning here on earth. We do not think of them so joyously. Oftentimes they rather embarrass us. Often we tax our ingenuity in order to explain them away. But in spite of this fact, it is my purpose to speak to you about them for a dozen or more Sundays. This sermon is by way of introduction.

The miracles of Jesus fall roughly into three groups.

1. There are his miracles of healing—miracles that he wrought upon the diseased and maimed bodies of men. As I re-read the Gospels in preparation for this series of sermons, I was astonished at how large a place the ministry of healing had in the brief record of the life of Jesus. He did not heal on rare occasions and grudgingly, as some seem to fancy. He healed lavishly and joyously. He seems to have taken the greatest delight in ministering to suffering bodies. This, of course, is only natural. We can think of few privileges so thrilling as being able to lift some despairing sufferer upon his feet.

Jesus healed those who came to him individually. Matthew tells how, when he came down from the mountain, after his immortal sermon, a leper flung himself at his feet, with this honest prayer: "Lord, if thou wilt, thou canst make me whole." He was sure of the power of Jesus, but he was not quite sure of his love. Life has dealt too harshly with him. The best he could say to Jesus was, "If you choose." And what did Jesus reply to this imperfect faith? He said, "I do choose." And immediately the leper was cleansed. And Jesus was constantly choosing health for those about him, instead of sickness. There was never an instance where he refused to cure because he thought it best for the patient to remain a sufferer.

On another occasion, when Jesus went into the synagogue, he encountered a poor woman who was suffering from a dread disease that had almost bent her double. He at once healed her, and sent her on her way joyfully erect. When the ruler of the synagogue saw her, he was filled with anger. "There are six days in which folks can come to be healed," he declared; "why, then, desecrate the sabbath?" But Jesus turned on him in indignation and said, "You hypocrite, if your ox falls into the pit on the sabbath, you lift him out. And should not this woman, whom Satan has bound all these years, be released on the sabbath?" He regards the woman's infirmity as a part of the kingdom of evil. Therefore, as any good physician would, he fights to set her free.

But not only did Jesus heal when folks came to him individually, but again and again we read of his healing when they are brought to him in groups. Here and there we find such words as these: "And Jesus went about all Galilee, teaching in their synagogues, and preaching the gospel of the kingdom, and healing every sickness and every disease among the people." Then, there is that beautiful picture in Capernaum: "At even, when the sun was set, the whole city was gathered about his door, and he healed them all." Then, in the fourteenth chapter of St. Matthew we read that when he came to Gennesaret the people went into all the country round about and brought to him all that were sick. And he healed them every one. Then, in the fifteenth chapter, we read that great multitudes came unto him, bringing to him the lame and the maimed and the blind. And he healed them all. It is evident, therefore, that Jesus gave a large place to the ministry of healing. And when he sent out his disciples, he told them to heal the sick. And I fear that in our dread of fanaticism we have turned this gracious ministry too largely into the hands of the cults and the faddists.

2. Jesus wrought miracles within the souls of men. There is no argument about this among Christian people. He changed the fluctuating son of Jonah into a rock. He changed John, with his high capacity to hate, into the apostle of love. He found the demoniac of Gerasa, a disintegrated personality, a menace, and made him into a missionary. It was to miracles of spiritual healing that Jesus gave supreme importance.

13

And we are right in putting the emphasis there still. We know that it is possible for one to be sound physically and rotten spiritually. But we also know that there are many whose physical diseases would vanish like mist before the sunrise if they only found spiritual healing. Then, there are multitudes who are able to suffer bravely and even joyously because they have inward peace. There is no greater miracle than the courage to say in the midst of life's disasters, "We know that all things work together for good to them that love God."

3. Finally, Jesus worked miracles in the realm of nature. These are the ones that the modern man finds it hardest to believe. We read that when Jesus was surrounded by hungry multitudes, he fed them upon resources totally inadequate. On another occasion, when he, with his disciples, was crossing the sea and a sudden storm threatened to wreck his little vessel, his disciples appealed to him for help, even as you and I should have done under similar circumstances. What was the response of Jesus? He did not simply stay the tempests within their hearts and give them courage to see it through with honor. This he will always do when we pray to him aright. This is the best possible. But here he saw fit even to still the sea itself, so that there was a great calm. He believed that it was in the hollow of God's hand that the seas rage and roar, and that they could be hushed at His bidding.

Then, Jesus raised the dead. A dead body is a part of nature. It is a "brother to the clod which the rude swain turns with his share and treads upon." But Jesus did not believe that death was any match for God. When on the way to the house of the ruler of the synagogue he was met by neighbors, telling him that the patient was dead, he did not turn back. "He paid no attention to what they said," is Goodspeed's translation. He went quietly on his way and gave the child back to those who loved her. He was not afraid to have the stone removed from the grave of Lazarus. He knew that there was One present who was mightier than death and that the victory was sure to be with Him. Jesus, then, worked miracles on the bodies of men, within their souls, and within the realm of nature.

III

Not only does the Apostle remind us that Jesus wrought these mighty deeds, but he tells us the power by which he was enabled to work them. He makes it very clear that Jesus did not perform his miracles in the power of his innate deity. When Jesus was born of Mary, he emptied himself. He lived his whole life, not as God, but as man. If Jesus met his temptations and did his mighty works as God, then his incarnation loses most of its meaning for us. Jesus' power was that of a perfect man perfectly filled with the Holy Spirit. So says Peter: "God anointed Jesus of Nazareth with the Holy Spirit and with power: who

15

went about doing good." With him agree all the evangelists.

The power of the Spirit that Jesus realized in its fullness was released in response to the prayer of faith. Where there was no faith, there were no mighty deeds. Where there was no faith, nothing great and thrilling was possible. Where there was faith, everything was possible. Impossibilities could be broken through like so many gossamer threads, and mountains of difficulties could be tossed aside like children's toys. This Jesus declared with his lips, and this he declared also by his deeds. Jesus set no limits to the power of faith. Again and again, when he cures, he attributes the cure to faith.

One day, for instance, when a woman who had been a sufferer for twelve years came to him and touched the hem of his robe, he healed her. When he dismissed her, he said to her this significant word: "Your faith has cured you." When blind Bartimaeus appealed to him for release from his blindness, he restored his sight, and said exactly the same word, "Your faith has cured you." Again, when the Samaritan who, with nine others, had been cured of his leprosy came back and fell down at his feet to give thanks, Jesus sent him on his way with exactly the same word, "Your faith has cured you." As we read the record we are impressed by the fact that nothing seems to have given Jesus greater pain than the lack of faith that he was constantly encountering. We are also made to realize that nothing so thrilled him as the discovery of faith, either in the heart of Jew or Gentile. This was the case because without faith nothing of worth was possible, while with it everything was possible.

But did not Jesus call Lazarus from the dead in the power of his own deity? Did he not say, "Lazarus, come forth"? And have we not heard it emphasized that if he had not specified Lazarus by name, all the dead might have risen? On the contrary, Jesus fairly goes out of his way to tell us that this was not the case. Standing before that grave, he offers a brief prayer of thanksgiving, "Father, I thank thee that thou hast heard me. I know that thou hast heard me always." Jesus won his victory in the secret place of prayer, before he reached that grave. Lazarus was raised from the dead, according to the clear statement of Jesus, in answer to the prayer of faith. And the significant fact is that the resources that Jesus used for the doing of his work are available for every man and woman today who will claim them.

IV

Now, what are we modern Christians living in this scientific age to do with these facts? The Gospels teach, with one voice, that Jesus worked miracles in the power of the Holy Spirit. What does this mean to us?

1. There are those who reject the miracles of Jesus

17

either wholly or in part. They believe that these stories grew up about Jesus in an unscientific age as stories are prone to grow up about any conspicuously great man. They have the same amount of truth that the story of the cherry tree and the hatchet has regarding Washington. These affirm that miracles cannot happen because nature is a rigid affair, a closed system, where only physical causes can bring about physical effects. They, therefore, dismiss the miracles as at once irrelevant and impossible.

2. Then, there are those who accept the miracles, but accept them only as evidences of the unique deity of Jesus. These declare that Jesus wrought miracles to prove that he was divine, and that, having demonstrated that fact, miracles were no longer useful. Hence they say now that the days of miracles are past. But those taking this position are about as greatly embarrassed as the ones who reject them altogether. This is true, in the first place, because the writers of the New Testament take no such view. Jesus never once worked a miracle just for display. When asked for a sign his answer was, "A wicked and adulterous generation seeketh after a sign." And no such request was ever granted.

This view is embarrassing also because, if the day of miracles is past, it is hard to tell just when it passed. It certainly did not do so at the death of Jesus. If we give credit to the Book of Acts, miracles went right on taking place, not only in the souls of men, but in their bodies, and also in the realm of nature. In the Acts, men were healed of bodily disease. Prison doors were opened, and men facing shipwreck were saved, all in answer to the prayer of faith. But the most embarrassing question of all for those taking this view is, why was this power withdrawn? If the power to do the impossible was needed in the long ago, surely it is not less needed now. If ever the Church was confronted by tasks that call for supernatural power, it is today. And I for one believe that all the power that was available in the time of Jesus is available now.

3. Finally, there are those who accept these miracles substantially as related in the Gospels. They find it easier to do this today than it was three-quarters of a century ago. This is the case because we have learned that nature is not a rigid affair, that it is not a closed system. We have had this fact demonstrated before our eyes again and again. We have discovered, for instance, something of the amazing power that the mind has over the body. We have seen folks stone blind, when there was nothing wrong with their eyes. We have seen deaf folks who had perfect ears, lame folks whose limbs were unimpaired. The trouble with all these was not in their bodies, but in their minds. We know that a hypnotist can put his subject to sleep, press the end of a pencil in his palm, and say, "I am burning you with a red-hot iron." Then he can tie up that hand. Wake the patient, and unwrap it, and there will be a blister burned there, not by a hot iron,

but by the mind. There is no tissue in the body, the *British Journal of Medicine* tells us, that is not influenced by spirit.

Now, if my mind can so influence this physical house in which I live, and there is no measuring how great that influence is, is it too much to believe that the divine mind can influence this physical universe? Jesus did not think so. He believed that the universe was God-made, and that it was plastic in His hands. Such a faith seems to me altogether reasonable. It would seem queer indeed that God would shut Himself up in a universe that He could not control. As I was driving along the road the other day, I saw a sign advertising brakes. It read, "If you cannot stop, don't start." And in all reverence, that would apply to God. If He cannot control His universe, He should not start it. We believe that He can control it. Why did men once say that nature was absolutely rigid? Because they did not know any better. Personally, I believe that the more we learn, the more credible will become the miracles of Jesus.

What, then, does this mean? It means that every human need may be a matter of prayer. It means that we can pray for spiritual blessings, for inner strength, and courage, and peace. It means, also, that while we recognize these as supreme, we can also pray for temporal blessings. We can pray for daily bread, as we do, when we use the prayer that our Lord taught us. It means that absolutely nothing is outside God's interest and God's power. Why, then, is the modern Church so often weak and discouraged and defeated? The answer is plain. It is because it is living beneath its privileges. The vast majority of modern Christians are sub-normal. Wherever any individual or group has become possessed of the simple faith of the early Church, the impossible has become possible, and spiritual winter has been changed into glorious spring. May God give us grace to claim our privileges! And of us, too, it may be written, "God anointed him with the Holy Spirit and with power: and he went about doing good."

II

THE BEST IS YET TO BE

*"Thou hast kept the good
wine until now."*

THE TEXT IS PART OF THE STORY OF THE FIRST
miracle of our Lord, the turning of water into
wine.   Indeed, the Apostle does not call this homely
service that Jesus wrought a miracle at all.   He calls
it a sign.   "This beginning of his signs did Jesus in
Cana of Galilee, and manifested forth his glory."
That is, while this kindly deed is important in itself,
it owes its chief importance to what it has to teach us
regarding our Lord.   To the mind of John this sign,
in a very profound sense, holds the mirror up to the
face of the Master.   It reveals something of his character and purpose in the world, also something of his
method of achieving that purpose.   For this reason it
is highly significant to all of us.   What are some of
the lessons it has to teach?

I

First, it is a revelation of the interest of Jesus in
the commonplace.   He is interested in ordinary folks

and in their ordinary joys and sorrows. The scene is
a wedding in an obscure country village. Who is the
bride? We do not know. John leaves her nameless.
She is evidently some peasant girl whose family has
no place in the social register. Who is the bridegroom? He also is nameless—just some ordinary
rustic "to fortune and to fame unknown." But when
Jesus receives an invitation to the wedding of these
commonplace young people, he accepts with gladness.
This he does, not condescendingly, nor from a mere
sense of duty. He does it rather because he is keenly
interested in them; not because of who they are, but
because of what they are, human personalities.

Now, what Jesus did here is typical of his conduct
throughout his entire ministry. Whenever he received
an invitation into anybody's home he accepted it. This
he did whether the giver of that invitation was rich
or poor, friendly or hostile, socially prominent, or an
outcast. That is, he was interested in folks as such.
Never once do we find him paying particular attention
to any man or woman because of his or her wealth,
or rank, or achievement, or intellectual gifts, or social
position. He leaves all that for us. He knew too well
that "the rank is but the guinea's stamp." But we still
bow down to what is outside and accidental. I heard
a woman say that she went shopping one day wearing
a very ordinary costume; but that the day following
she went again wearing her best, and there was a vast
difference in the consideration she received. That is,

23

we are interested in certain kinds of folks, but Jesus is interested in just folks.

Now, since Jesus was interested in this bride and groom, all that concerned them concerned him. When, therefore, an embarrassment arose because the bridegroom was too poor to furnish refreshments in sufficient quantity, Jesus threw himself into the breach. This he did, not because wine was an absolute necessity. It was not a matter of life and death. Wine was, however, part of the daily diet of that time. The bridegroom was expected to furnish it, and his failure to do so would have been very embarrassing. It was to save him from such embarrassment that Jesus worked this miracle. During his earthly life he was constantly interesting himself in the ordinary joys and sorrows of the folks about him.

And what he was before he came to the cross, he was after he had risen from the dead. That is a beautiful story that John gives us in the latter part of his Gospel. Peter, with a few of his friends, has returned to his old vocation of fishing. They toil all night, but catch nothing. In the early morning, as they come in from their fruitless labors, they see somebody standing on the shore. At first they do not recognize him. It is the gloaming of the early morning. Then, a question is shouted to them across the waters. It was a question that made their hearts beat quicker: "Lads, have you caught anything?" He is still interested in their interests, just as in the old days. When they tell him of their failure, he tells them how to cast their net so as to be successful.

Then, when a little later they reach the shore, dragging their net full of fish, they find that a fire has already been kindled, and that breakfast is being prepared. "Come and break your fast," he says a moment later. How beautiful it all is! This amazing Christ who has just conquered death and the grave still has time enough and love enough to give himself to the lowly task of preparing breakfast for a little handful of hungry fishermen who have just come in from a fruitless night of toil. And the Christ we see here is the same yesterday, today, and forever. He is the Christ who is interested in our commonplace selves and in our daily joys and sorrows.

II

Second, this is a sign of the purpose of Jesus in the world. What has he come to do? What is he here to accomplish? He is not a thief who is come to steal and to kill and to destroy. He is not come to rob us of our laughter or to cheat us of our joy. He is not come to take one single gleam of sunshine out of our skies. "Pale Galilean, thou hast conquered, and the world has grown gray at thy birth." So sobbed one of the spiritually blind. But a word more utterly false was never uttered. Not only is this untrue; it is the very opposite of the truth.

What, then, is Jesus here to do? He is here to

25

transfigure and to transform. He gives new glory to everything upon which he lays his hand. He makes the useless into the useful. He lifts the lower into the higher. He makes the colorless water of the worthless blush into the fine red wine of the worthful. He is here to change desert into garden. He is here to transmute the world's moral waste into the world's moral wealth. A man died in the West some years ago named Luther Burbank. Burbank said that every weed was a possible flower. What an amazing confidence he had in his vegetable kingdom! The only reason he thought that that old burweed did not have its hands full of blossoms instead of cockleburs was because no man had cared for its soul.

Now, in proof of the truthfulness of his contention, Burbank undertook the transformation of the cactus. I do not know whether you are personally acquainted with the cactus or not. If you are, you will recognize the fact that it is one of the best armed plants in the vegetable kingdom. It believes in preparedness. You could not slip up on the blind side of a cactus the darkest night that ever came. It is always ready for battle. But Burbank met this unfriendly plant and seemingly fell in love with it. Anyway he gave himself to its training till one day, in a moment of confidence, that cactus responded by putting down all its swords and bayonets, and filling its hands with flowers. When we see it today, we no longer gather our garments about us lest it touch us, but we should like to wear its colorful beauty over our hearts, or rub our cheeks against the soft velvet of its petals. He found what was a positive foe, and made it into a friend.

But the supreme artist in this work of lifting the lower into the higher is none other than Jesus himself. He finds a blundering fisherman named Simon, a creature of impulse, as unstable as water, and makes him into a rock of Christlike character. He finds a thunderbolt named John, capable of such hot hate as to be able to call down fire from heaven on certain misguided villagers who refuse a night's lodging to his Master and himself, and changes him into the Apostle of Love. He finds a grasping tax collector named Matthew and sets him to writing a Gospel. He finds a demon-possessed woman named Mary and makes her the first herald of the Resurrection. He finds an intellectual giant named Paul, the greatest menace of the early Church, and makes him into its greatest missionary. And he is the same Christ still. He still touches every life that will surrender to him, every gift we put into his hands, not to cheapen and to spoil, but to transform and to glorify. He is here to lift the lower into the higher.

III

Then, this is a sign of the method of Jesus.

1. It indicates his method of working his marvelous transformations. How did he change this water into wine? I have no doubt that he could have wrought

the change without any assistance. But he did not see fit to do so. How did he accomplish the task? He did it through the aid of human hands. These servants had to co-operate with him. In fact, they had to do all that they could do before this miracle was made possible. It is ever so. When the hungry multitude is to be fed, he must have the assistance of his disciples. Not only so, but he must lean especially hard upon the shoulders of a nameless laddie who happens to have a bit of lunch in his pocket. When he cures a paralytic and sends him away sound in body and soul, he must have the assistance of four resolute friends who refused to be balked by any difficulties. When he raises Lazarus from the dead, human hands must roll away the stone, and human fingers must loose him and let him go. When the night had settled over Europe, and he wants to bring in the dawning of a new day, he must have the assistance of a Martin Luther. When he would breathe a new spiritual springtime upon a morally dead England, he must have the aid of a hot-hearted Wesley.

In fact, all the transforming work of our Lord waits upon your co-operation and mine. If we would have abundant harvests, he must send the sunshine and the rain, but we must do our part. If we are to have strong physical bodies, we must co-operate with him. A perplexed and worried woman came to see me some time ago to ask me if I thought it would be a sin for her to take the medicine that her physician had prescribed. She had been told that she must leave it all to the Lord. Possibly I misled her, but I advised her to take the medicine. It might be within the power of God to keep me physically strong without my ever eating, but my faith does not work in that direction. I believe that it is my duty to co-operate with Him in eating the right kind of food. I believe, also, it is my duty to co-operate with Him in taking the remedy that the physician prescribes. God's work is not less miraculous because He is assisted by human hands. "I bound up his wounds," said Galen, "and God healed him."

It is my very firm conviction that God wills that we should have a strong and conquering church at the heart of this city. Vigorous churches are needed everywhere, but nowhere, it seems to me, so much as in the downtown sections of the city. A downtown church is to the spiritual life of a city a bit like what the heart is to the human body. If the heart is strong, it pumps the stream of life and power into every part of the body. If it is weak, it weakens the whole body. Even so, if a downtown church becomes weak, it tends to weaken the spiritual life of the whole city. If it is strong, the spiritual life of the city is strengthened. But how are we to have a conquering church? It is up to you and me. God cannot do it alone. The same is true in the world at large. If there is anything to be done in this generation toward the building of a new and better world, we that are alive today are the ones who are going to have to do it. Our Lord has no other way.

2. This is, also, a sign of Christ's method of giving results. When these servants co-operated with him, there was wine and to spare. Our Christ is ever the Christ of abundances. When he wants space, he spreads it out to the point of the infinite. When he wants suns, he kindles them by the million. When he wants stars, he sows them heaven-wide. Even in our little world he does things on a grand scale. When he wants mountains he piles up the Andes and the Alps, the Himalayas and the Rockies. When he wants flowers, he decks the hills and the fields with them. When he wants water, he scoops out the seven seas, and ribbons the world with rivers, and veils the rugged faces of the cliffs with myriad waterfalls.

And if our Lord is lavish in the realm of the physical, he is even more lavish in the realm of grace. When he offers redemption, it is not a scanty gift. "With him is plenteous redemption." When he pardons, he does not do so in a niggardly fashion. "Let the wicked forsake his way, and the unrighteous man his thoughts: and let him return unto the Lord . . . and unto our God, for he will abundantly pardon." When he gives salvation, he purposes to save unto the uttermost. When he promises to answer our prayers, "He is able to do exceeding abundantly above all that we ask or think." When he offers the gift of life, it is not a meager rivulet, it is a brimming river: "I am

30

come that ye might have life, and have it in abundance." When he offers us welcome into his house on the other side, he does not compel us to slip through a mere slit in the door; he gives us an abundant entrance. Thus he is ever the Christ of abundances.

3. This is the sign of Christ's method of meeting our needs. He does so with an ever-increasing satisfaction. He brings life to an ever-growing climax. When the governor of the feast tasted this new wine, he was astonished at its fine quality. "Every man," he said to the bridegroom, in amazement, "every man at the beginning doth set forth good wine; and when men have well drunk, then that which is worse: but thou hast kept the good wine until now." Such a procedure was altogether out of the ordinary. It is so still. The world ever gives its best first. There are many joys that it has to offer, but the thrill grows less and less with the passing of the years. However hopefully we begin the voyage, soon the anchor drags. However brilliant the feast, it soon loses its tang, the wine gives out, and we become wearied. This somber realization sobs its way through some of our best literature. We hear it bitterly from the lips of Byron:

> " 'Tis not on youth's smooth cheek alone,
>   The blush that fades so fast,
> But the tender bloom of heart is gone
>   Ere youth itself is past.
>
> O could I feel as once I felt,
>   And be what I have been,

And weep as I could once have wept,
  O'er many a vanished scene,

As springs in deserts found seem sweet,
  All brackish though they be,
So midst the withered waste of life
  Those tears would flow to me."

We hear it with less of bitterness from the lips of
Wordsworth:

"Heaven lies about us in our infancy!
  Shades of the prison-house begin to close
    Upon the growing Boy;
But He beholds the light, and whence it flows,
He sees it in his joy;
The Youth, who daily farther from the east
  Must travel, still is Nature's Priest,
    And by the vision splendid
Is on his way attended;
At length the Man perceives it die away,
And fade into the light of common day."

We hear it also plaintively from Hood:

"I remember, I remember
  The house where I was born,
The little window where the sun
  Came peeping in at morn;
He never came a wink too soon
  Nor brought too long a day;
But now, I often wish the night
  Had borne my breath away.

I remember, I remember
  The fir-trees dark and high;
I used to think their slender tops
  Were close against the sky:

32

It was a childish ignorance,
But now 'tis little joy
To know I'm farther off from Heaven
Than when I was a boy."

How many a weary heart, I wonder, feels with
Hood that their life journey is taking them each day
a little farther away from heaven? "For the wettest
of wet blankets," says Lord Morley, "give me the man
who was most enthusiastic in his youth." Another,
realizing how life tends to put out the holy fires of
our enthusiasm and reduce us to dull and disillusioned
plodders, expresses a longing that we might reverse
the order of things and begin at the end and work back
toward the beginning. That is, instead of being born
a baby boy and gradually growing into a disillusioned
old man, he longs to be born old, and gradually to grow
back to middle life, and from middle life to youth,
and from youth to the sweet innocence of childhood.
That, of course, is a futile longing. It is utterly impossible of realization, in the first place. But even if
it could be realized, it would make of life only a pathetic anticlimax.

But in the fellowship of Jesus we find all for which
this man yearned, and far more. With him life is
always climbing toward an ever-growing climax. The
feast is forever getting better, the tides of joy rising
higher. The buds of the heart's springtime are bursting into ever-increasing beauty. For the real Christian, always the best is yet to be. The Golden Age

is never of yesterday, but always of tomorrow. "Thou hast kept the good wine until now"—This we shall say at our first meeting with our Master when, with Thomas, we exclaim: "My Lord and my God." "Thou hast kept the good wine until now"—This we shall exclaim as the years come and go, and we get deeper into the intimacies of his friendship. "Thou hast kept the good wine until now"—This we shall say when we awake with his likeness on the other side. "Thou hast kept the good wine until now"—This we shall say as we climb one Alpine height after another with him in eternity. For "we know not what we shall be: but we know that, when he shall appear, we shall be like him; for we shall see him as he is."

Finally, we are to keep in mind how Christ's amazing dream for us is to become a reality. What are we to do that we may assist Jesus in his work of remaking the individual and the world? What are we to do in order to find life better at every step of the way? Mary put the answer into a single sentence: "Whatsoever he saith unto you, do it." Ours is to be a life of surrender, of complete consecration to God. This is the whole of Christianity. It is Christianity in its beginning, Christianity in its course, Christianity in its consummation. If we do this, we shall find that our path shall be, as the path of the just ever is, "as a shining light, that shineth more and more unto the perfect day."

III

ADVENTURING FOR WORLD PEACE

*"Nevertheless at thy word
I will let down the net."*

LUKE 5: 5

PETER IS COMMITTING HIMSELF TO A COURSE THAT he knows will make him look ridiculous in the eyes of every sane fisherman. To cast the nets under the present circumstances is the height of absurdity. But Peter is going to do it because of his confidence in his Master. He does not believe that Jesus will send him on a fool's errand. It is in this high faith that we adventure for world peace. Our Lord has pronounced a blessing upon the peacemakers. Evidently he believes that peace can be made. He expected a good day when men should beat their swords into plowshares and their spears into pruning hooks and learn war no more! Because we share this faith, we dare to adventure for world peace.

I

It is heartening that more people are thinking in terms of world peace today than ever before. This

35

does not mean necessarily that we are better or wiser than our fathers. The tragic experiences through which we have passed have compelled us to think. We have come to our thoughtfulness over roads strewn with human wreckage, wet with human tears, and crimsoned with human blood. We have tested on a larger scale than any other generation just what war is able to accomplish.

A little less than a quarter of a century ago, a small avalanche started in central Europe. This avalanche so increased in momentum and volume that soon two-score nations had been swept into an abysm of blood and tears. We fought on a grand scale. We are far enough away from the tragedy now to realize that while the war promoters were equally wrong, those whose duty it was to fight and die were equally heroic.

You remember the call that came to us from the battlefields of Europe:

> "In Flanders fields the poppies blow
> Between the crosses, row on row,
>   That mark our place; and in the sky
>   The larks, still bravely singing, fly
> Scarce heard amid the guns below.
> We are the Dead. Short days ago
> We lived, felt dawn, saw sunset glow,
>   Loved and were loved, and now we lie
>   In Flanders fields.
>
> Take up our quarrel with the foe:
> To you from failing hands we throw
>   The torch; be yours to hold it high.
>   If ye break faith with us who die

We shall not sleep, though poppies grow
In Flanders fields." [1]

You remember our heroic response:

"Rest ye in peace, ye Flanders dead!
The fight that ye so bravely led
    We've taken up. And we will keep
    True faith with you who lie asleep,
With each a cross to mark his bed,
And poppies blowing overhead
Where once his own lifeblood ran red!
    So let your sleep be sweet and deep
    In Flanders fields!

Fear not that you have died for naught,
The torch you threw to us we caught.
    Ten million hands will hold it high,
    And Freedom's light will never die.
We've learned the lesson that you taught
    In Flanders fields!" [2]

If the outcome of this war was disappointing, if our winnings were far too small, it was certainly not due to the smallness of our investment. Too often our best enterprises fail because of our lack of consecration. Too often we bring to our most worthful tasks in church and state efforts that are half-hearted. But such was not the case in our prosecution of the war. Here we gave our best. We gave our newspapers and our magazines. We had to have the press to propagate the multitudinous lies that are so necessary for the prosecution of a modern war. The press must beat

[1] By John McCrea. Used by permission.

[2] By R. W. Lillard.

37

down the individual mind and change it into a mob mind. In the business of fighting, therefore, lying is just as necessary as bayonets and bullets and deadly poisons. We gave to our task not a few of our pulpits. Some of us preached war as zealously as if our Master had been a military hero. We gave to this undertaking our treasure—all we had, and mortgaged the future. We gave our man power by the million. Our investment was immeasurably great.

From such an investment, we had a right to expect enormous winnings. But here we were doomed to disappointment. When we received our dividend, it consisted of a world-wide economic depression. It consisted of a moral and spiritual depression which was far more terrible and tragic. All our wild dreams of a better day turned to dust and ashes. Entering the war to make the world safe for democracy, we seem to have made it safe for autocracy. More people are living under despotisms at this hour than at any other time in all human history. There are pathetically few real democracies left in the world today. We were fighting to end war, but we seem to have made war all but inevitable.

"But, at least, we won," you answer, in a natural effort at self-defense. But even that is not quite so evident as we thought. A few months ago, Germany marched in and took over the Rhine. When that happened, one of our shrewd militarists declared that Germany had thus won the war; that, therefore, we ought to go over and whip them again. He did not say just why. But of course, the reason is simple. We ought to whip them again in order that they might march back twenty years later and win the war once more. Thus, if any were left alive, we could keep up the vicious circle like a squirrel chasing himself in a cage. But be that as it may, since Germany has taken over the Rhine, the value of our victory does seem a bit more doubtful than we once thought.

There are even those who are convinced that our boasted victory was a liability rather than an asset. Recently Dr. F. W. Norwood, of London, England, startled us by declaring that the entrance of the United States into the war was a genuine calamity. "Had you not entered," he said, "neither side would have won. We would have fought to a muddled draw. Having done so, we would have made peace on a basis of humility and compromise. But by your entrance, you made our victory decisive. Therefore, we made peace, not on a basis of humility and compromise, but of arrogance and pride. We dealt as conquerors with the conquered. Thus we recarved the map of Europe, and made future wars all but inevitable." From all these considerations, it is evident that the greatest war ever fought was a total loss.

II

Since our greatest adventure at war has proved such a failure, many of us have come to mistrust war altogether. It is estimated that only two-fifths of one per cent of our people really want war. Now, the question is, what are the other ninety-nine and three-fifths per cent of us going to do about it? On this question, we divide into various groups.

First, there are those who say that we can do nothing about it. Those who take this position are composed mainly of two groups:

1. They are people without religious faith. They share the pessimism of the preacher of Ecclesiastes. They believe that what has been will be, that the crooked can never be made straight. "Man is a fighting animal," they say. "He fought yesterday, he will fight today, tomorrow, and to the end of the chapter."

2. The other group sharing this pessimistic outlook, strange to say, is made of people who are very religious. One of their number preached on world peace in my pulpit some months ago. He is a man of especially high character and one for whom I have a deep respect. He deplored war as a horrible and hellish thing, but ended by telling us that nothing could be done to prevent it. He declared that the scriptures say that there are to be wars and rumors of wars to the end of the age. Therefore, there is nothing for us to do but to go ahead and kill each other.

Now it seems to me that this is fatalism pure and simple. Surely, it is little short of treason to our Lord and Master. His name was to be called Jesus because he was to save his people from their sins.

Now there is hardly a sin that war does not beget, and make to grow and to multiply. Lying, lust, hate, prejudice, murder—all these and far more are begotten and made strong by war. War is our supreme evil. It is the deadliest foe of mankind. If, therefore, our Lord cannot save us from this sin when we co-operate with him, from what sin can he save us? When he taught us to pray for the coming of his kingdom, he was not teaching us a prayer impossible of realization. But we have little to hope for in the way of world peace at the hands of those who do not believe anything can be done about it.

Second, there are those who hate war, but expect to prevent it by preparedness. Now I am not arguing, at the present, whether we should prepare or not prepare. But what I am saying is this: Preparedness is certainly not the road to peace. Of that we may be absolutely sure. This I say realizing that, though this claim has been made over and over again in such a way as to seem to smack of wisdom, yet in reality, it does not rise to the height of dignified nonsense. To make such a claim is to fly into the face of all history. To make such a claim is fairly to throw dust in the eyes of reason and spit in the face of common sense.

If the way to have peace is to prepare for war, then the way to have educated people is to exile our teachers and destroy our institutions of learning and burn up our libraries. If the way to have peace is to prepare for war, then the way to promote religion is to kill off the ministers and dynamite the churches. If the way to have peace is to prepare for war, then the way to have good health is to wreck our sewage system and disregard all laws of sanitation. If the way to have peace is to prepare for war, then we have learned how to reverse the laws of nature and gather grapes of thorns and figs of thistles. If the way to have peace is to prepare for war, then this is the only realm in all the universe of God where the law of sowing and reaping does not operate.

But the law of sowing and reaping does operate here as elsewhere. What a man sows, he reaps. What a nation sows, it reaps. The nation that is physically prepared for war is also mentally and spiritually prepared. In truth, that mental and spiritual preparation was an absolute necessity before the physical preparation could take place. If, therefore, we prepare the way of Mars, Mars will travel over it. If we prepare the way of the Prince of Peace, the Prince of Peace will travel over it. If that is not true, we are in a world of confusion. How peace will come, we may not know, but of one thing we can be sure, and that is, it is not going to come through battleships and bayonets.

Third, there are those who look for peace for ourselves in America through isolation. In the realization that we are separated from Europe by 3,000 miles of sea, we are going to let Europe and the rest of the world work out their own salvation while we remain safe in our natural isolation. Now, nobody is farther than I from any desire to be involved in another foreign war. If war breaks out in Europe or Asia, I am for the strongest of neutrality laws to keep us from getting involved. Furthermore, if our neutrality is violated, I am for suffering it rather than resorting to war. If, on the way home from this service, a highwayman should approach me and ask me for my dollar, I would give it to him. This I would do, not because of any great desire to be charitable toward him, but because I considered such a course the lesser of two evils. Weaker nations have to suffer the violation of their neutrality. For that very reason, they often fare far better than their strong neighbors. It is better to lose a hundred men than to lose millions.

But while isolation may be helpful, I seriously doubt if it offers the final solution to our problem. This is the case because we are a part of a constantly contracting world. This summer while fishing, I got poison oak on my left ankle. When it began to give me trouble, I remembered a remedy that I used as a boy— carbolic acid. But one important fact I forgot, that was that I used to dilute the acid. Therefore, I put it on straight and rubbed it in with vigor. When that acid began to eat to the bone, there was an insurrection. My hand said, "I am separated widely from this offending ankle, I will have nothing to do with it." My head said, "I certainly had nothing to do with the applying of the remedy, therefore I will have nothing to do with the suffering." But when bedtime came, as well as I remember, we all lay awake together. We are a part of the world, therefore we may count on this: America is either going to help the world make peace, or it is going to help the world make war. It is up to us to choose. The road to peace is not isolation.

Fourth, if the road to peace is not pessimism, not preparedness, not isolation, where shall we find it? I believe it must come out of our building a new world order. It must come through our cultivation of a new spirit of brotherhood. We must really "make" peace. Pacifist is not a winsome word. This is true because to many, a pacifist is one who simply does nothing. But that is not the case. The word pacifist has a "fist" in it, as another has pointed out. It is not a mailed fist, but it is one that requires a far higher courage. We must seek to remove these economic evils that make some nations so desperate as to be willing to fight. The nations that have must be willing to co-operate with those that have not. We must aggressively cultivate a new patriotism.

III

This new patriotism differs markedly from the old.

1. The old patriotism said, "My country, may it always be right; but right or wrong—my country!" The new patriotism says, "My country, may it always be right; but if I am convinced that it is wrong, I will

44

say so and act accordingly." This will be the case not because this new patriotism means a lesser love. As a pacifist, I concede nothing to the militarist in point of patriotism. As a father, I say, "My son, may he always be right; but my son, right or wrong." That means that I am going to love him whether he is right or wrong, but it does not mean that I am going to aid and abet him when I see him take a course that I believe will end in disaster. I will refuse to do so for love's sake. For love's sake also I will refuse to aid and abet my nation in a course that I believe fatal to its highest interests.

2. The old patriotism was so intense that it made its possessors antagonistic to every other country. The new patriotism enables its possessor to interpret the patriotism of those of another nation through his own. So often, the patriotism of the one hundred percenter, that patriotism that sends us to flout our navy in the eyes of another nation in order to impress them, succeeds only in making enemies. Now, as another has pointed out, a man might as well be an enemy to his country as to make an enemy for his country. That, I think, is self-evident.

A good friend told me this story. He was celebrating Armistice Day in his own church. Out in front was a veritable forest of flags. One of his stewards rushed into the office full of excitement. "A bohunk made a slighting remark about our flag," he said, "and I socked him in the jaw. He is lying out there now."

45

The preacher, who happened to be a very sane Christian, answered, "I venture that made a patriot of him. I bet the first thing he does when he picks himself up is to crawl to the flag and kiss it." "Now," he said, "let's go out and see if that is not the case." So the preacher and his steward went out together. The man had just picked himself up and was walking a bit groggily down the street. They overtook him and the steward said, "I am sorry I hit you like that." But the man glared and said never a word. "I am sorry I socked you in the jaw," he repeated, but still no answer. Then the preacher broke in. "What my friend is trying to say to you is that he is sorry." But the bohunk was still silent. Then the steward said in disgust, "That's the way with these foreigners; you can't tell them anything." So he went on his way.

But this friend of mine was not satisfied. He ducked into a door till he saw the offender against the flag start for home. He followed him at a safe distance down one street after another till he came to a miserable shack in the slums. When the foreigner had entered this shack, the preacher knocked on the door and was reluctantly admitted. It took him six months, he declared, never seeing him as far apart as two weeks to get into his confidence. Then he told my friend how he was reared in central Europe. He was told that if he would raise $500 he could go to America, the land of brotherhood and opportunity. He slaved for it, then they brought him over in the steerage, kept

46

him a prisoner at Ellis Island, then farmed him out. He said that since his coming he had never had a kind word, and that he came to hate America with all his soul. A few days later, this man asked to be received into the Church. When he had taken the vows, my friend gave him a private vow. "Will you," he asked, "be loyal to America, too?" To which he answered with tears, "I will be loyal to America, too." But a man had just as well be an enemy to his country as to make an enemy for his country.

3. The old patriotism reached its climax by death on the battlefield. This was its highest expression:

> "Theirs not to reason why,
> Theirs not to make reply,
> Theirs but to do and die!"

There was something very heroic in this type of patriotism. But you will notice that the horses on which these cavalrymen rode took the same position as their riders. It was also "Theirs not to reason why," and "Theirs but to do and die!" Surely, the new patriotism calls for something finer than this. It is not only our privilege, but our duty to reason why. If we reason and find that the orders given clash with conscience, then it is our solemn duty to obey God rather than man. But this is the greatest impeachment of the whole military system: It leaves no place for the conscientious objector. In the Gospels we read this significant word: The soldiers crucified Him. Why did

47

the soldiers crucify Him? Because they hated Him? Because they had reached the conclusion that He stood in the path of human progress? No! They crucified Him because their one task was to obey orders. "Theirs not to reason why, theirs not to make reply."

4. Finally, the old patriotism fixed its faith in force. The new patriotism believes there is a greater god than the god of force. About the saddest word, I think, that ever fell from the lips of Jesus was said to his disciples just before the crucifixion. He was under arrest, his friends now saw that he was going to allow himself to be killed. All their big dreams for him were coming to just nothing. Their disappointment was unspeakably bitter. Jesus understood and could hardly endure the heartbreak of it. "Don't you know," he said, trying to save them from the worship of force, "don't you know that I could pray to the Father, and he could send me twelve legions of angels?" But had he thus resorted to force, he might have escaped crucifixion, but he would not have a worshiper in all the world today. He died in the faith that the mightiest power in the world was not physical force, but love and good will.

That high faith must be ours if we expect to win in this great adventure for world peace. We are yet far from the goal, but we are making progress. The nations have passed up more good opportunities to fight in the last five years, I dare say, than in the previous five thousand. Why is this the case? The reasons are partly economical. Some have refrained from war because they were not financially able to fight. But another reason is that in almost every nation today there is a strong minority group of convinced pacifists who are determined at all costs to avoid war. It is these daring souls that are the supreme hope of the world. They are not unmindful of their difficulties. They fling themselves against the clinched fists of stark impossibilities, saying with Peter, "Nevertheless at thy word"—I make the adventure! May their number be increased!

IV

DISTURBING PUBLIC WORSHIP

"And when they could not come nigh unto him for the press, they uncovered the roof where he was: and when they had broken it up, they let down the bed wherein the sick of the palsy lay."

MARK 2: 4

HERE IS A STORY OF A SERVICE THAT WAS INTERrupted. The Preacher was not allowed to finish his sermon. There was a disturbance that made it impossible for him to go on. There are disturbances for which we devoutly thank God. They hearten us and leave us with some of our most bracing and inspiring memories. Many ministers, I am happy to believe, have had disturbances of this kind. But there are others that are very annoying and that leave behind them a sense of defeat and failure. Few, I imagine, even in this enlightened age, have preached for many years without experiencing disturbances of this type.

Some years ago I was preaching to a congregation in a little country village. Quite a goodly company was out, but they heard me on the installment plan. That is, they would come into the house in shifts of twenty or thirty, remain a few minutes, then go out and allow another shift to take their places. But there was one brave woman who remained through the entire service. She had with her two husky boys of about three and five years of age respectively. That she might not be disturbed by them, she had brought along an iron ring for them to play with. I think it had been taken from the hub of a wagon wheel.

Her plan worked with perfect success. The boys gave her no trouble at all. With a loud yell the younger, who sat upon her lap, would throw this ring upon the floor, and let it roll away till it crashed against the wall. With a yet louder yell, the older would fly in pursuit, never stopping till he had recovered it and restored it to his brother. Then they repeated the performance, keeping it up with unflagging zeal till the service was over. I do not think anything I said in my sermon registered. I hope, however, that my patience made a lasting impression.

But, I confess that I have not always done so well. My patience at other times has not been so much in evidence. On a few occasions, in fact, especially when big babies were doing the disturbing, I have allowed myself to get all hot on the inside, if not without. I have also known other ministers far better than

SERMONS FROM THE MIRACLES

myself to do the same. A few years ago an exceptionally able and consecrated evangelist was preaching to a great congregation in one of our Southern cities. Near the front was an old gentleman who coughed and wheezed and cleared his throat in a manner that was most distressing. At last the preacher seemed completely to lose his temper. He rebuked the disturber in no uncertain fashion. But the outcome was not happy. The preacher soon realized that by losing his temper he had also lost his congregation.

But if there are disturbances that are vastly annoying, there are others that are very thrilling. Such a one occurred when Peter was preaching in the house of Cornelius. The Apostle was delivering an excellent sermon, one into which he was putting his whole heart. But just when he was coming to his climax, just as he was telling how salvation was for everybody on the simple condition of faith, he was interrupted. "To him give all the prophets witness, that through his name whosoever believeth in him shall receive remission of sins." That was as far as the preacher got. He was then shouted down. "While Peter yet spake, the Holy Spirit fell on all them that heard the Word." But Peter was not annoyed. He even remembered that interruption with unspeakable gratitude and joy.

That was a magnificent interruption that occurred when Charles G. Finney was preaching in a certain city in the State of New York. Far back in the balcony sat the Chief Justice of the Supreme Court of that State. As this able lawyer listened to the preacher, he said to himself, "What he is saying is true. Since it is true, I ought to act upon it. Since I ought to act upon it, I ought to do so now." Therefore, he arose, made his way out of the balcony, down the long aisle of that crowded church, and up into the pulpit. Plucking Mr. Finney by the sleeve, he said, "If you will call for decisions for Christ now, I am ready to come." Mr. Finney did not get to finish his sermon, but he did not grieve over being thus disturbed. He rather thanked God. Now it was an interruption somewhat like this of which we read in our text.

I

Look at the story. The scene is a certain house in the city of Capernaum. Just what house this was it is impossible to say. Some think it was the house of Simon Peter, where the Lord was a guest. Others think that it was the house of the Master himself, since he was living in Capernaum at that time. David Smith argues that it was the synagogue. Now, since there were scribes and doctors of the law present from all over the country, even from places as far away as Jerusalem, this view seems the most reasonable. So many notables could hardly have been accommodated in a house as small as that of Jesus or of Simon, even if no others had been present. But there were many besides these. Therefore, it is safe to conclude that this was a week-day service in the synagogue.

The congregation on that day was unusually large. The atmosphere was tense and expectant. Some of these people were heart-hungry. They were there because they were in need of help. There were others who were merely curious. They saw a great crowd of people thronging into the church, and that awakened their interest. Nothing draws a crowd like a crowd. "Something out of the ordinary must be going on," they said to themselves. And at once they determined to find out what that something was. Then, there were others still, including these scribes and doctors, that were present in the role of critics. They were bent on catching some word from the Preacher that would discredit him. All these made a large and eager audience.

The Preacher was holding the fascinated attention of his hearers. He was always vastly interesting. This was the case for many reasons. He was interesting, in the first place, because he was interested. That is, those that heard him felt that he cared. He was interesting, also, because he talked to people about their fundamental needs. Then, he was interesting because he spoke a language that all could understand. The masses always heard him gladly. But he realized before he finished this sermon that he was losing the attention of his audience. Their eyes began to stray from his face to the ceiling where queer noises could be heard. Particles of dust and plaster began to drop, some even falling upon the dignified heads of the doctors of the law. Then, a queer object came floating down from above, to rest on the floor at the Master's feet. It was a bed upon which lay a wreck of a man who was so motionless that he seemed utterly dead except for his haunted and wistful eyes. At this, the Master's sermon came to an abrupt end.

II

Who was responsible for this disturbance? Of course we know that more than one was implicated. There were five. But, I am confident that there was one ringleader upon whose shoulders rested most of the responsibility. This was a man who had doubtless met Jesus before. He had come to know him, to believe in him, to love him. Having found the Master for himself, he began at once to think of a friend of his who was sorely afflicted. He had perhaps known this friend for years. He had caroused with him during a misspent youth. Having a strong constitution, he had weathered those years of riotous living without becoming a wreck. But it was not so with his friend. He was now paralyzed. In utter helplessness, he was compelled to face a past that was a blot, a present that was a blank, and a future that was a nightmare. Naturally this man who was whole was eager to bring his afflicted friend to Jesus.

His first step in that direction was to secure the consent of this friend, to arouse in him hope and confidence. Having succeeded in this, he next enlisted three others who were to help. Perhaps they had all been boon companions in their younger years. They talked things over as they sat beside the sick friend and perfected their plans. Jesus was out of the city at the time, but they decided that immediately upon his return they would certainly bring their afflicted friend into his presence. Then, one day the news was flashed about the city that the Master had returned. These four went at once to the house of their unfortunate friend. The whole committee was present. That speaks well for them. Not one of them had something more important to do. Each man took his corner of the mat and away they went on their mission for healing.

But when they reached the church, they ran into difficulties. They found such a mob within and without as to make any approach to the Master through the door an impossibility. Some doubtless were for taking the poor fellow back home and coming another day. But this leader would not hear of it. He was resolute. He was determined to see the matter through then and there. "Lay him down a minute," he said, "while I look the situation over." He glances here and there and discovers a stairway leading up the outside of the church. He bounds up these stairs two steps at a time. He pauses at the top, looks the situation over, and hurries back with sparkling eyes.

"Take hold," he says, "and let's go." They mount the stairs, and again lay down their burden. Then

56

the leader begins tearing up the roof. "It is against the law," says one. "Never mind," is the answer, "we have got to get this man to Jesus." And soon all four are working away at it. When the opening is large enough, the four of them take their sashes and each ties his to a corner of the bed. Then they lower it through the ceiling until their friend is right at the Master's feet. Then, without a word they lay prone upon their faces and watch to see what the Master will do.

Now, this is as far as they can go. They have done all that is humanly possible toward the helping of their friend. Maybe nothing will come of it all. Maybe, when the services are over, they will have to pick up their pathetic burden and trudge home again with their friend not one whit better, but just a little more wretched and a little more hopeless. But if such should be the case this at least will be true, the fault will not be theirs. What happens, now that they have done their best, is up to the Master. If there is failure, if it all ends in grim tragedy, it will not be their failure, but his.

III

Now, what actually does happen? Is Jesus impatient because he has not been allowed to finish his sermon? Not in the least. I think he is greatly rejoiced. Mark tells us of the reaction of Jesus in these words: "When Jesus saw." What did he see?

1. He saw past what was outward in this sufferer

and his friends to what was inward and fundamental. He saw their beautiful eagerness to get the sufferer into his presence. But he saw something more fundamental than that. He saw the high courage that enabled them to do this daring and unconventional thing. But he saw something that was deeper and more important than that. He saw their patient and dogged persistence that refused to be balked by difficulties. But he saw something even finer than that. He saw what lay behind all these, what made all these possible. He saw their faith. It was their deep conviction of the power and willingness of Jesus to help that made them so earnest and courageous and persistent.

2. Not only did Jesus see their faith, but he also saw the supreme need of the sufferer. What was the matter with this man? He was paralyzed. Anybody could see that. He could not move a muscle. But his paralysis was only a symptom of an inner disease. While I was pastor in Washington I was rather a zealous tennis player. But my tennis arm got to paining me so badly that I feared I would have to give up the game. I made up my mind to consult a physician. Desiring the best possible, I picked out the physician to the President of the United States. Having put me through a careful examination, he gave me relief, and I have never had any trouble with my arm since. How was this cure wrought? He did not cure me by treating my arm. He did not have me to rub it with a certain liniment, or to put it into a sling.

But what he did was to remove my tonsils. That is, instead of treating the symptoms, he treated the disease.

This was the method of Jesus. He always saw into the heart of things. As he looked into the wistful face of this sufferer, he saw there a deeper tragedy than mere physical helplessness. He saw the tragedy of sin. There were outward consequences of this man's wayward life that all eyes could see, but there were inner consequences known only to the sufferer himself and to the tender Christ who was now bending over him. This man was suffering in his body, but he was suffering yet more in his mind. As he lay there, his very helplessness and wretchedness were pleading with the Master and saying:

> "Canst thou not minister to a mind diseased,
> Pluck from the memory a rooted sorrow,
> Raze out the written troubles of the brain,
> And with some sweet oblivious antidote
> Cleanse the stuffed bosom from that perilous stuff
> Which weighs upon the heart?"

And Jesus answered that inarticulate prayer by saying, "My son, thy sins are forgiven thee."

Now, when Jesus said that he spoke home to the deepest needs, not only of this man, but of every man. This is true because of what forgiveness involves. Forgiveness is not merely the remission of a penalty. Forgiveness means the restoration of a broken fellowship. It means that we trust God, and that He trusts us, that He takes us back into His confidence, and forgets that we have ever sinned. It means a new nature. It means that God comes to possess us, and we come to possess Him. Therefore, if we have forgiveness and nothing else, we are still unspeakably rich, because we have God. On the other hand, if we possess all else and miss forgiveness, we are unspeakably poor, because we are without God and without hope.

Not only did Jesus forgive this man, but he saved him from the consequences of his sin. This he did by healing his body. Of course there are certain types of physical disease for which forgiveness is an effective cure. This is true of all those diseases that are the result of an inward conflict, of a quarrel of the soul with God. There are people, for instance, whose minds are so poisoned by hate that they are sick in body as well as sick in soul. I have in mind now one who, I am sure, is a case of this kind. She is unspeakably miserable. Her physical health is wretched. All the strength she has seems to spend itself in intense hatred. Now, if she would only accept the forgiveness of God and thus learn to forgive, the chances are that she would be healed in body as well as in mind. At least, such has been the case with many another.

But generally speaking, forgiveness does not save us from the consequences of our sin. David was forgiven, but in spite of that fact the sword of tragedy continued to pursue him to the very end. I was called to see a woman some time ago who was slowly dying of a poison that was self-administered. During her long hours of suffering she had been made to think. Thus thinking, she had become sorry for her deed. As we talked together, she turned her pain-pinched face toward mine and asked if I thought God would forgive her. I told her that I was sure of it. Then I was privileged to preach the gospel to her. Not only so, but I became confident that she had accepted the forgiveness that Jesus was so eager to give. But one thing that forgiveness did not do for her—it did not take away the poison that was slowly destroying her life.

But here Jesus did the unusual. He not only said, "Thy sins are forgiven thee"; he also said, "Arise, and take up thy bed, and walk." And immediately the sufferer was healed in body as he had been healed in soul. How did Jesus come to perform this lesser miracle? On the surface it seems to have been wrought in answer to the doubts of the doctors of the law who were accusing Jesus of speaking blasphemy when he claimed power on earth to forgive sin. But such is not the case. Of course Jesus claimed the right to forgive. He not only claimed it, but proved it here, and countless millions of times. But this man was healed in body as he was healed in soul, not in response to doubt, but in response to faith. To those who merely seek a sign, no sign is ever given. But to those who believe, all things become possible.

Now, the Jesus about whom this crowd gathered

in Capernaum long ago is with us still. He still has power on earth to forgive sin. Maybe you have a friend who needs him. Maybe there is one dearer to you than life who is desperately in need of one who can save. Why not use the wisdom of these four friends? Bring him to Jesus. He will not disappoint you, as he did not disappoint them. Maybe the sufferer is none other than yourself. Maybe you are experiencing even now the restlessness and wretchedness of separation from God. If so, it need not be the case a moment longer. There is one present who is eager to say to you, "Courage, my child, thy sins are forgiven thee." Just accept that forgiveness, and you will go away singing with the saints of yesterday:

> "My God is reconciled,
>   His pardoning voice I hear;
> He owns me for His child,
>   I can no longer fear:
> With confidence I now draw nigh,
> And 'Father, Abba, Father,' cry."

V

THE WHINER

"Sir, I have no man, when the water is troubled, to put me into the pool: but while I am coming, another steppeth down before me."

JOHN 5: 7

HERE IS A STORY THAT WILL LIVE FOREVER. IT will live because it is so genuinely human and so refreshingly hopeful. The scene is one of the porches at the pool of Bethesda in Jerusalem. It is a Sabbath day and the city is thronged with worshipers that have come up to the feast. Many are now passing through these porches on their way to the temple. All about them is a depressing company of sick and blind, lame and hopeless. But these eager worshipers do not see them. They are too busy, or too selfish, or too cowardly. They are far too absorbed in their religious duties to take knowledge of this broken earthenware that the world of their day has ruthlessly tossed aside.

But there is One among them who is beautifully different. He has an eye for those who have fallen behind the procession. Therefore, he comes of set purpose to this cinderpile, this human dumping ground, and picks out the man for whom the world has least hope and who has least hope for himself. This man has lain here thirty-eight years. For half a lifetime, he has waited for something to happen that has never taken place. Now, thirty-eight years is a long time in any man's life. It is a long time for one whose hands are busy with great and thrilling tasks. It is doubly long for one whose hands are weak and empty. It is all but interminable for one who is sick, without friends and without hope. Such is this paralyzed man to whom Jesus comes.

There had been a time when he had stood upon his feet as other men. Possibly, he had been the leader of a group of boon companions. Jesus indicates, you remember, that his present plight is the result of his own wrongdoing. "Behold, thou art made whole," the Master warns; "sin no more, lest a worse thing come unto thee." No doubt when his sickness first came upon him, these friends were shocked and grieved. They came to see him. They sent him flowers. But he neither died nor got well. Therefore, their visits grew less and less frequent, their offerings of flowers dwindled to nothing. One by one, his old friends moved away, or died, or forgot. He made no new friends. Thus, after thirty-eight years he is hopeless and alone.

But on this day of days, he finds himself face to

face with a new experience. He is being searched by
the most kindly eyes into which he has ever looked.
He does not know who Jesus is. Perhaps he has never
even heard of this amazing Prophet who is causing so
great a stir among the people. But while he is wondering, this winsome Stranger asks him a question.
It is a queer seeming question. "Wilt thou be made
whole?" he asks. "Would you like to get well?"
"Would you like to stand on your feet and play a man's
part in the world?"

I

What did Jesus mean by this queer question? What
is implied in it?

1. Jesus is facing with this man the fact of his sickness. He is meeting him on his own ground. He is
seeking the man's confidence by telling him that he
knows what the invalid knows about himself. When
he asks, therefore, "Wilt thou be made whole?" he is
saying, "I know that you are sick. I know just how
harshly life has treated you. You are not shamming.
You have not lain here all these years with nothing the
matter. You know and I know that there is something
wrong." Jesus knows that he will have little hope of
helping this man unless he faces with him the fact
that he is sick and in need of help.

Now the question that Jesus puts to this man is intensely individual and personal. It is also universal.
He asked it 1900 years ago; he asks it today. He asks

it of you and of me, of all of us. Perhaps there are those who resent this question because it implies that they are morally sick. But resent it how you may, the fact remains that our gospel is a gospel for sinners and for sinners only. Jesus declares emphatically that he has not "come to call the righteous." If, therefore, you are all that you ought to be, then his message of salvation has no meaning for you.

But when we face the facts about ourselves, we know that we are not whole. Paul's declaration that all have sinned may leave some of us a bit cold. But as he goes on to add that we have come short, we know that he is telling what is true of all of us. We are not crooks. We are not gangsters. We are neither rakes nor libertines. But, in spite of the fact that we are as decent as decency, we know that we are not living as abundantly as we ought. We have come short. We are not whole. It is the candor of Jesus in telling us this that is his first step toward winning our confidence.

2. Not only does Jesus imply the reality of this man's sickness, but also the possibility of his cure. There is hope in the question. There is the expectation of the dawn of a better tomorrow. If this is not the case, then Jesus is guilty of sheer cruelty. Suppose after saying to a hungry man at my door, "Would you like a good dinner?" I should hasten to shut the door in his face; would I not be cruel? Suppose I should give hope to a drowning man by asking, "Would you

like to be saved?" and then refuse to help him; would that be kind? Did you ever see a boy hold a piece of bread just out of reach of a hungry dog, have the poor fellow jump for it till he tired, and then end by eating it himself? It is a thoughtless and cruel procedure. We resent such treatment, even toward a dog. Surely, therefore, the tender Christ will not tantalize this poor wretch by a dream of wholeness when he knows his dream is impossible of realization.

Now since this question implies the possibility of wholeness for this man of the long ago, it implies no less for you and me. Jesus is always seeing possibilities in us that no one else sees. He is a Christ of infinite hope. He believes that fluctuating Simon may become a rock. He believes that narrow, sectarian John may become a prophet of love. He believes that gloomy Thomas may become spiritually radiant. He is also certain that we can live more richly, more courageously, and more helpfully than we are living. "However you may have failed up to this hour," he is saying, "you need not continue to fail. You may yet do something far bigger and better than what you have done. However mean and lean your life may have been, you may yet find your place at the feast of the fullness of life."

3. Then this question implies that if the man is made whole he must put himself unreservedly in the hands of his Questioner. Should a modern physician say to one who was ill, "Would you like to get well?" his question would imply, not only that the man was

sick, not only that the physician saw a possibility of recovery, but that, in order to realize that recovery, the patient must put himself fully into the hands of his physician. "You are sick," Jesus is saying to this man, "but there is a chance for your recovery. That chance can only be realized by your following my directions. If you give yourself in wholehearted obedience to me, then your recovery is sure. If you do not, I can do nothing for you."

And this word is just as pertinent for you and me as it was for this paralytic. If we are to find individual wholeness, we must find it at the hands of Jesus. If we are to come to possess the fullness of life, we must receive it from him. He is come that we might have life and have it in abundance. If we are to build a strong and victorious church, we must build it in obedience to him. If we are to find social salvation, he is our hope. If we are to build a new and better world, we must build it under his leadership. "There is none other name under heaven given among men whereby we must be saved."

4. This question implies, finally, that if this man is to receive the wholeness that Jesus is eager to give, he must be willing to receive it. Our Lord will not and cannot give what we are unwilling to receive. The same is true of ourselves. However eager you may be to give your boy an education, you cannot give it to him if he will not take it. You cannot give even so trifling a treasure as a coin to any man who will not

receive it. Jesus, therefore, is saying to this paralytic, "You are sick. You can be made whole. If you put yourself in my hands, I am both willing and able to cure you, but I cannot cure you against your will. I can only stand at the door and knock. Weak as you are, you can keep me shut out of your life, if you want to. But if you are willing, I can meet your needs."

Since this is the case, if this man continues prone upon his back, missing all that makes life worth living, it will be his own fault. He will have none to blame but himself. The Church has been careless of him, his friends have forsaken him, but that need not prove fatal. The only disaster that can spell utter ruin is his refusal to take what Jesus so freely offers. That is the only disaster that can work your ruin and mine. He is here offering you healing—he is doing far more, he is offering you the all-inclusive gift of himself. His word is "receive ye." We do not have to wrench his gift from clinging and unwilling fingers. All he asks of us is our willingness to receive.

II

Now, what reply does this man make to this question that is so full of hope? Listen! "Sir, I have no man, when the water is troubled, to put me into the pool: but while I am coming, another steppeth down before me." That is, he accepts readily the implications of Jesus that he is sick, but that is as far as he is willing to go. He does not confess the slightest expectation of recovery. I am persuaded that his long dead hopes are beginning to stir with some slight promise of a resurrection, but he is not yet willing to acknowledge this. He is further still from accepting any responsibility for either being or remaining what he is. Instead, he seems to say, "I can never be whole. But it is not my fault. This is the case for two reasons: First, I am not able to attain wholeness in my own strength. Second, I have nobody to help me. It is every fellow for himself and the devil take the hindmost. Therefore, as a sick man in a sick social order, there is nothing for me but despair."

Now, this is a mood that is all too prevalent today. It is a heartening fact that so many people are keenly sensitive to the desperate needs of our present world. We realize as never before the cruel inequalities born of wrong economical conditions. We are alive to the insanity of war as no other generation has been. We grieve over the weakness of the church. We deplore race prejudice and the wide chasms that divide nation from nation. But too often we are so conscious of our own personal needs and of the appalling greatness of the task that we are stricken with paralysis. Having failed to find inward peace, we despair of bringing about peace throughout our troubled world.

III

Now, what does Jesus say to this man who has despaired both of himself and of his fellows? He calls him to the facing of his own personal responsibilities. Of course no man can preach an adequate gospel who deals solely with the individual. Our gospel is both social and individual. But there is a way of preaching the social gospel that merely leaves the individual with a sense of bewilderment and helplessness. Having heard of appalling world conditions, he asks himself, "What can I do about it?" And the answer oftentimes is, "Nothing." But such answer is always wrong. When a hunter flushes a covey of birds, he does not let the fact that he cannot kill them all prevent his shooting at any of them. He singles out one bird and tries to bring him down.

This is the equivalent of what Jesus says to this man. He tells him to begin with himself. That is always a right starting point. The first duty of every reformer is to reform himself. The first duty of everyone that would give life is to find life for himself. We shall do little toward saving a whole world unless we have done something toward saving ourselves. Therefore, Jesus gives this man a threefold command. It is personal and individual: "Rise, take up thy bed, and walk." It is also logical, as another has pointed out. We must keep the divine order. It is not, "Walk, take up thy bed, and rise." Before we are ready to walk, we must get on our feet. A good many forget this. But the man who undertakes to walk when he is flat of his back can do nothing but kick. Most of the kickers that worry us are folks who never dare to get upon their feet. Look now at these commands in their order.

1. "Rise!" While this whiner is telling the Master how impossible it is for him to be made whole, Jesus speaks to him this word of authority, "Get up!" That seems a strange command. That is the very thing that this paralytic cannot do. Jesus is, therefore, challenging him with the impossible. But this is his method always. We are prone to excuse ourselves for the sins and shortcomings that have an unusually tight grip on us. We say, "That is my peculiarity—that is my weakness." But Jesus is not come to save us from the sins from which we can save ourselves. He is come to enable us to do the impossible.

One day, for instance, he went into the temple and found a man with a withered hand. He said to him, "Stretch forth thy hand." That was the very thing that the unfortunate man could not do. Yet, as he undertook it, the impossible became possible. He is constantly calling us to these big impossibilities. He is calling us to be born anew. He is calling us to love, not only the decent and kindly folks that love us, but to love our enemies as well. He is calling us to be the salt of the earth, to make disciples of all nations, to establish the kingdom of God in a world. His call is constantly to the impossible. What happened when He commanded this prostrate man to get on his feet? Even while he was telling Jesus how utterly hopeless his case was, he was doing what Jesus had commanded.

72

How did it come about? He simply willed what Jesus willed for him. When a man does that, all of the energies of God become available for him.

2. Having gotten this man upon his feet, the next command of Jesus is, "Take up thy bed." Why did he tell the healed man to do that? Is he urging him to save this worthless old mat that has served him for so long? No. He is still trying to save the man. He told him to take up his bed, according to Dr. Marcus Dods, to keep him from making any provision for a relapse. I think that is a wise word. Suppose this healed man had said to himself, "I am cured, it is true, but there is no telling how long I am going to stay that way. My weak knees are liable to buckle under me before I have gone half a block. Therefore, I will just leave my mat here so that I may have a resting place, in case of failure." Had he taken that course, he would have been flat on his back within the next thirty minutes.

"Take up thy bed" is the wise command of Jesus. That is, make no provision for returning to the old life; burn your bridges behind you. I used to have a friend who had a persistent habit of quitting tobacco. It would be impossible to tell how many times he swore off from the use of the weed. But whenever his wife would go through his pockets, she would almost invariably come upon a half plug of tobacco. When she questioned him about it, he had a standing answer. "I am not carrying that with me to chew, but only to smell." Naturally, he was constantly falling back into his old habit. Some time ago, I was talking to a young man who had come forward in token of the fact that he was going to be a Christian. I asked him to unite with the Church. But he refused. He said, "I intend to join the Church sometime, but not now. I want to see if I can hold out before I take that final step." When he said that, I knew that he was not simply going to backslide, but that he had already backslidden. The only way to live a new life is to make a clean break with the old.

3. The final command of Jesus is, "Walk." You have been carried long enough. You have been out of the game long enough. You have whined about your own weakness, about the faults of the Church, about the rottenness of society, long enough. Try carrying your part of the load. If things are not what they ought to be, then get up on your own feet and help to make them better. Bernard Shaw gives a rather refreshing definition of a gentleman. "A gentleman," he says, "is one that puts more into life than he take out of it." And Jesus is calling this man to be a gentleman. "Rise, take up thy bed, and walk." Begin here and now to face up to your own personal responsibility. Set yourself today, this moment, to doing what you believe God would have you do. To take this course is surely to find life and victory.

Some twenty-five centuries ago there was a brilliant young man who was all but overwhelmed by his own desperate needs and by the appalling needs of his people. "Woe is me," he sobbed bitterly, "woe is me. I am undone. I am a man of unclean lips and dwell in the midst of a people of unclean lips." But if this man had stopped there, his name would have perished long ago. But he found personal cleansing. Then as he heard the voice of God saying, "Whom shall I send, and who will go for us?" he dared to answer, "Here am I; send me!" Thus, Isaiah not only found peace, but he made the whole world richer because of his full and courageous life. And this is the way out for you and me. We are to begin, as Carlyle said, by doing the duty that lies closest to us. If we dare to do this, our victory is sure. "Wouldst thou be made whole?" Begin now to follow him. "Rise, take up thy bed, and walk."

VI

HOW TO GET ANGRY

*"He looked round about
on them with anger."*

MARK 3: 5

UPON ENTERING THE SYNAGOGUE ON THIS OCCAsion, Jesus found himself face to face with a man with a withered hand. Luke tells us that his right hand was withered. He was, therefore, a man with a handicap. He was forced to meet the demands of life at a disadvantage. He represented that great class of hampered and underprivileged people that ever made a strong appeal to the heart of Jesus. The people standing about were naturally on tiptoe of expectancy. They knew that, now that a man with a need was standing face to face with Jesus, something wonderful was likely to happen. Their faces, I can well imagine, were all aglow with eager interest.

But there were those present to whom this expectancy brought no glow of soul. They viewed the scene with hard eyes and sour faces. These were the Pharisees. They were there as the custodians of the law. They felt that it was their business to see to it that this

76

young Carpenter did not desecrate the Sabbath. By their very attitude they were saying to Jesus, "Don't you dare heal this man on the Sabbath day. If you do, it will be an affront to us who are the religious leaders of the people. You will fly in our faces, who are the people of power, and we will never forgive you."

Naturally Jesus, with his fine sensitiveness, was conscious of their opposition. Having invited the man whom he was to heal to stand forth, he asked them a question, "Is it lawful to do right on the Sabbath, or to do wrong? to save life, or to kill?" That was a simple question, and they knew the answer. But they maintained a stony silence. Then it was that Jesus looked round about upon them with anger, being grieved at the hardness of their heart. Then with flaming eyes and glowing cheeks, he bade the man to stretch forth his hand. And as he willed to do what Jesus willed for him, the impossible became possible, and he was cured.

I can see the light of a great joy break over his face. But there is no light upon the faces of these religious leaders. Instead, as Luke tells us, they were filled with fury. In hot anger they went from the synagogue with their minds made up that they would never rest till this man, who cared so much more for personalities than he cared for institutions, was destroyed. But as angry as they were, I dare say they were not one whit more angry than Jesus, who had wrought this miracle of healing.

I

Now the fact that Jesus, the tender and loving Christ, got angry is to some a bit bewildering. This is true because anger is not generally regarded as a virtue, but as a vice. It is so often a mark of littleness rather than of bigness. No greatness of intellect is required to get angry. The most stupid can do it quite as well as those that are wise. It is an achievement that is as readily within reach of the young as of the old. We have all seen babies far too young to talk, but never one too young to lose his temper, and become blood-red with rage.

Since this is the case, it is not surprising that the Bible does not encourage anger. The author of the thirty-seventh Psalm, for instance, bids us "cease from anger, and forsake wrath." "Don't fret in any way," he urged, "because it tends only to evil." Then another psalmist whom Paul quotes with approval writes, "Be angry and sin not." That is, he permits anger, but recognizes the fact that it is a close neighbor to sin, that the man who is angry is more likely to do some ugly wrong than one who is not. And the writer of the Proverbs has this wise word: "He that is slow to anger is better than the mighty." To fly off the handle, to go into a rage, he feels is a mark of weakness, while to control one's temper is a mark of strength. And with this wise man we agree.

When we turn to the New Testament we find the same attitude of disapproval. "Put away anger," Paul writes to his converts at Colosse. In his immortal ode to Love, he tells us that love is sweet-tempered. In his letter to Titus, when he speaks of the qualifications for a bishop, he says that he must not be hot-tempered. We can all see the wisdom of that. A bishop has considerable power over his brethren. Therefore one is not to be trusted with this high office unless he is able to control his temper.

But it remains for Jesus to say the sharpest and most convincing word. "Ye have heard," he says, "that it was said by them of old time, Thou shall not kill; and whosoever shall kill shall be in danger of the judgment: but I say unto you, That whosoever is angry with his brother shall be in danger of the judgment." The law only forbade striking the deadly blow. Jesus went back of all that to the deadly passion that prompts the blow—the passion of anger. "Anger," he says, "is incipient murder." No wonder, then, that Jesus warns against it.

Now since the Bible thus discourages anger, we naturally look upon it with suspicion. Folks that readily lose their tempers, we cannot regard as well-developed Christians. Some time ago a certain preacher was disturbed while he was doing his best to deliver his sermon. The disturbance was annoying. But the saddest part of the whole unfortunate affair was that the preacher lost his temper, made himself quite ridiculous, and sent many of his congregation away, seriously discounting his Christianity. And more than one minister has fallen into this slippery pit. Right or wrong, we tend to question the genuineness of those Christians who cannot control their tempers.

Some time ago a minister told me this story. He had in his congregation a woman who was very active and effective. But her husband, though a good man, did not identify himself with the Church. One day this minister went to him and pressed him for a reason. They were close friends, and at last, in confidence, he gave his reason. "My wife," he said, "is a good woman and one of the best workers you have in your church, but she has a perfectly hellish temper. Now and then she goes into a rage and the children and I simply have to hide out. This," he said, "is not my idea of what it means to be a Christian."

Now this preacher was a brave man. He went away from this interview to another with the wife. He told her frankly what her husband had said. By a desperate effort she controlled her temper. Then she and the minister knelt in prayer. A few days later that husband was going fishing. He came into the house with his fishing rod on his shoulder, and in turning about he touched a new swinging lamp that had just been put up. It fell with a crash that was a bit like a hardware store being swept away by a thunderstorm. The amazed husband stood waiting for the next storm to break. But it did not break. And he joined the Church the next Sunday. It is evident that our ordinary brand of anger does not look good either in the Bible or out of it.

II

Why is this the case? It is true because so much of our anger is like that of these Pharisees. Why did they get so furious at Jesus on this occasion? What was wrong with their anger?

1. It was purely selfish. They were not interested in this man with his pitiful handicap. They were not concerned with personal values. They were concerned about the law. They felt that a violation of the law governing the Sabbath was an affront to themselves. They felt that the conduct of Jesus tended to weaken their position and to undermine their authority. It therefore wounded their pride. They could endure any amount of injustice toward others, but when their own pet pride was stepped on, it filled them with rage.

Now this is the most common brand of anger among us today. Some of us can stand with complacency any amount of criticism directed against others. It is only when it is directed against ourselves that we become indignant. We can be very sweet-tempered while others are robbed of their rights. It is only when we ourselves are robbed that we get hot and angry. It does not greatly disturb us to see our fellows wounded, but we can let out howls of sheer rage when the wound is suffered by ourselves. About the only time we ever become indignant is when we are not made chairman

81

of the committee, or not invited to the party, or suffer some other affront to our pride.

There was a preacher once that was sent to minister to a great city. He entered that city with a message of doom upon his lips, and with little pity in his heart. He went through its streets shouting, "Yet forty days, and Nineveh shall be destroyed." When the folks heard that startling warning, they were arrested by it. They repented of their sins and thus averted the threatened doom. But Jonah, instead of shouting over it, got angry. "I told these folks," he informed the Lord, all hot and indignant, "that you were going to destroy them, and now you are pardoning them. Such mercy as that will ruin my reputation as a prophet." The sufferings of thousands counted for nothing; his own wounded pride counted for everything. Such anger is utterly hellish.

2. The anger of these Pharisees was not only wrong in its motive, but wrong in its objective. When they got angry, they wanted to destroy the one against whom they were angry. That is what selfish anger always seeks to do. When we are angry at any one, our first impulse is to hurt, to give pain, to wound. Selfish anger is deadly cruel. Sometimes it wounds to the death. How many lives have been snuffed out in a fit of anger! The first impulse of anger is to strike, to become greedy for another's pain.

Now, there are times when our desire for vengeance takes a more refined form. Instead of wounding with our hands, we wound with our tongues. When angry people substitute the sword of their tongues for the sword of steel, they seek to wound; but they strike not at the body, but at the heart. We study to say the thing that we believe will cause the most agony, will bring the deepest shame and humiliation. So eager are we to make the object of our anger writhe that we often have no regard whatever for the truth. We say not only the worst that we know, but what we frankly realize to be false.

Then there are those whose anger takes on a still more refined form. These do not stab either with a dagger or with their tongues. They just break off diplomatic relations. They cease to speak to the object of their anger. They send in their resignation. They quit the game. They withdraw from the Church. They act like the Elder Son in the immortal story that Jesus told. He did not shoot up the town. He just refused to go into the banquet, remained outside and pouted. Why? Because he was trying to hurt somebody. He was eager to cause somebody pain. The some one that he was seeking to hurt was his own kindly father. And his ugly and babyish efforts were not in vain. His father was deeply grieved. Selfish anger, therefore, is always a deadly cruel thing, whether it expresses itself in a fashion that is refined and fastidious, or crass and vulgar.

3. Then this anger of the Pharisees was silly. Our selfish anger always is. We have a way of saying, "I

83

got mad." It is an altogether proper word. It means that we ceased to act under the impulse of either love or reason. It means that for the time being we became insane. How many foolish and utterly stupid things we say and do when we are angry simply because we have lost our heads!

There was a man in our community when I was a boy who owned and operated a sawmill. He was a good mechanic and had plenty of push and driving power. He should have been a useful and prosperous man. But he had a terrific temper that he did not control. Now and then something would get wrong with his engine. He would set himself to the task of fixing it, but the wrench would slip, or some false move would cause him to hurt himself in some fashion. Immediately there would be an explosion. He would whack the engine with his wrench and then throw the wrench as far as he could into the pond. What was the result? The engine did not burst into tears. It just stopped running. The workers would have to be idle at the expense of the owner while a new piece of machinery was brought from a distant city. At last he went broke, not from lack of ability, but because he could not control his temper. He was too silly to be successful.

But selfish anger is always silly. This is the case not only when we try to wreak our vengeance upon inanimate things; it is even more true when we try to avenge ourselves on others. If I am angry at you, I may wound you, and wound you deeply, but always I will inflict the sorest wound upon myself. When Edmond Dantes escaped from prison, he gave his life to the punishing of those who had wronged him. He made them suffer. But he himself was the greatest sufferer. Selfish anger, therefore, is a deadly and damning thing that we do well to avoid at all cost.

III

But how about the anger of Jesus? His was righteous anger; not because it was his, but it was right in the nature of things.

1. It was right because it was born of a right motive. It was born of love. When Jesus himself was wronged, he bore it. One day a Pharisee invited him to his home. But when Jesus arrived, his host seems to have done his best to make him feel small and uncomfortable. But Jesus was not in the least offended. Later, when his best friend, the man who a few hours before had asserted emphatically that he would go with him to prison and to death, swore that he had never met him, Jesus did not grow indignant. When he turned and looked upon his faltering disciple, there was no anger in his eyes. They were rather full of tenderness and love. Then, at last, when they hung him on the nails and tried to poison the solemn and holy hours of his dying by vile railings, he was not angered in the least. Not once did he try to strike back. It was this, I think, that gripped the heart of Peter as

nothing else. Years later, looking back at those terrible hours, the biggest thing he could say of Jesus was this: "When he was reviled, he reviled not again."

But there were times when Jesus did get angry. When he saw right trodden underfoot of might, then he blazed. When he saw here in the synagogue these religious leaders so totally unmindful of human values, declaring by their conduct that man was made for the Sabbath instead of the Sabbath for man, then he flamed with holy indignation. When on another day he went into the temple and saw how men had made his Father's house into a robbers' cave, that incensed him. When he saw strong men take advantage of the weak, when he saw religious men rob widows' houses and try to atone for it by long prayers, then his eyes flashed fire, and he uttered words that flame to this hour. "Ye serpents," he cries, "ye generation of vipers, how shall you escape the damnation of hell?"

And those who are like Jesus share in his anger. If he were here today, he would burn with holy indignation against all wrong as he did in the long ago. I think his anger would flame against many of us who are trifling with his Church, and thus treating supreme values as if they were worthless gewgaws. He would certainly blaze against those who seek special privileges for themselves and are unmindful of the common good. He would burn with indignation against those men who are willing to make drunkards and orphans and warped and twisted souls for the sake of satisfying their own appetites for drink, or for the sake of growing fat on the proceeds of liquor. He would burn with unspeakable anger, I am sure, against those munition makers who are willing to plunge the whole world into an abysm of blood and tears, if only by so doing they can further smother their souls under an avalanche of profits.

2. It was a righteous anger because it sought a righteous end. When we get angry we wish to hurt. When Jesus got angry it was his passion to help and heal. When he was angry here in the synagogue it was not alone to this man with a handicap that his tender heart went out. It went out no less to these blind and stupid and self-destroyed Pharisees. He rebuked them in "thoughts that breathe and words that burn." But he never hated them; he only hated their sin. Righteous anger is righteous because it seeks to help, and not to hurt.

3. Then the anger of Jesus was sane and dynamic. It was not simply a fit of madness that often leaves its possessor weakened and ashamed. The fire of his anger was what the fire is in a locomotive. It made the steam that gave him driving power. Had he been less passionate he would have accomplished less. It was this holy indignation that helped him to do his work. And what was true of Jesus is true of the greatest of his saints. The outstanding leader of the Old Testament is Moses, and his is the hottest heart in the Old Testament. He could blaze and burn with anger. The greatest man in the New Testament is Paul. And his,

too, is the hottest heart in the New Testament. He could write: "Who is offended, and I do not burn with indignation?"

What, then, shall we do with anger? We shall realize that while selfish anger has no place in the life of a Christian, righteous anger has. The reason most of us blaze so little against the wrongs of our day is not because we are too Christian, but too un-Christian. Much that passes for tolerance among us is not in reality tolerance at all. It is nothing more than indifference. If we loved men as Jesus loved them, we would hate all that oppresses and thwarts them, as he hated it. There is no surer sign that one is rotting down in his inner life than a lost capacity for holy indignation.

Some time ago a young woman told this story. There was a rehearsal for a play. A young bud of a girl who was evidently fresh and clean and modest was openly insulted by the manager. More than a score of men were present when the dirty deed was done. But no cheek glowed in anger, and no eye flashed fire. Why? Because these men were broad and tolerant and Christian? No! It was because their souls had become so honeycombed by moral rottenness that they had lost their capacity for a clean and cleansing anger. Give us men today who can love as Jesus loved, and they will blaze with holy indignation as he blazed. Give us a few such men, and many of the evils that now swagger boldly among us will shrink away in fear, and we will move with irresistible strides toward a better day.

VII

A GLAD SURPRISE

"He was astonished at him."

LUKE 7: 9 (GOODSPEED)

I

HERE IS A MAN WHOSE SERVICE TO THE MASTER was unique. So far as the record goes, he gave Jesus the one glad surprise of his ministry. Our Lord was surprised one other time, but that surprise brought him pain. But this one filled him with boundless joy. You can see the gleam of gladness in his eye and the glow upon his cheek. You can hear the joyous enthusiasm in his voice across the far spaces of the years. There was something in the heart of this Centurion that thrilled him as no miser was ever thrilled by the discovery of hidden gold. What was this priceless treasure? He was amazed by this man's faith. He declared with joyous surprise, "I have not found so great faith, no, not in Israel."

Here, then, in this unsuspected place, Jesus found that treasure upon which he set supreme store. He always gloried in faith. It was the choicest posses-

89

sion of his own soul. Faith was the power by which he lived and did his work. When he hung on the nails the charge that his enemies threw in his face was this, "He trusted in God." Through his own experience he knew that faith was something that made its possessor invincible. He knew that the man of faith can hurl mountains of difficulties into the sea, and break through impossible barriers as though they were a spider's web. No wonder, therefore, he was thrilled by the faith of this Centurion.

II

But why was he so surprised?

1. He was surprised because of who this Centurion was. Such faith in the heart of a Jew would not have been so astonishing. The Jews had as their ancestor a man who was known as the father of the faithful. Their greatest heroes, their greatest prophets and statesmen had been men conspicuous for their faith. They had been trained to faith from their infancy. Jesus expected to find faith among them. The only other time he is represented as being surprised was by their lack of faith. But this Centurion had had no such opportunity. He was a Gentile. He had not been born in a home where one God and one God only was honored. He had grown up under the influence of an enervating polytheism. He had not had a great opportunity. Jesus was astonished, therefore, because he had so little and made so much out of it, just as he

was surprised at the Jews because they had so much and made so little out of it. And if Jesus was astonished at these Jews for their lack of faith, how much greater must be his amazement over us! So many of us believe so little in spite of the fact that our opportunities are far greater than were those of the Jews of Jesus' day.

Not only was this man a Gentile, but he was a Gentile soldier. Now the life of a soldier is not conducive to faith. The profession of killing tends to demoralize and brutalize. This is not to say that there have not been many eminent soldiers who were also eminent Christians. That was far truer of yesterday, I am sure, than it will be of tomorrow. There are many things that our fathers could do and still be saints that we, their sons and daughters, cannot do. New light is constantly breaking upon us, and we must live up to that light or lose our souls.

There was a time, for instance, when one might own slaves and be a Christian, but that would be impossible today. There was a day when even ministers of the gospel might fortify themselves for preaching by taking liquor, but we should not trust such a minister today. One of the sweetest hymns in our hymnal, a song fragrant with the breath of the cross, was written by a man who was engaged in the opium traffic. We are not going to question his Christianity, but we should certainly question the Christianity of such a man today.

And this new day is forcing us to take a new attitude toward war. Amidst our feverish piling up of armaments, there is this encouraging feature: we are facing, as never before, the fact that war is a deadly and damning thing; that it is so deadly and damning as to be the supreme foe of mankind. We have realized that, as horrible as are the brutalities that take place during a wholesale slaughter on the battlefield, this is not the greatest of its evils. The most terrible thing about war is the unmeasured tragedy that follows in its wake. More horrible than the death-dealing shells that we fire when our blood is hot, is the aftermath of broken hopes, blasted ideals, lowered moral standards, wrecked economic systems, blighted bodies, unbalanced minds, and damaged souls. With all these we have to reckon when the smoke of battle is cleared away. Surely it is hard to engage in a business so damning as war and be a man of faith. Yet this Roman soldier had managed it.

2. Not only was Jesus astonished because of who the man was that possessed this faith, he was also astonished at the high quality of his faith. His was a faith strong enough to walk without the crutches of the visible. The Jews needed the assistance of signs. The nobleman whose son Jesus had recently healed is a typical example. "Come down," he prayed. He could not conceive of Jesus' being able to heal at a distance. But this Roman soldier prayed no such prayer. According to Matthew's version, he asked for nothing at all.

He merely laid his desperate plight before the Master, virtually saying to him, "This is my situation; deal with it as you think best." And when Jesus turned his face toward his house he stopped him, saying, "Never mind about coming; just speak the word only, and my slave will get well." How marvelous! No wonder that Jesus was amazed and gladdened. Such a faith creates an atmosphere in which it is possible for him to work. We are not surprised, therefore, that this slave was instantly cured.

III

Now how did this man come by his faith?

This is a vastly important question. It is important because a vital faith is the deepest need of our day. It is the supreme need of the individual. There is nothing that the fathers and mothers who have the shaping of the generation that is to rule the world of tomorrow so need as a genuine faith. It is the supreme need of the Sunday-school teacher. It is the supreme need of every official of the Church. It is the supreme need of the minister. It is the supreme need of the Church as a whole. It is the supreme need of the nation. We can hope for national greatness and national security only through a vital faith in God. How, then, I repeat, did this man find such a faith?

1. His first step was hearing. "Faith cometh by hearing." We must hear before we believe. In the good old days of the mourners' bench, we have heard

some very bewildering instructions given to those who were seeking salvation. "Just believe," some saint would say fervently. "Only believe." But too often this eager teacher would forget to tell the seeker what to believe. "Hold on," another would say. "Just hold on." While yet another would admonish with equal fervor, "Turn loose. Just let go." But unfortunately the inquirer was left in the dark both as to the something that he was to let go, and as to that to which he was to cling. I shall never forget the first man who told me, not simply to believe, but gave me a definite promise on which to rest my faith. Then and there I ventured on that promise and found that it was true.

Now this Roman soldier, coming to live among the Jews, had learned something of their religion. He had been impressed by its high morality. Then, rumors of the teachings and doings of Jesus began to come his way. He was, I imagine, thrilled from the first. "Here is one," he doubtless said, "who seems to embody all that I have dreamed, all that I have longed to be." Then one day he was gripped by a pressing need through the sickness of his slave. While he was struggling under the weight of this burden, I feel confident that this faith was strengthened by the testimony of a friend. That friend was the nobleman whose son Jesus had just healed. These two men lived in the same town, and worked for the same master. This nobleman told him how Jesus, while still at Cana, had cured his boy away at Capernaum. And the Centurion listened and believed.

2. A second step toward victorious faith was obedience. Year by year this Centurion has bravely lived up to the best that he knew. This is ever a sure roadway to faith. There are some for whom faith is far harder than for others. There are those who are beset by intellectual difficulties. There are those who do not believe because of muddy thinking. But there are infinitely more who do not believe because of muddy living. Of all the handicaps to faith, there is none so deadly as disobedience. However clear of vision you may be, if you refuse to be obedient to that vision, it will fade into darkness. However keen of hearing you may be, if you refuse to heed, you will become deaf to the Voice Divine. On the other hand, however dim your vision, if you will live up to it, you will come into the fullness of the light.

(1) He has been loyal to the best that he knows in the use of his money. He has learned that money is power, that this power is not to be used simply for himself, but in the service of others. When these Jewish elders come to plead his cause, they call the Master's attention to the fact that he has built them a synagogue at his own expense. Jesus had doubtless preached in that synagogue. I think it was through its roof that the paralytic was lowered to receive the Master's healing and the Master's forgiveness. Now the man who takes a right relation to his wealth is on the way to a richer

faith. "Prove me now herewith, saith the Lord of hosts, if I will not open you the windows of heaven, and pour you out a blessing, that there shall not be room enough to receive it."

(2) Then this man is beautifully humble. He possesses a winsome modesty that makes him irresistible. When he turns his eyes away from the sufferer in whom he is so keenly interested, and sees Jesus coming to his house, he is overwhelmed by a sense of his own unworthiness. The Master's amazing love fills him with awe. In deep humility he calls some friends who are watching with him and dispatches them posthaste to say to the Master, "Do not trouble yourself further. I am not fit to have you under my roof, nor do I think myself worthy to come to you; but speak the word only, and my servant shall be healed." How beautifully modest! "I am not worthy," he says of himself. But his friends tell a different story. "He is worthy," they say. The man who boasts and swaggers, the man who is constantly praising himself, will usually have a monopoly on that particular job. He will say so much about himself that he will leave nothing to be said by his friends.

This man possesses faith just because he is humble. Pride kills faith. It not only fails to find God, but does not even desire to find Him. Jesus tells the story of two men who one day went to church. It may have been to the same church. One of them was a decent, respectable man. The other man was an outcast, a hireling of a foreign power. They both prayed. But the upright man prayed without humility. He merely thanked God that he was not as other men. The result was that he went down to his house no richer than when he came. Pride had shut the door of blessing in his face. But the publican—he was humble. And through the door of humility he entered into the richness of the forgiving grace of God.

(3) Last of all, and above all, this Roman soldier has lived up to the best that he knows by exercising an unfailing friendliness toward all men. The story of the amazing good will of this man is one of the most winsome that we meet on the pages of the Bible. His friendliness has literally overcome all barriers, and bridged all chasms. First, it has bridged the wide chasm between master and slave. Who is this individual about whom this Roman soldier is so exercised? He is an utter nobody, a slave, a chattel. Yet his master does not look upon him as such. He regards him as a man. He does not even call him slave. He calls him "boy." His friendliness has transformed a slave into a warm, human friend whose sickness breaks his heart, and whose returning health makes him sing.

Then, think how fertile is the soil that his situation offers for the growing of mutual hatred between himself and the people among whom he has come to live. Remember that he is a Roman soldier, a member of a proud and conquering race. Remember, also, that these Jews over whom he has come to stand guard are members of a yet prouder race, in spite of the fact that they have been conquered. All their lives they have been taught to thank God that they were not born Gentiles. Naturally, therefore, they hate their conquerers with a fierce and bitter hatred. Always there are mutterings of rebellion. Again and again this fierce hatred flames into action, to be repressed only by the sternest of measures. Many of their choicest patriots have hung on forests of crosses. And now this Centurion has come to keep up this shameful subjection. No wonder they hate him even before they have ever seen him!

But this soldier meets this hot hate with genuine friendliness. With an invincible good will he bridges the wide chasm of race. He forgets that these among whom he has come to live are turbulent and narrow-minded Jews. He remembers only that they are human beings, men of like passions as himself. Their religion is different from his, but his friendliness bridges that chasm. Then he is the conquerer, and they are the conquered, but his good will even spans that wide chasm. He does not lord it over them. He does not try to make them feel that they are subjects; he ever seeks to make them realize that they are friends. This he does, not for just one day, but for many days. At last he convinces them that he does really care. At last he compels them to this beautiful confession: "He loves us." What an amazing and worth-while victory!

Now, what response do these proud Jews make to this man of good will? Well, they simply find it impossible to continue to hate him. In fact, they find it impossible to refrain from loving in return. When, therefore, trouble comes to his home and he is anxious and worried, they do not rejoice over it. They do not declare that God is punishing him for his sins. Instead, they gather about him, eagerly asking if there is anything they can do. When he tells them that they might see Jesus on his behalf, they are all eagerness. They hurry away and present his plea as forcefully and earnestly as possible.

It worked then. It will work today. A friend of mine tells this story. A certain friend of his, who was an unusually beautiful Christian, bought a lovely home in the suburbs of one of our Southern cities. He had his goods moved out one day, but he himself did not arrive till the late afternoon. While he was out walking over the wide lawn that was part of his newly acquired property, he saw his next-door neighbor hurrying to meet him. He was glad, for he was always eager to make friends. But this neighbor did not greet him in the kindly fashion that he had expected. "Did you buy this property?" he asked in a voice tense with anger. "Yes," came the quiet reply. "Well, you have bought a lawsuit, that's all. That fence is seven feet over on my land, and I am going to have every inch of what is mine if it costs me the last dollar I have."

Now, what answer would you have made to an onslaught like that? I tell you what this Christian did. He said, "My friend, there is no need of a lawsuit. I believe that you are perfectly sincere in what you say. Therefore, though I bought this land in good faith, I am not going to claim it. I will have that fence moved the first thing in the morning." The angry man looked at his new neighbor in wide-eyed amazement. "What did you say? Do you really mean that you will have this fence moved?" "That is exactly what I mean," came the quiet answer. Then the astonished neighbor broke into a string of oaths that were about as earnest as prayers. "Blankety, blank, blank," he said, "no, you won't. This fence is going to stay right where it is. Any man that is as white as you are can have the blank land. And that's not all, you can have anything else that I have that you want." Thus he won his neighbor by his invincible good will.

Are you desirous of a larger faith? Do you yearn for a faith that will satisfy your own deep needs and make you a transmitter of the power of God to a needy world? You can have it. This is just as certain as that you are listening to me at this moment. It is as sure as the fact of God. You will find it if you walk the road that this man walked—the road of obedience. Begin here and now to use your money as God's steward, to walk in humility, to meet the world with an invincible good will, and then one day you, too, will come to a radiant faith that will be a surprise to your own heart. You, too, will thrill your Lord with unspeakable joy as did this Centurion of the long ago.

VIII

DEFEATING OUR FEARS

". . . Why are you afraid?"

MATTHEW 8: 26 (MOFFATT)

JESUS WITH HIS DISCIPLES IS CROSSING THE SEA
of Galilee. He is a bit weary, therefore he goes
into the stern of the boat, makes himself as comfortable
as possible upon a pillow, and is soon fast asleep. While
he is sleeping, a sudden storm breaks upon them. The
savage winds soon lash the sea into wild fury. The
waves begin to spit their rage into the face of heaven,
and to toss the puny vessel as a juggler might toss a
ball. At first the disciples bear up bravely. Some of
them are men of the sea and are not easily frightened.
They will hold on their course in spite of the storm.
But their situation becomes more threatening each moment. Meantime, they begin to turn perplexed and
fear-filled faces toward their Master. Is he never going to awake? Is it possible that with Death blowing
its chilling breath in their very faces he is going to
sleep through it all?

At last they can stand the strain no longer. They are
loath to wake him, but they feel that they must. There-

fore, frantic with fear, one grasps him rudely by the shoulder and shakes him into wakefulness. "Master, wake up," he cries; "don't you care if we drown?" It is a very human question. It has been asked in one way or another countless millions of times. Jesus opens his eyes, rebukes the sea, and there is a great calm. Then he turns to these friends of his and asks in bewilderment not unmixed with pain, "Why are you afraid?" And strange to say, these men who could have given such an excellent reason for their fears a few moments ago are utterly silent now. Their terrors seem positively silly in the presence of this Man who speaks to them with such calm confidence, and looks at them with such quiet eyes.

"Why are you afraid?" This is a question that Jesus is constantly asking. He asked it long ago when life was haunted by so many fears. He is asking it in the enlightened day in which we live.

1. This is the case because fear is so widespread. So many of us are afraid. Poor folks are afraid. Of course. They have no sense of economic security. They do not know how they are going to keep the "wolf of want" from their doors. But many rich, who are fairly smothered in their luxuries, are even more afraid. The ignorant and superstitious are frightened. They do not know when a black cat might run across their pathways or they might get a glimpse of the new moon in an unlucky fashion. But many who are educated are also constantly dogged by fears. Irreligious

people—those who have no sense of God in their lives —have fears. But sad to say, this is also true of many who belong to the Church and who are earnestly religious. Old folks who are coming close to the sunset and evening star are sometimes fearful. Their strength is failing and they know that their day will soon be over. But many who are in life's green spring are even more afraid. Fear constantly dogs the steps of vast multitudes in every walk of life.

Then we are afraid of all sorts of things. We fear for the health of our bodies and for the health of our souls. We are afraid that we cannot secure a desirable position, or that we may lose the one that we have. We are afraid of what happened yesterday, it may track us down and bring us shame. We are afraid of what might happen tomorrow. Tomorrow some lurking tragedy may spring upon us and lay waste our lives. We are afraid for ourselves. We are afraid for our children. We are afraid for our friends. We are afraid lest someone may get ahead of us. We are afraid of what others may think or say about us. We begin, psychologists tell us, with only two fears, but soon they become a multitude. There is nothing too big or too insignificant to make us afraid.

2. Then this question is pertinent because fear is so harmful. There are few foes so utterly ruinous as fear. This is true in spite of the fact that fear has a legitimate place in our lives. There are fears that safeguard and protect us. The man, therefore, who

tells us that he is absolutely afraid of nothing is not speaking complimentarily of himself. There are certain things of which every sane man ought to be afraid. For instance, every man ought to be afraid to take a needless physical risk. Life is far too priceless to be flung away for naked nothing. There are many high values for which we may wisely venture our all, but to venture that all for nothing is plain stupidity. The man, for example, who is not afraid to mix gasoline and liquor is not showing himself to be wise, but foolish. We ought to be afraid of needlessly violating the laws of health. Every sane man ought to be afraid to take any needless physical risk.

Then every sane man ought to be afraid to take a needless moral risk. Everyone, therefore, who flirts with uncleanliness and everyone who toys with some practice that is likely to enslave him is simply playing the fool. This was the trouble with Samson. He thought he was smart enough to have his fling and get away with it. He therefore exposed himself to the direst moral risks. But regardless of the fact that he was not afraid, his venture cost him his freedom and ultimately his life. The man who is not afraid of sin does not for that reason escape fear. He only makes his bondage to fear an absolute certainty. For every man who is not afraid of sin sooner or later is made afraid by his sin. In the old Genesis story, the first face upon which Adam looked after he broke with God was the face of Fear. Every wise man, therefore, will be afraid of a needless moral risk.

But it is not of our legitimate fears that I propose to speak now. I am to speak rather of our foolish and needless fears. It is these that do so much to mar and lay waste our lives.

II

What do these fears do to us? Why are they so ruinous?

1. Fear is creative: "The thing which I greatly feared is come upon me." This pathetic wail that we hear from the lips of Job is the soundest psychology. The experience of this ancient sufferer has been that of countless multitudes. Fear is always creating the thing it dreads. The man who is constantly fearing for his health—the one who gets up every morning with his fingers upon his pulse and with his tongue poked out before the mirror—that is the man who is most likely to be sick. I have a friend who rushes home and makes his will every time he hears of any sort of epidemic, even one so common as colds. He constantly goes about armed with various remedies. He haunts the offices of doctors. He is therefore sick, or fancies himself so, about 365 days each year. Fear tends to create the thing it fears.

Then fear is creative in another sense. It is creative in that it is contagious. When I was a country schoolteacher, I remember a story—a fairly silly story

—that was in one of our readers. It told how Chicken Little was in the garden one morning when a cabbage leaf fell upon her tail. She at once concluded that the sky was falling. Therefore, crazed with terror, she began to run. By and by, she met Henny Penny and told her the fearful story. Seized by panic, she, too, began to run. Soon all the other fowls of the barn-yard heard the horrible news and joined in the stampede. Off they went, running for their lives. At last, they met Mr. Fox, who offered them refuge in his den, where he made of them a gorgeous feast. Now, we men and women are very much like that, and can be stampeded almost as easily. By our fears, we can take the heart out of others. Fear is contagious.

2. Fear makes us wretched. If we are to find life joyous, we must get rid of fear. What agony, born of sheer fear, have we seen in the faces of men and women. At its mildest, fear is a kill-joy. At its worst, it is very hell. A few years ago I read the story of a hobo who slipped into an empty banana car to steal a ride to a neighboring city. He lay down upon a pile of straw and soon dropped off to sleep. By and by, he was awakened by something crawling on his face and hands. He brushed it away, but the crawling kept on. At last he sprang to his feet, more annoyed than afraid. He fumbled in his pockets for a match, and found only one. This he struck and held aloft till it burned his fingers. He was too frightened to be at once conscious of the pain, for the straw seemed alive with tarantulas. When

the match had gone out and black darkness had fallen upon him, he sprang for the door only to find it fast. He then proceeded to pound it till his fists were bloody. But there was no response. When he was released the next morning, he was little better than a maniac. This was the case not because of any physical pain. Not a single tarantula had harmed him. He was driven half mad by fear. Fear is a sure road to wretchedness.

3. Then fear is paralyzing. When I was a student at Harvard University, for quite a season, I used to meet each morning, as I went to my first class, a huge dog. Now I am afraid of dogs. I do not need any psychiatrist to tell me why. I was bitten by one when I was a child. But I spoke to this dog at each meeting as if I loved him. But he seemed to sense my lack of sincerity, and to resent it. At least, when we met one day he made no polite response to my greeting. Instead, when he was a few feet past me, he wheeled with a roar and came at me. And I did just what all dog psychologists say do. I stood perfectly still and looked him squarely in the eye. But this I did, not because I knew it was the wisest course—I did it because I was scared stiff.

What was the matter with the man of one talent? It was not that circumstances were against him. It was not that a man with such a meager gift has no chance —he had every chance. He was afraid. Therefore, he did nothing but bury his talent in the earth. Why did not the Rich Young Ruler follow Jesus? It was not because Jesus did not appeal to him. He did appeal and that greatly. This young ruler was paralyzed by fear. Why do we so often do nothing in the presence of appalling wrongs? We are afraid. Too often we are so afraid that we will do the wrong thing, that we do nothing at all.

4. Not only does fear tend to paralyze, thus preventing our doing what we know we ought to do, it often drives us to do things that we know we ought not to do. How many lies we tell, not because we are naturally dishonest, but because we are afraid. Why do such a vast number of women smoke cigarettes today? It is not because they have any greater desire for tobacco than their sisters of a few years ago. Smoking became a fad, and they were afraid not to conform. Why do so many, who have been reared in homes where liquor was never allowed, join in the drinking of cocktails today? It is not the result, at least at the beginning, of any appetite for liquor. They drink because they are afraid to say "No." Fear often leads us to spit in the face of our deepest convictions. "The fear of man," says the wise man, "bringeth a snare." That has been proved true countless millions of times.

Not only does fear often cause us to outrage our convictions by engaging in practices to which we object, it often makes us cruel. This is true of the group. Fear is perhaps the supreme factor in bringing about the red hell of war. It is true also of the individual. Some time ago, I read anew the story of the sinking of the Titanic. The writer said that many of the life-boats that put out from this ill-fated vessel were not half full. Yet people by the hundreds were left behind to drown. Why this cruelty? It was born of fear. The author told of a certain swimmer who succeeded in making his way to one of these half-empty boats. He clutched the side and tried to climb in. But no one lent him a hand. Not only so, but a woman took an oar and pounded his hands until he could cling no longer, and he dropped back to his death. Why did she do that? It was not because there was no room in the boat, there was plenty. She was brutalized by fear. Fear at its worst blasts our convictions and changes us into beasts.

III

If fear then is such a ruinous and deadly thing, we ought to be rid of it—but how?

Well, we cannot be rid of it by simply clinching our fists and resolving to banish it altogether. There are certain fears that might be banished in some measure by this method, but this is not enough. In one of Mc-Guffey's readers, there is a story of a lad who saw a guidepost one night, and was terrified by it. In the gloom it looked like a forbidding monster. But when he discovered what it really was, he was ashamed of his foolish fears. He then reached the following con-clusion:

"Ah well," thought he, "one thing I've learned,
  Nor shall I soon forget;
Whatever frightens me again
  I'll march right up to it!"

That might serve for the specters of the mind. But it would be a poor way out if what you feared happened to be a rattlesnake or a speeding car. Our cure must go deeper than this.

Nor are we going to get rid of our fears by simply ignoring them. There are some foes that we fear that are very real. Since they are so, we are not going to destroy our fear of them by merely shutting our eyes. There are those, for instance, who seek thus to banish sin, sickness, and death. But these grim realities persist, however hard we try to ignore them. Since we know this, our fears are likely to persist, unless we find a better remedy. Too often, when we say we are not afraid of these things, we simply drive our fear down into the subconscious mind and thus sow the seed for future trouble.

How then can we conquer fear? One prime essential, as others have pointed out, is the living of a clean and upright life. No man can be really fearless who hides guilty secrets in his heart. If your yesterday has been stained by faithlessness or crime, the nemesis of fear is upon your track today. Think of the tormenting fears of Arthur Dimmesdale in Hawthorne's *Scarlet Letter*. Nobody knew his guilt save himself and the woman who shared his sin. But every moment of his waking existence was a hellish nightmare of fear. Think of the terror that dogs the steps of the professional criminal. Many a fugitive from justice has surrendered of his own accord, because he felt that the penitentiary, or even the gallows, would be better than being tortured by the fiendish fears that constantly hung upon his heels. To be rid of fear then, a clean and upright life is an absolute necessity.

But the supreme antidote against fear is faith. "Why are you afraid?" Jesus asks; and then he adds this further word, "How little you trust God." By this he means to say that fear and faith cannot at the same time keep house in the same heart. When faith comes in, fear flees like a guilty thing afraid. Jesus knew this from his own experience. His was a tempestuous life. When he began his ministry, there was a bit of calm, but soon the skies were overcast. He had to see his popularity change into hate. He had to face day by day the bitterest of opposition. At last, he had to see the high mission to which he had given his life seemingly fall into utter ruins. He himself was nailed to the cross. But through it all, there was never a moment of fear. In the face of defeat and death, he bore himself with a calm courage at which all the centuries have wondered. What was his secret? It is found in the words that were howled at him by the mob that watched him die. "He trusted in God." A faith like that of Jesus makes fear an utter impossibility.

Now this faith that casts out fear is a big and brawny

something. It is far more than a mere belief that we have a good and fatherly God who will keep us out of all difficulties. A faith that expects God to still all storms may calm our fears for a while, but such relief is only temporary. We shall become only the more fearful when we realize that God does not save us from all hard situations. When these disciples appealed to Jesus, he stilled the storm, but others who have prayed just as earnestly have gone down at sea. "God sends his rain upon the just and the unjust." The same also is true of droughts. In the old Sunday-school stories, there were usually a good boy and a bad boy. The good boy was always coming out on top and the bad boy was forever getting stung. But that is not altogether true to life. Bad men do sometimes go to the wall, but so do good men. A man's faithlessness often gets him into trouble, but so does his faithfulness. It was Paul's faithfulness that caused him to be scarred from head to foot by the stones and scourges of persecution. A faith, therefore, that saves from fear must be more than a faith that expects deliverance from hardship and difficulty.

What then is this faith? It is a faith that trusts God so completely that it puts His will first in all things. It is a faith that believes that the will of God is so perfect that nothing can harm us so long as we live within that will. This was the faith that gave Paul his undaunted courage. "We know," he declares boldly, "that to them that love God, all things work together for good." If a man is really convinced of that in the deepest depths of his soul, then nothing can make him afraid. He may be called upon to face loneliness, unpopularity, bitter loss, intense suffering. But these will not frighten him because he knows that God can change his foes into friends, his calamities into capital, his losses into gains. "This is the victory that overcometh the world" with all of its fears and with all of its terrors—"even our faith." If we trust God enough to put His will first, if we have no fear save the fear of disappointing Him, then that fear will banish all others as the sunrise banishes the stars.

IX

THE DISTURBING CHRIST

*"And they began to pray
him to depart out of their
coasts."*

MARK 5: 17

I

HAD YOU PASSED THROUGH THIS VILLAGE OF Gerasa a week before the events here recorded, you would doubtless have been impressed by its quiet restfulness. There was an atmosphere of contentment that pervaded the people, as

> "Along the cool sequestered vale of life
> They kept the noiseless tenor of their way."

Even that notorious madman, who now and then stirred a few waves of excitement upon the sea of their complacency, was behaving fairly well. At least, he was living among the tombs down by the lake. Perhaps, not recently, had he upset the villagers by coming to town and getting himself bound with fetters and with chains.

But today, all this is changed. The once placid calm

has given place to a fever of excitement. If you have ever gone into the forest in early spring and over-turned a rotting log and watched the twilight life that had its home underneath as it scurried here and there; if you have heard, even with the ears of your imagination, these disturbed creatures shriek at you to go away and stop annoying them, you can appreciate what is happening among these villagers. They are being disturbed by the new light that is shining upon them. They do not like it. Therefore, their one prayer is to be let alone.

Who has caused this fever of excitement? Who has dared to shake them, for the moment at least, out of the deep ruts in which they were so content to abide? It is none other than the Young Carpenter from Nazareth. He is doing here what he was constantly doing throughout his entire ministry. He is doing here what he has done through all the subsequent centuries. He is the most disturbing personality that the world has ever known. I know that he comes to us with the promise of rest. But he usually has to make us restless before he can give us rest. He is a persistent disturber.

One Sabbath day, for instance, he attended services at his own home church. He stood up to signify that he desired to read the lesson for the day. He turned to that thrilling passage in Isaiah that begins, "The Spirit of the Lord is upon me." Having read, he began to tell them how that scripture was then and there being fulfilled. At first, the people listened, charmed by his gracious words. But he proceeded to tell them that, while they might be God's children, they were not his only children. This was indicated by the fact that while there were many widows in Israel during the days of Elijah, when God wanted somebody to provide for his prophet, he sent him, not to one of themselves, but to a woman who was a pagan. He told them that, while there were many lepers in Israel during the days of Elisha, not a single one of them had the faith to be cured. The only one that was healed was a man without the covenant, named Naaman. And the service that had begun so peacefully broke up in a riot.

When Jesus was brought before Pilate, most of the testimony given against him was utterly false. But there was one bit that was true. His enemies declared that he had stirred up the people throughout the whole nation. There was no denying that. He did throw the people of his day into a ferment of excitement. And he has been disturbing us ever since—this strange Man upon his cross. Since then, he has lifted empires off their hinges and changed the whole course of human history. Jesus was and is the supreme disturber.

II

How does Jesus disturb us?

1. Our Lord disturbs us by the very processes of living in the kind of world in which he has placed us. Ours is a world of constant flux and change. Nothing

remains quite the same. No sooner do we adopt one style of dress than we have to throw it away for another. No sooner do we accept one mode of travel than we have to discard it for another. We changed our oxcarts and prairie schooners for horses and buggies. We changed our horses and buggies for automobiles and airships. We throw away our candles for kerosene lamps, and these we must exchange for the incandescent. We discard our old books for new ones. We exchange the statement of the faith of our fathers for one more suited to our own needs. We leave the old home to establish one of our own, only to have this one broken up, in its turn, by the ruthless hand of change. To live in a world like ours is constantly to be disturbed.

This is the case whether we like it or not. A great many of us do not like it. We do not accept change graciously. We like to sink down complacently into our well-worn ruts and be at ease. But life refuses to treat us that way. The passing years bring changes that all but compel us to make new adventures. To refuse to do so, is to be thrown into discard. You remember that lovely old couple in Goethe's *Faust,* who stood in the way of the building of the City Beautiful. They refused to accept change, so one night their house burned to the ground and they burned with it. Our Lord is constantly saying to us what he said to the children of Israel long ago, "You have dwelt long enough in this mountain." Day by day we are being called to strike our tents and move on to other camping grounds. We are born on an incline—everyone of us—where there is no standing still. We must either climb or slip down the hill. Our Lord is constantly disturbing us by setting us to live in a changing world.

2. He disturbs us by being what He is. In his presence, we see ourselves. One day, a city missionary sat by the bedside of an outcast woman who was ill. She was not talking to this woman about her sins, she was simply paying her a friendly visit. But suddenly, the sick woman burst into tears. As her visitor sought the reason, this woman of the street reached out her thin finger and touched the white flower that her friend held in her hand. "I am not like that," she said; "I used to be white like that, but I am not any more." Against the white background of that lovely flower, this woman had seen herself.

It is in some such fashion that Jesus disturbs us. Our first impression as we come into his presence is this, "I am not like that." We can compare ourselves with each other with fair complacency. "I am not anything to brag on," a chap said the other day, "but I am as good as the average." Possibly so, but we do not talk like that in the presence of Jesus. When we see ourselves against the white background of his pure and radiant life, we cry with Isaiah, "Unclean, unclean."

Here, for instance, is a robber who is dying by the most fiendish mode of torture that the ingenuity of man has ever contrived. This man has led a hard and bloody life. He has been a highwayman, a knight of the road.

He has swooped down upon his fellows as ruthlessly as a beast of prey. But now he has reached the end of the trail. He is suffering the pangs of death. But, as he thus suffers, he declares that it is just, that he is receiving the due rewards of his deeds. How has he come to make such a confession? None such is being made by his fellow in crime. What has happened? This man has seen himself and his deeds against the white background of the personality of Jesus. Therefore, as he suffers the very pangs of hell, he cries, "I suffer justly." As we see Jesus, we see ourselves.

Not only does Jesus disturb us by showing us ourselves, he disturbs us no less by showing us what we may become. If, when we stand in his presence, our first word is, "I am not like that," our second surely is this: "I may be like that. As he used his life, so I ought to use mine. As he flung himself away for the good of others, so ought I to fling myself away. I am not like him, but I can be, I ought to be, I long to be like him." So men felt who really saw him in the long ago. So they feel to this day. Jesus is constantly disturbing us by compelling us to see the larger and better men and women that he makes it possible for us to be.

3. Then our Lord disturbs us by the call of human need. Here is a story from the life of St. Paul. He is telling us how he came to invade Europe with his revolutionary gospel. One night in Troas, he had a vision

of a man of Macedonia. The hungry face of this man so haunted him as to make restful indifference impossible. His outstretched hands were so appealing as to disturb his very dreams. To his ears there came a call as disquieting as the call of a sick and frightened child to its mother. "Come over into Macedonia and help us," was the appeal. That appeal made further sleep for Paul impossible. It upset his plans. It compelled him to new adventures. Our Lord was disturbing him by the call of human need.

So men have been disturbed through all the centuries. They have been made restless and eager by the needs, the burdens, heart-hungers of their fellows. "Why do you wish to return to China?" Dr. Jowett asked of a missionary who had come home as an invalid. "Because I cannot sleep at night for thinking of them," came the answer. The empty lives of those who needed him took the softness out of his bed and stuffed his pillow with thorns. Why did Walter Reed and his companions brazenly flirt with death in their fight with yellow fever? They had been disturbed by the call of human need. Thus through the years, our Lord has disturbed heroic men and women who have gone forth to brave all sacrifices and to dare all deaths in order to serve their fellows. These have been so disquieted by their brothers' burdens that they could find no peace till they took them upon themselves.

And our amazing Christ is doing today what he has always done. He is disturbing some of us by the needless suffering and the needless waste of life among underprivileged people of other lands, and we are going as missionaries. He is disturbing others by the injustices of our own social order so that they must be giving themselves to the changing of the things that are into the things that ought to be. Our fathers looked upon war with more or less complacency. But this is today impossible for an ever-increasing multitude. We are being disturbed by it. We are realizing that war really is hell, and that we must learn to live together or we are not going to live at all. Our Lord is calling us through this great need to give ourselves to the high task of peace-making. Thus, through what he is, through the very process of living, through the call of need, through countless other voices, our Lord is disturbing us.

III

Why does Jesus disturb us?

He does not disturb us because he enjoys our restlessness. It seems hard for some of us to get away from that strange conviction that religion is a kill-joy. "Pale Galilean, Thou hast conquered, and the world has grown gray at Thy birth." But really a more colossal lie was never told. About all the radiance and beauty that has come to our world has come through this amazing birth. But in spite of this fact, there are still those who seem to feel that Jesus has come "to steal and to kill and to destroy," rather than to give us life in abundance. You remember how Thomas Hardy ends one of his depressing stories. Tess has died after meaningless suffering. "Thus," concludes the author, "the President of the Immortals had finished his sport with Tess." His idea seems to be that the God whom Jesus came to reveal is, after all, only a cruel devil who takes pleasure in torturing His own children.

Now, our Lord does disturb us. He frankly tells us that he has come not to send peace, but a sword. But this does not mean that he does not give peace to those who give him a chance. He is the Prince of peace. Giving peace is his specialty. "Peace I leave with you, my peace I give unto you." What, then, does he mean? He means that he has not come to bring a wrong kind of peace. There is a peace that is born of stagnation and death. He must often take his sharp sword and stab us into wakefulness and restlessness before he can give us real peace. But he never disturbs us just because he delights in our unhappiness. He does not disturb us because being disturbed is an end in itself.

Why then, I repeat, does he disturb us? He does so in order to bring us to the realization of our best possibilities. Not to be disturbed is to sink into a complacent self-content. To be content with ourselves, to be content with things as they are, means arrested development. Such contentment strikes a deathblow to all progress either for the individual or for the group. If we are as good as we desire to be, we are not likely to become any better. If we are as wise as we care to be, we are not going to grow any wiser. If we are as high up the hill as we long to be, we are not going to climb any higher. It is only as our Lord disturbs us that he can get us to move on.

In one of the most tenderly beautiful and poetic passages in the Old Testament, God's care of His people is compared to that of the mother eagle for her young. "For the Lord's portion is his people; Jacob is the lot of his inheritance. He found him in a desert land, and in the waste howling wilderness; he led him about, he instructed him, he kept him as the apple of his eye. As an eagle stirreth up her nest, fluttereth over her young, spreadeth abroad her wings, taketh them, beareth them on her wings: so the Lord alone did lead him, and there was no strange god with him." That is, God disturbs us as the mother eagle disturbs her young when she stirreth her nest. There are the eaglets safe and comfortable in their rugged home high upon a shelf of the cliffs. But one day, the mother comes without bringing her young their accustomed food. Instead of feeding them, with ruthless claws, she tears their home into shreds. Not only so, but she flings them from their place of safety out into space. Helpless and frightened, they begin to fall to where the ragged rocks are waiting to pound out their lives.

Why does this mother do this seemingly cruel thing? Is it that she may laugh in fiendish glee at the terror of her falling young? Not a bit of it. She does not allow them to fall. Just when they are thinking that

123

they are doomed, she dashes underneath them, takes them upon her wings and bears them up so that they suffer no hurt. What, then, is she trying to do? She is trying to teach these eaglets to realize that for which they were born. They were not made simply to be coddled in safety. They were made for the cloudland and for the upper air. They were not made to be sheltered in a nest. They were made "to bathe their plumage in the thunder's home." And that is the reason that our Lord disturbs us. We, too, are meant for flight sunward and Godward. As our Master, we have not come to be ministered unto, but to minister. Therefore, our Lord is constantly seeking to arouse us from a low content in order to bring us to our best.

IV

Now, what response are we to make to this disturbing Christ? When our Lord awakens us, what are we to do about it? This is the big question. It is not ours to decide whether we shall or shall not be disturbed. Again and again our Lord awakens us, whether we will it or not. Again and again his voice breaks upon our indifference and complacency, even though we may be unwilling. But, while it is not ours to decide whether we shall be disturbed or not, it is ours to decide what we shall do, once we are disturbed. If an alarm clock rings in your room, it is likely to wake you whether you wish it to or not. But when it has gotten you awake, that is as far as it can go. It cannot drag you out of bed. Whether you get up or go back to sleep depends entirely upon yourself. And that, with all reverence, is as far as our Lord can go. All he can do is to disturb us. This he does in a thousand ways. But having done that, the rest is left to us. He can wake us, but the getting up must be done by ourselves.

Now, what response do we make? Broadly speaking, we make one of two. We either get up or we remain in bed and go back to sleep. These villagers took the latter course. They were disturbed by Jesus, but nothing worthwhile came of it. All the change it made in their lives was to cause them to hurry to him with this terrible prayer upon their lips, "Depart out of our coasts." He was interfering with their business. They were afraid that he would cut down their profits. Therefore, there was but one thing for them to do and that was to get rid of him.

You will agree that theirs is a terrible prayer. Yet awful as it is, there is not one of us that has not at some time prayed it. Of course, we do not word it just as they did. We never quite dare to say to Jesus openly and frankly, "Leave us alone." But we tell him to do so in language just as emphatic. This we do by refusing to give up some practice to which we know he objects. This we do when we are content with the second best, when he is calling us to the best. We thus pray when we turn a deaf ear to needs that we know we ought to meet, when we stand idle in the presence of pressing calls to which we know we ought to respond.

We have all, at one time or another, asked to be let alone. Some of us are praying that prayer even now.

What response does Jesus make to such terrible prayers? He makes the only one that he can make. He grants our request. So he did in the case of these Gerasenes. So he ever does. When he stopped on one occasion to spend the night in a certain Samaritan village, they refused to receive him. What then? He did not call down fire from heaven as the Sons of Thunder asked him to do. He did something more tragic still. He passed on to the next village. Our Lord will not and cannot force himself upon any of us. Persistently, he stands at the door and knocks. But it is ours to open. If we fail, we little by little get used to being without him, till we all but cease to care. There is more of truth and pathos even than of humor and poetry in those words of Kenneth C. Kaufman:

> "I think my soul is a tame old duck,
> Dabbling around in barnyard muck,
> Fat and lazy, with useless wings.
> But sometimes when the north wind sings,
> And the wild ones hurtle overhead,
> It remembers something lost and dead,
> And cocks a wary and bewildered eye,
> And makes a feeble attempt to fly.
> It's fairly content with the state it's in,
> But it isn't the duck it might have been." [1]

But if it is within our power to resist our Lord when

[1] From *Level Land,* published by Kaleidograph Press, Dallas. Originally published in the *Daily Oklahoman.* Used by permission.

he disturbs us, it is also within our power to yield to him. If we can say "No" to him, we can also say "Yes." And it is this that makes the real difference between the spiritually victorious and those who go down in defeat—one yields to God's awakenings, the other does not. How great was the disturbance that our Lord wrought in the heart of Paul! After he had witnessed the stoning of Stephen, he was a haunted man. His soul was as a sea whipped by a tempest. He could never forget the shining face and the Christlike prayer of that great saint. But the disturbance wrought in the heart of Paul was no more real than that wrought in the soul of profligate Felix under Paul's preaching. As the great apostle reasoned of righteousness, temperance, and judgment, he was made to shudder. But here the similarity ends. Felix said, "Go thy way for this time," and sank into the sleep of death. Paul said, "Lord, what wilt thou have me do?" and henceforth went to live in the freshness and beauty of an eternal springtime. Which course will you take?

X

GREAT THINGS

*"Go home to thy friends,
and tell them how great
things the Lord hath done
for thee."*

MARK 5: 19

THE STORY OF WHICH THIS TEXT IS A PART HAS
certain details that are thoroughly bewildering.
Some of its language sounds like a foreign tongue to
our modern ears. But we must not allow this fact to
blind us to its central message. This queerness as to
details has to do with the nonessentials of the story,
rather than with its essential truth. It has to do with
the setting of the jewel, rather than the jewel itself.
And there is real jewelry here and that of priceless
worth. This story tells what Christ did for a poor
demented wreck in the long ago. It tells also what
he does today for the soul that gives him a chance.

He does "great things!" I like that word. There
are many who seem to think that our religion has in
it more of weight than of wings; that at best, its
benefits are rather paltry and worthless trifles. But in
reality, these seeming trifles are the great things, the

priceless things, the supreme things. "Tell how great things the Lord hath done for thee." Have you such a story to tell? Is there anything taking place in your life day by day that can only be described by this word "great"? If there is nothing, then you are not claiming your spiritual birthright. If there is nothing, then your religion is not doing for you what God intended that it should do. But this is not the fault of your Lord, nor is it the fault of the Church. It is your own fault. Wherever Christ has his way, he does great things. Such was the case here. Such has been the case throughout the centuries.

I

Look at this man as Jesus found him. The description given of him is so clear that it would seem to have come from the pen of an eyewitness. The keel of the boat in which Jesus is sailing has hardly touched the shore before a ghastly figure rushes out from one of the tombs. He is wearing practically no clothing. He is disheveled and unkempt. To his wrists and ankles probably still cling the fragments of fetters with which men have vainly tried to bind him. He is a poor half-mad creature with whom we feel little kinship. But when we face the facts, we are made to realize that we have much in common. Of course, we are far more sane than he, far more decent and respectable. Yet we differ from him in degree rather than in kind. This we realize as we study his story. What was the matter with him?

1. He was a divided personality. When Jesus asked him his name, he gave a ready answer: "My name is Legion." That is, he was not one, but many. He was not so much a personality, as H. G. Wells would say, as a battleground. He was at war with himself. He was being tugged in a thousand different directions. A thousand different impulses and passions were warring within his soul. We meet such divided and disintegrating personalities today in the psychopathic wards of our hospitals. But we do not find them there alone. We often meet them as we mingle with our fellows. We sometimes even meet such as we live with ourselves. Of course, this inner conflict is far less pronounced with some than with others. But all of us know something of the tragedy of a divided personality.

The truth of this is emphasized by modern psychologists. They tell us, for instance, that we are possessed of a conscious and a subconscious mind. In the subconscious mind are the driving instincts that have come to us from our ancestors. These instincts are without conscience. They have no moral sense. They seek their gratification, the pleasure of their own fulfillment, with not the slightest attention to the question of right and wrong. But in the conscious mind, there is a sense of oughtness. Here is that which makes us say "I owe" and "I must," or "I must not." Therefore, the conscious mind rises up against the subconscious. Our ideals fight with our instincts. Our higher self battles with our lower self. Hence we become divided personalities, incarnate civil wars, victims of the direst of all conflicts—the conflict within ourselves.

The writers of the Bible discovered this long before the birth of modern psychology. Here is a man, for instance, who is conscious within himself that he fears the Lord. He is a man of piety and prayer. Even now, he is upon his knees with his face turned wistfully toward the heights. But there is another self within him that refuses to kneel. There is another self that jeers and sneers while the higher self seeks to pray. It is out of the agony of this conflict that he cries to God. For what does this earnest soul make request? What is his prayer? This: "Unite my heart to fear Thy name." He has a fear of the Lord that is altogether genuine. But in spite of this, he is conscious that he is only half-hearted in his fear. He is, therefore, praying for a unified personality, a wholehearted devotion to God.

Here is another man who is also deeply religious. But he seems more sensitive to the lure of evil than to that of good. He is more conscious of the call of the depths than the call of the heights. He has a keener sense of his baser self than he has of his better self. The voices that call to him to take the lower road seem more appealing than those that call to him to take the higher. But in spite of this, he cannot wholly give himself to the base and to the unclean. He cannot fling himself with abandon away from all that is beautiful and best. He has gone into the far country of his own choice, yet he cannot be at home there. Therefore, he cries, "My soul cleaveth unto the dust: quicken thou me according to thy word." If with one hand he is grasping at the mud, with the other he is reaching for the stars. Therefore, like this demoniac and like ourselves, he is at war with himself.

2. This poor fellow, being at war with himself, was naturally wretched. "Always, night and day," the story says, "he was crying and cutting himself with stones." Always he was fighting himself. Always he was wounding himself. Always he was his own worst enemy. Thus warring against himself, he was a stranger to real happiness. That is ever the case. No divided personality can ever be happy. However beautiful our surroundings, however large our bank account, however great our success, however thunderous the applause that may ring in our ears—if we are at war with ourselves, we are miserable and will continue to be so till our conflict is hushed into peace.

This is not theory, this is experience. Here is a great soul that is in the midst of this age-old conflict. He is lured by the heights. But when he sets out to climb, he somehow gravitates toward the depths. He hates the unclean and solemnly vows that he will never stretch forth his hand to it again. But while his vow is yet upon his lips, he finds himself guilty of the very deed that he has solemnly foresworn. At last in desperation he utters a wild cry that comes to us across the far spaces of the years. It is a cry that was uttered countless millions of times before it became articulate upon Paul's lips. It has been uttered countless millions of times since then. What is this divided man saying? Just this: "O wretched man that I am! who shall deliver me?" It is a cry of sheer agony. It is wet with the tears of frustration and bitter heartache. I read recently of a man in excellent circumstances who committed suicide. The one reason he gave for his rash deed was this, "I am tired of fighting with myself."

3. Then this man being divided and wretched was also antisocial. He had separated himself from his fellows. He lived alone. Nobody could live with him. He was too thoroughly disagreeable. Warring with himself, he also warred with his fellows. And that is the case in some degree with all divided personalities. When we get to fighting with ourselves, we tend to fight with everyone else. When we go to pieces and explode over nothing, when we lose our tempers and slam doors and break up dishes, when we unsheath the sword of our tongue and stab right and left, we call it "nerves." We tell how poorly we slept last night, and how badly we feel. But often the real reason is that we lack inward harmony. We are at war with ourselves. Those torn by inward strife are generally hard to live with.

Being unable to live with his fellows, he was equally unable to live for them. He was, therefore, rendering no high service. He was too busy fighting with himself to have any time for the needs of others. In fact he was a liability rather than an asset, a hindrance rather than a help. Instead of making the burdens of others a bit lighter, he made them the more difficult. Inward conflict always prevents us from enjoying that leisure from ourselves that is necessary to our highest usefulness. In extreme cases, it does for us what it did for this demoniac: makes of us burdens rather than blessings; places us among those who lean rather than among those who lift.

4. Finally, this man was rated as an incurable. He had no hope for himself. Nobody had any hope for him. He was beyond help. "No man," the story says, "could tame him." Thus he was, when Jesus found him, divided, wretched, unable to live with and for his fellows. His is an extreme case, I know, very extreme. But there are few of us that cannot recognize our kinship to him. His needs, therefore, are our needs. What Jesus did for him, is what we long that he should do for us. What Jesus did for him, he surely can do for us. He is still able to save unto the uttermost.

II

Now, what did Jesus do for this demoniac?

1. He gave him a unified personality. That he can do for you and me. And we are not likely to reach

this high goal except through him. Certainly no man can ever find inward peace by yielding to his baser self. However fully he may seem to do so, he can never quite hush the voices that call from the heights. One of the most heartless women of all literature is Lady Macbeth. It would seem that the fiends had heard her prayer when she prayed that they would take her milk for gall. She could turn a loyal husband into a murdering traitor, seemingly without compunction. She could plot the death of a royal guest with devilish eagerness. She seems so utterly bad as to be past feeling. But such was not the case. In her waking moments, by sheer force of will, she could hide the terrible war that raged within. But not so in sleep. Then the conflict reveals itself as she seeks to cleanse her bloody hands, crying, "Out, damned spot! out, I say!"

We find the same truth in Jack London's *The Call of the Wild*—the best dog story, in my opinion, ever written. You remember the hero of the story, a splendid Newfoundland, named Buck. Now Buck was stolen from his home in the States and shipped to Alaska. Here he had to begin life anew. He was no longer a fireside pet. He was in a harsh world where in order to survive he had to learn to live according to the law of the club and fang. He became a husky, the pride of his new master. He was the best and strongest dog that ran the trail. But it came to pass by and by that his master became ill. As a result,

Buck had more leisure than was good for him. In his restlessness, he began to make excursions into the forest. At first these were brief, but gradually they became longer. Soon he was a good hunter, amply able to provide his own food. One night while on a hunt, he heard the howl of a wolf. At once his bristles went up. He was prepared to do battle with this wild thing that he felt was a natural enemy.

But as time went on, and the master continued ill, Buck became accustomed to these weird howls. One night, therefore, when he came face to face with this wolf whose mere howls had once raised his bristles and made him eager for battle, there was no conflict at all. Instead, the dog and the wolf put their noses together in token of the fact that they had buried the hatchet. Together they trotted through the aisles of the forest. Together they sat upon their haunches and howled to the distant stars as their ancestors had done centuries before. But always, with the breaking of the day, Buck would return home. At last, his master died and the big tie that bound him to the old life was broken. Soon after that, Buck began to run with the pack, seemingly the wildest wolf of them all. Yet, I daresay, he could never quite throw off all restraints of his former life. He could never become completely a wolf. Certainly this is true with ourselves. Therefore, to take the lower road is to be a divided personality to the end of the day.

But if we cannot find a unified personality by taking the lower road, we can find it by taking the higher. Here again we are not talking the language of theory, but of experience. Listen, once more, to Paul's anguished cry: "O wretched man that I am! who shall deliver?" Who indeed? Is there a satisfactory answer to that pressing question? There is. Paul answers it out of his own experiences: "I thank God through Jesus Christ." "There is therefore now no condemnation," no inner conflict. He has won as we may win, not by fighting against God, but by surrendering to him. This is what our Lord longs to do for every one of us. He gave and gives to those who fully surrender to him a unified personality.

2. Jesus gave to this tempest-tossed man inward peace. This is ever the result when we make our surrender to God full and complete. For when we have peace with God, we have peace within ourselves. Some years ago, I had a good friend, a minister, who made shipwreck of his faith. But after much inward conflict and much suffering, he turned back to the Christ that he had forsaken. One day in the course of an intimate conversation he told me his experience. "Have you recovered your old joy?" I asked him when the story was ended. "Better than that," he answered, "I have peace." That is our Lord's special legacy to every one of us: "Peace I leave with you, my peace I give unto you." This is one of the great things that Jesus did and does for those who give him a chance. Every

man's religion ought to give him that inward unity that has its issues in inward peace.

3. Jesus enabled this man to live with and for his fellows. He sent him back to the intimate circle of his own family. He sent him to those that we either love the best or hate the most. He sent him back to live with those with whom, till this experience, he could not live. A prominent physician who lives in another city came to see me the other day. He had but one object in his visit and that was to tell me his experience. After lean, gray years, Christ had come into his life. And among the winsome changes that Christ had wrought, this seemed to give him greatest joy, that he had enabled him to rebuild his broken home. And right here is one of the sharpest and highest tests of our religion. Does it make us easy to live with? If we are cantankerous and disagreeable, if everybody is sorry when we come and glad when we go, then however Christian we may think ourselves, we have missed the mark. Here is a test that every man ought to put to his religion: does it enable him to live with his fellows? A real Christian will certainly be able to meet this test.

Not only did Jesus enable this man to live with folks, he also enabled him to live for them. After this experience, this one-time demoniac had enough leisure from himself to care for those to whom he had once been indifferent, to help where he had been only a hindrance. He helped by what he did. He helped even more by what he was. There is no measuring the service that anyone renders, out of whose eyes looks the peace of a great discovery. "Go home," says Luke, "and show how great things the Lord hath done for thee." Show by what you do. Show by what you are.

Stanley Jones tells of a physician who found a stray dog with a broken leg. He took that dog to his home, put the leg in splints, and soon he was able to walk again. Then one day the seemingly ungrateful animal disappeared. The doctor was surprised that after so much kindness the dog should leave him. But he was away for just one night. The next morning there was a scratching at the door. When the doctor opened the door, there was the dog whose leg he had healed. But he was not alone. With him was another dog; lame, as he himself had been, but who had come at the invitation of his friend to be healed. It is as we are gripped by a passion to share that we build up our own personality, and the personalities of others as well.

III

Here, then, are some of the great things that our Lord can do for us. He can give us a unified personality. He can give us inward peace. He can enable us to live with and for our fellows. Of course, we are not claiming that he does all these instantly. But instantly he can make a beginning. How, then, are we to set about the realization of the great things that he longs to do for us?

Our first step is to be converted. That sounds a bit old-fashioned, I know. Conversion is a word that has lost cast among church people in recent years. But if it has lost in one group, it has gained in another. When the teachers and the preachers began to forsake it, then the psychologists took it up. Conversion is a fact. We may be born anew. We can be born from above or from below. I have seen both kinds, and so have you. Sometime ago I met a girl whom I had known in former years as a beautiful and devoted Christian. She had been a life volunteer. But how she had changed! Her face was different. There was a different look in her eyes. She carried herself in a different fashion. Her very walk had a swagger about it that was all but vulgar. What was the matter? She had become the intimate companion of a scoundrel, and in his fellowship she had been reborn, born from below.

But it is our privilege to be born from above. To do this, we must change the master passion of our lives from self to Another. We must become Christ-centered instead of self-centered. When Jesus passed by and said to Matthew, "Follow me," instantly he rose up and followed him. That was Matthew's spiritual birthday. That was his first step toward a unified personality. Why was this the case? Because he had found One whom with deeper and deeper loyalty he could call Master. What did Buck need to steady him when the spell of the wild was upon him? It was not a new kind of collar. It was not a stronger chain. What he needed and all he needed was a master. No dog ever arrives without a master, and this is just as true of a man as of a dog. What do you need with your soul as full of jarring discord as clashing instruments played out of tune? You need a master, The Master. Put the baton into his hands and he will change your discord into winsome music.

"I walked life's way with a careless tread,
I followed where comfort and pleasure led;
Till at last one day in a quiet place,
I met my Master face to face.

I'd reared my castles and built them high,
Till their turrets touched the blue of the sky.
And I'd vowed to rule with an iron mace—
When I met my Master face to face.

I met Him and knew Him and blushed to see
That His eyes in pity were fixed on me,
And I faltered and fell at His feet that day,
And my castles melted and vanished away.

They melted and vanished, and in their place
I saw naught else but the Master's face.
And I cried aloud, 'O make me meet
To follow the path of their bruised feet!'

My care is now for the souls of men.
I've lost my life to find it again,
E'er since that day, in a quiet place,
I met my Master face to face."

XI

THE HIGH ART OF NOT PAYING ATTENTION

*"But Jesus paid no atten-
tion to what they said."*

MARK 5: 36 (GOODSPEED)

"BUT JESUS PAID NO ATTENTION TO WHAT THEY
said." How magnificent! What high courage
it took to do that! What daring faith! But this was
what Jesus was constantly doing. There were always
voices clamoring for his attention to which he turned
a deaf ear. This is one of the secrets of his victorious
life. For instance, there were those who said that the
way to win was to be a "go-getter." But Jesus paid
no attention to what these said, declaring rather that
the meek should inherit the earth. There were multitudes that were contending that the sword was the
pathway to power. But Jesus paid no attention to
these, knowing that he that takes the sword shall perish
by the sword. There were those who warned him
earnestly against the cross, but Jesus paid no attention
to what they said. He rather accepted the cross in the
faith that, lifted up by it, he would draw all men unto

himself. Jesus had the high art of not paying attention developed to perfection.

The story of which our text is a part furnishes a striking example of this. A desperate man, Jairus by name, has come to him with a pressing request. He flings himself at the Master's feet and tells him that his little daughter is very ill, that even now she is swinging like a pendulum between life and death; but that there is still hope if he will only make haste to come and lay his hand upon her. Jesus cannot resist this pathetic appeal. At once he turns his face toward the house of suffering, and the heart of the anxious father fairly sings within him for joy. But there is an interruption. Jesus stops to deal with a needy woman who has touched him in the crowd. He is so leisurely about it that the father becomes almost frantic with fear. He can hardly keep from turning in hot anger upon the woman who has appealed to the Master at this inopportune time. "She could have waited," he doubtless says to himself. "But in the case of my child there can be no delay. It is now or never."

Then, what he so desperately fears actually happens. The Master has hardly resumed his journey when messengers come with devastating news. They seem quite officious, these messengers. They delight in telling news. They seem to be of those who would rather tell bad news than to tell none at all. There are those, you know, who would almost be willing to die themselves if they could be privileged to announce their own funerals. "Thy daughter is dead," they announce brutally. "Why trouble the Master any further?" At that the father's hope dies, and his face becomes wet with tears. "Too late," he whispers to himself bitterly. The crowd looks on in sympathetic silence. Perhaps the light even fades from the face of the woman who has just been healed, as she feels that her healing has been bought at too great a price.

But there is One present upon whom this fatal and final news has no effect at all—that is the Master. The same calm assurance looks out from his eyes. There is the same high courage in his voice. He acts in every way just as he would have acted had these messengers of despair never spoken. "Jesus paid no attention to what they said." On the contrary, he turns to the heartbroken father with this word of quiet confidence: "Be not afraid, only believe." Then, instead of apologizing, instead of saying, "I am sorry that I am too late," he continues his errand, never stopping till he has changed death into life, and the house of mourning into the house of laughter and joy. Thus Jesus won because he refused to pay any attention to the prophets of doom.

I

The first word that this story has for us is this: When we set out on any high quest, we, too, may count on meeting with prophets of disaster. There is absolutely no escape. Every Columbus who would discover a new continent must encounter those that will warn him of the futility and madness of his undertaking. Every astronomer that would think God's thoughts after Him must do so amidst the shrieks of those who tell him of the utter hopelessness of his enterprise. Every perfecter of a new invention must transform his dream into reality while the prophets of doom are doing their best to persuade that he cannot succeed. No man ever undertakes anything that is really worth doing but that somebody tells him that all hope of victory is dead, and that the only wise course is to quit and give over his dream.

This morning I am talking to some youth whose heart has been taken captive by Jesus Christ. You are out on the highest of all quests—the quest of Christlike character. You yearn to receive of his fullness. You long that the beauty of the Lord your God shall rest upon you as the sunshine rests upon the hills. You are praying hopefully:

> "O for the man to arise in me,
> That the man I am may cease to be."

And the wonder of it is that yours is an altogether possible achievement. But, I must warn you that there are many voices that speak to the contrary. Some of these voices come out of the past. They are the memories of your failures of yesterday. Some of them come from certain sane and practical folks that look upon Jesus as a dreamer. Others still are the unconscious

145

voices of nominal disciples whose faulty and shabby lives so proclaim their own spiritual poverty as to make Christianity seem either worthless or impossible. Every Pilgrim setting out for the Celestial City, with the cry of "Life, Life, Eternal Life!" upon his lips, is sure to have insistent voices calling after him, and bidding him stay.

The same will be true if you set yourself to render any high and worthful service. Perchance God has put it into your heart to be interested in boys and girls. You have come to believe in the supreme importance of right training. You are convinced that under such training, these young lives will blossom into the knowledge of Jesus Christ as naturally as a rose blooms at the kiss of the springtime. But, there are other voices that seek to upset this brave faith. They tell you that a child must become morally sick before it can be morally well, that it must be lost before it can be found. They affirm that the best equipment for being at home in the Father's house is a sojourn in the far country. They contend that prevention is a rather dull and unexciting something, little worthy of the power of God; that His might is shown at its best, not in prevention, but in cure.

But, while clinging to our faith that our biggest opportunity is with childhood and youth, we must not despair of those who have gone into the far country. Cynical voices, of course, will tell us that the crooked can never be made straight. They will warn us of the utter impossibility of reaching certain damaged souls. A friend pointed out one such to me some time ago. He warned me of the foolishness of speaking to him. I took him at his word till I was practically forced to speak by a combination of circumstances over which I had no control. Then, to my amazement, I found him with a sense of desperate need. I found, also, that his heart was as tender almost as the heart of a child. But I warn you that you will never undertake the introducing of one single soul to Christ but that there will be numerous voices that tell you that you cannot succeed.

Then, there are some who are looking forward to a world where economic injustice shall be done away. You are dreaming of a time when all race hatreds shall be healed. There are those who are even daring to look forward to, and to work toward, a warless world. But, how many voices there are that seek to deter us from dreaming these daring dreams! They wail, "Human nature can never be changed. Man is a savage under his skin and always will be. While there is more talk of a warless world today than in any other time in human history, there were never before such frantic peacetime preparations for war." Thus it is that all who are bent on any high quest must constantly encounter those who tell us that our hope is dead, and that there is no use in making any further effort.

147

II

What are we to do about this?

1. We can give ear to these prophets of despair. But if we do this, one of two tragic results will doubtless follow. We shall either become half-hearted in our efforts, or quit altogether. Of course to become half-hearted is to fail. A double-minded man is unreliable in all his ways. Years ago, when we were boys, my brother and I were making our way to a certain goal at the back side of our farm. We came to what was normally a rivulet so narrow that one might step across it. But there was a rise in the river, and the flood waters had backed up this little stream until it was now some twelve feet wide. But we would not be turned back. We, therefore, decided to jump across it. I was to jump first. I took a good running start and could have succeeded easily enough, but just before I made the effort my brother changed his mind and shouted, "Stop, stop, stop!" Instead of paying no attention to what he said, I listened to him, with the result that I made a half-hearted jump, and hit right in the middle of the stream. There are many in the Church that are failing in the same fashion. They have not surrendered. They have become half-starved. They are, therefore, possessed of a religion that satisfies neither God nor man.

Then, sometimes these prophets of doom cause us to give over our high quest altogether. There is a significant verse tucked away in the Gospel of St. Mark: "There followed him a certain young man, having a linen cloth cast about his naked body; and the young men laid hold of him and he left the cloth in their hands, and fled from them, naked." It is Thursday evening in Jerusalem. Some Roman soldiers, followed by a mob, are hurrying down one of the narrow streets of the city. In a certain house on that street is a young man who is preparing for bed, or who is just from the bath. He hears the tumult. His curiosity is aroused. He opens the door to a slit and asks what is happening. "We are going out to Gethsemane to arrest Jesus of Nazareth," is the reply. By this news the young man is transformed. He knows Jesus. He has wished to follow him, but possibly has never quite dared. But, now a noble madness is upon him. Not taking time to dress, he grabs a sheet and wraps it about his body, and flees into the night to die, if need be, by the side of Jesus. But something happens to break the spell. He runs into a group of young fellows who see the madness of his high quest. He comes to himself, leaves the cloth in their hands, and flees naked into the night. His tragedy was that he paid attention to the wrong voices.

This is the case with entirely too many today. That was a pathetic wail that a certain group of ministers sent out the other day. They proclaimed the utter bankruptcy of Protestantism, and warned that our one hope was to flee to Rome for refuge. Of course this does not mean that what they said is true. It only means that these have been so attentive to the prophets of despair that they have become unmanned, and have given over the fight. This is also the tragic plight of not a few in the pew. Some time ago a layman said in my presence, "The devil has my church, therefore I am not going any more." But a robust old saint, who belonged to the same church, answered, "He may have your pew—I never see you in it; but he hasn't mine yet. I occupy it every Sunday." The trouble with this quitter was that he had failed to cultivate the high art of not paying attention.

2. But we may follow the example of our Lord and pay no attention to these sad wails. That has been the method of every man that has ever made a success of any worthy enterprise. When as a young chap I was preparing to get married, I confided the good news to a few of my mature friends. I expected their faces to light up and their eyes to sparkle. But, to my amazement, this did not happen. For the most part they merely looked sad and undertook to warn me of the risk I was running. But, thank God, I paid no attention to what they said. A man told me recently, with a voice of despair, that with the depression, and with the death of so many of our older members, our church was headed for the rocks. But instead of bursting into tears and getting ready to move, I paid absolutely no attention to him. This is a habit I have

tried, with some degree of success, to cultivate throughout my ministry.

I had to begin this habit early. After I had been preaching for only five months I was sent to follow a pastor who had been distressingly popular. The congregation was angry at him for leaving and at me for coming. Soon after my arrival, a gentleman came with this pleasing announcement: "Mr. A. is going to quit this church." "Why?" I asked. "Because you are not big enough for the job, and he is not going to stay here and see it topple about his ears." A few days later another came with a similar message with regard to Mr. B. Then, another with regard to Mr. C. Being quite young, I had an idea that these ought to help all the more since things were so shaky. But they did not think so, and I was naturally greatly distressed. But even a worm will turn sometimes. So, after listening to these voices of doom for some six weeks I decided to quit it. The next Sunday I stepped into my pulpit, held up some paper, and said: "All who desire to leave this church because it is dying may have their certificates at the close of this service."

Then, I continued: "This week I witnessed a scene that heartened me greatly. I saw a man buy a bottle of soda pop. (It was one of the old-fashioned kind that opened with a loud noise, a bit like the report of a revolver.) When he had uncorked it, it began to splutter and bubble furiously. I could hardly keep from shouting at the fellow, though he was a stranger,

'Drink it, man, drink it, else you will lose every drop of it.' But he waited and watched with placid indifference. By and by it grew quiet. Then I looked, and, to my amazement, the bottle seemed just as full as at the beginning. Nothing had escaped but a few bubbles and a little wind. 'Now,' I said, 'you bubbles and wind, come and get your letters.'" And not one came, and the situation was saved. There are always those who wail, but we can refuse to listen.

III

But how can we help paying attention? How did Jesus do it? He did not do so by merely stopping his ears. There are those who seek to silence these clamorous voices by a monkish withdrawal from the world. That is entirely futile. If you have a radio, you can keep it turned off and thereby refuse to hear anything objectionable. But, in that case, your radio is entirely useless. The better way is to tune out the worthless by tuning in the worthful. The air is full of voices. You can hear the choicest of arias, if you desire. But, if your taste runs in another direction, you can listen to that masterpiece, "The Music Goes Round and Round." The air is also full of voices that call to faith and courage and of voices that call to doubt and despair. In the old Genesis story, we read, "God said," and we read, also, "The serpent said." God is still broadcasting, and so is the serpent. It is our high privilege to tune in on God and thereby hush these lower voices into silence. This has been the way of the saints through all the centuries.

Take Abraham, for example. You will notice that when the writers of the New Testament want to tell us what religion is at its best they keep turning back to this strange old hero, who left Ur of the Chaldees at God's call to journey into the unknown. He was lured on by the promise that he should become the father of a great nation. But the swift years slipped by, and nothing came of it. Now, he is an old man, and Sarah has passed from life's springtime into withered winter. How the devastations that the years have wrought shriek at him! How insistently they say, "Look at your age-worn body, and see how impossible your dream is." But Abraham paid no attention to what they said. He was too intent upon the voice of God. "He considered not his own body, now dead . . . but was strong in faith, giving glory to God, being fully persuaded that what He had promised, He was able also to perform."

Some years ago one of my dearest friends, who increased the loveliness of heaven recently by passing into it, told me this intimate and personal experience. He did not tell it in public. He was a man of beautiful spiritual modesty. "Once," he said, "my little girl was desperately ill with membranous croup. Late one afternoon I lifted her into my arms to rest her a bit. She looked pathetically into my face and said: 'Daddy, am I going to get well?' 'Darling,' I answered, 'Daddy doesn't know. I am hoping that you will.' Then," he continued, "it came to me that I might know, for there was One willing to tell me. I then gave her into the arms of the nurse and hurried to my place of prayer. I did not ask for the life of my child; I only asked to know the will of God in the matter. As I prayed I became sure that she was going to recover. I hurried home to tell my wife the good news. The night came on, we went to bed as usual, and I was soon asleep. How long I slept, I do not know. But when I awoke my wife and the nurse were bending over the baby's bed, and I heard the mother say, 'Is she dead?' " Now, there was a test. What did this man do who had gone to sleep so sure of the recovery of his child? Did he spring from bed frantic with fear? Did he conclude at once that God had let him down? That question, "Is she dead?"—no voice could have been more disconcerting than that. But this strong saint turned his face to the wall without a word and went back to sleep. In other words, when doubt and despair clamored for his attention, he paid no attention to what they said. The next morning, he learned the reason for the mother's question. The child had been breathing so quietly that she feared she was not breathing at all. But what she had taken for death was in reality the return of life.

"Faith, mighty faith, the promise sees,
  And looks to God alone;
Laughs at impossibilities,
  And cries, 'It shall be done.' "

XII

HOW TO TALK TO YOURSELF

*"What she said to herself
was this . . ."*

MATTHEW 9: 21 (MOFFATT)

I

HERE IS A WOMAN WHO IS HAVING A CONVERSA-
tion with herself. We all do that at times, and
what we say to ourselves is vastly important. Of
course, we recognize how tremendously we are influenced by the words of others. A wrong word has
often meant the utter marring of a life. Many a child
foolishly rebuked for stupidity, for instance, by a
parent or a teacher has gone out under that influence
to a lifelong battle with an inferiority complex. Words
of abuse have so convinced many another child of his
badness, that, in utter discouragement, he has gone to
a life of wrongdoing, and, at times, to one of positive
crime. There is, in fact, no measuring the possible
harm of one wrong word.

But if wrong words can do endless harm, right
words can do endless good. "A word fitly spoken,"

155

said a wise man, "is like apples of gold in pictures of silver." There are words that have power to grip us by the shoulder and shake us out of our sleep, power to turn indifference into wide-eyed awareness. There are words that tell us of the hidden gold that is in our own undeveloped personalities. There are words that have skill to break up the drought of the soul and set the fields of the heart to flowering. I am thinking of a man now, a successful minister, who as a boy was so careless and indifferent that he was all but the despair of his family. But when tragedy came into the home in the death of his father, Jim chanced to overhear an older brother comforting and encouraging his mother. It so happened that the word he overheard, not meant for his own ears, ran something like this, "You can count on Jim. He is gifted. He will certainly make something some day." And Jim thinks with gratitude of that word to this day. It thrilled him like a trumpet call, and sent him out with a keen zest for battle.

Then when things have gone wrong and life has crashed into ruins, how much the word of a friend can often do for us! When we walk in slippery places, when we need a strong staff upon which to lean, when we need a sturdy something against which to lean our backs, we find that something oftentimes to be a word fitly spoken. "Your words have kept men on their feet," was a compliment, a rather grudging compliment I think, to Job from one of his comforters. Few bigger things than that could be said about any man.

We ought to be exceedingly careful what we say to each other, for our words have power to hurt or power to help. They have power to kill or power to make alive. It is next to impossible to overestimate their might for weal or for woe.

But, if what we say to each other is important, what we say to ourselves is even more important. Tell me what you habitually say to yourself, and I will tell you the kind of man you are. Tell me what you say to yourself, and I will tell you what you are likely to become. Take the Rich Farmer of whom Jesus spoke, for instance. He was a successful man, honorable and upright. No doubt, he was a pillar in church and state. But how little his neighbors really knew about him! We should never have known him at all if we had not overheard a conversation that he had with himself. If we had only overheard him talking to his minister, we might not have known him. If we listened as he talked to his wife, we might still have been in doubt. But when we hear him as he talks to himself, we know him for what he is.

Listen to him! He is looking out over a fertile farm that is growing golden with abundant harvest. The rain and the sunshine have come in just the right proportions. He himself has enjoyed excellent health. His fellow-workers have been energetic and faithful. Therefore, as he looks over his bumper crops that are far beyond his own needs, he begins to talk to himself. As we listen, we naturally expect him to say something like this: "God has been most gracious to me. Those who have been in my employ have been very faithful. I have made far more than I need. Out of sheer gratitude, I am eager to use some of this abundant harvest for the common good."

But unfortunately, that is not what he said. As we listen to him, we learn that he has no slightest appreciation of the help of either God or man. He has no sense of obligation. His one thought is how he can conserve all his wealth for himself. He knows no better bank in which to deposit his gains than a barn. "I will pull down my barns, and build greater; and there will I bestow all my fruits and my goods. And I will say to my soul, Soul, thou hast much goods laid up for many years; eat, drink, have a good time." It was by such talk as this that he showed himself to be an utter fool, a pathetic moral imbecile, with no more appreciation of life's finer values than a pig would have for a sunrise. We know him for what he is by what he said to himself.

II

Now what did this woman say to herself? She might have said some very distressing things, and have told the strictest truth. Life had dealt very harshly with her. In the springtime of her years, she had become the victim of a shamefaced disease. It was a disease that made her morally unclean. It was a disease that had robbed her of almost every worthy prize.

It had robbed her of about the only vocation open to women in that day—the vocation of wifehood and motherhood. This heavy handicap seems to have been softened in some measure, at the beginning, by the fact that she was a woman of independent means. But she was a resolute woman. When her sickness came upon her, she determined that she would not die without a fight. If there was any cure to be had, she would have it. Therefore, for twelve long years she went to one physician after another. But these relieved her of nothing but her money. Today she is a little more faded, a little more weak, a little nearer the cemetery than ever before. And to the burden of her sickness has now been added the burden of poverty.

How easy, under these circumstances, it would have been for her to have had a grudge against life. "I am suffering," she might have told herself, "and that through no fault of my own. I have not been a coward. I have tried hard to be well. I have spent my very all. But there is no hope. The cards are stacked against me. Life has cheated me. I no longer believe that there is a good God back of the universe. If there were, He could not allow me to suffer so deeply and so needlessly." This would have been an easy conversation for this woman. But if she had talked to herself in this fashion, she would either have sunk into hopeless invalidism, or have chucked the whole business and jumped out the window.

What then did she say? She said: "I am sick, it is

true, but I am not dead yet. I have seemingly exhausted all of my resources, but that is not exactly the case. A new Personality has come upon the horizon, Jesus by name. They tell me that his hands have cunning to work cures that none other can work. I have heard that the very might of God is in him. Maybe he can help me. At least I am going to try him. I am going to him with the conviction that if I do my part, he will do his. If I win, I win. If I fail, after having done my best, I shall certainly not be any worse off than I am. But I will not fail. If I touch but the tassel of his robe, I shall be healed." Thus this brave woman talked to herself.

III

Now what was the outcome of this daring conversation?

1. By thus talking to herself, she kept alive her hope. By thus talking to herself, she kept her courage from dying utterly. Of course, you know that when we lose heart and hope, we are through. If you think you are licked, you are. If you believe you are whipped, then you are whipped. If you have been knocked down flat and have convinced yourself that you can never get up, you are likely to lie there and whine the rest of your days. If you have made up your mind to die, then die you will, in spite of all that physicians can do for you. But no man is ever quite beyond the possibility of help till he concedes defeat within his

own soul. This woman talked to herself in such a fashion as to keep alive her courage and hope.

2. By keeping up her hope, she was able to keep up the struggle. When we lose hope, we stop trying. That is true in every department of human endeavor. Tell yourself you cannot hold your job, and you are likely to quit even trying to hold it. Tell yourself that you can never be well, and you will give over the fight for health. Tell yourself that the life abundant is not for you, that all Christ's wealthy promises are but empty nothings so far as you are concerned, and your soul will forget its high quest and accept failure without a struggle. There are multitudes today who no longer make any serious effort at being Christians, not because Christlikeness no longer appeals to them, but because its attainment seems so impossible. But as long as we hope, we can keep up the struggle.

One day, therefore, when the exciting news is brought that Jesus is in her neighborhood, she resolves to go to him. But she meets with difficulties. Multitudes of curious people are thronging him. They are not crusaders. They are just vagrants. They are, therefore, in the way. But in the face of opposition, she keeps encouraging herself with this word, "If I may touch but his clothes, I shall be healed." So she struggles on till at last her finger touches the tassel of his robe. At once she is healed—not by her finger, but by her faith. Thus by talking to herself in terms of faith, she finds the bodily healing for which she seeks. Not only so, but she finds what is far more priceless, healing of heart. As she kneels at the Master's feet, he bids her go in peace.

IV

Now, what are we saying to ourselves? Some of us are talking to ourselves in a fashion that makes only for our weakening.

There are those, for instance, who are soothing themselves by enervating alibis. Perhaps you are conscious of the fact that you have not played the game very well. You have been untrue to your convictions. You have flung away your former ideals. You have chucked your moral standards. You can be at home today in a companionship that once would have disgusted you. You have learned to take on the color of your crowd as readily as a chameleon. "It is true that I drank a bit at the party the other night. It is true also that I have pronounced convictions against drinking. But everybody else drank, therefore I went with the crowd. What else could I do? Surely you could not expect me to be peculiar. I played the weakling and the fool, but it was not my fault. It was the best I could do under the circumstances." Thus, some of us weaken ourselves by soft alibis.

Then, others of us weaken ourselves by baby talk. Life has dealt us some rather hefty blows. We have not had as good opportunities as some of our friends. We have handicaps that it seems impossible for us to overcome. Therefore, we tell ourselves that we are pitiable creatures, shut out from any possibility of playing the game well. If we only had a better chance, we should doubtless do big things. But under the circumstances, anything worthwhile is impossible. Therefore, we coddle ourselves and kill our possibilities by self-pity. This we do, while all about us are those in far worse circumstances who are fighting their way to victory.

Then there are not a few who talk themselves into doubt, and even into positive unbelief. A certain psalmist knew a man of this kind. God became an embarrassment to him. Just as a son of the parsonage who is going wrong is often angered by being reminded that he is a minister's son, so this man was angered and annoyed by being reminded, even by himself, that he was a son of the Most High. The fact of such a relationship laid demands upon him that he was unwilling to meet. He came to see with increasing clearness that he had either to get rid of God or give up the selfish life that he was living. Lacking the courage to change, he decided to ditch God.

And how did he go about it? Just as millions of others have done. He had a conversation with himself. He told himself frankly that God did not exist. "The fool hath said in his heart," that is to himself, "there is no God." Having gotten rid of God, he continued his conversation to its inevitable conclusion: "Since there is no God, I am not really a child of the King.

I am the product of blind forces that had no prevision of what they were creating. I am a child of the mud. I can now go my own filthy way and still be quite worthy of such a sire. Thus not a few, lacking the courage to live up to the demands of a vital faith, talk themselves into unbelief.

But if it is possible to talk ourselves toward defeat, it is also possible to talk ourselves toward victory. If you can lessen your chances of health by forever telling' yourself that you are sick, so you can help yourself toward health by talking encouragingly to yourself. This is especially true of nervous diseases. I knew a man some years ago who had a bad nervous breakdown. Now the psychologists tell us that all such breakdowns are subconsciously desired. That is, we get into a hard situation where we tell ourselves that there is no good way out but to get sick. Then we proceed to act accordingly. Be that as it may, such sickness is a most depressing experience. Our nerves are good liars. They tell us all sorts of horrible stories: That we have not slept, even when we have, and will never sleep again; that we are the greatest sufferers in the world, and always will be. So it was with this gentleman: once sunny, he became about as cheerful as a dust storm.

But one day he took himself in hand. He told himself plainly that something had to be done, and that he was the one to do it. "You are going to quit moping about, looking like a chicken with a bad case of cholera," he told himself; "you are going to brace up and get well." And, as Ripley would say, "believe it or not," he began from that day to improve. Soon he was enjoying vigorous health. Of course, this would not work with every kind of sickness, but I doubt if there is any that it would not improve. Then, too, such a course would make it easier for the sick body to live with himself. It would also make it easier for others to live with him.

Now, if talking to ourselves aright is a help toward physical recovery, it is certainly not less so in the realm of the moral and spiritual. You remember that tenderly beautiful story that Jesus told. It is of the graceless laddie who went away from home. This boy was eager to be on his own. He desired to get some place where he could be independent of his father. So he went into a far country. Here he ran through with his wealth and came down to utter poverty. He had to go out seeking for a job, and the best that he could find was the herding of a bunch of swine. The whole adventure had proved bitterly disappointing. And now, we find him in the hogpen, having a talk with himself. Let us draw near and hear what he has to say. His conversation might have run something like this:

"My father is a graceless old fossil. The mess I am in is all his fault. He ought to have refused to have given me my share of goods. He might have known that something like this would happen. Why did God make it possible for a man to sin anyway? Why did He give us the power of choice? Of course, I know that the price a man pays for the capacity to climb is his capacity to go down; that if he is capable of doing right, he must also be capable of doing wrong. If he has the possibilities of heaven in him, he must also have the possibilities of hell. But while I can't think of a better way, this one is all wrong. Then there is that brother of mine, cold as ice and hard as nails. I might never have left home but for him. And what fine friends I've had! They helped me spend my money, then threw me to the hogs. Everybody has played me false. Therefore, I am just going to lie down and die. Then they'll all be sorry they treated me as they have."

Many a man has talked to himself after this fashion, and, thus talking, has slipped into the pit. But this prodigal did infinitely better. What really did he say? Listen: When he came to himself, he said: "I was an awful fool to have left my father as I did. But it was my own choice. I have nobody to blame but myself. I thought I was going to have a great time down here. I looked forward to an endless round of feasts. But what I have really found is hunger to the point of starvation. Now, though my friends have thrown me down, and though my brother will likely not give me welcome, I am going back. There is one who will welcome me. He has the tenderest of hearts. His very servants have bread enough and to spare. He will not refuse me, unworthy as I am, for I am his son. Therefore, I am going to rise and go to my father. I am going openly. I left openly. I am going back the same way. I am not going to spare myself. And when I get back, I am going to tell my father the plain truth, just as I am now telling it to myself."

That wholesome conversation got action. Having thus told himself the truth, he picked himself up and turned his face toward home. And you know the happy ending: "When he was yet a great way off, his father saw him and had compassion on him, and ran and fell on his neck and kissed him." Then his father gave him the best robe and the best possible feast and the best possible home. He gave him also, not the place of a servant, but of a son. And so God will do for us, if we will tell ourselves the truth about ourselves, and act accordingly. He is our Father and is eager to give us his best. Frankly face your own spiritual poverty. But as you do so, face the further fact that you may be rich. Tell yourself that He that spared not His own Son, but delivered him up for us all, will also with him freely give us all things. Thus talking to yourself, you, too, will find a place at the feast of the fullness of life.

XIII

OVERSTATING OUR POVERTY

"We have here but five loaves, and two fishes."

MATTHEW 14: 17

THESE DISCIPLES ARE OBVIOUSLY WORRIED. THEY have come out to this lakeside for a bit of rest. They have come hoping for a little private picnic with their Master. But their hopes were doomed to disappointment. The keel of their boat has hardly touched the shore before they begin to be besieged by a great multitude of troublesome people. These take up all their Master's time, so that they have not a single moment alone with him. The hours are hectic and toilsome, even beyond the ordinary. At last, the shadows are lengthening and the day is almost over. Still these troublesome creatures refuse to leave. By this time, they have become a serious problem. Having been all day without food, they are hungry. But there is no bread to be had in this lonely spot. Besides, if there were, these disciples have no money with which to buy.

Then, to make matters worse, Jesus seems entirely

unconscious of their plight. He is so busy with his teaching that he seems to have forgotten where he is. He is so taken up with the work of healing that he has lost all track of time. They love this Master of theirs. They have no end of admiration for him. But they do not quite trust him. They feel that he requires a good bit of managing. In fact, at present he is more of a liability than an asset. Therefore, there is nothing for them to do but to take matters into their own hands and make the best of a hard situation.

I

Now this is a very human story. It is also very modern. It belongs not simply to a far-off yesterday, it belongs also to today. Life is constantly bringing us both as individuals and as groups into trying and perplexing situations. Again and again we come to veils through which we cannot see and doors to which we find no key. Over and over we are met by demands for which our resources seem entirely inadequate. Some of us are facing such trying situations even now. And, sad to say, our religion does not seem to be doing very much for us. Even our Lord appears to be either totally unmindful of our pathetic plight, or as inadequate to its demands as ourselves. We, as these disciples, feel that the whole burden must rest upon our shoulders and ours alone. No wonder, therefore, we are worried. But what are we to do about it? What did these disciples resolve to do? They resolved to escape. That was a resolution that had in it very little heroism, and none too much good sense. But it is one that we ourselves have tried again and again. We seek to escape by various methods.

1. We employ that of these disciples. They simply stood from under. They "passed the buck." "Send the multitude away," they ordered. "Whatever is done for these hungry men and women will have to be done by somebody else." How familiar that is! There are thousands in this city, for instance, who believe in the Church, who are altogether friendly to it, who would not think of living where there were no churches. But what do they do about it? Naked nothing. They simply stand from under. They allow all the responsibility for their support to rest upon other shoulders. We want a clean city, a wholesome place for our boys and girls to grow to manhood and womanhood. But we refuse to take any part of the responsibility for building such a city.

What a human story is that in the second book of Kings! A small boy has gone out into the field to be with his father. It is harvest time and the day is hot. The blazing sun is too much for the boy. He becomes desperately ill. In his agony, he hurries to his father, crying, "My head, my head." Now, what does this father do? Does he gather him in his arms and do his best to minister to him? Not at all. He does what too many busy fathers have done through the centuries. He "passes the buck." "Take him," he says, "to his mother." But it is not fathers alone who take this cowardly and selfish course. There are multitudes, both men and women, who are seeking to meet their trying situations by simply shirking them or putting the responsibility upon others.

2. Then there are those who seek to escape their hard situations by running. There was a psalmist once who found himself in a situation that literally bristled with difficulties. Old friends had proven unfaithful. Treachery stalked abroad. War and rebellion were in the land. He was sorely troubled. Then he saw a dove rise on swift wings and fly away into the far-flung vault of blue. He watched her as she became first a speck and then faded into utter nothingness. Then he wiped his eyes that had grown moist, partly from looking upon the brightness without, but more from looking upon the darkness within, and he muttered something to himself through lips that were white and drawn with pain. What was he saying? This: "I wish I had wings like a dove. How soon would I fly away and be at rest."

How many have felt like that! There was a certain preacher named Jeremiah who had an appointment that he did not like. His congregation almost drove him to desperation. But one day he thought of a possible remedy. "I wish," he said, "I had a lodging place in the wilderness for wayfaring men, that I might leave my people and go from them." There was another prophet who was appointed to Nineveh, but just

as Jeremiah, he did not like his appointment. Therefore, he resolved to run away: "Jonah rose up to flee
unto Tarshish from the presence of the Lord." Faced
by demands that they felt themselves unable or unwilling to meet, these prophets wanted to escape by
running.

But this desire to run is by no means confined to
the prophets. We have all felt it. A member of my
church, who was having more domestic difficulties than
he knew what to do with, said, "My best friend is my
hat. Whenever things get too stormy at home, I seize
my hat and make my escape." There is a tragically
large number who are trying to escape their domestic
difficulties by running even to the divorce court. But
to run off from a situation just because it is hard is
always cowardly, and often futile. This is the case
because the trouble from which we are flying is often
within ourselves. Of course, we cannot escape that by
running. We take it with us. Milton's Satan found
that out:

"Infinite woe and infinite despair:
Which way I fly is hell; myself am hell!"

3. Then there are those who in their eagerness to
escape fling out of life altogether. We have about
22,000 suicides in this country every year. Why do
these take this desperate course? Why do they thus
dare to quit before the whistle blows? It is generally
because they find themselves face to face with trying

situations to which they feel inadequate. They are met by problems they have not the gallantry to try to solve. Of course, as a matter of fact, there are always tens of thousands in situations just as trying as theirs who go bravely forward. Challenged by stark impossibilities, they refuse to surrender, but see the battle through with honor. These, therefore, who slip out of life by the back door do so, not because they must, but because they have not the heroism to face their trying task. Suicide is for them a way of escape from a situation that they have not the gallantry to meet.

II

Why did these disciples seek to escape? It was not because they were altogether selfish. It was not because they were entirely indifferent to the needs of this hungry crowd. They were not indifferent. They were genuinely concerned. No more did they seek to escape because they felt that the physical needs of this multitude were no business of theirs. They were not among those who believe that the one concern of the Church is the spiritual needs of their fellows. Why then, I repeat, did they undertake to send these hungry folks away to shift for themselves? There is but one answer. It was because they felt that there was nothing else to do. There was no other way out. They were plain, practical men, not fanatical dreamers. Therefore, there was nothing to do but to face the ugly facts in the case and act accordingly.

Now what were the facts? When they found themselves face to face with this hungry crowd, with commendable sanity they took account of their resources. Upon so doing, they found those resources entirely inadequate. Then, with a stupidity that has a striking resemblance to good sense, they brought in the following report: "Having made a thorough canvass of our assets, we find that we have but five loaves and two fishes." Having thus faced their pathetic poverty, they quite naturally proceeded to pass the following resolution: "Whereas we are in a desperate situation to which we are entirely inadequate, be it resolved that there is but one sane course open to us, and that is to send the multitude away." How modern it is! It is quite evident that these disciples, though willing to serve, were at once hopeless and helpless in the presence of the pressing demands of the hour.

Why was this the case? It was because they had so grossly overestimated their poverty. "We have here," they said, "but five loaves and two fishes." "Really, is that all?" it seems someone would have asked. "Does that sum up *all* your resources? Do you have no wealth at all except these five loaves and two little dried fish?" "That is all," they answer stupidly. "But how about your Lord and Master?" this questioner might have persisted. "Has he ever failed you? Has he ever let you down? Is it not possible that he might enable you to see this desperate situation through with honor? Instead of looking solely at your

174

material wealth, why not look to him of whom it is written, 'He shall not fail nor be discouraged'?'' But they, refusing to reckon with their matchless Master, headed toward utter defeat.

Now, I am convinced that this brings us face to face with the greatest weakness of the modern church. We have far saner views of the Bible than our fathers had. I believe we have a clearer conception of what Jesus is trying to do in our world. I am convinced that our beliefs, for the most part, are more intellectually respectable. But in spite of this, we are sadly lacking in dynamic. Intellectually sane, we are often morally and spiritually impotent. In our efforts to preach to the scientific mind, we have been frightened to death of anything that smacks of the supernatural. Sometimes, therefore, we have left God out altogether. Even when we have suffered Him to remain in the picture, we have too often conceived of Him as so imprisoned in His own universe as to be all but powerless. Now, "Men are like the Gods they serve," Carlyle tells us. A mighty God makes mighty men. But our God is not vastly able, therefore our power is anything but impressive.

How up-to-date is this old story! The prophet Elisha has a price on his head. He is now spending the night in the city of Dothan. While the city sleeps, a hostile army surrounds it. The one purpose of this army is to capture the prophet. Now Elisha's servant is totally unaware of their danger. When, therefore, he goes out in the morning and discovers that an army is encircling them, he is overcome with fear and despair. "Alas, my master," he cries desperately; "how shall we do?" At once the prophet begins to pray. But he does not pray for deliverance as this servant expects him to do. He rather prays that the eyes of this frightened servant might be opened. When that prayer was answered, when this timid man comes to realize something of the infinite resources of God, his fear gives way to faith and courage. So it was for these disciples when they realized that they did not have to meet this trying situation alone. This day, that seemed destined to end in defeat, ended in victory.

III

How did it come about? The difference was made by their Lord. He was the way out for them, as he is for us. Behold the difference that he makes!

1. These disciples discovered with amazement that their Master had a plan. "Himself knew what he would do," John tells us. How heartening! Then this emergency has not taken him by surprise. He is neither frightened nor worried by it. He has foreseen it and made his plans for meeting it. Therefore, the whole responsibility is not on their weak shoulders. It is on the shoulders of One infinitely wise and infinitely able. Now, this heartening realization is needed by ourselves. We, too, need to know that God has a plan for His world. He has neither forgotten nor

forsaken it. He is now in the midst of it, moving to meet its desperate needs. He will never give over till the kingdoms of the world have become the Kingdoms of our Lord and His Christ.

Not only are we to believe that God has a plan for His world, we are also to believe that He has a plan for each individual soul. Horace Bushnell preached a sermon years ago on the subject, "Every Life a Plan of God." A better statement of the case would possibly be "God Plans Every Life." "As the Father hath sent me into the world," said Jesus, "even so send I you into the world." This does not mean, of course, that God has fixed a certain groove in which we are to run whether we are willing or not. We can thwart God's plan for our lives if we so desire. It simply means that He is the Architect and we are the builders. He makes the plan; we are to execute that plan. To do this, to fulfill God's plan in our lives, is the ultimate in victorious living.

2. Not only did these disciples discover that their Master had a plan and a program for the situation, they discovered also that his was a positive and constructive plan. When these disciples made their plan, it was purely negative. They sought only to send the multitude away—to stand from under. "This situation is bad, therefore we must get out of it," they said. But, that is not our Lord's way. He rather says, "The situation is bad, therefore change it; make it over into what it ought to be." In spite of this, there are many

good people today who believe that God has no better plan for the saving of this world than deserting it. They believe that things are going from bad to worse till they become utterly and hopelessly rotten. Then the Lord will rapture away the little handful of saints that may yet remain, and leave the world to welter in its own ruin. That seems to me to be pessimism at its worst. Our Lord is not here to desert, but to save.

That also is the reason for our being here. Years ago, when I was a teacher in a certain town, I undertook to establish a public library. My first move was to invite my old teacher, Sawney Webb, to deliver a lecture in the opera house. By charging a small admission, I was sure I could get the first few hundred dollars for this undertaking. I advertised thoroughly and looked toward the big event with high hopes. But I was doomed to disappointment. The audience was shamefully small. As we were going back to the hotel after the lecture, I was bewailing the lack of interest in matters worthwhile on the part of the people. But my wise old teacher made this reply: "Son, if everybody were just as they should be, and every situation just as it ought to be, the Lord wouldn't need you and me. But because they are not, that is the reason that we are here." "I pray not," said Jesus, "that thou shouldst take them out of the world." It is not ours to run away; it is ours to stand in our place and thus change our moral doubts into positive convictions.

Our Lord not only calls upon us to do this, but he

makes us equal to the task. "They need not depart,"
said Jesus. This was the case for at least two reasons:
First, because Jesus was present and fully adequate to
the situation. He always is. "He is the same yesterday, today, and forever." He is able now as then to
supply every need of ours. Then, "they need not depart," because there was no hope elsewhere. And that
holds true still. If Christ has not the answer for our
bewildered day, then there is no answer. If he cannot
show us the way out as individuals and as a world,
then there is none who can. All schemes for human
betterment that leave him out of consideration are
doomed to disappointment. Multitudes, both within
and without the Church, are today coming to realize
that there is none other Name under heaven given
among men whereby we must be saved.

3. These disciples came to understand the simplicity
of Jesus' method. The needs of this multitude were
met. "All ate and had enough," the story tells us.
How was it brought about? It was not brought about
by Jesus alone. No more was it brought about by the
disciples alone. It was brought about by Jesus and
his disciples working together. That is how all great
tasks are accomplished. When Paul was explaining
how Christianity was sweeping over the Roman world,
he used these words: "I planted, Apollos watered; but
it was God who made it grow." That is, the Kingdom
of God is to come, a new world is to be made, by God
and man working together.

This means, of course, that in the making of this new world God is dependent upon man. He walks to His missions upon human feet. He ministers through human hands. He speaks His message through human lips. If anything, therefore, is to be done in our day toward the saving of our humanity, if anything is to be done toward building a better home life, a stronger and more spiritual church life, a more just social order, we are the ones that are going to have to do it. He is the vine, we are the branches. The vine has no way of bearing fruit except through the branches. That simply means that God has no way of bringing in His Kingdom except through you and me. He is absolutely dependent upon ourselves.

But if this is true, it is certainly equally true that we are absolutely dependent upon God. How strangely prone we are to forget this! How prone we are to take the whole task of building a new world upon ourselves, and leaving God out altogether. This is the reason that so many of us are tired, weak, and discouraged. We fret and strain in our own strength and make little progress. But such need not be the case. All the while, God is saying to us, "It is not by might, nor by power, but by my Spirit, saith the Lord." "Ye shall receive power, after that the Holy Spirit is come upon you." "I will give you a mouth and wisdom that men cannot gainsay nor resist." Through our very failures, he keeps impressing upon us this truth:

"Apart from me ye can do nothing." We are absolutely dependent upon God.

What, then, is our present duty, our high privilege? Instead of bewailing our poverty as did these disciples, instead of taking account only of our material resources, we are to take account also of those that are spiritual. We are to count upon God and to co-operate with Him. This we are to do by putting what we have, whether large or small, into His hands. We are to give Him our all—our very selves. This, and this alone, will bring us victory. For, if we give God ourselves, He will accept us. This is true regardless of how weak and futile we may be. If we give Him ourselves, He will cleanse us and fill us with His Spirit. If we give Him ourselves, He will use us for the accomplishment of His purpose. This is not theory; it is experience. "In him who strengthens me," shouts Paul, "I am able for everything." To that tremendous assertion the choicest of the saints say, "Amen." Such a rich experience may be yours and mine. May we begin entering upon it even now!

XIV

SURVEYING THE WIND

"But when he saw the wind, he was afraid; and beginning to sink, he cried, saying, Lord, save me."

MATTHEW 14: 30

"BEGINNING TO SINK . . ." THAT IS AN ARRESTING and tragic word. A few moments ago Simon Peter was daring the impossible. With the rude winds pounding him, with an enraged sea spitting its spray into his face, he was climbing down out of the boat to go to Jesus. "Lord, if it be thou," he had prayed, "bid me come unto thee on the water." And Jesus, instead of reminding him that he was in sufficiently great danger where he was, granted his request. "Come," he invited. At once, with the light of a great faith in his eyes, Peter planted his feet on that word "Come," and began to walk on the water to go to Jesus. But his success proved to be short-lived. Soon his faith had changed to fear, his victory to defeat. He is beginning to sink. Unless a hand is stretched forth to help him, he will soon be at the bottom of the sea.

I

Now it seems to me that this sinking man is a picture of much that we see in our modern world.

It is a description of many of ourselves. We are not living as victoriously as we once dreamed that we should. While we have not given over the fight, have not wholly surrendered, still we do not seem to be getting anywhere. There are even those who have quit trying. One such came to see me a few days ago. He told me with frank desperation that all of his inner and outer resources had broken down, that he had completely lost his grip. According to his own confession, he was not simply sinking, he had already gone down and the waters of utter defeat were rolling over him.

This sinking man reminds us also of much that we see in our churches. It is at times hard for us to sing "Like a mighty army moves the Church of God" without a sense of unreality. When we realize the terrific moral slump that has overtaken our church life in recent years, we feel that the only army that we greatly resemble is one that is disorganized and discouraged and in retreat. Too often our services are pervaded by an atmosphere of defeat rather than of victory. Many of our churches are more conspicuous for their empty pews than for their growing and enthusiastic congregations. Now, I believe that the worst is over and that the present trend is upward. But in spite of this fact, the average church still reminds us more of one who is sinking than one who is moving victoriously forward on a mission of conquest.

Then what is true of the individual and of the church seems equally true of civilization as a whole. A few years ago we were very sure of ourselves. Just before the outbreak of the World War, we thought we had won the fight and had planted our feet firmly upon the road of an inevitable progress. But all that has changed. Today there is widespread pessimism regarding the future. Every great nation of the world is girding itself for war. The nations of Europe and Asia are threatening at any moment to be at each other's throats. If any two of these nations fight, the chances are that the conflict will be world-wide. Many thoughtful people believe that we cannot bear the strain of another World War. There is, therefore, widespread fear that our present civilization is even now on the verge of the abyss. No wonder then that floundering Peter reminds us of ourselves.

II

How did Peter get that way? How did he come to be sinking?

It was not because he had lost all interest in the enterprise that he had undertaken. That is, of course, the case with many that are in our churches. They are failing at the big task of being Christian because they have either never been greatly interested or have lost that interest. If these were to treat their business as they do their religion, they would be bankrupt in less than a week. If they were to treat their amusements, their bridge-playing, their golf, their dancing, in the slipshod fashion in which they treat their religion, they would be ostracized so far as these games were concerned. Nobody would have them for partners. Yet these often sadly bewail the fact that they are getting very little out of their religion. Of course not. They are putting nothing into it. Peter was failing, but it was not from lack of interest or effort.

Nor was Peter's failure born of the difficulty of his task. His task was difficult. It was difficult to the point of impossibility. But that fact does not account for his defeat. It does not account for your defeat and mine. Jesus is constantly calling us to the impossible. He calls us to be what in our own strength we cannot be. ˙We are to be born anew. We are to become partakers of the divine nature. We are to possess the very mind that was in Christ Jesus. Then he calls upon us to accomplish tasks that in our own strength we cannot accomplish. We are to disciple the nations. We are to bring in the Kingdom of God. These are impossible tasks. "Apart from me," he tells us with engaging frankness, "you can do nothing." But with him the impossible becomes possible. "In him who strengthens me," shouts Paul, "I am able for anything." Peter's failure, therefore, was not born of his difficulties.

Why, then, did Peter fail? Here is the answer:

185

"He saw the wind." Peter was getting on beautifully until he decided to make a survey of the wind. He walked victoriously until he began to tabulate his problems. But when he got absorbed in the enumeration of his difficulties, at once he began to sink. When he became obsessed by his problems, the angry waves laid violent hands on him and began to drag him to the bottom of the sea. This was the case because his hindrances so completely filled his horizon that he saw nothing of what was helpful. He was so taken up by the forces that were unfriendly that he forgot those that were friendly. He became so completely wind-conscious that he ceased altogether to be Christ-conscious.

Now this is certainly one of the outstanding characteristics of our day. We are no doubt the best surveyed generation that this world has ever seen. Our age is perhaps the most problem-conscious age of all history. We see our individual problems with bewildering clearness. We also have a keen realization of our church problems, our social problems, our national problems, our international problems. These are so obvious that we cannot but see them. In addition, they are being persistently pointed out to us by pulpit and press. Naturally, these problems often so fill our horizon that we become utterly depressed and bewildered. The very keenness of our analysis of ourselves and of our situation has all but brought on paralysis. Therefore, looking only at the opposition, many of us, as Peter, are beginning to sink.

Now, this does not mean, of course, that the need of the hour is a greater blindness. Though it may seem folly to be wise, our bliss is not to come at the hands of ignorance. It is altogether to the good to face all the facts, however unpleasant they may be. Our weakness is born not so much of our facing our difficulties as of our overemphasizing of them. That always makes for weakness. There are few of us who could not walk from end to end of a fifteen-foot plank that was ten inches wide, provided that plank were lying flat on the ground. But if that same plank were made a bridge between the roofs of two 30-story sky-scrapers, to walk it would be a far more difficult matter. This would be the case not because the plank had become more narrow, but because the walker had become more conscious of his difficulties. Physicians, when sick, generally are bad patients. This is the case because they are too problem-conscious. Therefore, while to know our problems is good, to be obsessed by them is a source of weakness.

It was just this problem-obsession that worked the undoing of the ten spies. These went out with Caleb and Joshua, you remember, to explore the Promised Land. The purpose of this exploration was not to determine whether or not the land could be taken. That had already been decided. It was to determine how best to accomplish the task. All of the spies undertook the exploration, it would seem, with equal enthusiasm. All found the land to be an exceedingly good land, flowing with milk and honey. All also saw the giants, the sons of Anak. But Caleb and Joshua saw these giants in the light of God. Therefore, they were in no sense terrified by them. They represented only an opportunity. "They will be bread for us," they declared with daring faith. But when the ten saw them, they so filled their horizon that they had no eye for God at all. Therefore, they were completely unmanned. "We were in our own eyes as grasshoppers," they wailed pitifully, "and so we were in their eyes." Naturally, the only contribution they could make upon their return was one of discouragement and despair. In fact, the whole enterprise of possessing the land had to wait till their generation had slipped into their coffins, because they had become too problem-conscious to be of use.

III

But the wonder of this story is that Peter changed his fear into faith and his defeat into victory. How did he do it?

He did not win by denying, or altogether ignoring, his difficulties. He did not tell himself that there really was no wind, that the waves were all a myth, that the storm had no reality except in his own mind. The fact that we overemphasize our problems does not mean that we are to shut our eyes to them altogether. When pursued by an enemy, we do not find victory by merely thrusting our heads into the sand as the ostrich is incorrectly supposed to do. Even an ostrich has too much sense for that. There is one thing, if possible, worse than a blind and stupid pessimist who sees nothing but shadows, and that is a blind and stupid optimist who sees nothing but rainbows. Peter's way out, therefore, was not to shut his eyes to the facts just because they were unpleasant.

How, then, did Peter win? When he saw that he was sinking, he frankly faced the fact. He knew that he was a disappointment to himself, a disappointment to his friends, a disappointment to his Lord. Realizing his failure, he dared to take his eyes off the wind and the waves long enough to fix them on Jesus. Fixing them on him, he prayed this simple prayer, "Lord, save me." I like the directness of it, and the brevity of it. When we are not greatly in earnest, when we neither desperately desire nor expect anything, we can pour out whole Niagaras of words before the Lord. But when the storm breaks upon us, when it is a matter of life and death, we can come to the point very quickly. "Lord, save me," cried Peter. Then what happened? "Immediately," the story says, "Jesus stretched forth his hand, and lifted him up."

Now, as old-fashioned as it may seem, I am confident that the way out for Peter is the way out for you and me. Suppose you have come this morning with a sense of defeat. You realize that you are not getting anywhere religiously. Your life seems a lean and mean affair when compared with the wealthy promises and with the wealthy personalities that you meet on the pages of the New Testament. Somehow the whole business of being a Christian has been for you little better than a failure. Your religion has been far more weight than wings. But even if this is the case, you need not despair. There is a way out. You may yet find victory. Try Peter's way. Take your gaze off your own weakness and follies and failures and fix it on Jesus. Pray his simple prayer, "Lord, save me." If you do this, a hand will surely be stretched forth to you, a hand that is mighty to save.

"But, I have prayed," some of you answer desperately. "Far into the night have I agonized in prayer. But it has got me nowhere." With Kipling's Fool, you can say, "I asked God to help me, but He didn't, He didn't." Now, we must confess that there are times when prayer seems to do no good at all. In fact, it is possible to pray in such a fashion as to do positive harm. This is the case when we focus all our attention upon our needs rather than upon Him who is able to supply our needs; when we concentrate upon the temptation from which we seek deliverance rather than upon our Deliverer. Such prayer is a source of weakness rather than of power because it enlists our imagination on the side of our temptation rather than on the side of Him from whom we seek help. Now, when there is a conflict between our will and our imagination, the psychologists tell us that the imagination always wins, and that the will goes down in defeat. Therefore, if we are going to find victory in prayer, we must fix our minds not upon our needs, but upon our victorious Lord. "Look unto me, and be ye saved." This is at once good theology and sound psychology.

That is what Jesus meant when he told the story of the embarrassed host. "Which of you shall have a friend, and shall go unto him at midnight, and say unto him, Friend, lend me three loaves; for a friend of mine in his journey is come to me, and I have nothing to set before him? and he from within shall answer and say, Trouble me not: the door is now shut, and my children are with me in bed; I cannot rise and give thee. I say unto you, Though he will not rise and give him, because he is his friend, yet because of his importunity he will rise and give him as many as he needeth." Here is a man who has an unexpected guest who has come at midnight. When this host goes to his larder to see about some food for his guest, he finds it as empty as the cupboard of Old Mother Hubbard. Then what does he do? Does he gaze with fear-filled eyes upon that emptiness while his guest has to go hungry to bed? No. He turns from his own inadequacy to the adequacy of his friend. He is so friend-conscious that he defies all difficulties, and thus receives all that he needs.

Now, just as this is the way out for the individual,

so it is for the Church. It is my firm conviction that there is no hope for the world except through the establishing of this Kingdom of God. If the Kingdom of God is not established in America, then America is doomed. If the Kingdoms of this world do not become the Kingdom of our Lord, then the world is doomed. But, how is the Kingdom of God to be established? It is my further conviction that this can only be done through the Church. This is not saying that there are not many organizations that are seeking to do good. But everyone of these that is exerting the lifting power of an ounce receives its inspiration directly or indirectly from the Church. If the Church is to establish the Kingdom, it, of course, needs to be alert and alive to the difficulties involved. But above all else, it needs to be alive to its resources, especially to those resources that are available through him who said, "All authority in heaven and in earth is given unto me." In other words, to be a victorious church, we must be a God-conscious church.

How strikingly this is illustrated by the history of the early church. Could any situation be more hopeless than the one it faced just after the Crucifixion? Its members were only a handful of scattered, discouraged, and defeated men and women who were hiding behind locked doors. They were without money, without social position, without church buildings, without schools, without any visible assets whatever. And these, whose assets were naked nothing, were confronted by stark impossibilities. But something took place that caused them to brush these impossibilities aside like so many cobwebs. In spite of seemingly irresistible foes, they went forth conquering and to conquer. How did they do it? What changed them from whipped and frightened creatures into dauntless heroes? The answer is Pentecost. And what is Pentecost? Stripped of what is merely incidental, it means just this: That these people came to realize that their Lord had come back to them in the power of the Holy Spirit. Through this experience they were made sure that henceforth he would be both with them, and within them, as their abiding Leader and Friend. It was this overwhelming consciousness of their risen Lord that made them the victorious saints that they were. This experience did for them at least four things.

First: It welded them into a brotherhood. They became united. They faced the world wearing upon their hearts the one sure badge of discipleship, love one for the other. "By this shall all men know that ye are my disciples, if ye have love one to another." By this mutual love wide chasms were bridged, and old barriers were broken down. "How these Christians love each other," said the awed and heart-hungry pagan world. And because these pagans desired to love and be loved, they were drawn into this group of brothers. A God-conscious church, a church that has experienced Pentecost, is brotherly. A brotherly church is always a growing church.

Second: This experience made these early saints shockingly aggressive. "And they called them, and commanded them not to speak at all nor teach in the name of Jesus. But Peter and John answered and said unto them, Whether it be right in the sight of God to hearken unto you more than unto God, judge ye. For we cannot but speak the things which we have seen and heard." That this was no idle boast was proven by the fact that when they were arrested again a few days later, they were sharply rebuked for their disobedience. The authorities flung the charge into their faces that though they had been commanded not to speak at all nor teach in the name of Jesus, they had filled all Jerusalem with their teachings. They were so bent on sharing that they laid almost violent hands on every passer-by to tell him of their transforming experience. Today we are timid in our witnessing. The very word "evangelism" seems to frighten us. But this is an indication of our spiritual poverty rather than of our wealth; for when the Church loses its evangelistic fervor, it is either dying or already dead. A God-conscious church is an evangelistic church.

Third: Through this experience these people became possessed of an unbelievable confidence. No difficulties, no opposition, no persecution could daunt them. They were undergirded by an abounding hopefulness. No foes could make them afraid. Publicly whipped, they departed rejoicing that they were counted worthy to suffer shame for His name. Cast into prison, they sang till their prison doors were opened and till the hearts of those who had them in charge were opened also. They were absolutely sure of final victory. "I am always confident," shouts Paul, as he faces gigantic impossibilities. And Paul's shout is the shout of this early church. They were confident because they were so sure of God. A God-conscious church is always a confident church. Its face is ever flushed with the sunshine of a dauntless optimism.

Fourth: This experience made them a powerful church. They were so powerful that they were absolutely irresistible. Age-old religions and age-old abuses vanished before them as mists vanish before the sunrise. No weapon that was formed against them could prosper. Wherever they went, the wilderness and the solitary place became glad and the desert rejoiced and blossomed as a rose. They met stern opposition, but the more they were opposed, the more they triumphed; the more they were slain, the more they lived. Why were they so mighty? The only answer is this: They were God-conscious. They had entered into the experience promised by their Lord, "Ye shall receive power, after that the Holy Spirit is come upon you."

Today, we are all but infinitely ahead of them in point of numbers and material resources. We have many large churches that are well-housed and well-organized. We have many that are possessed of wealth and culture and moral earnestness. We have the best-trained ministers in our pulpits and the best-trained teachers in our church schools of any generation since Pentecost. We have an intelligent awareness of our goals and of the problems involved in reaching them. But in spite of this, we lag. Our conquests are not vastly impressive. Though we have large and influential churches, we have too few powerful churches. What we need, therefore, is the realization that all the spiritual resources that were available for those of the long ago are available for us. We need above all else to claim their awareness of God. If we do this, we, too, shall become united, daring, confident, and powerful. Then, instead of sinking, we shall increasingly go from victory to victory.

XV

THE GIVING OF SELF

*"Have mercy on me, O
Lord, . . . my daughter is
grievously vexed with a demon."*

MATTHEW 15: 22

HERE IS A MOTHER WITH A SHADOW OVER HER home and a shadow over her heart. She has an afflicted daughter. Just the nature of this affliction, we are unable to say. According to the belief prevalent at that day, she is possessed by an evil spirit. But whatever her malady, it is robbing her of her opportunity. It is laying her life in ruins. But hard as it is on the daughter, it is harder still on the mother. Suffering with her child as she does, she is ready to pay any price within her power to bring her healing. Therefore, when she hears of Jesus, she hurries to him and prays this prayer: "Have mercy on me, O Lord; my daughter is grievously vexed with a demon."

This prayer is beautifully unique. This mother is not praying as we should have expected her to pray. She is not praying as we usually pray. Instead of say-

197

ing, "Have mercy upon my child," she rather prays, "Have mercy upon me." Her prayer, therefore, is not an effort to stand from under, as ours so often are. She is not seeking simply to push her burden upon other shoulders, while she goes her easeful way. Her prayer is not a cheap prayer. It is costly, as real praying ever is. It costs the giving of self. She has made the burden of her daughter her very own.

Now, it is such self-giving that is required of all true prayer. We cannot really pray except at the price of self-surrender. If we refuse to surrender ourselves as we pray, then sooner or later we surrender prayer. This you have discovered for yourself, if you have ever tried to pray when there was a controversy between you and God. Did you ever try to pray when you knew there was a surrender you ought to make that you were unwilling to make? Did you ever try to pray when you kept realizing that God was pointing out a road which you ought to walk that you were refusing to walk? If you have, you know that under such circumstances one of two things always happens—either you give up yourself, or you give up prayer. Real prayer always involves surrender. God can only trust this amazing power to those that are willing to give themselves.

It is such self-giving also that is of the very essence of Christianity. "Bear ye one another's burdens," says Paul, "and so fulfill the law of Christ." What does the Apostle mean? He means, first of all, that this law of self-giving is the law by which Jesus lived. He was and is the great burden-bearer. He is constantly putting himself under our load. He takes upon himself the burden of our sin. He takes upon himself the burden of our hungers and thirsts. This he does, as he offers himself as the bread of life and as the water of life. He takes the burden of our weariness and of our restlessness, saying, "Come unto me, all ye that labor and are heavy-laden, and I will give you rest." He is constantly offering himself as the bearer of our burdens. This sums up the whole meaning of his life from the manger to the cross.

But, not only is this the law by which Jesus lived, it is also the law by which he expects us to live. What he did and does, he counts upon us to do also. We are to have his mind, his disposition, his way of looking at things. We are to have his way of doing things. We are to give ourselves for the good of others, even as he. "If he laid down his life for us, we ought also to lay down our lives for the brethren." It was in this spirit that the early Christians lived. It is in this spirit that we are to live. We cannot be truly Christian in any other way.

> "Must Jesus bear the cross alone,
> And all the world go free?
> No, there's a cross for every one,
> And there's a cross for me!"

It is only as we bear one another's burdens that we can fulfill the law of Christ.

II

Why does Jesus make self-giving the law of life for you and me?

He does not do so because he looks upon sacrifice as an end in itself. To afflict ourselves, to cause ourselves needless suffering, is not in itself a virtue. I read some time ago of a girl who sought to atone for some wrong that she had done by beating up glass and putting in her shoes. But God was not honored by her thus making herself a cripple. Suffering is never an end in itself. Simon Stylites standing for years upon his pedestal certainly practiced self-sacrifice, but I am not at all sure that by so doing he rendered the slightest benefit either to himself or to anyone else. Self-giving, even to the last limit, is not necessarily a good. "If I bestow all my goods to feed the poor, and give my body to be burned, and have not love, it profiteth me nothing."

If sacrifice in the sense of surrendering something of value were an end in itself, then those who are farthest from wishing to make any sacrifice at all would be the most enriched. This is the case because nobody gives up quite so much as those who are most determined to give nothing. When the Prodigal went into the far country, he certainly had no thought of making any sacrifice. But in spite of this fact, he found the adventure to be very costly. It cost him the companionship of his father. It cost him gnawing hungers and burning thirsts. It cost him his usefulness. It cost him everything. He literally spent all that he had. It is true, therefore, that none surrender so much as those who are most bent on surrendering nothing at all.

Why, then, I repeat, does Jesus ask you and me to make self-giving the law of our lives?

1. He does so because he knows that it is only as we give ourselves that we can achieve our highest usefulness. But this self-giving, to be of supreme value, must have at least two characteristics. First, it must be voluntary. It is only thus that it is shot through with the spirit of the cross. We sometimes speak of certain burdens as our cross, when those burdens are thrust upon us. We have to bear them whether we are willing to do so or not. But we can only count that as our cross that we bear of our own choice. That was the case with the cross of Jesus. He did not have to bear it. When he spoke of the giving up of his life on the cross, he said, "No man taketh it from me, but I lay it down of myself."

Not only must the burdens we bear be borne voluntarily, they must be borne from a worthy motive. Jesus never looked upon any form of suffering as an end in itself, not even that of the cross. Why did he put himself under the burdens of others, even to the point of going to Calvary for them? It was for the joy that was set before him that he endured the cross, despising the shame. This joy was not the joy of suffering, but the joy of winning the world through suffering. He suffered because of the conviction that after he was lifted up, he would draw all men unto himself. It was through his self-giving on the cross that he expected to attain his highest usefulness. And all the subsequent centuries bear witness to the fact that his expectation was well founded.

Now we, too, can only serve in a superlative way at the price of life laid down. This, of course, does not mean that we cannot render many helpful services at a lesser cost. We can and do give and serve in such fashion as to win high commendation without going to such extremes. But, in spite of all that, it still remains true that we never accomplish our best, never realize our highest, except at the price of the giving of self. This is true in every department of human endeavor.

Take literature and art, for instance. There are comparatively few books that are of permanent value. Many are timely, but it is an exceedingly rare book that is also timeless. What are the books that live? Milton describes such when he declares, "Books are not absolutely dead things; they are the precious lifeblood of a master spirit, embalmed and treasured up on purposes to a life beyond life." That is, the book that lives is the costly book. It is one into which the author has poured his lifeblood. He has written it at the price of life laid down.

This is equally true in the realm of art. No great picture is painted except at a great price. That is the lesson of that oft-told story of the artist whose pictures had in them an inimitable coloring, a bewildering crimson, that caused them to cast a spell upon every beholder. Other artists, charmed by their beauty and power, sought to learn the secret, only to give up in despair. At last, the great painter died, and everyone thought that his secret had perished with him. But when they were preparing him for burial, they discovered above his heart an old half-healed wound. Then they understood. As this artist had painted, he had dipped his brush into his own heart's blood. That is, his painting was a parting with life. His work was done, as all really superlative work is done, at the price of life laid down.

This is equally true of all high service. This week, a man who gave away more in terms of money, I dare say, than any other that ever lived, passed to his reward. His gifts amounted to more than five hundred and thirty millions of dollars. Not only did he give lavishly, but he gave wisely. His money will doubtless be serving humanity centuries from now. Yet, strange as it may seem, the world will still remember the meager gift of a certain widow of the long ago, will still grow tender-hearted over it, when the gifts of this multimillionaire have been forgotten. Why is this the case? What comparison is there between five hundred and thirty millions of dollars and two mites? Surely none in quantity. The gift of Mr. Rockefeller was almost infinitely greater than that of the widow. But there was a quality about the gift of this woman that does not belong to the gift of the billionaire. He gave out of his superfluity, as the scriptures would say, just as those other rich men of the long ago. But she gave out of her want. She gave her all. Her gift was crimsoned with the blood of sacrifice. And we never give our best except at this high price.

As with giving, so it is with all service that is superlative.

"I sometimes think that never blows so red
The rose, as where some buried Caesar bled."

There is a sense in which this is profoundly and literally true. Flowers of Christlike character certainly grow in their richest profusion only where the soil has been fertilized by the lives of those who have given themselves. This is true of the homes where boys and girls have the best opportunities of growing into fine men and women. This is true of every church, every community, where the fields grow golden with harvests of transformed lives.

Some years ago, a missionary went to preach in an obscure Chinese village. When the people gathered about him, he began to tell them about Jesus. He told how he went about doing good, how he suffered in the sufferings of others, how he made every man's burden his burden. As he spoke, their faces took on a new radiance and their eyes became bright with understanding. "We know him," they said eagerly. "He has been here. He used to live among us. He is buried in our cemetery." The missionary was amazed and bewildered. "Where is he buried?" he asked. And they led him to a well-kept grave whose headstone bore the name of a Christian physician whom the outside world had forgotten. This man had flung himself away on those obscure villagers. And though the big world had forgotten him, this soil that he had fertilized by his life had become colorful with human flowers.

2. Then Jesus urges us to the giving of self, not only because this is the way to our highest usefulness, but also to our highest self-realization. When we talk about self-giving, the thought that persistently haunts so many is this: Such self-giving is well enough for those who are on the receiving end; but how about the givers, where do they come in? It is fine, of course, to have somebody to sacrifice for you, somebody willing to part with life on your behalf. There is often no measuring the value of such sacrifices to those in whose behalf they are made. But how about those that have to make them? Surely they are doing more than their part, and are, therefore, allowing themselves to be cheated.

But instead of this being the case, the very opposite is true. If giving self for others enriches the receiver, it enriches the giver even more. Much is being said today about personality. We once thought that personality was purely a matter of gift. We either had it or did not. But we are learning now that personality is something that we can develop. How are we to go about it? By self-giving. One of our leading psychologists tells us that our personalities grow just in proportion to our ability to do things with and for others. That is, other things being equal, the greater the abandon with which we give ourselves away, the greater and richer our personalities become.

Who is it, then, that lives most abundantly? It is the one who flings his life away in the service of others. A few years ago a young Japanese student left our shores for his home with the sentence of death passed upon him. His physicians told him that he had only one lung and, therefore, could live but a brief while. He decided, since this was the case, to make the short hour that was left him count for the most possible. He therefore buried himself in one of the worst slums in his native land. He gave himself so lavishly that the tides of spiritual power that flowed into him made death impossible. He is living still—creatively and mightily. In fact, this man with his physical handicap is perhaps the most powerful and influential Christian in the world today. To fulfill the law of Christ, then, by self-giving is at once the way of highest usefulness and of highest self-realization.

III

Look at what such self-giving did in this story before you. "Have mercy upon me," prayed this sorrowing mother; "my daughter is grievously vexed with a demon." What was the worth of that prayer to the one on whose behalf it was offered? Was it of any value at all? I was reading recently a book on prayer written by one of our most earnest young ministers. Much in the book was at once sane, scriptural, and helpful. But with youthful arrogance he threw intercessory prayer completely into the discard. To his way of thinking, it is utterly useless for one man to pray for another. But to take such a position is to make nonsense of much that is most beautiful and helpful in both the Old and the New Testaments. Jesus himself offered such prayers again and again. Paul never wrote but one letter, the one to the backslidden church at Galatia, without asking an interest in the prayers of those to whom he wrote. He believed that the humblest of the saints could thus anoint his lips with grace and power. And such has been the faith of the saints throughout the centuries.

That there are mysteries connected with intercessory prayer, I am not denying. Nor am I undertaking at this time in any way to clarify these mysteries. But what I do affirm is this, that we are taught throughout the Bible to pray one for another. "God forbid that I should sin against the Lord," said the prophet of the long ago, "by ceasing to pray for you." Such praying does make it possible for God to do for us what otherwise He cannot do. It was so here. It was through this woman's prayer that healing came to her daughter. By her prayer, she took her afflicted child in her arms and fairly laid her upon the lap of God. So saintly mothers have done countless numbers of times. We remember such this day with tenderness, for many reasons; but for none more than this, the prayers they offered on our behalf.

But, though this self-giving prayer brought help and healing to the daughter, that was but the lesser of its benefits. It did even more for the mother. However much, therefore, this mother gave, it was little in comparison with what she received. I know of nothing in the entire experience of our Lord that brought him greater joy, nothing over which he showed a greater enthusiasm, than over the persistent, faith-prompted prayer of this mother. He who had at first seemed to meet her request with flat refusal, turned at last to say, "O woman, great is thy faith. Be it unto thee, even as thou wilt." Thus while her prayer brought a blessing to her child, it brought an even greater blessing to herself.

It is ever the case. It was by such self-giving that our Lord won his crown. "Have this mind in you, which was also in Christ Jesus: who, existing in the form of God, counted not the being on an equality with God a thing to be grasped, but emptied himself, taking the form of a servant, being made in the likeness of men; and being found in fashion as a man, he humbled himself, becoming obedient even unto death, yea, the death of the cross. Wherefore also God highly exalted him, and gave unto him the name which is above every name; that in the name of Jesus every knee should bow, of things in heaven and things on earth and things under the earth, and that every tongue should confess that Jesus Christ is Lord, to the glory of God the Father." Thus, according to St. Paul, Jesus climbed to the highest heights because he was willing to stoop to the lowest depths of humiliation and shame.

There is a story that, once on a time, a certain Chinese King ordered his chief minister to make a bell that would ring with a note of flawless sweetness. This King put all the treasures of his vast kingdom at the disposal of his minister. Therefore, having received such a commission, the minister went out and gathered together the choicest silver and gold of the realm. He flung this into a great caldron, melted it, and cast his wonderful bell. But when it was swung in the tower and the King and his subjects were gathered to hear it ring, they were disappointed. While there was music, it was soulless and metallic, with no note of tenderness. It was, therefore, as jarring as instruments played out of tune.

The King, therefore, ordered that the bell be recast. This was done. Again it was swung in the tower and again the King and his subjects gathered to hear the music. But again they were disappointed. There was still that soulless tone that jarred rather than soothed and healed. Then the King became angry. He summoned his minister and commanded him to cast the bell a third time. He further warned him that, unless it should ring with flawless sweetness this time, his life would be the forfeit. That evening, therefore, the minister went home with a heavy heart. He knew not what to do. When his wife and daughter pressed him for the reason for his sadness, he told the story of his pathetic plight.

Now, it so happened that this daughter loved her father with unusual devotion. When, therefore, she heard his story, it almost broke her heart. She resolved that at all cost she would do something to help. Therefore, that night, when all slept, she slipped out of the house and down the street to where the Wise Man lived. She told him her story and asked how the bell might be made to ring with a note of flawless sweetness. With deep solemnity, the Wise Man gave the answer: "If the bell is to ring with flawless sweetness, it must have in it something more than silver and gold. With the metal, there must be mingled the blood of a devoted heart."

Pondering this truth in her mind, the girl went home again. She had resolved what to do. Therefore, the next day when the metal was seething and hissing over the hot fires, before any hands could stay her, she threw herself into the boiling caldron. With the silver and gold was mingled the blood of her devoted heart. Then the bell was cast once more. Once more, it was hung in the tower. Once more, the King and the people gathered to hear it ring. And what a change had taken place! This time, as they listened, tears wet every face, every heart grew soft and tender, for such heavenly music had never been heard before. And our lives are like that—yours and mine. They never reach their best, they never attain their highest possible sweetness and beauty, except at the price of utter self-giving.

XVI

ON THE SIDE LINE

*"Blind Bartimaeus, the son
of Timaeus, sat by the highway side begging."*

MARK 10: 46

HERE IS A PATHETIC CHARACTER. HE IS A MAN
that nobody envied. A few perhaps pitied him,
and many despised him. He is a blot upon the landscape, a bit of human wreckage that tends to raise in
our minds questions of the goodness and love of God.
Of course the fact that he is what he is, is not altogether his fault. He is far more sinned against than
sinning. Most of the blame rests upon the society of
his day that made no provision for men of his kind.
But regardless of who is at fault, Bartimaeus himself
is a mere ragged pocket that calamity has turned inside
out and emptied of everything of worth.

I

What is wrong with this man?

1. He is blind. That is always a tragic loss. He
has been born blind. He has never been privileged to

witness the miracle of a sunrise nor the blazing glory of a sunset. He has never looked into the blue of the sky, nor into the face of a little child. But this fact need not have resulted in utter disaster. Many have lived in the light in spite of their blindness. John Milton was blind, yet he was not for that reason a creature of the dark. He was rather a child of the flaming dawn. He was speaking out of his own experience when he sang:

> "He that has light within his own clear breast
> May sit in the center and enjoy bright day:
> But he that hides a dark soul and foul thoughts
> Benighted walks under the midday sun;
> Himself is his own dungeon."

2. Not only is Bartimaeus blind, but he is also poor. He is so poor that he is compelled to wear the threadbare and ragged castoff garments of others. He is so poor that he has often to suffer the pangs of hunger. Such poverty is a tragic something. It tends always to suppress our noble rage and freeze the genial current of the soul. But even poverty need not prove fatal. Many have, through high faith and courage, changed their poverty into spiritual plenty and their want into wealth.

3. The supreme tragedy of Bartimaeus consists in what he has allowed his blindness and poverty to do for him. They have put him on the side line. He is out of the game. He is not one of the world's workers. He is an idler, a parasite, a blind mouth,

living off of the work of others. Thus compelled to live on charity, his morale has been destroyed. He has lost his self-respect. He is not only a beggar, but content to be one. He has reached the conclusion that the world owes him a living. He lives only for himself. Every footfall that he hears along the highway sets him to asking this one question: "What can I get out of this passerby?" He has become so utterly blind spiritually that he thinks the big business of life is not giving, but getting.

II

Now, this type of spiritual blindness has lived through the centuries.

We meet it in the long ago. Here, for instance, is a story out of Mythology: When Achilles was born, his mother went to consult the Oracle of Delphi as to his future. The Oracle told her that her son would either live a long life of inglorious ease, or a short life of battle and victory. With the blindness of Bartimaeus, she chose for her son the long life of uselessness. Therefore, she dressed him up like a girl and put him out on an island where nobody lived but girls, where he seemed destined to live and die in idle worthlessness.

By and by, however, the Greeks went to war against the Trojans. For a long time they fought about her walls in vain. Then, they went to consult the Oracle of Delphi as to how they could win the victory. The

Oracle told them that they could never win except Achilles fought with them and for them. But nobody knew where Achilles was. But that wily detective among the Greeks, Ulysses by name, undertook to find him. He traveled over all lands until he came to that island where nobody lived but girls. Then, disguised as a peddler, he went among them to sell his wares. They bought eagerly, all except one. At last he lifted from among his feminine trinkets a suit of armor and a sword. At sight of that this girl sprang forward eagerly, fitted on the armor and began to wield the sword. Thus Ulysses recognized Achilles, the hero. He chose that with which he might serve instead of that with which he might be served. But his escape was not by virtue of, but in spite of, the blindness of his mother.

But this blindness is not simply of yesterday, it is also of today. In a recent issue of the *American Magazine,* there was an article by a young man of more than ordinary intelligence. He was propounding this question: "Why should I be honest?" He shut out all religious and idealistic answers by saying: "I do not wish to be great, I only desire to be comfortable." But no man could write after this fashion who was not stone-blind spiritually, blind to the fact that he himself is something more than a mere animal. A pig may be comfortable if he has plenty to eat, even if his swill is stolen. The herd of hogs that the prodigal fed were comfortable enough, but their fare did not suffice for the prodigal himself. He was tormented by dreams that made his soul sick and restless. Of course he might have disregarded this restlessness till he had become possessed of a certain content. But this would have been the contentment of death rather than of life. The trouble with this young man is just plain blindness.

Too often we meet this same type of blindness in the world of business. A bright young chap said the other day: "I'm not in business for my health; I'm in it strictly for the money I can make out of it." And, sad to say, there are those who are not shocked by such a devilish declaration. These rather nod their heads sagely as if he were talking the language of wisdom. Recently a gentleman gave me a letter written by a man who claimed to be a churchman. This man was railing against the Federal Council of Churches because this organization had objected to the profit motive in business. This good brother was outraged, and was threatening to wreck the Church by withdrawing from it altogether. Of course there are certain types of so-called business with which no one but selfish getters will have anything to do. Take the liquor business, for example. What is the motive of the liquor dealer? Crass and utter selfishness. He is out for number one. He is out to get all he can, even at the price of blood and tears. Gambling is very prevalent among us today. What is the motive of the gambler? He is seeking to get something for nothing. At his best, he is a parasite; at his worst, he is a fool.

But when we come to the realm of legitimate business we expect something better. In many instances I am happy to say that our expectations are not disappointed. Why should not this be the case? Why, in all common sense, should the motive of the business man be less high than that of other workers? Suppose I should announce from this pulpit: "I am not preaching for my health. I am preaching strictly for the money." Every one of you would despise me. Suppose the physician should stand in the presence of pain and death and never undertake to aid unless he saw the glint of a dollar. You would look upon him with contempt. Every man, regardless of the nature of his work, must recognize the fact that he is not come to be ministered unto, but to minister. The business man who fails to realize this is blind, and such blindness is not only bad morals, but bad business.

III

But one day blind Bartimaeus was utterly changed. He ceased merely to exist and began to live. How did this come about? Of course the first move was made by Jesus. That is always the case. He ever seeks us before we seek him. His help here, too, was brought, in part, as almost always, through human hands. Look at the steps by which Bartimaeus came into the light.

It is quite evident that this beggar had heard of

Jesus before his encounter with him here on the highway. One day, doubtless, there had passed along his road a man who was more kindly than the average. After he had dropped a penny into the clutching fingers of the beggar, he looked at him with a mingling of loathing and pity. Then, he asked him a question: "Bartimaeus, why don't you get well? Why don't you quit this sordid business of begging and do something worthwhile?" "Get well," he answered with pained amazement, not unmixed with anger. "Get well? How can I get well? Don't you know I was born blind? My father was blind before me. I have always been like this, and there is no chance of my ever being different. Why do you mock me by a question like that?"

"I did not mean to mock you," came the kindly answer. "You can get well if you will. Is it possible that you have not heard of the amazing Prophet that has come among us? He has power beyond the human. I have known him to heal the sick by a word. I have known him to touch lepers into purity. He has even made the roses of life to bloom upon the frozen cheeks of death. I tell you, there is a chance for you." And the beggar's face becomes one lean wistfulness. "What is his name?" he inquires eagerly. "His name is Jesus, and he is of the house and lineage of David," is the answer. "Jesus, the Son of David!" the beggar murmurs to himself. "Jesus, the Son of David. Well, if he ever comes my way, I'm going to ask him."

During the days that followed, Bartimaeus was filled with a growing discontent. The meanness of his lot was increasingly distasteful. But along with his discontent was a strange, new expectancy. He did not know what day Jesus might come his way. Every morning, though he awoke in the dark, he was thrilled by the thought that something big might come into his life that day. "With a Prophet like Jesus abroad in the land, anything wonderful is likely to happen," he told himself. And he was right. We are not half as expectant as we should be. There is nothing too good to take place in the meanest of our lives when a Christ like ours is so eager and so near.

Then, at last his great day dawned. There was the tramp of many feet along the highway. Something was happening that stirred his heart and set his soul to dreaming. Could it be Jesus? He was not quite sure. He needed somebody to interpret to him these movements along the highway. That is often the case with ourselves. Samuel needed the wise old prophet to explain to him that the voice that called him in such a human fashion was after all God's voice. What is the meaning of the stirring of your own heart? Why is it that sometimes, in the most unlikely situations, at a cocktail party, or down at the Sunday show, you are suddenly strangely disgusted and sick of it all? What does it mean that there are times that you feel that you would give your very life to break with sin, and be what you ought to be? O heart, it means for you what it meant for Bartimaeus in the long ago. It means that Jesus is passing your way. To all he comes, though sometimes we fail to have ears to hear and eyes to see.

When Bartimaeus heard that Jesus was passing, what effect did it have on him? Did he pursue his beggar's trade as if nothing big and worthwhile were afoot? No. The great news electrified him. It set his sluggish heart to pounding as if it would leap from his bosom. Of course some of us can hear such news without the tremor of an eyelash. But not so, this beggar. It thrilled him. Not only so, it set him to praying. His was not a long prayer, but it was intense and to the point. When we neither desire anything nor expect anything, we can pour out torrents of words in the form of prayer; but when the sword of a great need has pierced our hearts, then we come to the point. So it was with this blind beggar. "Jesus, thou Son of David, have mercy on me." Bartimaeus put all his knowledge and all his soul into that prayer. The man who told him that Jesus was passing called him "Jesus of Nazareth"; but this beggar recognizes him as the Messiah and calls him the Son of David.

But, there were those present who were shocked by the loud outcries of this beggar. They felt that such tumultuous praying was unseemly. They believed in dignity. They were convinced that even prayers to be effective ought to be built on the Gothic style of architecture. Of course real dignity is quite worthwhile.

But there is a type of dignity that has been well described as "a pose of the body to conceal the defects of the soul." Such is the case with those who are more concerned with being dignified than with being helpful. They ordered this beggar to keep quiet. We never do that, in so many words, but sometimes we silence the supplicants just as effectively by our knowing looks, by our smugness, by our lack of sympathy.

But Bartimaeus was not to be silenced. He was a stout-hearted man. He was bent on winning through to daylight. Seeing the crowd was against him, he only shouted the louder. The greater the opposition, the more determined and desperate became his efforts. I feel like reaching a hand across the centuries to congratulate him. And above the hot words of those who would stop him, Jesus heard his cry. Of course we are not to understand that it was the prayer of this beggar that made Jesus willing to help him. But it was through this prayer that Bartimaeus opened the door of his heart and invited Jesus to enter. And his invitation was not in vain. Jesus stopped and commanded him to be called. And those who have just been his foes are now his friends. Those who a moment ago were getting in his way and commanding him to silence now hurry to his side eager to help. "Courage," they say; "He is calling for thee."

What a thrill this must have brought to Bartimaeus! Nobody had ever wanted him before. Nobody had ever called him. But now this is the word: "Page

Bartimaeus." Who wants him? Jesus wants him. He is eagerly waiting for his approach. And that is my message to you. He is calling for thee. He knows where you sit. He knows the longings of your heart. He knows how dismally and how desperately you have failed. He knows how marvelously you may succeed. He knows all your possibilities. He is looking wistfully at you this moment, singling you out from all that have lived and from all that do live. He knows that he can do something for you that nobody else can do, and that you can do something for him that nobody else can do. "He is calling for thee."

And what did Bartimaeus do, when he heard that good news? He threw aside his beggar's cloak and came at once to Jesus. This man was putting first things first. He would not cling to anything that would hinder him. It was not a sin to wear that old threadbare coat, but it was in the way. Therefore, he parted with it at once. If you come, you must fling away all known sin. You must go even further than that. You must throw away those practices that are not in themselves sinful, but that hinder your usefulness. "Therefore, laying aside every weight and the sin that doth so easily beset us, let us run with patience the race that is set before us." That was what this beggar did. Let us be wise with his wisdom!

Now, because Bartimaeus was willing to give up all for Jesus, Jesus was willing and eager to give all to him. "The eyes of the Lord run to and fro throughout the whole earth, to show himself strong in behalf" of such surrendered souls. It is to these that Jesus can say, "Son, thou art ever with me, and all that I have is thine." Bartimaeus had little enough to give up, a beggar's life in darkness, and a beggar's ragged coat. But, in exchange for these worthless nothings, Jesus put the key of heaven into his hand. "What wilt thou that I should do unto thee?" he asked. "Lord," came the answer, "that my eyes may be opened." And with that the day dawned and the shadows fled away.

IV

What was the outcome? Bartimaeus was not only healed of his physical blindness, but he was healed of his spiritual blindness as well. In fact, this is the supreme miracle of the story. If Bartimaeus had continued in the dark physically his experience would have lost little of its winsome wonder. Having found Jesus, he got off the side line. He got into the game. He began to follow Him whose road always leads where battles for righteousness are to be fought, and where wounds are to be healed. Thus following, he experienced for the first time the high luxury of usefulness and the sweet joy of being wanted. Paul, writing to certain friends of his, said: "Whenever I think of you, I thank God." So, Luke tells us, it came to be with this one-time beggar. When folks thought of him, they thought of God and gave Him thanks.

I heard Dr. Luccock say that while he was in Europe he visited two rooms that impressed him deeply. One was the Hall of Mirrors. In this hall, he could see nothing but repeated images of himself. In one nook he could see himself seven times at a single glance. But in a certain Swiss village, he went into another room that was so full of windows that he called it the "Room of Windows." Here he could not see one single image of himself. But his compensation for this loss was the fact that he could look out and see the wide world. Before Jesus came, Bartimaeus lived in the Hall of Mirrors where he saw nobody but himself. But through this experience he entered "the house of windows" where he no longer saw himself, but Jesus and a needy world. God grant that a like experience may come to ourselves.

BOOK 3

QUESTIONS
JESUS ASKED

CONTENTS

I

THE FOLKS WHO ARE DIFFERENT

"What do ye more than others?"

MATTHEW 5:47

THIS is an arresting and searching question. It is evident that Jesus expects his followers to be vastly different from those about them. He came at a cost to himself beyond our powers to understand, to do something for us that we cannot do for ourselves. It was for the joy that was set before him, a joy measured in terms of transformed lives, that he endured the cross, despising the shame. Just what difference then has his coming made in your life and mine? What is there about us as professing Christians that is special? If there is nothing, then our Christianity is a futile something, a disappointment to ourselves, and a far keener disappointment to him whom we claim as our Lord and Master.

Naturally this difference between the man who is a Christian and the one who is not is not so sharp in our own land today as it was when Christianity was young. This difference is not so pronounced among us as it is in pagan lands where the gospel has been only recently proclaimed. Our society has been so leavened by Christian teaching and preaching that there are multitudes who are Christian in certain of their attitudes, though they acknowledge no loyalty to Jesus Christ. Yet there is something really distinctive about those who know Jesus Christ. A little girl in India, when questioned about the Christians in her village, described them as "the folks who are different." That description holds good in every land and in every age.

As there is a marked difference between the man who follows Christ and the man who does not, there is also a marked kinship between one Christian and another. It is a matter of deep regret that we are divided into so many different sects and denominations. But in spite of this, as others have pointed out, real Christians are more alike than any other people in the world. Henry P. Van Dusen calls our attention to this in his book *They Found the Church There.* In telling how the Christians of the South Sea Islands took care of our soldier boys, he declares that this tender care was the same whether those showing it were Methodist, Catholic, Episcopalian, or any other denomination. As those who know Christ differ from those who do not, even so, real Christians are more alike than any other group in the world.

Assuming then that our Christianity is genuine, what is there distinctive about us? Perhaps we can get a clearer answer to this question by looking at the early church. Often we can see what is far off better than we can see what is near. As we turn the pages of the New Testament, what do we find that the Christian possessed that his unbelieving neighbor did not possess? Of course our answer to this question can be only in part.

I

These early Christians specialized in what, for lack of a better word, I call brotherliness. As T. R. Glover would say, the Christian of the first century outloved his pagan neighbor. He was far more brotherly. There was a breadth and depth about his love that was beautifully distinctive.

1. These early Christians specialized in love one for another. They had been so taught by their Master. How, according to Jesus, are we to distinguish one who is a Christian from one who is not? "By this shall all men know that ye are my disciples, if. . . ." If what? Not if you belong to a certain denomination, not if you hold to certain beliefs or forms of worship. This is the one mark of genuineness: "If ye have love one to another."

It was by one Christian thus loving his fellow Christian that these early saints made perhaps their most profound impression upon the world of their day. "How these Christians love each other!" men exclaimed in awed wonder. And because these pagans longed to love and be loved, they were drawn into these Christian groups that Paul called colonies of heaven. To this day there is nothing so winsome as an atmosphere made warm and vital by the presence of those who really love each other. Such atmosphere belongs to every truly Christian group. This is the case because every Christian loves his fellow Christian.

13

2. Not only did these followers of Jesus love one another, not only did they love the brotherhood, but they loved those outside the brotherhood. If you read *Out of the Night,* a best seller a few years ago, you must have been impressed by the author's emphasis on the devotion of one Communist to another. I could not help being amazed at the price that one fellow traveler seemed willing to pay to serve and protect another. But as impressive as was their loyalty to each other, so was their hatred of all outside their organization. There was no sacrifice too great for them to make in seeking to destroy all who happened not to be of their faith.

But not only did these early Christians love each other, they also loved strangers, foreigners, and outsiders. If our world is divided today by deep and wide chasms, that ancient world was divided by chasms that were deeper and wider still. Yet there was no chasm that separated people in that day that Christianity did not bridge. It bridged the chasm between man and man and between race and race. It bridged the chasm between people who were respectable and those who were outcast. It gave to social nobodies and slaves healing for their wounded self-respect by bringing them into the brotherhood. These early Christians were possessed of an eager interest in every human soul. They not only loved one another, but they loved strangers and outsiders.

3. Finally, these disciples of Jesus not only loved one another, not only did they love strangers and foreigners, but they loved their enemies. That is something that the man of the world not only does not do, but does not even

desire to do. In *Quo Vadis* Petronius is writing a letter to his nephew who has been converted to Christianity. This nephew has been impressing upon his uncle the fact that if he becomes a Christian he must love everybody, even his enemies. "Must I love Nero?" writes the uncle in reply. Then he answers his own question: "I swear by the white knees of the Graces that I couldn't love him if I wanted to." What is implied is that such love is not only impossible but undesirable.

But these Christians did love their enemies. Real Christians do so still. If they do not they are simply not Christians. Of course Christian love does not mean fondness for or delight in one's enemies. They are not the ones that we would choose as our guests. We love our enemies when we exercise toward them an active and sacrificial good will. Such love Jesus taught, such love Jesus practiced. "Bless them that curse you, . . . pray for them which despitefully use you, and persecute you," is his exacting word. So he himself did. He did it even as he hung on the cross. Here he threw about the shoulders of his murderers the sheltering folds of this protecting prayer: "Father, forgive them; for they know not what they do."

Here is another scene. A brilliant and gifted young man, Stephen by name, has become a follower of the Christ. He proclaims his faith with irresistible power. His foes, being unable to answer him with words, resort to stones. They drag him outside the city and mob him. There is no effort at justice or fair play. He is done to death without even a mock trial. How does he meet this terrible ordeal? He meets it in the spirit of his Master.

15

When we hear him pray this prayer, "Lord, lay not this sin to their charge," we know that we are in the presence of a Christian. These early Christians specialized in brotherliness in that they loved one another, they loved outsiders, they loved even their enemies. Such love is characteristic of Christ's real followers today.

II

Then these early Christians specialized in a fine gallantry that made them dare to live life the hard way. They went out, not simply to follow Christ, but to reproduce him. Thus they sought to make him king over all that pagan world. Their adventure was costly. Their Master had made this fact plain to them from the beginning. They had become followers of Jesus knowing that such would be the case. They knew that they would have to pay much, even their very all.

Jesus also makes this plain to us. He declares that there is a wide gate and an easy way, but that this leads to death. If we are bent on life we must enter by the narrow gate and travel the hard way. It was so hard for Jesus himself that it involved the cross. He never promised that it would be easier for us. He said: "If any man will come after me, let him deny himself, and take up his cross, and follow me." At the very door of entrance to life there stands a cross upon which we must die to self. This dying to self is often as painful as physical death. But there is no beginning of the Christian life without this dying to self. There is no continuing it without this daily dying to ourselves. There simply is no cheap and easy way to be a Christian.

If you will turn the pages of your Bible with this in mind, you will be impressed by how little God seems to care for the ease and comfort of his saints. Take those men of the Old Testament who were most loyal to him and who became his closest friends. These heroic souls were willing to dare any danger, brave any death rather than prove disloyal. What response did God make to them? Did he see to it that no rude wind blew upon them? Did he shelter and coddle them? Here is the answer: "They were stoned, they were sawn asunder, were tempted, were slain with the sword: they wandered about in sheepskins and goatskins; being destitute, afflicted, tormented. . . . They wandered in deserts, and in mountains, and in dens and caves of the earth."

In the New Testament there is the same seeming indifference. For instance, when Jesus kneels in prayer for the last time with his little handful of friends he makes no plea that they be sheltered and protected. He knows the harsh and cruel world in which he is leaving them. They are destined, almost to a man, to die for their loyalty to him. Yet this is his prayer: "I pray not that thou shouldest take them out of the world, but that thou shouldest keep them from the evil." He is concerned not for their comfort, but for their character.

What is perhaps stranger still, this indifference on the part of God to the comfort and ease of his saints was shared by these saints themselves. Notice in the New Testament how the followers of Jesus prayed when they

17

found themselves with their backs to the wall. Their prayers were never for escape. Those who prayed only to escape were not followers of Christ. Here are the two revolutionaries who died at the side of Jesus. One of them is a truly great soul. After he has taken the part of Jesus against those who are doing him to death, he prays this prayer for himself: "Lord, remember me when thou comest into thy kingdom." He wants deliverance, not from where he is, even though he is suffering the pangs of hell. He rather seeks deliverance from what he is. But the lesser revolutionary does not mind being what he is; he only hates being where he is. Therefore he prays this prayer: "If thou be Christ, save thyself and us."

Simon Magus has sought to buy the Holy Spirit on a cash basis. With righteous indignation Peter turns on him with this word: "Thy money perish with thee. . . . Repent therefore of this thy wickedness, and pray God, if perhaps the thought of thine heart may be forgiven thee. For I perceive that thou art in the gall of bitterness, and in the bond of iniquity." Then answered Simon and said: "Pray ye to the Lord for me." But what are Peter and John to ask for him? Not that he be forgiven, but "that none of these things which ye have spoken come upon me." He had no desire for any kind of heaven; he only wanted to escape hell.

But listen to the saints as they pray: "And now, Lord, behold their threatenings." Who are doing the threatening? The very same men who had crucified their Master. They know, therefore, that these are not vain threats. Their danger is real. For what then do they pray? They

18

do not ask for escape. This is their prayer: "Grant unto thy servants, that with all boldness they may speak thy word." They do not ask for an easy way. They ask rather that they may see their hard way through with honor.

Here is Paul writing a letter from a prison in Rome. By and by he comes to the matter of prayer. "Praying always with all prayer and supplication in the Spirit, and watching thereunto with all perseverance and supplication for all saints," he urges. Then he remembers his own needs. Therefore he requests prayer for himself. But for what are his friends to ask on his behalf? That he might be free? That his health might no longer be endangered by his hard prison life? By no means. "And for me," he writes, "that utterance may be given unto me, that I may open my mouth boldly, to make known the mystery of the gospel, for which I am an ambassador in bonds." Thus in a fashion characteristic of the saints, he does not ask for an easy way; he rather seeks for strength and courage to walk the hard way. These early Christians dared to walk the difficult road. The same must be true of us.

III

But here is a lovely paradox. If these early Christians did have the hardest time of anybody, they also had the best time of anybody. When we get our first glimpse of them as a group they are so absurdly joyous that the worldlings as they look on can find no explanation of their joy but that they have had a few too many drinks. "These men," they declare, "are full of new wine." But from that intoxication they never recovered. It did not leave them with an ill head and an aching heart. It rather sent them laughing and singing over all that hard Roman world.

Real Christians are joyful. We cannot be like our Master in any other way. I know that we have a tendency to gasp with amazement when we hear Jesus say "My yoke is easy." What was his yoke? It was the yoke of a perfectly dedicated life. It was a yoke that made his life one long toil up Calvary. Yet he tells us that the yoke that cost him so much was kindly. This was certainly true. In spite of the cross, yes, and because of the cross, Jesus lived more richly, more joyously, I take it, than any other man who ever set foot upon this planet.

The abundant life that Jesus lived he shares with his followers. Take another look at Paul, for example. What a hard life he lived! He went to the whipping post so many times that his body must have been little more than one huge scar. He tells us frankly that he suffered the loss of all things. Yet how richly he lived! Absolutely nothing could rob him of his radiance. But this radiance belongs not simply to the Christian of the first century, but of every century. This is the case because specializing in loving and in self-giving, he specializes also in the fellowship of his Lord. The Christian thus possessing Christ possesses all that makes life supremely worth while, both in time and in eternity.

II

THE ANTIDOTE FOR WORRY

"Which of you by taking thought can add one cubit unto his stature?"

MATTHEW 6:27

WHAT warning is Jesus giving us by this arresting question? To begin negatively, he is not warning us against taking life seriously. Jesus was tremendously in earnest. No man was ever more so. One day as his disciples looked into his face they read there the interpretation of a text that they had not understood before. That was this: "The zeal of thine house hath eaten me up." That is, Jesus was fairly burning himself out because of his intense earnestness. He desires us to be in earnest. Therefore he is not urging upon us that happy-go-lucky attitude toward life that some pretend. There are those the soil of whose souls is so shallow that it cannot even grow a decent worry.

No more is Jesus warning us against the thought-out life. Few words of Jesus, in my opinion, have been more grossly misunderstood than what he had to say about

21

taking thought. When, for instance, he said, "Take therefore no thought for the morrow," he was not forbidding us to look ahead. If ever a man took thought for tomorrow, Jesus was that man. It was he "who for the joy that was set before him endured the cross, despising the shame." Since he thought of tomorrow he would have us do the same. Therefore he is not warning here against the thought-out life.

What then is he warning against? He is warning against our taking anxious thought for tomorrow. He is eager that we face the future with an attitude of faith instead of an attitude of feverish and fretful anxiety. Thus he appeals to our common sense with his question: "Which of you by taking thought [or being anxious] can add one cubit unto his stature?"

I

Why do we need a word like this?

1. We need it because so many of us are worried. Perhaps there was never another day in all history when there were so many worried people as there are at this moment. Nor can we explain this widespread worry merely in terms of our circumstances. Many of our circumstances are bad enough, it is true. But worry is not a child of circumstances. Whether you worry or not depends not upon your situation but upon you. Whenever you are robbed by worry it is always an inside job.

But be the causes what they may, multitudes are worried today. Ignorant folks worry. Of course they do not know any better. Educated folks worry. Certainly. They know so much to worry about. Old folks worry. Yes, indeed. They are coming close to the sunset of the evening star. Young folks worry. Naturally. They have so many years ahead of them in our topsy-turvy world. Irreligious folks worry because they have no faith. Many religious folk worry because they have an inadequate faith. All sorts of people worry.

Not only do all sorts of people worry, but they worry about all sorts of things. We worry about our bodies and we worry about our souls. We worry about the pulpit and the pulpit worries about the pew. We worry about getting married and we worry because we have got married. We worry about calamities that actually take place. We worry far more about calamities that never take place. If you are a good worrier and put in more than a forty-hour week, as many of us do, you can count on it that at least 75 to 90 per cent of the tragedies about which you have worried never have and never will take place.

Not only do all sorts of folks worry about all sorts of things, but, as another has pointed out, they worry at the worst possible times. If you would only do all your worrying while on vacation, then it might not be so bad. But instead of picking a good leisurely time, you wait until the going is hard and until the burden is heavy. You wait until you are most in need of steady nerves and a clear head. Then you unfit yourself for coping with your situation by giving way to worry.

2. Then we need this word of warning because worry is so useless. This is the very heart of what Jesus is implying. "Which of you by being anxious can add one

23

cubit unto his stature?" If it so happens that you are not as tall as you desire to be, you will not grow taller by merely worrying about it. We have all done plenty of useless things, but nobody ever did anything more useless than to worry. It never gets us anywhere. It never lifted a single load. It never solved a single problem. It never rubbed out a single wrinkle. But it has rubbed in billions of them.

It has been well said that there are two classes of things about which nobody ought to worry. First, we ought not to worry about those things that we cannot help. There are some things that, if we are wise, we simply accept. We may object to the law of gravity, but it is not wise to argue with that law. This is the case because it will not argue with us; it will only break our bones. There are many things that we might like to avoid if we could, but we simply cannot. Therefore we ought to meet them without anxiety.

Take the matter of growing old, for instance. I have known those who lived in deadly fear of the almanac. There are perhaps some of you who would not tell your ages for any price. There is no gain in that. Folks are guessing at you. By telling your age you might save yourself a year or two. Why should we fear to get old? Does not God have as much plan for December as for June? Yet a friend said to me the other day: "You ought not to get old." I replied: "The only way I know how to avoid it is to die and that is too heroic a remedy for me to be willing to apply it at this time."

A second class of things that nobody ought to worry

about are those things that we can help. Instead of worrying about them, we ought to get so busy helping that we shall not have time to worry. But did you ever wake up on a winter's night about two thirds cold and remember that there was a blanket not six feet away? But instead of getting up and getting the blanket you simply lay there and worried the rest of the night. Of course such conduct did not get you warm, but you had a good time worrying. We ought to avoid anxiety because it is so useless.

3. We need this warning because worry is so harmful. It is harmful to the one who worries. It takes a great deal of work to kill if there is peace within the heart of the worker. But it does not take worry long to make us face toward the cemetery. This ugly sin is the mother of many a disease, and there is no disease known to medicine that it does not aggravate.

Not only does worry hurt the one who worries, but it makes such a one hard to live with. I have known husbands who would be cheerful all day long at their work, then come home at eventide and spill out all their worries about the dinner table and spoil everybody's appetite except their own. I have known a few wives who were so worried that the best they could offer their husbands and children when they came home from the day's work was a face that looked like a dead ache. Those who worry are a burden to themselves, a burden to others, and above all else, they are a disappointment to our Lord. When Jesus was here how often he had to say to his friends with pained amazement: "O men, how little you trust me!"

25

II

Since worry is such an ugly foe we ought not to tolerate it. It is more than a misfortune; it is a positive sin. Therefore we must get rid of it. But how?

There are two so-called remedies that are very popular, but they can be guaranteed not to work. For instance, some of us who are worried now are going to quit worrying just as soon as we get into an ideal situation. But that remedy is an utter failure. This is the case for at least three good reasons. It is a failure in the first place because there is no ideal situation. It is a failure in the second place because if there were an ideal situation, the chances are that you and I would not get into it. It is a failure in the third place because even if there were an ideal situation and you and I were so fortunate as to get into it, the first thing we would do would be to mess it up.

If we cannot conquer worry by getting into an ideal situation, no more can we conquer it by merely clenching our fists and squaring our jaws and saying: "Go to, now, I am never going to worry again as long as I live." I used to have a friend who, when she began to become feverish with anxiety, would say over and over again: "I am not going to worry about that, would you?" But the more she resolved the more desperately worried she became. I have an idea that she got to heaven several years ahead of time because she found no better remedy against worry than grim determination.

What then are we to do?

1. First, I think it might help if we bear in mind that

worry is an acquirement. Nobody was ever born worried. You doubtless caused somebody else to worry soon after you got here, but nobody was ever born worried. If it so happens that you are an excellent violinist or a skilled golfer, it is not because you were born that way; it is rather because you have practiced and practiced and practiced. Even so, if it happens that you are good at worrying, that is the case because you have practiced and practiced and practiced. Worry is an achievement. Anything that we can learn can be unlearned.

2. If we are to conquer worry we must keep on good terms with our consciences. We are gifted with a conscience, every one of us. If we are to have peace we must give ear to that inner voice. H. G. Wells says of a certain character that he was not so much a personality as a civil war. Such civil wars we have all met. These have little chance of making a winning fight against an outside enemy; they are too busy fighting themselves.

Is there a certain course of action that others seem able to follow with impunity but that always leaves you with a feeling of being defeated and morally run down at the heel? If such is the case, however innocent such conduct may seem, you will never know peace until you give it up. Does God seem to be pointing down a certain road saying to you, "Walk that way"? Then you will never find peace until you obey. When Isaiah said, "There is no peace . . . unto the wicked," he was uttering a truth that is as up-to-date as your latest heartbeat! We can never find peace until we stop fighting with God and our own consciences.

3. If we are to find peace some of us will have to re-

direct our thinking. We will have to look sometimes upon the things that we approve and not sorely upon those of which we disapprove. Paul put it in these words: "Whatsoever things are true, whatsoever things are honest, whatsoever things are just, whatsoever things are pure, whatsoever things are lovely, whatsoever things are of good report; if there be any virtue, and if there be any praise, think on these things."

The apostle is not urging us to a blind optimism. He is not trying to make us into starry-eyed Pollyannas. He is not even telling us to look on the bright side. He is rather urging upon us the sanity of seeking in our world, in our situation, in our church, in our friends, in our loved ones, the things that are lovely instead of fixing our whole attention upon those things that are ugly and that fill us with horror and disgust. If we are going to conquer worry we must give attention to the beautiful as well as to the ugly. We must seek to think white instead of allowing ourselves constantly to think black.

4. Finally, the supreme antidote against worry is faith in God. The same fatherly God, Jesus reminds us, who looks after the needs of the birds can be trusted to supply our needs. We are to rest in the Lord and wait patiently for him. We are to cast all our care upon him in the realization that he cares for us. Above all else, we are to make a habit of prayer. Paul, who shared the mind of Christ to an unusual degree, gives us this wise word: "In every thing by prayer and supplication with thanksgiving let your requests be made known unto God. And the peace of God,

which passeth all understanding, shall keep your hearts and minds through Christ Jesus."

I read somewhere of an aviator who was making a flight around the world. After he had been gone for some two hours from his last landing field, he heard a noise in his plane which he recognized as the gnawing of a rat. He realized that while his ship was grounded the rat had entered it and was now getting in his work. Not knowing what bit of his delicate machine those sharp teeth might be cutting, he was filled with fear. At first he did not know what to do. It was two hours back to the landing field and more than two hours to the next one ahead.

Then he remembered that the rat is a rodent. It is not made for the heights; it is made to live on the ground and under the ground. Therefore the pilot began to climb. He went up a thousand feet, then another thousand, and still another thousand, until he was twenty thousand feet in the air. Then the gnawing ceased. When more than two hours later he came down in safety at the next landing field, there was a dead rat in the pit of the plane.

Worry is a rodent. It cannot live "in the secret place of the most High." It cannot breathe in an atmosphere made vital by prayer. Therefore "in every thing by prayer and supplication with thanksgiving let your requests be made known unto God."

> "Drop thy still dews of quietness,
>   Till all our strivings cease;
> Take from our souls the strain and stress,
> And let our ordered lives confess
>   The beauty of thy peace."

III

THE HABIT OF FAULTFINDING

"Why beholdest thou the mote that is in thy brothers' eye, but considerest not the beam that is in thine own eye?"

MATTHEW 7:3

THERE is a delicious touch of humor about this text. Jesus is deadly serious, but that fact does not interfere with his laughter. There are those who confuse seriousness with solemnity. Such people are convinced that to be serious one must be very solemn. Now, while it is possible for one to be very serious and have his eyes bright with tears, it is possible for another to be very serious and have his eyes bright with laughter. Jesus had a sense of humor. He knew that laughter is a good medicine. He knew also that it is a very effective weapon. What could be more absurd than for a man with a log in his eye to minister to another who is afflicted with a mote, a mere speck? Thus did Jesus seek to make the sin of faultfinding look ridiculous, and to laugh it out of court.

It is well to bear in mind that in rebuking the seeker

after specks Jesus is not forbidding us to reach a conclusion as to the degree of worthfulness of those with whom we have to do. Such conclusions are at once inevitable and necessary. This is indicated by the Master's next word: "Give not that which is holy unto the dogs, neither cast ye your pearls before swine." It is impossible to carry out this command unless we reach some conclusion as to who is swinish and who is not. What Jesus is really rebuking is faultfinding—the looking for the worst instead of the best.

I

Why do you see the mote in your brother's eye? It is not because it is so large and glaring that it cannot be overlooked. It is not because it shrieks at you and demands attention. When you see a thing so small that it can float in a sunbeam it is because you are looking for it. You cannot help seeing a log. It compels your attention. But no one is likely to see a mote, an insignificant speck, unless he is a keen-eyed searcher.

And why do we search for specks? Generally speaking, we do so because we hope to find something wrong. We feel that we cannot afford to give the individual thus criticized a clean bill of health. Satan, in the immortal drama of Job, is of this type. When the Lord calls attention to the high character of his servant Job, Satan fairly shakes with laughter. He cannot help being amazed at how easily the Lord is taken in. "Doth Job fear God for nought?" he questions. What he is suggesting is that Job is not really a good man. In fact, there is no such thing as goodness. Decent in his outward conduct he may be, but

31

he is rotten in motive. Thus Satan was so keen-eyed that he could see a speck that was at once invisible and non-existent—a bad motive. Even so, when we see motes it is because we are looking for them and hope to find them.

Why do we hope to find something wrong? We do so for a variety of reasons. Sometimes we look for the worst in order to salve our own consciences. When our own faults and follies and failures make us uncomfortable we often seek to gather a bit of comfort by saying, "I am not the only one." Such people feel that the number of the guilty in some way lessens the guilt of the individual. But of course that is not the case. If I am dying of a disease it will not help me in the least to know that thousands of others are dying of the same deadly disease. Yet we sometimes seek comfort in our moral sickness by looking at the faults of others and convincing ourselves that theirs are as great or greater than our own.

Then we often indulge in faultfinding because we have a strong conviction that by tearing the other fellow down we somehow build ourselves up. For instance, when I tell what a shabby and shoddy minister a certain pastor is, I do this in order that you may, by comparison, realize what a paragon of perfection I am. "Poor Mary," said an over-fed sister the other day. "Poor Mary, she really ought to reduce." Why this criticism? It was the critic's way of adding to her own slenderness without going to the trouble of changing her menu. But we really never build ourselves up by tearing others down. I have never known any man to build a house by tearing down the house of his neighbor.

Finally, we often find fault out of sheer envy. Of all the vices, surely envy is one of the most malignant. It is not, as another has pointed out, to be confused with jealousy. Jealousy may be a perfectly natural and right emotion. I know that at times it is "the green-eyed monster which doth mock the meat it feeds on," but when the meat is made to order by another, then jealousy is all but inevitable. If a husband gives his love to another woman who is not his wife, that wife has a right to be jealous. Jealousy is a child of love.

But envy is a child of hate. "Love envieth not." Envy has a long and ugly criminal record. When Cain's offering was rejected and Abel's accepted, Cain could not take it. Out of envy he struck his brother dead. Saul flung a dart at David and then drove himself mad out of envy. The elder son out of envy did his best to spoil the feast when his prodigal brother had come home. It was envy that helped to crucify our Lord. Sometimes we inflict the pangs of crucifixion by our tongues because of envy. Thus we find fault to salve our own consciousness, to build ourselves up, and out of sheer envy.

II

Why is this practice of looking for motes so wrong?

1. It is wrong in motive. Of course there is such a thing as constructive criticism. We realize the truth of this word: "Faithful are the wounds of a friend." A real friend may point out the faults of one he is earnestly seeking to help. This text does not urge us to go about soft-soaping all and sundry. But the man who is seeking

the worst is not actuated by good will. This man with a log in his eye claimed to be trying to help his brother, but in so claiming he was playing the hypocrite. His motive was one of sheer selfishness.

In one of the beautiful scenes of the New Testament, Mary broke a cruse of oil and anointed her Lord. Jesus saw in it something so lovely that he declared that he would never allow it to be forgotten. The perfume of that gracious deed filled the room on that distant day. Not only so, but it has helped to sweeten our world for nineteen hundred years. But Judas, with a keen eye for the worst, saw in it nothing beautiful at all. He saw in it only something to snarl over. "Why was not this ointment sold for three hundred pence, and given to the poor?" he asked in indignation. It seems at first glance a very reasonable question. But what prompted Judas to offer this criticism? He did not offer it for the sake of Mary, nor for the sake of the poor, nor for the sake of the Master. He offered it out of sheer selfishness. The faultfinder is wrong in his motive.

2. This practice of looking for the worst instead of the best is bad because it so often hurts the one with whom we find fault. There are those who are deeply wounded by such criticism. There are those who are discouraged by it. Then often the faultfinder steals the reputation and thus impairs the usefulness of the one criticized. My reputation is a part of the capital on which I do business. If one robs me of it, doors of usefulness will thereby be shut in my face that might otherwise have remained open. The faultfinder often hurts the one with whom he finds fault.

3. Finally, the habit of looking for the worst instead of the best hurts the critic himself. The faultfinder may wound his brother, but he inflicts the sorest wound upon himself. Why is this the case?

First, it is the case because the habit of faultfinding has a way of putting out our eyes. The faultfinder is never a dependable factfinder. This is true because to seek the worst is to find the worst. It is true here as elsewhere that he that seeketh findeth. To find the worst and to fix our eyes upon it is to miss the best. In looking for something to condemn we fail to see anything to commend. Even Jesus Christ himself had no moral beauty for those who were seeking only to find fault. To seek for the worst is to become blind to the best. You cannot count on the faultfinder as a reliable factfinder.

Tell me what you are seeking and I will tell you what you are likely to find in your brother, in your situation, everywhere.

> "Pussy cat, pussy cat,
>   Where have you been?
> I've been to London
>   To visit the Queen.
>
> Pussy cat, pussy cat,
>   What did you there?
> I frightened a mousey
>   Right under her chair."

Here is one who has been on a visit to the metropolis. London, I think, is the most interesting city in the world. But when this cat had returned and her friends, who had

35

never had an opportunity to visit London, gathered to hear of that famous city, they must have been sorely disappointed. This traveler had nothing to tell of London Tower with its heroic and bloody memories; nothing of Westminster Abbey, that poem in stone, with its sainted dead. She had nothing to say of the Houses of Parliament, nothing of Buckingham Palace, nothing even of the graciousness of the Queen. All she saw was a mouse. She saw only a mouse because, being mouse-minded, that was all she was looking for. She reported truly what she saw, but her report had no light to throw on the city. She had failed to see it.

If I were desirous of knowing the facts about a rugged land of poetry and beauty, I would not send a vulture to spy it out. In one respect he would be well-equipped for the task. But though he might fly over mountains crowned with forests, over many a lovely cottage nestling among the trees, and over waterfalls hanging like white ribbons from the cliffs, he would have nothing to say of any of these beauties. The one fact which he would report would be that he found a bit of carrion under a thornbush. Why would this be the case? It would not be so because that was all that was there. It would be the case because that would be all he was looking for.

One day you went to church in a critical frame of mind. You were in a mood to find fault. What was the result? Though the music was beautiful, the scripture lesson a gem, the sermon so full of truth that you agreed with it 99 per cent, yet you were not edified. This was because the minister said just one thing that offended you. There was

36

one word in the sermon that you did not like. But instead of rejecting the little that was bad and accepting the much that was good, you threw away the good and kept only the objectionable. Had I desired an accurate account of that service I could not have obtained it from you. The faultfinder cannot be counted on for the truth. He is a bad factfinder.

Not only does the faultfinder miss the facts about his brother, but he misses those about himself as well. Generally speaking, the keener our eyes become to the faults of others, the blinder do they become to what is wrong with ourselves. The more we magnify the vices of our brother, the more do we minimize our own. It is equally true that the more we minimize his virtues, the more do we magnify our own. Thus we still hear one who is doing nothing to help heal the world's open sore saying pridefully, "At least I am not a hypocrite." What a noble boast! Neither is a tiger or a jackal or a fishing worm. No man is a saint because of one ugly sin of which he happens not to be guilty.

This blindness to his own faults is just what has overtaken this man who was looking for specks. What a joke it was when, with a whole log in his eye, he goes to his friend and dares to say: "Pardon me, but there is a speck in your eye. Let me help you." But our laughter is changed to tears when we realize that the poor fellow is not joking at all. He is in earnest. Thus that which might have been merely ludicrous becomes genuinely tragic. So long had this man looked for the faults of others that he had become totally blind to his own.

4. Then the faultfinder cheats himself in the realm of friendship. If you really desire to know how to win friends and influence people, I cannot give you all the rules that will work, but I can give you one that will not work. You will not win friends by constantly seeking for the worst in those about you and then telling them wherein they are wrong. If you have a friend you may lose him just by persistently picking him to pieces. If you have an enemy you may change him into a friend by looking for what is best in him and by telling him of your appreciation of that best. Here the word of Jesus is emphatically true: "With what measure ye mete, it shall be measured to you again."

5. Finally, the habit of faultfinding so ministers to our pride that it makes repentance next to impossible. Generally speaking, the faultfinder is an egotist. He is proud of his capacity to see more through a keyhole than others can see through a wide-open door. Iago, the worst devil in literature, was a man of this type. This is his proud boast: "I am nothing if not critical." Instead of being ashamed of his wickedness, he took pride in it. He was therefore as far from repentance as the Pharisee who went to the temple to pray, but got so busy cataloguing the vices of others that he forgot to ask for God's mercy and pardon for himself. The lesser robber who died by the side of Jesus might have repented had he not been so busy criticizing others. The greater robber went right where his companion went wrong. He took a look at himself. Therefore he declared that though he was suffering the very pangs of hell, he was suffering justly. It was thus

that repentance was born. No man ever finds God by confessing the sin of his brother. He has to confess and repent of his own.

Why then do we so often cheat ourselves by looking for petty faults? Such a habit is as silly as it is wicked. It is a sure way of ministering to our own wretchedness. However fine your friend, however lovely your home, however adorable your wife, however faithful your husband, just practice the habit of looking for the worst and all the glamour will fade away. However loyal your employer or employee, however excellent your position, constantly seek to find something to criticize adversely and soon you will be changing jobs. The habit of looking for specks may hurt others, but it will certainly inflict its deadly harm upon the faultfinder.

III

How then are we to find a cure for this ugly habit?

1. Let us realize the wickedness of it. Such a habit is not simply our peculiarity, it is our deadly sin. It is a cruel weapon by which we wound ourselves, our fellows, and our Lord. Such conduct can be natural only to an unregenerate and unbrotherly heart.

2. Having faced the wickedness of this habit, we are to repent. Repentance means a change of mind. It is so to change our minds that we not only cease our faultfinding, but we go in the opposite direction. Just as we once cultivated the habit of looking for something to condemn, we are now, by the grace of God, to cultivate the habit of looking for something to commend. Thus looking for the

best we are sure to find it, for it is true here also that he who seeketh findeth.

One day years ago my small son came running into my study to invite me to come and see a strange dog that had come to visit us. I hurried out only to find about the most disreputable-looking cur I had ever beheld. "What a horrible-looking creature," I exclaimed. But the boy saw him through different eyes. Therefore he was quick in his defense. "But, Daddy," he said, "he wags his tail good." Thus looking for the best, he found it. We can cultivate this habit and thus help others as well as oureslves.

> "There are loyal hearts, there are spirits brave,
>   There are souls that are pure and true;
> Then give to the world the best you have,
>   And the best will come back to you."

IV

THE HAND OF FAITH

"O thou of little faith, wherefore didst thou doubt?"

MATTHEW 14:31

JESUS put this question to Simon Peter after that daring disciple had turned a triumph into a near tragedy. You will notice that to the Master's question Peter gave no answer. That is out of the ordinary. Doubt is usually quite vocal. It can pour out niagaras of words in defense of its position, and often look quite keen-eyed and broad-browed while so doing. But on the pages of the Bible, and especially in the presence of Jesus, it does not show up so well. Often it looks quite unreasonable. Such is surely the case in this fascinating story. If it is true that the parables of Jesus are miracles of wisdom, it is also true that his miracles are parables of teaching. They are at once both timely and timeless. Therefore they have something of value to say to us.

I

Look at Simon's fine beginning.

He with his fellow disciples is in a small vessel on the

Sea of Galilee. This little sea is being whipped into a rage by a tempest. Against the fierce opposition of the storm these fighting and frightened men are making little progress. Though it is now three o'clock in the morning they are but little nearer their goal than when they set out hours ago. More than once have they said to themselves and to each other that they wished that the Master would come. Then, as if in answer to their longing, they see him coming across the waves.

But his coming at first brings them no gladness. Our Lord often comes to us in a fashion that fills us more with fear than with comfort. Sometimes he comes in the guise of a keen disappointment or a heavy heartache. Sometimes he comes in a call to a high adventure of faith that we are not willing to make. I think it might amaze us to realize how many of us are really afraid of God— afraid, not in a beautiful and filial fashion, but rather in a fashion that makes us unwilling to surrender to him wholly lest he should demand too much of us.

Jesus, realizing that they were afraid, spoke to them this word of comfort: "Be of good cheer; it is I; be not afraid." "Be of good cheer." That word was upon the lips of Jesus again and again. He uttered it in the face of the ravages that sin had made; he uttered it as he reached the end of the journey and faced what seemed to be disastrous defeat. "In the world," he declared, "ye shall have tribulation: but be of good cheer; I have overcome the world." He implied: "I have overcome the fear of it and the love of it; I have overcome the worst it could do to me, and have changed that worst into the best."

Now, on hearing that word, "Be of good cheer," Simon's fear gave way to faith. He at once began to dream of doing the impossible. Jesus ever inspires faith. When one day his disciples came upon him at prayer they were deeply moved. Here was prayer that was so beautiful and real that it made their own prayer life seem paltry and cheap. They realized that they had never really prayed, at least not in this fashion. But if what they saw rebuked them, it also gave them hope. As they thus looked upon the Master they said, "We too can pray." Therefore they came eagerly and expectantly saying, "Lord, teach us to pray."

Not only does Jesus inspire faith by what he says and by what he does; he inspires faith through the faith of others. How much we owe to our fellow believers! There are those in whose presence it is easy to doubt. But there are also those in whose presence it is easy to believe the highest and the best. When my own lamp of faith has burned low I have gone again and again to relight it at the glowing torches of some of the choice believers whom I have known along the way.

Now as soon as Simon began to believe, he was ready for action. Faith is an active something. A Gallup poll revealed the fact that some 99 per cent of the American people claim to believe in God. But what is their faith doing for them? Is it helping them to conquer their lust for power, for money, for the unclean? What we really believe shapes our character and our conduct. When a certain crackedbrained adventurer decided centuries ago that the world was round instead of flat, he could not rest until he had done something about it. It is impossible to take very seriously the professed faith of many of those composing this 99 per cent. Too many of them act as if the Bible were a myth and God a lie.

When Simon reached the conviction that with the presence of Jesus the impossible was possible he did something. He said: "Lord, if it be thou, bid me come unto thee on the water." How did the Master answer him? He did not rebuke him. Instead of telling Simon he was foolish, instead of warning him against being a starry-eyed fanatic, he rather invited him to adventure.

Just as Jesus inspires faith, he also encourages it. As we turn the pages of the New Testament we find that nothing thrilled him more than faith. Here is the story of a pagan who fairly swept Jesus off his feet by the fullness of his faith. He was a Roman centurion. When a slave of this officer became ill he so took the illness of that slave upon himself that he asked certain Jewish friends to appeal to Jesus on his behalf. This Roman soldier must have been a great soul. His brotherliness bridged the chasm between master and slave, Gentile and Jew, conqueror and conquered. In spite of the fact that he belonged to an army of occupation he had won the confidence and the friendship of the people he had been sent to rule. Therefore when these Jews appealed to Jesus they said he was worthy, "for he loveth our nation."

In answer to their prayers Jesus at once set out to visit this sick slave. But when this officer saw him coming he sent a messenger saying, in effect: "Never mind about coming. I am not worthy that you should enter my house,

44

but speak the word only and my servant shall be healed. As a Roman soldier I have soldiers under me. When I give them orders they obey. You who have under you the healing might of God himself need only speak the word and my slave shall be healed." At that Jesus declared joyfully that he had not found so great faith even in Israel. Jesus always appreciated and encouraged faith.

When, therefore, Simon sought to do the impossible Jesus encouraged him. He did so with one word: "Come." When the Master said "Come," Simon at once began to climb out of the boat. That was faith. Had I been in Simon's place I should have desired far more than that one word of invitation. I should have wanted specific assurance on the part of Jesus that he would help me see it through. But Simon knew that the invitations of Jesus are guarantees that power will be given to the invited to accept. If this were not the case such invitations would not in reality be invitations at all, but mere mockery. Therefore believing that he can do what Jesus invites him to do, Simon boldly climbed out of the boat. Does it look silly? By no means when we face the facts. Upon what was Simon depending for safety while he remained in the boat? Upon a few planks. What was his confidence when he climbed out? His confidence was in the everlasting arms. He was depending upon the power of him in the hollow of whose hand the seas rage and roar.

Now thus depending upon the word of Christ, for a time at least he triumphed. No subsequent failure can do away with that fact. He did the impossible. So have countless thousands of others. There are those of us who

45

have thus won through difficulties that we could not have faced in our own strength. To the man who believes, always the impossible becomes possible. While Simon trusted he triumphed, and thus he was an inspiration to his friends and a joy to his Lord.

II

But when we look again something has gone wrong. Simon is sinking as if his Lord were out of the picture altogether. What is the matter? It is not that his Master's arm has grown weak or weary. It is not that the tempest has become too strong. The cause is rather this: Simon's faith has given way to fear. He has come to doubt. That is ever a supreme cause of failure. To doubt is always to sink.

"Without faith," says the writer to the Hebrews, "it is impossible to please him." We might leave off the latter part of the sentence and it would still be true. "Without faith it is impossible." What is impossible? Everything constructive is impossible. Without faith it is impossible to get married; it is impossible to build a home or to keep one; it is impossible to run a bank or any other business. Without faith it is impossible to win a permanent peace. It is faith that does all the constructive work that is done in the world.

Just as nothing of worth is possible through doubt, everything is possible through faith. So Jesus declared in language that sounds to us extravagant, even incredible. He said that a bit of faith that is genuine, even if no larger than a mustard seed, is mightier than an atomic bomb.

46

He was sure that such faith could toss mountains about. For instance, one day a father brought to him his afflicted son. Jesus was away at the time. Therefore his disciples tried to heal the boy, but failed. In the presence of their failure the father's faith began to slip. When Jesus came, the best that this father could pray was this: "If thou canst do any thing, have compassion on us, and help us."

At this Jesus looked at him with mingled amazement and pity. He was putting the "if" in the wrong place. "If thou canst believe, all things are possible to him that believeth." Then the father cried out with tears: "Lord, I believe; help thou mine unbelief." His was not a perfect faith, but it made the impossible to become possible. That is a unique and yet oft-repeated story. Jesus is saying today when we give him the opportunity what he often said in the long ago: "Go thy way: thy faith hath made thee whole." But without faith we constantly thwart his purpose for us. He can still do no mighty work for those who refuse to believe.

III

To faltering Simon, Jesus puts this question: "Wherefore didst thou doubt?" Why indeed? We do not all doubt for the same reason.

1. Some doubt is born of wishful thinking. I know that we who believe are accused of being the victims of wishful thinking. At times this may be true. But wishful thinking certainly works both ways. There are those who doubt in order to evade moral responsibility. The fool of whom the psalmist writes was such a man. "The fool hath said in

his heart, There is no God." He did not deny God in his head but in his heart. The fact of God put him at a high altitude where breathing was a bit difficult. It compelled him to face responsibilities that he did not desire to face. Therefore he dismissed God. Sometimes we doubt because we will to doubt.

2. There are those who doubt because of God's strange ordering of things. John the Baptist is a good example of this kind of doubter. He was a great and loyal soul. He had staked everything on his faith in Jesus Christ. For his loyalty he is now languishing in prison instead of carrying on his work in the big outside world. Rumors are being blown to him in his gloomy prison of how the Young Prophet is working wonders in the outer world. He is cleansing lepers and opening blind eyes. If he can do these impossible tasks for others, why does he not open the prison cell of one who has been a loyal friend? To this question John finds no satisfactory answer. Therefore, filled with doubt, he appeals to Jesus with this question: "Art thou he that should come, or do we look for another?" His doubt was born of God's strange dealing with him.

3. There are those who doubt because of their willful disobedience. This, I am convinced, causes more doubt than all else. However little you may believe, if you live up to that little it will grow from more to more. But however strong your faith, if you become deliberately disloyal to that faith it will inevitably die. Here that word of Jesus is supremely true. "Unto every one that hath shall be given, and he shall have abundance: but from him that

hath not, shall be taken away even that which he hath."
The way to spiritual certainty is the way of obedience.
"If any man is willing to do his will, he shall know."

4. Finally, there are those who fall into doubt because
they become obsessed by their difficulties. This was the
cause of Simon's failure. He was getting on quite well
until he saw how boisterous the wind was. Then he took
his eyes off the Master and fixed them on the raging sea.
Looking at the storm he came to believe in its might more
than in the might of his Lord. He saw Jesus through his
difficulties instead of looking at his difficulties in the light
of his Lord. Thus his problems loomed so large that they
blinded him altogether to the presence of Christ.

This is an ever-present danger. It threatens us especially
today as we face our national problems. The clouds that
gather on the horizon of the world at present are very
black. So black are they that for multitudes they have
hidden the face of God. Many are so obsessed by their
dangers that they are blind to their advantages. They are
like the ten spies who went to spy out the Promised Land.
These became so keenly conscious of the giants that they
forgot utterly the leadership of their victorious Lord.

Just as this is true among the nations today, it is also
true of many of us individually. There are those who are
so obsessed by their personal difficulties that they can see
nothing else. Even when they go to pray they too often
fail to look to him who "is able to do exceeding abundantly above all that we ask or think." They rather look
at their own weaknesses and pressing needs. Thus their
prayers often become a source of weakness rather than of

strength. Our one hope is to look to God. This is his word: "Look unto me, and be ye saved, all the ends of the earth."

IV

Even in his defeat Simon has a helpful message for us. Though he made a failure he did not allow his defeat to discourage him. He recovered his faith and ended in a triumph that thrills us to this hour. How did he do it?

1. He faced the facts about himself. When he found himself sinking he did not shut his eyes to that depressing fact. He did not try to bluff it through. He did not tell himself that while he was making a mess of things such failure was all he had a right to expect. He faced the fact that though Jesus had invited him, he was sinking right in his presence. Then he faced the further fact that he could not manage the situation alone. Simon faced these two facts: I am sinking; I cannot save myself.

2. Having faced the facts, Simon looked to him who is able to help. Simon took his eyes off the storm and fixed them again on Jesus. Then he prayed. I like his prayer. I like the intensity of it. I like the brevity of it. When we have no burden we can pray wordy prayers. But when we face a problem that is a matter of life or death, then we come to the point. This Simon did. He simply cried, "Lord, save me." Then what? Jesus saved him. That mighty hand that is always feeling for yours and mine in calm and in tempest, in the daylight and in the dark, gripped the up-lifted hand of Simon and lifted him out of defeat into victory. So it may happen to us. Let us reach our hands to him in the faith that his hand is reaching for ours.

V

THE SUPREME QUESTION

"Who say ye that I am?"

MATTHEW 16:15

JESUS had gone with his disciples to the district of Caesarea Philippi for a brief retirement. Here he asked this inner circle of friends two questions. The first of these questions had to do with the impression that he had made upon the people during his brief ministry. "Who do men say that I am?" he asked. I dare say that Jesus already knew the answer to this question quite as well as his friends. He was therefore not so much seeking information as he was seeking to help these friends to a clear and solid affirmation of their own faith.

In answering this question his disciples did not tell the whole story. They passed over the ugly criticisms that they had heard. They said nothing of those who had accused their Master of being a winebibber and a glutton and a friend of publicans and sinners. Instead, they told him only the complimentary things that they had heard. They declared that some had been so impressed by his fiery earnestness that they thought he might be John the Baptist come back from the dead. Others had felt the rugged strength of him and had called him Elijah. Others had been gripped by his tenderness and had named him Jeremiah. Others still, feeling that he embodied the very finest qualities of the heroes of the past, said that he was one of the old prophets.

This was the very climax of the complimentary. To be likened to a living prophet might be anything but flattering. Real prophets, while they are alive, generally manage to get themselves heartily hated. But to be likened to one of the great prophets long since dead was praise indeed. Yet Jesus heard these words of high commendation without the slightest enthusiasm. I dare say he was no more thrilled by them than he is thrilled today when we see in him only a personality so great that he cut history squarely in two.

We are accustomed to honor our illustrious dead. We celebrate the anniversaries of certain select souls whose achievements in point of character and conduct have been outstanding. We write books to remind ourselves of the virtues that made these great personalities what they were and to quicken our sense of gratitude for the high service they rendered. We impress upon our children a sense of obligation and responsibility to pass on to others the lighted torches that we have received from their hands. But when life grows hard and we find ourselves in the midst of bleak winter, none of us turn to George Washington in memory of his heroic struggle at Valley Forge. As much as we honor him, we do not seek help from him.

Those who think of Jesus as a great prophet are altogether right, but that is not enough. That answer aroused no enthusiasm in Jesus.

Having asked this question about other men's opinion, Jesus asked the disciples to speak for themselves. He put the question to them personally: "Who say ye that I am?"

This is a question to which we might well await the answer in breathless anticipation. Other men spoke from hearsay or from seeing Jesus once or twice. But these disciples are the star witnesses. They have been with him constantly. They have heard all his words; they have seen all his deeds. What is their answer?

When they first began to follow him, they had no clearly defined answer. They found him amazingly exciting. They found him by far the most winsome personality they had ever known. At times he shocked them. At times he thrilled them. At other times he filled them with awe and wonder. He set them whispering to each other, "What manner of man is this?" Whoever he was, they were sure that he was vastly greater than any other they had ever known.

Now the cross was only about six months away. The Master had taken them for a retreat to Caesarea Philippi. Evidently he thought that they had been with him long enough to have reached some definite conclusion. They had seen him in solitude and in the midst of crowds; they had been by when he had prayed, when he had preached, when he performed his works of wonder. So he now put to them this question, "Who say ye that I am?"

Impulsive Simon speaks up for them all. In a tremendous answer he affirms his faith: "Thou art the Christ, the Son of the living God." That is, Simon is saying, "I have found in thee the very values that I seek and that I find in God."

And what was the reaction of Jesus? Did he rebuke Simon, as any honest man who was mere man would have done? When a few years later Paul and Barnabas had created such enthusiasm in Lystra that the people were on the point of offering them sacrifices because they thought they were gods, what was the reaction of these good men? They were horrified. They repudiated such honor though it came very near to costing Paul his life.

But what, I repeat, was the reaction of Jesus to Simon's answer? He did not rebuke Simon. He rather pronounced a blessing upon him. With wholehearted enthusiasm he said: "Blessed art thou, Simon, Bar-jona: for flesh and blood hath not revealed it unto thee, but my Father which is in heaven." He thus declared that the conviction of Simon is the truth, a truth that he had come to possess because he had been illuminated by the very light of God.

"Thou art the Christ, the Son of the living God." That was no passing notion, no spur-of-the-moment guess later seen in another light. The certainty of Simon and his fellow disciples that Jesus is God come in the flesh did not weaken with the passing of the years, but rather grew stronger. Having witnessed the death and resurrection of their Master, and having experienced Pentecost, these men became aboslutely certain that the same Jesus with whom they had walked the roadways of Galilee was alive forevermore. They became certain that he was both with and within them as a living presence. Not only so, but

54

they became the kind of men and did the kind of deeds that we should expect God-possessed men to become and to accomplish.

I

Is the faith of these disciples your faith? Today Jesus is searching our hearts with this question: "Who say ye that I am?" This is an abiding question. In every age it is the most important question with which men have to deal. It is therefore the most important question that confronts you and me today. This is not simply my conviction; it is the conviction of Jesus himself. It is so important that if we give it a wrong answer, though if it were possible we might give a right answer to every other question, life must be an adventure of failure and of tragedy. It is so important that if we give it a right answer, though if it were possible we might give a wrong answer to every other question, life would still be an adventure of joy and victory.

Listen to these daring words of Jesus: "Whosoever heareth these sayings of mine, and doeth them, I will liken him unto a wise man, which built his house upon a rock. . . . And every one that heareth these sayings of mine, and doeth them not, shall be likened unto a foolish man, which built his house upon the sand." Thus does Jesus claim to be the arbiter of human destiny. He claims that whether nations or individuals rise or fall, survive or perish, depends upon their attitude toward him.

If you remind me that Jesus is here talking about his sayings, his teachings, and not about himself, I answer

55

that Jesus and his teachings are one. He did not claim merely to teach the truth. He said: "I am . . . the truth." He himself is Christianity: Listen to him: "Blessed are they which are persecuted for righteousness' sake. . . . Blessed are ye, when men shall revile you, and persecute you, and shall say all manner of evil against you falsely, for my sake." "For righteousness' sake" and "for my sake" are synonymous. This is the case because Jesus is the very incarnation of righteousness. He and his teachings are one.

Recently a distinguished minister declared that in order to be a Christian it is only necessary to share the faith of Jesus. This faith he summed up as faith in a fatherly God and in the brotherhood of man. He asserted that our attitude toward Jesus himself is not of prime importance. However much truth there may be in that assertion, this I can say with absolute conviction: such is not the Christianity of the New Testament. It is not the Christianity possessed by the disciples, nor is it the Christianity taught by Jesus. The supreme question of the New Testament is not, "What think ye of the faith of Jesus?" but, "What think ye of Christ?" It is, "Who say ye that I am?"

How flatly this contradicts the conviction held by so many today—that what one believes is a matter of no great importance! There are still intelligent churchmen who are lukewarm in their attitude toward the missionary enterprises of the church because they are possessed of a hazy belief that one faith is about as good as another. Christianity may be good for Occidentals, but it might not work so well for those living in the Orient. Yet the law of gravitation works just as well for the one as for the other.

I read somewhere that a committee of Japanese waited on the philosopher Herbert Spencer years ago to discuss with him the wisdom of adopting a state religion for Japan. He thought that such a step might be wise. Then when they asked what religion they should adopt, he agreed that their own Shintoism, being a native religion, might be quite as good for them—if not better—as any other, not excepting Christianity.

Now, had a friend told Herbert Spencer after this interview that he had assisted in placing an infernal bomb under the Japanese nation that would one day blow it to bits and leave black wounds on the rest of the world, he would have heard him in utter incredulity. This would have been the case because Spencer was an unbeliever and looked upon one faith as about as good as another.

But regardless of what Spencer had to do with it, what actually came of the adopting of a religion on the part of Japan that taught that the emperor is divine? Multitudes took that creed seriously. Believing that they had the Son of Heaven for their emperor, they naturally came to believe that a people so highly favored were destined to rule the world. One who had lived long in Japan declared that when he would tell a Japanese friend that he did not share his faith that his nation was destined to conquer the world, this friend would not become angry; he would just be astonished that one should be so ignorant and illogical. Thus the attack on Pearl Harbor, the fanatical heroism with which the Japanese fought, was the natural outcome of their faith. What they believed wrecked them and caused them to seek to wreck the world.

The greatest threat to modern civilization today, in my opinion, is atheistical communism. What is wrong with the Communist? It is not that he by nature differs from ourselves. If you were to prick him, he would bleed. He is not made of the slime and ooze of things while we are made of far finer material. Yet here is a man who acknowledges no loyalty except that to his political party. There is no other trust that he will not betray. There is not a crime that he is not ready to commit. Why is this the case? It is because of what he believes.

What one believes, therefore, is a matter of great importance. This is the case because beliefs are creative. As a wrong faith issues in wrong character and wrong conduct, even so a right faith issues in right character and right conduct. Therefore when Jesus searches us with this question, "Who say ye that I am?" he is asking a question of supreme importance. Upon the answer we give to that question depends the destiny of the individual and the destiny of the world.

II

"Who say ye that I am?" That question is intensely personal.

Some time ago a friend of mine sent a manuscript to his publisher. It happens that this friend is a great reader. In writing his book he seems to have said to himself: "Why should I read so widely and not use what I have read?" Therefore he fairly crowded his manuscript with

58

quotations. The result was that it was returned a few weeks later with this notation: "Too many quotations. We want to know what you think."

When Paul reached Rome as a prisoner, his fellow Jews gathered about him to hear what he had to say. "We know," they declared, "that this sect to which you belong is everywhere spoken against. You Christians have a bad reputation. But we desire to know what you think. Evidently," they seemed to say, "something big has happened to you. Something has brought you through. Tell us what you think of the Christ whose you are and whom you serve. Who do you say that he is?"

In the same way I bring this question to your own heart and mine. Who do you say that Jesus is? I am happy in the conviction that there are those who find in him just what these early saints found. He is to many of you a "friend that sticketh closer than a brother." He is your Lord and Master, your personal Saviour. You too can sing:

"Thou, O Christ, art all I want;
More than all in thee I find."

For those of you who have not come to this bracing certainty I have this good news. You too may give a satisfying answer to this question out of your own experience. You too can say: "I know whom I have believed, and am persuaded that he is able to keep that which I have committed unto him against that day." Certainly that is a consummation devoutly to be wished.

Christianity is a religion of giving—worldly goods, time, talents, love, our very selves. But it is also a religion of receiving. When God gave himself in the person of Jesus Christ in that distant day, some refused to receive the gift. Here is one of the saddest sentences ever written: "He came unto his own, and his own received him not." But there were those who did receive him. That sad sentence is followed by one of the most thrilling ever written: "As many as received him, to them gave he power to become." That is what Jesus is constantly doing for those who receive him. He gives them the power to become. Simon received power to become a rock of Christlike character. Fanatical and narrow John received power to become an apostle of love. To all he gives power to become new creations in Christ Jesus.

Receiving him, we not only receive power to become Christlike, but we also receive power to give somewhat as he gave. There were those in that distant day who declared, "We have no king but Caesar." Built upon that foundation, their houses were swept into oblivion long centuries ago. There was a far smaller group who went out saying, "We have no king but Christ." These still enrich us, these still breathe upon us like the breath of an eternal springtime. Receiving power to live, they also received power to give. So it may be for us.

I think about the most needlessly cruel deed I ever witnessed took place at a Christmas celebration in our little village church. The tree must have been quite a crude affair, but to my boyish eyes it had the beauty of paradise. Santa Claus was present in person. We boys and girls gathered about him while he called our names and filled our hands with presents.

But there was one boy whose name was not called. He was the village idiot. He stood with his ugly face turned toward the tree, one gaunt wistfulness. Then Santa Claus took down the largest box that was on the tree and called his name. He reached for his present with eager hands. He untied the string with fingers that trembled. Then he lifted the lid to find the box empty. Somebody, mistaking a tragedy for a joke, had given him only an empty box.

We are hanging presents upon the world's great Christmas tree, each of us. The presents we hang are the lives we live. Some give lives that are empty of goodness and empty of God. But it need not be so. It will certainly not be so for him who shares the faith of the disciples that Jesus is "the Christ, the Son of the living God" and receives this Christ into his own heart. This is the case because "he that believeth on me, . . . out of his inner life shall flow rivers of living water."

"Who say ye that I am?" To answer that question aright is to receive power to live and power to give.

VI

BREAD

*"Why reason ye, because ye have no bread?
. . . Do ye not remember?"*

MARK 8:17-18

DO ye not remember?" This question was born of
pained amazement. Jesus was finding it difficult to
be patient with his blundering disciples. When he warned
them to beware of the leaven of the Pharisees they missed
the point altogether. They failed to understand that his
warning was against the doctrine of the Pharisees. The
word "leaven" had misled them. They saw in that word
nothing but bread. Therefore when they took account of
their assets and found that they had only one loaf, they
were in a perfect fever of anxiety.

Now it was this anxiety on the part of his disciples
that filled the Master with pained amazement. He could
not see, in the light of their own experiences, how they
could be so worried about bread. Since he had met their
needs in the past, they should have trusted him to meet
them in the future. Thus it was not a too great interest in

bread on the part of these disciples that disturbed Jesus, but rather their lack of faith. The Master is not here minimizing the importance of bread, as a surface reading of the story might suggest. He is rather magnifying its importance. He is seeking to teach his disciples that he is both willing and able to supply all our needs. Therefore he questions: "Do ye not remember?" What then are we to remember?

I

We are to remember the interest of our Lord in those needs that we are accustomed to call physical and temporal. He knows that man cannot live by bread alone. He also knows that man cannot live without bread. He is therefore as truly interested in the bread that gives life to the body as he is in the bread that gives life to the soul. Our failure to realize this has led to a conviction regarding Jesus that has resulted in untold harm. That conviction is that Jesus is not quite practical. His teachings are of course unspeakably beautiful. He is indeed "the sweet Galilean dreamer." If we only lived in castles in the air, or if we were souls without any bodies, then his teachings might be excellent. But since we have bodies that must be housed and clothed and fed, we had better look elsewhere for teaching that fits us to live the life that now is.

But this view is flatly contradictory to the teaching of Jesus. Our Lord is interested in all our interests. He never drew any sharp distinction between the secular and the sacred as we are accustomed to do. When a housewife makes a cake she does not put the sugar in one compartment and the other ingredients in another. The sugar permeates the whole cake. Thus with Jesus religion permeated the whole of life. He knew that for one to be religious on holy days and in holy places was not in reality to be religious at all. Jesus therefore was interested in the temporal as well as the spiritual.

Since this is the case, our Lord never concerned himself merely about the souls of men. I do not read that he ever asked any man: "How is your soul?" Of course he knew that man is both body and spirit. But he was interested not in bodies and not in spirits. He was interested in folks; in men and women, boys and girls. He knew that while man is both a son of Adam and a son of God, he is also a unit. What therefore God had joined together he did not put asunder. He was interested in the whole man.

Jesus realized, I am sure, something of the tremendous influence of the mind over the body. We are told today that some 60 per cent of those occupying beds in our hospitals became ill mentally before they were ill physically. A sick mind is very likely to eventuate in a sick body.

But if the mind influences the body, so does the body influence the mind. This body is the house in which I live. If it comes to be a tumble-down ruin, I may still be sound in my soul, but such an achievement will not be easy. Other things being equal, it is far easier to be genuinely Christian with a sound body than with one that is tortured by disease. It is easier to be sunny and optimistic when we feel fit than when we feel unfit.

We recognize this every day by the apologies we make, both for ourselves and others. When one we love is rude we say "he is not himself today." Even on the radio we hear one rail out in anger and then apologize by laying his loss of temper on a headache. Personally I have little respect for such excuses. I am exceedingly selfish if, just because I am miserable, I seek to make everybody about me miserable too. But when we do become peevish and fretful we often plead our pain for an excuse. Even so great a man as Thomas Carlyle sought to explain his years of snarling by saying nothing better could be expected of one who had dyspepsia gnawing like a rat at the pit of his stomach.

Elijah was a tremendous man. Both by nature and by grace he was one of the greatest of the prophets. But in spite of his greatness we find him one day whining and complaining like a spoiled child. He tells God frankly that he has had enough, that he wants to die. Great saint that he is, he is not even honest. He did not really wish to die. Had that been his desire he would not have had to pray about it. All he would have needed to have done would have been to stop over in Jezreel for a day or two. Jezebel would have fixed him up without any prayer. Why then is he thus playing the baby? It is in part because he is physically and nervously exhausted. Therefore the first step God took toward bringing him to himself was to feed him and give him a good night's sleep.

Since our Lord is concerned with the whole man he is keenly interested in bread. This interest runs through his entire ministry. When he passed through a wheat field with his disciples one Sabbath and these disciples gathered a bit of the grain to eat, the Pharisees were outraged. But the Master defended his offending friends both from scripture and common sense. Having cited the example of David he uttered this word of wisdom: "The Sabbath was made for man, and not man for the Sabbath." By this he was not minimizing the importance of the Sabbath. The Sabbath is of vast importance. But he was saying that no institution is so important as to be above human need. Then, in the passage of which our text is a part, Jesus reminds us that on two occasions he met the physical needs of the multitudes that gathered about him.

Just as our Lord was concerned about bread in the days of his flesh, so was he concerned after his resurrection. Listen to this winsome story. A little group of disciples who have been fishing are coming home in the gloaming of early morning. They see a stranger on the shore. Then this stranger speaks: "Lads, have you caught anything?" When they answer that they have caught nothing he tells them how to cast their net in order to be successful. Then when they reach the shore they find breakfast waiting for them. Who prepared it? Their risen Lord. How wonderful that those mighty hands that created the universe, those hands that had just throttled death and the grave, were not above the lowly task of getting breakfast for a few tired fishermen who had just come in from a night of toil. Remember that our Lord is interested in all our needs. That means that he is interested in bread.

II

We need to remember that bread is God's gift. When Jesus taught us to pray he taught us this petition: "Give us this day our daily bread." It seems to me significant too that he told us to ask for bread before we ask for forgiveness, as important as that is. We are to pray for bread before we pray for victory over temptation. This is the case because Jesus knew that we are not apt to be greatly concerned about forgiveness if we are being tortured by hunger. He knew that we are not likely to pray very earnestly not to be led into temptation if starving children are tugging at us asking for bread that we cannot give. We are to ask for bread because all bread comes from God.

It is not always easy to realize this in our land of plenty. It is far easier for us to realize our dependence upon God for the bread of life than it is for us to realize our dependence upon him for material bread. Of course the bread of life is a gift. "The wages of sin is death; but the gift of God is eternal life through Jesus Christ our Lord." But we save ourselves spiritually quite as easily as we can save ourselves physically. All the scientists of all the centuries could no more create a loaf of bread in independence of God than they could create a universe.

"Remember," Jesus might urge, "that I am interested in bread, and that all bread comes from God." To fail to realize this is not the part of wisdom but of folly. Why was the rich farmer a fool? For a number of reasons, this among them: He thought because he had barns filled to overflowing that he could get on without God. But every man must lean upon God for the supply of every physical need. Even the fact that bread can meet our physical needs is a mystery. The fact that the same loaf could give strength to Judas for treachery and to Jesus for bearing his cross is a mystery. Both bread and its power to give life come from God's hands. Remember then that bread is God's gift.

III

We are to remember that God gives bread as we co-operate with him and with each other. This feeding of the five thousand was a co-operative enterprise. All successful dealings with the bread question must be so.

1. To produce bread we must co-operate with God. My father was a Christian farmer. He was a man of prayer. He prayed about all his needs, but when the spring came he did not ask God to plant corn in one field and to sow oats in another. He had me to do that. He knew that the cultivation and reaping of a harvest was a matter of co-operation between man and God.

2. Not only must man co-operate with God, but he must co-operate with his brother. When Jesus taught us to pray for bread he taught us to say "give us," and not merely "give me." If therefore I am an employer, when I pray this prayer, if I pray it intelligently and sinecrely, I am asking for bread not simply for myself, but for the man who works for me and with me. Therefore I will help to answer my prayer by paying a living wage. Even so, if I am an employee and pray this prayer, I am asking bread not for myself alone, but for my employer. I will therefore do an honest day's work. How much precious bread has been wasted because of a lack of co-operation between employer and employee!

This is also a prayer for the nations. How many wasteful wars have been fought primarily over the bread question! For us in rich America to help the devastated nations of the world is good religion. It is far more than good religion; it is sound economics. One group cannot have an abundance, and the other be tortured by want, without tragedy. Jesus gave some stern warnings of the perils of refusing to share. On the surface these warnings may sound arbitrary, but in reality they are not. They are true in the nature of things.

Look, for instance, at the picture of the Last Judgment. To one group the King says: "Depart from me, ye cursed." To the other: "Come, ye blessed of my Father." Why this difference? Why was the one group turned away while the other was made welcome? The charge against the group that was banished was in part this: "I was an hungred, and ye gave me no meat." The commendation of those who were welcomed into everlasting life was this: "I was an hungred, and ye gave me meat." It would seem therefore that our heaven or hell depends on our willingness to share our daily bread.

Here is another story that, if possible, seems even more stern. "There was a certain rich man, which was clothed in purple and fine linen, and fared sumptuously every day: and there was a certain beggar named Lazarus, which was laid at his gate, full of sores, and desiring to be fed with the crumbs which fell from the rich man's table: moreover the dogs came and licked his sores. And it came to pass, that the beggar died, and was carried by the angels into Abraham's bosom: the rich man also died and was buried; and in hell he lift up his eyes."

What was the sin of this rich man? It was not that he set the dogs on this helpless beggar. It was not that he had him stoned. He rather allowed him to die of neglect. Therefore in hell he lifted up his eyes. Are we then to understand that to refuse to share our bread means that in the afterlife we shall be cast into hell? About that I cannot speak with authority. But what is certain is that such failure means that we shall be cast into hell in the here and now. That is not theory; that is experience. It is what has taken place over and over again. It will continue to take place until we become Christian in our attitude toward bread.

IV

Now suppose we do remember. Suppose we take Jesus seriously when he tells us that he is concerned about bread, that bread is his gift, and that he can only give it to us when we co-operate with him and with our fellows, what happens?

1. Such an attitude brings a sense of God into our daily lives. The earning of our daily bread becomes a beautiful and sacred task. It enables us to handle the tools of our trade as religiously as we handle our Bibles and our hymnbooks on Sunday morning.

2. To take Jesus seriously means that every meal becomes a sacrament. When Cleopas and his companion were going home after the crucifixion they were utterly heartbroken. But a winsome stranger joined them. This

stranger so charmed them by his conversation that they almost forget their sorrow. When they reached the door of their humble little home they felt that they could not let this companion go on his way: "Abide with us," they urged, "for it is toward evening, and the day is far spent."

Their urgent invitation was accepted. Soon supper was announced. Then what? "And it came to pass, as he sat at meat with them, he took bread and blessed it, and brake, and gave to them. And their eyes were opened, and they knew him." The risen Christ was known to them in the breaking of bread. We too may so see the finger marks of our Lord upon our bread that every meal will become a sacrament.

3. Finally, this taking of our Lord seriously in the matter of bread is a fundamental step, not only toward the saving of our bodies and our souls, but of our civilization as well. To look on bread as a gift from God to be earned and shared in co-operation with him and with our fellows is a necessity for right living. This also is the one way of preventing the ghastly waste, both in bread and blood, that the past centuries have witnessed. Shall we not remember?

VII

PROFIT AND LOSS

"What shall it profit a man, if he shall gain the whole world, and lose his own soul?"

MARK 8:36

JESUS was never interested in winning disciples whose loyalty was born of blindness or lack of understanding. When a young man came to him one day all aflame with enthusiasm vowing: "I will follow thee whithersoever thou goest," the Master did not respond with a kindred enthusiasm. He saw that this eager volunteer did not understand what discipleship involved. Therefore he quenched the fires of his youthful ardor with this dash of cold water: "The foxes have holes, and the birds of the air have nests; but the Son of man hath not where to lay his head."

Sometime ago I gave myself the trouble of boarding a train when I did not know where the train was going. I thought it was going to Washington, D. C., but I found that it was headed for Washington, N. C. When my mistake was discovered I had to get off and walk about a mile back to the station carrying two heavy grips. Not only that, but by taking the wrong train I missed the right one. Our Lord urges that we count the cost, that we know where the train is going before we get on board. Therefore he arrests us with the question: "What shall it profit a man, if he shall gain the whole world, and lose his own soul?"

I

This text sounds a bit old-fashioned, but it has in it one word that is thoroughly up-to-date. In fact, this word is quite as much at home in our day as when it was uttered nearly two thousand years ago. That word is "profit"— "What shall it profit a man?" Everybody is interested in profits of one kind or another, and rightly so. This therefore is a sane question that we may ask either selfishly or unselfishly. It is perfectly right to ask it. The tragedy is that so many ask it with an eye only for one kind of profit, that which is of the earth earthy.

Years ago, as an enthusiastic young teacher, I sought to erect a new high-school building in the village where I was teaching. To this end I invited some of the leading citizens of the town to a meeting. When I had outlined my plan, one of them, the wealthiest of the group, said: "I am all for it if you will show me the dividends." By this he meant that he was willing to help construct the new building provided I could show him how it would pay him in dollars and cents. The dividends that it would pay in terms of better trained boys and girls and better citizens did not interest him in the least. He was interested in financial returns and those only.

73

One of the most crucial problems of our day is the liquor problem. We are on the way to becoming the drunkest nation on the face of the earth. What makes liquor a problem? It is made so by two classes of people. Eliminate these and liquor will be no more a problem than sassafras tea. The first class is composed of those who desire to drink liquor. Some of these are quite decent and respectable people who are in search of a thrill. Some are seeking momentary escape from the dull monotony of life or from a sense of inferiority. Then there are those who are in bondage to liquor and have become such hopeless slaves that they are willing to pay any price for a drink.

The second group, the one in my opinion that is far the more dangerous and selfish and wicked, is made up of those who are bent on making money out of liquor. These manufacture it, sell it, rent their property for its sale, vote for it, all in order to gain financial profit. Naturally these have no desire to make drunkards; they have no joy in robbing children of their chances or in sending a father staggering down the street to make a hell of his home. But they are willing to run the risk of doing this in order to make money. Take the profit motive out of liquor and I am sure this deadly evil could soon be brought under control.

Sad to say, there is no crime that men have not been willing to commit in an effort to win worldly gain. This question therefore may be asked selfishly, but it may also be asked unselfishly. There is a profit that we cannot measure in terms of dollars and cents. Here, for instance, is a lonely man in the heart of Africa. He has had one attack of fever after another. Because he is suffering from scurvy he is having to knock his own teeth out one by one. Why does David Livingstone not go home where he can keep his health? What is he seeking to gain by his mad adventure? He is out after profit. He is seeking the profit that comes from helping to heal the world's open sore. He is seeking profit for others rather than for himself. By so doing he is being vastly enriched.

Now these are the two kinds of profit between which we are to choose. Of course we often choose now one and then the other. But at long last there is one that we make central, one that we put first. Jesus sums up these two types of profit in two words: the world and the soul. "What shall it profit a man, if he shall gain the whole world, and lose his own soul?"

What is the world? It is all in the way of fame and fortune that our present dwelling place has to offer. Of course the world in itself is not an ugly and evil thing. It is beautiful and desirable. God himself called it very good. The world only becomes an evil when it ceases to be a servant and becomes a master. As a master it stands for that spirit of self-pleasing that is so prevalent today and everyday. To choose the world therefore is to seek to please ourselves, to save our own lives, to be independent toward God.

Jesus indicated this in his reply to Peter. The Master has just declared that he must suffer and be rejected and be killed. But Peter cannot stand for this, so he took him and began to rebuke him saying in effect: "Be it far from thee, Lord. What is the use in having power if you do not capitalize on it for yourself?" At this the Master turned upon Peter saying: "Get thee behind me, Satan. . . . Thou savourest not the things that be of God, but those that be of men." In other words: "You are talking the language of the world, you are not talking the language of God."

The other value offered for our choice is the soul. This word is also translated "life." Of course life as here used does not mean mere length of days. A man might exist for a century and never really live for a single hour. No more is this life a product of things. "A man's life consisteth not in the abundance of the things which he possesseth." To save the soul is to come into possession of values that are moral and spiritual. It is a quality of life that becomes ours when we surrender wholeheartedly to Jesus Christ. The salvation of the soul is the natural outcome of a vital faith in God.

II

What is involved in our choice of the world? What do we promise ourselves if we put the world first?

Our gain in terms of material values is uncertain. We may gain very little or we may gain very much. For the sake of argument, Jesus assumes that we may gain everything. He is assuming that by putting the world first we shall succeed in winning all that it has to offer. Of course nobody has ever really done that. Vast multitudes who have put it first have won exceedingly little.

But over against this uncertainty of worldly gain there is a certainty of tragic loss. The man who puts the world first will surely lose his soul. That fact ought to give us pause. There is such a thing as losing the soul. It is possible for a nation to lose its soul. It is possible also for an individual. One calls attention to the fact that when H. G. Wells was on his deathbed he answered a friend in this fashion: "Do not bother me. Don't you see I am busy dying." Busy dying! That is an arresting word. In recent years we have seen nations exceedingly busy doing just that. We have seen individuals doing the same. I visited a man sometime ago who gave me the impression that he was doing just that. As I came from that interview I said to my companion: "He impresses me as a man who is slowly rotting down." He was busy dying.

Now this loss of the soul is the supreme and all-inclusive loss. There are lesser losses that might give us pause. What shall it profit a man if he gain the whole world and lose his health? Many a man does just that. But how much in terms of material values would you charge to become a physical wreck? What would be the gain of being able to buy the daintiest of food, but be too sick to eat it; to have the money to buy the choicest of cars, but be too sick to ride in them; to possess the most comfortable beds and yet be utterly restless?

What would it profit a man to gain the whole world and lose his physical life? Many a man has paid this price for an insignificant fraction of the world, though few have paid it deliberately. In the backwoods community where I lived as a boy there was a man who had worked like a slave and lived a bit like a pig. Thus he managed to accumulate some $5,000 in gold. He would not trust it to

77

a bank, but kept it hidden in his cabin. One night a highwayman paid him a visit, and, putting his gun so close to the miser's face that he could almost smell the powder, asked him for a donation. The miser responded to that appeal by giving the highwayman all that he had. The next day an old friend came to condole with him.

"Homer, he asked, "did you give him all the money you had?"

"Yes," came the answer, "every bit of it."

"Why did you not argue with him?" the friend continued.

"Argue with him?" came the indignant question. "Argue with him? Hell was too close." He loved money, but he did not love it well enough to die for it.

Here is one who even did that. Nearly a century ago a boat whose passenger list was made up mainly of miners returning from the gold fields of California was making its way up the Mississippi. Suddenly that boat struck an obstruction that tore a great wound in its hull. At once it began rapidly to sink. There were not enough lifeboats, so many of the miners, seeing that they must swim for their lives, unfastened their belts heavy with gold and threw them on the deck of the boat. But there was one miner who thought these were mad. He therefore gathered up the belts one by one and fastened them upon himself. Thus hampered he jumped into the water and sank as if he had been made of lead. They found his body a few days later, but no one congratulated him upon his vast wealth.

Now to lose one's soul is infinitely more than the loss of

78

physical life. There are treasures for which one might gladly die. But for me to lose my soul is to lose my very self. It means the loss of all of my finest possibilities. It means the loss of the privilege of Christlike character. It means the loss of all those values that come from faith in God. For such a loss there is absolutely no compensation. The man who loses his soul loses his all.

This is equally true of a nation. The nation that loses its soul always ends by losing itself. When we hold an autopsy over the once-mighty nations that are dead today how do we find that they came by their death? They were not destroyed by outside enemies. They did not starve for physical bread. They starved for the bread of life. The nation that loses God loses its soul. The secular nation, as the secular man, is not headed toward life, but toward death. Woodrow Wilson was right when he affirmed that a nation cannot be materially secure unless it is spiritually redeemed.

III

Now suppose we make the high choice, the choice of life. Suppose instead of seeking merely to save ourselves, we give ourselves in wholehearted surrender to God. Then what?

1. If we put God first in our seeking we are sure to find him. As we give ourselves to God he gives himself to us. This is not theory. This is experience. If everyone who has found this true were to say "Amen," it would boom like a cannonade and shake like an earthquake. "If any man is willing to do his will, he shall know."

2. In finding God we shall find all that life needs. "Seek ye first the kingdom of God, and his righteousness; and all these things shall be added unto you." Jesus in saying this is speaking to the group rather than to the individual. There is no doubt that the man who puts God first, generally speaking, has a better chance at things than the man who does not. But if there are those who would question that putting God first would guarantee that all our material needs would be met, this certainly does apply to society as a whole.

3. Finding God, we shall not only have our physical needs met, but we shall find satisfaction for the highest hungers of the heart. "If any man thirst," says Jesus, "let him come unto me, and drink." He has that to give without which we die. All our highest hungers, all our deepest thirsts, are met in him. "My God shall supply all your need according to his riches in glory by Christ Jesus."

Then everybody at his best desires to be useful. We cannot but realize the deep tragedy of missing the majesty and the mirth of being helpful to our fellows. This need is also supplied by our Lord. "He that believeth on me, as the scripture hath said, from within him shall flow rivers of living water." (A.S.V.) Thus putting Christ first we find satisfaction for ourselves. We also have something to share. Out of our inner lives "shall flow rivers of living water." We shall have power to break up the drought of the soul and to set the fields of the heart to flowering.

"What shall it profit a man, if he shall gain the whole world, and lose his own soul?" It is a choice between self-seeking and self-giving, between those values that are of the earth earthy, and of those values that are born of a vital faith in God. You have just one life to invest. Where are you going to invest it? Are you going to stake your all on a spiritual interpretation of life or a material one? Will you put yourself first, or God first?

One day I stopped and watched some young ants coming up out of the ground. They spread their silvery wings in the sunlight as if they were made for the skyland and the upper air. But before I could be thrilled over their beautiful destiny, they seemed to say to themselves: "Business is business, I cannot waste my time developing and using my wings." So they laid them quickly aside and went to the practical business of crawling.

Schiller tells this story. Once the bird had no wings. They merely walked about in the dust having no commerce with the sky at all. Then one day the Lord threw wings at their feet and commanded them to pick them up and carry them for his sake. At first it seemed very hard. They thought they were going to have a heavy handicap. But in obedience they held the wings close to their sides, and the wings grew. At last what they had once thought would be only a hampering weight lifted them into the heights. We can take the way of the ants or the birds. As we seek for ourselves we lose our wings. As we give ourselves we are able to mount up with wings as eagles. What is your choice?

VIII

BEING DECISIVE

"Why call ye me, Lord, Lord, and do not the things which I say?"

LUKE 6:46

THIS sane question is addressed to the undecided. In speaking to you on being decisive I am speaking on a subject of major importance. This is an essential for successful living. If you know where you are going and are determined to get there, almost any old jalopy will serve the purpose. But if you cannot come to a definite decision as to your goal, then a Rolls-Royce will be of little avail. It would wear out and fall to pieces before you would reach your goal. Truly, for the ship that is bound for no harbor no wind can be favorable. No wonder therefore that our Lord is constantly calling us to be decisive: "Let your language be, 'Yes, yes,' or 'No, no.'" (Weymouth.)

How essential that is, and yet how difficult! So often our "Yes" has in it a tincture of "No," and our "No" a tincture of "Yes." To give utterance to a "Yes" that is 100 per cent affirmation is about the most difficult task that we are called upon to perform. The burden of choice is so heavy that many people go to pieces under it. There are young men who were happier in the army than they have ever been before or since. This is the case because there they were in some measure relieved of the burden of choice.

It is difficult to get people to think. It is more difficult still to get them to be decisive. What a keen thinker was Hamlet, Prince of Denmark! There are those who believe that the story of this prince is somewhat autobiographical. They believe that Hamlet, with his vast ability to think and his inability to act, is in a measure a picture of the poet himself. Be that as it may, Hamlet found action next to impossible. He did not like his situation. He rebelled at the fact that his world was out of joint and that he was ever born to set it right. He contemplated suicide, thought of it with brilliant clearness, but could never quite decide to go through with it.

> "Who would fardels bear,
> To grunt and sweat under a weary life,
> But that the dread of something after death,
> The undiscover'd country from whose bourn
> No traveller returns, puzzles the will
> And makes us rather bear those ills we have
> Than fly to others that we know not of?
> Thus conscience does make cowards of us all;
> And thus the native hue of resolution
> Is sicklied o'er with the pale cast of thought,
> And enterprises of great pith and moment
> With this regard their currents turn awry,
> And lose the name of action."

I

Now look at this question of Jesus: "Why call ye me, Lord, Lord, and do not the things which I say?" We can readily realize the kind of folks to whom this question was addressed. Our Lord is not speaking to those who are out and out against him. He is not speaking to his avowed enemies, nor to those who ignore him. Neither is he speaking to those who are wholeheartedly for him. He is rather speaking to people very like many of us. He is speaking to those who admire him, who honor him to the point of calling him Lord, and yet who are not fully persuaded to follow him. They give him an intellectual assent, but have failed wholeheartedly to give him themselves.

Mark tells us of a man of this type. One day this man came to Jesus with this question: "Which is the first commandment of all?" When Jesus answered that the greatest commandment is to love God and man, his questioner approved his answer. In fact, he gave the answer of the Master such wise approval that Jesus commended him for his answer and then paid him this compliment: "Thou art not far from the kingdom of God." It was a beautiful commendation, and yet it was not enough. Though so near the kingdom that his foot was almost upon the threshold, he was not in it. One decisive step would have brought him to life's finest adventure, but so far as we know, he failed to take that step.

Now this company of the undecided is a vast company. It is not uncharitable to say that it includes a large percentage of the members of our churches. This does not mean that these undecided folks are hypocritical. Very few of them are. It does not mean that they do not refrain from certain evils every day out of loyalty to Christ. It does not mean that they do not do certain deeds of service every day because of that loyalty. It does mean that while they are obedient in many things, they still do not put the Kingdom of God first. Though decent, religious, and respectable, there are areas in their lives that they have never dedicated to him whom they call Lord.

Not only does this company of the undecided include vast numbers who are in our churches, but it includes even more who are outside any church. As I have spoken to various clubs and organizations outside the church I have discovered that it is by no means unpopular before such groups to sound a definitely religious note. Any reference to Jesus Christ, any word honoring him, is met with almost universal approval. Also as I have spoken to men individually who were outside the church I have found plenty of those who were harshly critical. These were often critical of the ministry. They could point out numerous flaws both in the church as a whole and in the individual members. But when I confessed that we were a faulty group all of us, and then asked this question, "What about Jesus Christ? What fault have you to find in him?" I do not recall ever to have heard from these one harsh criticism. In spite of all our faults, there is a sense in which Jesus Christ is the most popular character in the United States today. Our tragedy is not that we are out and out against him; it is rather than we are not out and out for him.

II

"Why call ye me, Lord, Lord, and do not the things which I say?" Now what is he asking at our hands? Let us get away from what is incidental to what is really essential.

To begin negatively Jesus is not asking primarily for our church membership. By this I do not mean that it is not the duty of every Christian to belong to some church. I realize that there are many decent and right-thinking people outside the church. But it is my conviction that those who take Jesus seriously will join some church. The church at the time of Jesus was even more faulty than the church of today, yet Jesus did not stand apart from it and stone it. He rather attended it as a matter of habit and conviction. He knew that what help he brought he must bring as a member of the church and not as an outside antagonist.

Here and there I find people who have become too pious to belong to any church. I was preaching to a congregation some years ago in which was a brother who was giving me most encouraging backing by his hearty amens. Now I approve of saying amen. When a hearer makes such a response I feel he is on my side. But this man overdid it. He was talking almost as fast as I was. By this I knew I had not yet rebuked his particular sin.

Then it happened. I said: "I believe in the church."

"Amen," was the response.

"Now and then," I continued, "I have found people who were too good to belong to any church."

"Amen."

"If I lived next door to a man like that," I continued, "I would lock my garage every night."

He started to say amen and it slid off like a feather-edged shingle. When the sermon was over I learned the truth. He had quit the church because the Lord had said: "Come out from among them and be ye separate." Personally I believe that if you take Jesus seriously you will join some church. But our Lord is not asking for that first of all.

No more is Jesus asking first for our work. Of course if we are in earnest about following him we are certain to do something about it. But his first demand is not for our work. Neither is he seeking first for our money. Naturally if our Christianity is real we shall be glad to give, but money does not come first. No more is our Lord asking for some kind of emotional response. He is seeking neither for our laughter nor our tears. For what then, I repeat, is he asking? He is asking for ourselves. He is saying to us what he said to Matthew long ago: "Follow me." This publican was decisive. He at once left all, rose up, and followed. This also we are to do. Jesus is asking what Paul urged in these words: "Present your bodies a living sacrifice." He is asking for our complete and unconditional dedication of life. Nothing less than that will meet his demands.

If you think that sounds difficult I am ready to agree. Jesus never hinted that discipleship was easy. But when he set out to redeem us he did not seek an easy way. He took the way of the cross. "This is my body," he declares, "which is given for you." "This," he is saying, "is my-

self, my very all, my everything, and it is given for you."
He asks that in return we take our discipleship seriously.
As he gave his all, we are to give our all. We are to say
day by day: "Not my will but thine be done."

III

Why should we do this?

1. We ought to be wholehearted in our decision because nothing else will satisfy our Lord. He is never
pleased with half-hearted devotion. In fact, it would
seem, as we turn the pages of the New Testament, that
that is just the attitude that he hates most. He even
prefers out-and-out antagonism. "I would thou wert cold
or hot." What are we here to do? Not to win success
primarily. Certainly we are not here to fail. We are here
to do the will of God. It is only by a wholehearted dedication to him that we can please him and thus fulfill God's
purpose for our lives.

2. It is only by our wholehearted loyalty that we can
find satisfaction for ourselves. There is no peace for the
undecided. The most wretched hours of our lives are those
hours when we are unable to reach a decision. Even a
wrong decision brings more peace than does indecision.
The wise story of Jonah emphasizes this fact.

Listen to this: "The word of the Lord came unto Jonah
. . . saying, Arise, go to Nineveh, that great city, and cry
against it." There were two possibilities open to this
prophet: to go or not to go. He decided against the call of
God. We have that amazing power. Having reached a
definite decision to renounce God by disobeying him, he

went on shipboard and fell fast asleep. The days and nights that had preceded his decision had been full of agony. When he at last decided, even though his decision was wrong, that decision brought sufficient peace to make sleep possible.

But the trouble with the peace born of a wrong decision is that it will not last. This is the case because God simply will not let us alone. He refuses to leave off his loving efforts to win us. "No man can be as bad as he wants to be." We may reject the high calling of God, but our rejection will bring us no permanent peace. It is only when we have fully committed ourselves to God that we come to know the peace that abides.

Then a wholehearted decision to follow Christ brings peace because so many lesser questions are decided by it. There are those for whom no moral issue is finally decided. Every morning they must decide whether they will pray or not pray, whether they will look into God's Word or neglect it. Every Sunday church attendance is an open question. These people are therefore in constant conflict. They remind one of that old story of the man who possessed a dog whose tail was far too long, but desiring to give the dog the least possible pain, he decided to cut it off an inch a day rather than all at once. If you take Jesus seriously a thousand lesser decisions will then be made in advance.

Not only will this one great decision include many that are smaller, but it will make every other right decision easier. The choice you made today was born quite largely of the choice you made yesterday. Every wrong choice makes the next wrong choice the easier and the surer. When Rip Van Winkle used to swear off drinking he would return to his bottle saying: "I will not count this one." But even if he failed to count it his weakened will did not. It chalked that failure against him. Now just as every wrong choice makes the next wrong choice easier, even so every right choice makes the next right choice easier and surer. We can so cultivate our right choices in the fellowship of Jesus that they become all but spontaneous.

3. Then we ought to be fully decided in the matter of following Christ, because this alone brings us to our highest usefulness. Indecision means weakness. Years ago when we were boys, my brother and I in passing through the fields had to cross a spring branch which was normally two or three feet wide. But heavy rains had given this little stream a breadth of from ten to fifteen feet. In spite of this we decided we could jump it. I was to adventure first. So I gave myself a good running start and was on the way to victory when my brother changed his mind and shouted, "Stop! Stop! Stop!" The result was that I lost my decisiveness. The further result was that I landed in the middle of the stream. But my failure was not due to my lack of athletic ability. It was due rather to my indecision.

In those dark days when Israel was being swept off its feet by Jezebel, it was Elijah who saved the day. Standing before a great throng he flung at them this sane question: "How long halt ye between two opinions?" In other words: "How long are you going to allow yourselves to be crippled by your indecision?" To be thus undecided is as silly as trying to win a foot race with a ball and chain on your ankle. Indecision brings weakness. Decision brings strength.

Years ago I watched a company of men move the side of a mountain. They were not using bulldozers as we do today. They were using hydraulic pressure. When that water fell from the heavens it doubtless fell so gently that it would hardly have hurt a baby's face. But now, under its tremendous pressure, small trees were being uprooted and rocks were being rushed out of their places. Why the difference? This water was saying: "This one thing I do." It is only as we are wholeheartedly for Christ that we find our highest personal satisfaction and highest usefulness.

4. Then we ought to decide definitely for Christ, because by refusing to do so we decide against him. There is a fable that a donkey once stood between two delicious bundles of hay. The donkey was hungry. Both bundles offered just the satisfaction he needed. But when he would turn toward the one the other would seem to call to him. Thus he could never make up his mind just which bundle he would eat first. Therefore he hesitated between the two until he starved. His death was not the result of a decision to commit suicide. It was rather the result of his failure to decide to eat.

Even so we miss knowing Jesus Christ through lack of decision. Right now he is offering himself to us. Most of us have declared to him our allegiance in some fashion. But in spite of this some of us are keenly conscious of the fact that our religious lives often have been quite disappointing. We wonder at times if we had not better renounce the whole venture as a failure. What is the way to victory? Make a wholehearted decision. God longs to give you the best, but he cannot without your co-operation. Remember that God's one plan of salvation is for a surrendered heart.

IX

THE TRANSFORMING TOUCH

"Who touched me?"

LUKE 8:45

"WHO touched me?" Simon and his fellow disciples could hardly keep from laughing. What an amazing question for one to ask who was being pushed and elbowed on all sides by an eager and curious crowd. This Master of theirs was unspeakably winsome. He was fascinating beyond all words. They had never seen anyone like him. But what queer things he could sometimes do and say! The idea of asking "Who touched me?" when he was being half crushed by a mob! But they did not laugh at him; they loved him far too well for that. Yet his question did seem as silly to them as it would to us if a friend, while sitting by our side at a Rose Bowl football game, should ask: "Who is seeing the game with us today?"

Naturally Simon simply could not keep from setting his Lord right. Therefore he answered patiently, as to a small child: "Master, the multitude throng thee and press thee, and sayest thou, Who touched me?" What Simon is trying to get across to his Master is that his question is

93

rather ridiculous. He is saying: "Scores of people have touched you, perhaps hundreds. It is therefore impossible for any of us to give a correct answer to your question."

But Jesus was not satisfied with Simon's answer. He was, of course, as keenly aware of the thronging crowd as Simon. But he also knew what this disciple did not know—that one single individual had made contact with him and had thereby been the recipient of his healing power. Therefore, in spite of Simon's explanation, he affirmed: "Somebody hath touched me."

Our Lord found deep joy in being able to make this affirmation. That was the case because he was always eager to give of himself. He rejoiced with joy unspeakable when one needy soul was willing to receive at his hands. It would seem that his greatest heartache while he was here was that he was so eager to give while those about him were so reluctant to receive. Here is a word that is still wet with tears: "Ye will not come to me, that ye might have life." Perhaps the greatest grief of our Lord at this moment is that he longs to do so much for us and we permit him to do so little. Here he was able to say: "Somebody hath touched me." That fact made his heart sing.

But if there was gladness in this word there must have been sorrow as well. There were hundreds, perhaps thousands, in the crowd that thronged about him. Every one of them needed to touch him. Every one of them might have touched him. But only one claimed her privilege. Only one availed herself of her opportunity. The door to a richer and fuller life stood open before all, but only one had the faith to enter. Thus while our Lord rejoiced over the one who touched him, he could not but sorrow over the many who were content merely to throng him.

I

Who was this fortunate soul?

1. She was a woman with a heavy handicap. She had been suffering from a hemorrhage for twelve years. Twelve years is a long time when one is well; it is doubly long when one is fighting with illness. It is longer still when one is making a losing fight. Then hers was a shame-faced disease that made her ceremonially unclean. It seems also to have shut her out from the privilege of wifehood and motherhood. Then too she had consulted various physicians who had relieved her of nothing but her money. Thus to the burden of her illness had been added the additional burden of poverty.

2. She was a woman who clung passionately to life. She was determined not to die until something killed her. I like that. It has always been my conviction that the best way to get ready for the life to come is to love this life and to live it as bravely and faithfully as we can. She therefore did not make a tame surrender to her illness. Having made one effort at recovery she did not lie down in self-pity to enjoy bad health. She refused thus to become a burden both to herself and to others. In spite of all her failures she still possessed a fighting heart. It was this woman, handicapped by illness and many failures, who succeeded in touching Jesus.

95

II

How did she come to touch him?

1. Mark tells that she heard of Jesus. Naturally. "Faith cometh by hearing." The reason that you touched him in youth's bright morning long ago was because somebody told you about him. That is how I came to touch him. That is how our children will touch him, if at all. We must tell them about him. We must tell them by what we say and especially by what we do. Christianity can be taught. It can also more effectively be caught. This woman heard about Jesus.

Just who was the bearer of this good news we are not told. I imagine that it was some friend, some woman perhaps who had come to know Jesus and who had experienced his healing power. But whoever she was, one day she took time to sit down beside this faded and fading friend and tell her that a new physician had come. She told her further that the fact that she had spent all her money need not deter her from going to him. "He heals without money and without price," she may have declared boldly. "Not only so, but he is in our village today. If I were you, I would give myself a chance by going to him at once."

2. Not only did this woman hear about Jesus, but she believed what she heard. As she listened to her friend faith and hope grew strong in her heart. She said to herself: "I believe that he can heal. I believe that he healed this friend of mine!" Then she passed on to affirm that faith that is of supreme importance: "I believe he can and will heal me. Of course I do not expect healing without any

co-operation on my part. But if I do co-operate I can be certain of the results. If I but touch his clothes I shall be healed."

3. Having thus come to believe, she went into action. Faith that is real acts. Faith that does not act is not in reality faith at all. In spite of her weakness, in spite of the fact that some of her friends perhaps looked askance at her and told her how silly she was, she set out on her adventure of faith. In spite of the crowd that got in her way she persisted; she kept telling herself: "If I touch but his clothes I shall be healed."

This woman knew how to talk to herself. That is a fine art. What others say to us is often of vast importance. There are words that can weaken and torture us. There are other words that can strengthen us and that fall upon our wounds like healing balm. But if what others say to us is important, what we say to ourselves is far more important. Tell me what you habitually say to yourself and I will tell you what you are and what increasingly you are becoming.

Who would ever have called the rich farmer a fool had they seen nothing but his shrewd face and his obvious success? But when we hear him talk to himself, when we hear him tell himself that he alone is responsible for his prosperity and that therefore he owes no debt of gratitude either to God or man, then we begin to understand how only one word can adequately describe him and that is the word that God used—"Thou fool."

How did the prodigal son come to turn his steps home? It was because he knew how to talk to himself. When he talked to himself what did he say? Here is what he might have said: "I am the most wretched person in the world. Here I am feeding hogs. But it is not my fault. It is the fault of my father who is as soft-headed as he is soft-hearted. He ought not to have given me my inheritance when I asked him for it. It is the fault of my brother who is as cold as an icicle and hard as a nail. It is the fault of my friends who stood by when I had money and left me when I was broke. It is everybody's fault except mine." Had he talked like that he would have remained in the hogpen until he rotted.

What then did he say? When he came to himself he spoke somewhat after this fashion: "I have made a terrible mess. I came away to have a good time, but I am now literally dying of hunger. Not only so, but I have nobody to blame but myself. It broke my father's heart for me to leave him, but in spite of that I came. Now I am going back and tell him what a mess I have made. I came away in the open light of day; I am going back in the same fashion. I am not going to try to sneak in. I am going to face all the ugly facts and ask for a new chance." Thus talking to himself, he left the hogpen and never stopped going until he felt the hug of his father's arms and the kiss of his father's lips.

This frail woman setting out on her difficult mission might have said some very discouraging things to herself. "How silly you are," she might have said, "to keep trying. Here you are going to a physician who has no diploma from a medical school. Yet you know that the very best physicians have failed to help you." But instead of talking in this fashion she encouraged herself. She told herself that here was one who was different. She told herself: "If I touch but his clothes I shall be healed. Therefore touch I will, regardless of cost." Thus talking to herself, she accomplished her purpose.

III

What was the result?

At once she was healed. Just as an electric light bulb begins to blaze with light the instant it is brought into contact with the dynamo, so this woman received healing power the instant she touched him who is the source of power. Not only was she healed but she was conscious of her healing. She could join her voice with those who through the ages have come to certainty. A once-blind man can leave many questions unanswered without serious hurt if he can affirm: "One thing I know, that, whereas I was blind, now I see." At once this woman knew that she had been healed.

Then it was that Jesus asked: "Who touched me?" Why did he ask that question? It was not because he was seeking information. It was not because he was ignorant regarding this woman. It was rather because he knew that she was ignorant of him. He was not seeking to get her to reveal herself to him, but he was seeking to reveal himself to her. It was her purpose to steal away in silence and not tell the story of her illness any more. But Jesus had something better for her than that. Therefore he asked: "Who touched me?"

Now when the woman saw that the Master knew just

what had taken place, she came, as Mark tells us, "and fell down before him, and told him all the truth." It is well to follow the advice of James and confess our faults one to another and pray one for another. However, I am convinced that there are some confessions that we ought to make to God only. In his presence we can fully "unpack our hearts with words." Without reservation we can tell him all the truth. When this woman had done this Jesus fairly opened the door of a new world to her as he said: "Daughter, thy faith hath made thee whole; go in peace." And we may believe that the Christ who had given her salvation kept her to the end of the journey.

IV

What does this story have to say to us today?

We are separated from this scene by centuries and seas and continents, yet it has a word for us that is as fresh and up to date as our last heartbeat.

1. We, despite the centuries, have much in common with that multitude that thronged Jesus in the long ago. We are confronted with tasks that are too heavy for our strength. We need to be the recipient of his power. Some of us have come with empty lives that we need to hold up to his fullness. Some of us have fears that make us look with painful foreboding for the morrow. Some are lonely and need the comfort of him who has promised to be with us all our days. We have all come with our hungers and thirsts, with our burdens, our fears and our sins, even as these of the long ago.

2. The same Christ who was thronged by the multitude

on that distant day still moves among us. This is his own word: "Where two or three are gathered together in my name, there am I in the midst of them." We can count on this fact with absolute conviction. We can count on it, as Livingstone would tell us, because it is the word of a gentleman of the strictest honor.

3. Now since he is here among us we can do one of two things. We can either throng him or we can touch him. If we touch him we must co-operate with him. Doing this, the outcome is sure. We can touch him by our prayers. So the saints have found through the centuries; so some of us have found.

"Speak to Him thou for he hears, and Spirit with Spirit can meet—
Closer is He than breathing, and nearer than hands and feet."

Then we can touch him by our obedience. We can touch him by the dedication of our lives to him. This is his own promise: "If any man is willing to do his will, he shall know." This is not theory; it is experience.

"No fable old, nor mythic lore,
Nor dream of bards and seers;
No fact stranded on the shore
Of the oblivious years.

But warm, sweet, tender even yet
A present help is he;
And faith has still its Olivet,
And love its Galilee.

101

The healing of his seamless dress
Is by our beds of pain;
We touch him in life's throng and press,
And we are whole again."

Not only can we touch our Lord today, but the contact that we make in the here and now we can keep through all the changing years. Listen to these words: "I am the vine, ye are the branches." That is, we are related to our Lord as the branch is related to the vine. If this is the case our position then is to be one of constant contact. It is only as the branch remains in contact with the vine that it can live. To lose that contact is to wither. So our lives wither when we lose touch with our Lord. But if we live in his fellowship, it becomes true of us what the psalmist sang of God's blessed man in the long ago—"His leaf also shall not wither." To touch the living Christ and continue in his fellowship is surely to become one of God's evergreens.

This is a story of the long ago. But suppose that I had been an eyewitness to the transformation of this woman. All excitement, I tell you what I have just seen. "I was standing right by Jesus," I declare eagerly. "In fact, I was rubbing elbows with him when I saw a frail woman pressing her way through the crowd. My first thought was that she ought to be at home in bed. But I saw that she was bent on some definite purpose. At last she reached out a frail finger and touched the tassel of Jesus' robe. I then rubbed my eyes in utter amazement. I could hardly believe what I saw. At once the roses of health began to bloom on her faded face. Immediately she was healed.

Then I heard the Master say: 'Thy faith hath made thee whole; go in peace.' "

Now were I to speak to you after this fashion you could not leave my story just there. You would have to ask a few questions: "Are you telling me that the woman was healed by a mere touch and that you were fairly rubbing elbows with the Master when this miracle took place? Then what difference did his presence make in you? Were you also transformed?" Should I answer in the negative you would know that I had made no real effort to touch Jesus. I was satisfied merely to throng him. How about you? When he asks, as he is asking now, "Who touched me?" can you give a glad affirmative?

X

THE GREAT DISTURBER

"Suppose ye that I am come to give peace on earth? I tell you, Nay; but rather divi-sion."

LUKE 12:51

IT is well for us that Jesus answered this question. Personally I should never have given the reply that he did. On the contrary, I should have answered with a most emphatic affirmative. In so doing I should have had solid scriptural backing. That Jesus came to bring peace is affirmed by his very name. He is the Prince of Peace. This is further declared by the song that the angels sang at his birth, a song of peace and good will. Jesus himself affirmed it further during his ministry by saying to more than one tempest-tossed soul: "Go in peace." He affirmed it finally by the legacy that he left us when he went away: "Peace I leave with you, my peace I give unto you. . . . Let not your heart be troubled, neither let it be afraid."

But in spite of my confident affirmation that Jesus has come to bring peace, he answers his own question by an emphatic denial. "Suppose ye that I am come to give peace

104

on earth? ... Nay; but rather division." Instead of "division" Matthew substitutes the word "sword." This makes his answer even more shocking if possible. Here then is the Prince of Peace declaring that he has not come to bring peace, but a sword. In other words, this Prince of Peace has come as a disturber, a creator of discord. Surely this is a paradox that needs some explaining.

I

When Jesus declared that he is a disturber, a creator of division, he was speaking sober truth. In fact, he was and is the most disturbing personality that ever walked this earth. When he was on trial for his life much of the testimony offered against him was utterly false. But there was at least one charge that his accusers brought that was true. Had his prosecutors been so minded they could have called a thousand witnesses to prove it. That charge was this: "He stirreth up the people." Indeed he did. Wherever he went sedate and quiet villages came to seethe with turmoil and confusion. In fact, his whole nation felt the impact of his personality. It became as fretted and restless as a sea whipped by a storm.

One day, for instance, Jesus attended church in his home town. It was a Sabbath, and the atmosphere, I dare say, was pervaded by the serenity and calm of that holy day. When the congregation had assembled Jesus himself read the lesson of the day. It was that beautiful passage from Isaiah which begins like this: "The Spirit of the Lord is upon me, because he hath anointed me to preach." Then, as he proceeded with his sermon, his hearers were spellbound. They could not but wonder at the gracious words that fell from his lips. It seemed as if the service was destined to be one of the high spots in their lives.

But not only did Jesus have gracious words for his fellow worshipers, but he even had something gracious to say about certain rank outsiders. "There were many lepers in Israel during the days of Elisha the prophet," he declared in effect, "but not one of them had faith to be healed. The only man possessed of such faith was a foreinger named Naaman. There were many widows in Israel when Elijah had a price on his head and was hunting for a boarding place. But the only widow who dared give him shelter was a pagan of the land from which Jezebel came." At this the service was thrown into confusion. The Sabbath calm was shattered by the protests of angry men. A mob was formed, and those present could account for the escape of Jesus only by saying that it was a miracle.

On another day Jesus came to a bit of countryside near the village of Gadera. This too was in the main a quiet place. "Along the cool sequester'd vale of life" the native farmers and swineherds "kept the noiseless tenor of their way." True, there was a certain lunatic in the neighborhood who created a disturbance now and then. But he lived in the cemetery and gave only occasional trouble.

But with the coming of Jesus there was a real disturbance. For no sooner had he come upon the scene than he cured this lunatic. When therefore the neighbors saw this once-madman seated at the feet of Jesus, clothed and in his right mind, they were naturally excited. But far more exciting and disturbing was the fact that, seemingly in the process of working the cure, Jesus had had to sacrifice a whole herd of hogs. "What," they ask in terror, "is to be done with a man who thinks more of a bit of human wreckage than of a herd of good hogs?" They felt that something must be done and that at once. So not daring to try to drive out so powerful a personality, they sent a committee tactfully to request Jesus to depart out of their coasts. The man who puts human values first is always a disturber.

Then Jesus disturbed men individually. I dare say there was no man in his community more honored and respected than the rich young ruler. He possessed so much worthwhile treasure. He had youth, wealth, and position. He was earnestly religious. He was doubtless fairly contented with himself and his lot. Then rumors about Jesus began to blow his way. When he heard what this young rabbi was doing, how unselfishly he was using his life, he was disturbed. His inward conflict reached a climax one day when he heard that Jesus was passing along the highway. So disturbed was he that, patrician though he was, he ran to kneel at the feet of this peasant to ask how to find life. Sad to say, the price was higher than he was willing to pay. But though he went away he did not go joyfully. He rather went with an ache in his heart and a sob in his throat. Thus did Jesus rob him of the bit of false peace that he might have possessed.

That great revolutionary who died beside Jesus was no ordinary criminal. He was an ardent patriot who had dedicated his life to the service of his counquered country. Unable to organize armies and fight in the open, he had

107

staged one raid after another in which there had, no doubt, been considerable bloodletting. But he had become a revolutionary with his eyes wide open to its cost. So when he had been captured and brought to justice his one regret was that he had not inflicted greater injury upon the enemy. Therefore he walked bravely toward Calvary under the weight of his wooden cross. Like a man he had fought, and like a man he was determined to die.

But something happened that turned what tranquility he had into utter turmoil. Against the white background of the man on the central cross he saw himself. Therefore, though he was suffering the tortures of hell, he declared that he was suffering justly. In fact, so great was his inner agony that the agony of his tortured body was forgotten. His pain was not in being where he was, but in being what he was. Therefore he turned to his dying companion with this prayer: "Lord, remember me when thou comest into thy kingdom."

Thus Jesus divided men within themselves. Thus he divided man from man. Some who touched him loved him with a love that nothing could kill. Others hated him with a hatred that nailed him to a cross. These two groups, therefore, were separated from each other by distances wider than the spaces between the stars. Jesus was and is the great disturber. He has come to bring division.

II

Why is this the case?

1. Jesus disturbs us by being what he is. When I was a small boy my utter aversion to all schoolwork made me

the despair of my family. In sober truth, I never intended to learn to read. I did not even want to learn. There were so many other things that seemed more worth-while. But one day there came a little girl, some two years younger than myself, to spend the summer in our home. I showed her my prowess with the horses and the cattle. I was a good rider and her admiration thrilled my boyish soul. But I soon saw that she was far different from me. She was a great reader. She made me feel for the first time that my ignorance was an ugly and shameful thing. So much was this the case that I said to myself: "Someday I am going to know as much as she." And life for me at that time took on a new departure.

Years ago each worker in the Hugh Price Hughes Mission in London was accustomed to wear a white carnation. One day one of these workers sat talking to a young woman who was an outcast. Suddenly this young woman burst into tears. The worker was puzzled because she was not discussing anything to stir her emotions. When she sought to know the cause of her tears, the young woman touched the white flower and said: "I am not like that. I wish I were white and clean like that flower." Thus when we face Jesus we are forced to say: "I am not like that." He disturbs us by being what he is.

2. He disturbs us through natural law. This world is built on a basis of righteousness. When we do wrong we suffer. That suffering is not our foe; it is our friend. If you have a diseased appendix that disease announces itself in the convincing words of pain. That pain may be very unwelcome, yet it is the red flag that nature waves in

your face to tell you that something is wrong. If this disease were to fail to announce itself you might die without ever knowing what was the matter.

Now there are laws of spiritual health just as there are laws of physical health. When I sin against my body I suffer. When I sin against my better self I suffer too. Take hate, for instance. Hate may cause me to do injury to one against whom I hold a grudge. But if I am too civilized to try to injure my enemy, that hate will still tear my life to bits and make it a veritable hell. By making me sick spiritually it will often make me sick physically as well. I knew a woman who died not long ago, and it is my honest conviction that she died largely of hate.

Then we have social, national, even world-wide agonies. These at times express themselves in costly conflicts between capital and labor. They express themselves, though at rarer intervals I am happy to say, in terms of mob violence. They express themselves in terms of wars that all but wreck the world. All these tragic pains are the outward eruptions of an inward rottenness. They are voices calling to us, in language that we cannot wholly ignore, to set the house of life in order.

Today, for instance, there is widespread hunger for peace. It is not the result, I am sorry to say, of a new sense of brotherhood. I fear that we do not love each other any better than did our fathers. But we are driven to seek a warless world because of what we have suffered. Thus our Lord disturbs us by the painful consequences of our sins.

3. Then Jesus disturbs us of set purpose. There is a

word in Genesis that says: "My spirit shall not always strive with man." But God does strive with us here and now with patient persistence. Constantly he is saying: "Behold, I stand at the door, and knock." He will never permit any of us to sleep our way into disaster without doing his best to rouse us into wakefulness. Our dissatisfaction with ourselves, our longing to be better, our passion to be of service, all these are but the disturbing voices of our Lord calling us to our best possibilities.

III

Now what is the purpose of our Lord in thus disturbing us?

He is robbing us of our false peace in order to give us one that is real. For we may be sure after all that Jesus has come to bring peace on earth. But he can give us this peace only through our co-operation. This is the case because peace is a consequence. It is an effect rather than a cause. To find peace therefore we must be willing to meet the conditions of peace. We must be willing to give up whatever is antagonistic to peace. Unless we meet these conditions not even God himself can give us peace.

When I was a barefoot boy I would often have a stone bruise. This was a painful experience and I eagerly sought for peace. I would try one poultice after another. But all in vain. The only remedy that worked was the lance. The corruption caused by the bruise had to be let out. Even so our Lord declares that there are ills that demand spiritual surgery: "If thy right eye offend thee, pluck it out. . . . If thy right hand offend thee, cut it off."

That is, we must be willing to get rid of that which disturbs our peace, even though it prove as painful as the cutting off of the right hand or the plucking out of the right eye.

When the prophet said "There is no peace . . . to the wicked," he was not making a threat, but stating a fact. Paul was speaking to the same purpose when he said: "The kingdom of God is not eating and drinking, but righteousness and peace and joy in the Holy Spirit." (A.S.V.) We do not find peace merely by having plenty to eat and plenty to drink. Before there can be any real peace there must be righteousness. This means rightness—rightness with God, rightness within, rightness between man and man. Any temple of peace that we seek to build upon a foundation of unrighteousness and injustice will fall into ruins however full of promise it may seem.

How then shall we find peace? It is first of all an individual matter. We shall find it as we give ourselves in wholehearted obedience to the Prince of Peace.

Some years ago a returned missionary told this story. "As I was coming down from the Himalaya Mountains I saw a man in the distance climbing to meet me. When we drew closer together I heard the clank of chains. Closer still I could see that the man had a huge chain about his neck that had almost worn the flesh from his chest. I could not pass him by without a question, so I asked him to tell me his story. He then told me that a few years before he had gone to his priest in search of peace. This priest had told him to perform certain extremely hard penances. He had obeyed only to be disappointed. At last the priest had put

112

that heavy chain about his neck and had told him to climb to the summit of the mountain up which he was then toiling.

"When I had heard this story," the missionary continued, "I reached up and took the chain from his neck and asked him to sit down beside me. Then I told him about the Prince of Peace. I told him that peace was a gift of Jesus Christ, that he could receive it as a gift by the giving of himself. At once the light of understanding came into his eyes and the glory of God broke over his face. The last I saw of him he was going back to tell those of his native village about the Prince of Peace."

Yes, Jesus has come to bring peace on earth, peace to your heart and mine, and peace throughout the world. But he can give that peace only when we give our all to him.

XI

SIN AND SUFFERING

"Suppose ye that these Galileans were sinners above all the Galileans, because they suffered such things?"

LUKE 13:2

CERTAIN individuals had just rushed into the presence of Jesus bearing tragic tidings. I have an idea that these messengers were Judeans. If so they looked askance at these suffering Galileans as crude folks from the sticks. Therefore it was with more elation than tears that they told the Master of how these Galileans had come to worship, but had ended by having their own blood mingled with the blood of the beasts that they were offering in sacrifice. What terrible sinners they must have been! That is what they meant to imply as they told their heavy news.

But Jesus did not agree with them. Instead he told them frankly that this tragedy did not indicate that these slaughtered saints were worse than their fellows. If you and I are in an automobile accident and you are killed and I escape, that does not argue that you were wicked while I am good. Instead of agreeing with these men Jesus affirmed that they themselves were just as real sinners as those who had suffered. He declared further that unless they should repent they too would perish. It is evident as we read this story that these ancient bearers of evil tidings were possessed of certain convictions that were a strange mixture of truth and error, or of truth and half-truth.

I

There was one conviction that they held that is 100 per cent true. They were firm in the faith that sin always results in suffering. In their own scriptures they read this emphatic word: "Be sure your sin will find you out." This they steadfastly believed; this we should do well to believe. It was true in the long ago; it is true today. It was true in a primitive society; it is true in our scientific age. Every man who sins turns loose a nemesis upon his tracks that he can no more escape than he can escape his own shadow. "Be sure your sin will find you out." Your friends, your loved ones may never find you out. The officers of the law may fail, but your sin, never.

This is the case not because God is angry at the sinner. It is rather the case because we live in a law-abiding world. We live in a world where this law is forever true: "Whatsoever a man soweth, that shall he also reap." This is a solemn word of warning that we have chiefly used to cudgel sinners into being obedient. But it is more than a warning—it is a radiant promise. It tells us that we have it in our power to determine beyond a peradventure the quality of harvest we are going to reap tonight, tomorrow night, to the end of life, and to the end of eternity. That is something for which to be devoutly grateful.

In one of *McGuffey's Readers* there is the story of a man who barked his shins against this law of sowing and reaping until he cried out in bitterness: "I wish I were in a world of chance." Having thus wished, the author tells us that he went to sleep to awake in a world where law had ceased to reign. Suddenly he got the toothache. He sought relief by undertaking to make a pot of hot coffee. But when he took this supposedly hot coffee into his mouth he found it to be full of ice. "What does this mean?" he asked, as he spat it out in indignation. "It doesn't mean anything," came the reply. "We put the coffee on the fire. Sometimes the fire boils it and sometimes it freezes it. But it is your kind of world." Naturally, he longed to get back into his ordered world. That is the only kind of world in which life is livable.

But whether we appreciate the fact that ours is an ordered world or whether we resent it, the law of sowing and reaping still operates. Years ago when I was a pastor in Houston a good woman gave her son a secondhand automobile. This young man, who was just getting well into his teens, enjoyed driving his car at high speed around curves in order to hear the tires screak. One morning as he was indulging in this pastime his car skidded and ran into a telephone pole. He was thrown through the windshield against the pole and an ambulance came and hurried him to the hospital. They phoned for the minister and when I reached the hospital his mother was almost frantic. She

116

grasped my hands in both of hers and exclaimed: "Why should this happen to me?"

Her question silenced me for an instant, then I answered: "It did not happen to you, it happened to him."

"But why did God let it happen," she continued.

"Hold on," I replied, "don't blame God for permitting this accident. If our Lord were to snatch a telephone pole from in front of your son when he was driving recklessly, he might set one in front of me when I was driving carefully. In that case none of us could drive intelligently. All I am arguing is that every man must hit his own telephone pole."

So must every group; so must every nation. If the law of gravity operates for me when I walk on the ground and thus keeps me from flying out into space, I cannot expect it to go into reverse when I step out a tenth-story window.

Of course there was a sense in which this accident did happen to the mother. She suffered in the suffering of her son because she was bound up in the bundle of life with him. The vast majority of the suffering that we experience in this world, I am sure, comes from our own individual and collective wrong choices. But even when we are not personally guilty we often suffer because we are members one of another. Here, for instance, is a horrible sentence. On the surface it sounds positively devilish: "Visiting the iniquity of the fathers upon the children unto the third and fourth generation."

"How unjust!" I might exclaim. "Why should a guilty father have the power to visit his guilt upon me? How

117

unfair that I should be handicapped by the loose and lustful life of one in whose sin I had no share." But that is the price I pay for the capacity of being helped by a father and grandfather who lived clean and Christlike lives. If their sins are visited upon me, so also are their faith and goodness and Christlikeness. If by wrong living I have power to hurt my children, by right living I also have power to reach a hand even across the chasm of death to steady them and give them an upward lift.

Just as we are bound in a bundle of life with our children, so are we with our fellows everywhere. We are bound in a bundle of life with the nations. Not long ago I read a fiery speech that urged that we withhold our help from Europe and the rest of the world and spend our money making ourselves strong. In other words, we are to save ourselves as did the priest and the Levite, by passing by on the other side. But that is salvation that ends in damnation. This is the case simply because we are part of the world. We belong to the family of nations. We are bound even more closely with the Negroes who live among us. Therefore if one member suffers all members suffer with him.

Some months ago while fishing I got some poison ivy on my left ankle. Now if you have ever had anything to do with such poison you know that it can be very diverting. If any of you find difficulty in staying awake while your minister preaches, I can assure you that you will have no trouble at all if you manage to contract poison ivy. When I realized what had happened I remembered how I used to treat the ailment when I was a boy. I was accustomed to cure it by applications of carbolic acid. So I hurried to the drugstore and obtained a small bottle of the remedy.

But there was one item that I forgot. As a boy I used to dilute the acid. Instead, this time I took mine straight. I rubbed it on and rubbed it in. Then I got action. When the acid had eaten down close to the bone my whole body had an insurrection. My hand said: "I will have nothing to do with it. I am going to see to it that that offending member keeps its place." My head vowed that it would have nothing to do with it, saying: "That ankle is now burned black and red." But though every member of my body was an isolationist, when we went to bed that evening we all stayed awake together. Here then is a conviction held by the ancient Jews that is certainly true. Sin always eventuates in suffering. The sinner suffers, also those bound in a bundle of life with him.

II

But along with this certainty that is true everywhere and in every age there were other convictions that were mixtures of truth and of error.

1. Believing that sin always results in suffering, they affirmed with equal conviction that righteousness always escapes. They therefore would have said "Amen" to that mistranslated word of the first psalm that, speaking of God's blessed man, says, "Whatsoever he doeth shall prosper." Now the psalmist did not really say that, as we shall see later. But it was their faith that while the wicked man always went to the wall, the good man always won

the prize. He prospered physically and financially as well as spiritually.

Now there is a measure of truth in this. Certainly it is a fact, other things being equal, that the good man stands a better chance of physical health than the evil man. He also stands a better chance to prosper financially. A leading civic club has this as its motto: "He profits most who serves the best." Men in business have discovered that honesty and fair dealing are profitable. Thus a decent clean-living man has a far better chance at worldly success than his opposite.

But while this is true it does not mean that goodness is an infallible road to success. It might be very impressive to see all the rascals go bankrupt and all the saints get rich, but that is not the way life works. What therefore the psalmist really said is this: "In whatsoever he doeth he shall prosper." His bank may fail, his business may go to the wall, his physical strength may give way to weakness, but God's blessed man himself will prosper in spite of it all. The belief therefore that the righteous always succeeds is only a half-truth.

2. Convinced that sin always results in suffering, they believed that wherever any man suffered he suffered as a result of his own sin. Of course this is often the case. All of us have known those who have suffered the pangs of hell in their own souls and in their own bodies who had no one to blame for that suffering but themselves. Years ago I had a brilliant friend who threw away priceless possessions of ability to plunge into a mad orgy of dissipation. He held himself back from nothing that he thought

120

would give him a thrill. By-and-by, he became a sober clean-living man. He told his own story in this fashion. "I have given up my wild and foolish ways. This I have done not because I have become a Christian, at least I have not become a Christian yet. But I changed my way of living because I got tired of suffering." Many a man who has gaily sowed to the flesh is today reaping his harvest with bitter anguish and tears.

But while this is true it does not mean that all who suffer are paying the penalty for their own sin. When Job had lost his wealth, when he had lost his loved ones, when pain had come to walk with fireshod feet along every nerve of his body, three friends came to comfort him but remained to torture him. They had a very easy reading of the problem of his pain. They said that he was suffering as a result of his own sin. To their way of thinking it could not be otherwise. Therefore they asked him this quenching question: "Who ever perished being innocent?" The answer to that is "Multitudes." Jesus Christ himself was such a sufferer. If there are those who suffer because they are so evil there are also those who suffer because they are so good. Therefore we cannot say that everyone who suffers is paying the penalty for his own sin.

3. Being sure that sin always results in suffering, they reached the erroneous conclusion that because they themselves were not suffering they therefore had not sinned. This does not necessarily mean that they were claiming absolute perfection, but they were profoundly sure that they had not sinned so greatly as these miserable creatures

121

whom Pilate had slaughtered. This false conviction did not make them better. It made them far worse.

This was the case in the first place because it ministered to their pride and self-righteousness. They did not look at these poor Galileans and say: "There go we except for the grace of God." They rather said: "You ought to have been good like us then you would not have suffered." Therefore instead of looking upon those sufferers with compassion and humility they regarded them with prideful contempt.

A second result of their freedom from suffering was the conviction that even though they might have sinned in some respectable fashion they were getting away with their sin. They were still sure of course that men reap as they sow. That is, they were sure that the ordinary run of the mill do that. But such was not quite true for themselves. They were shrewd enough to manipulate the laws of nature and to gather grapes of thorns and figs of thistles. Thus they had not only become self-righteous and contemptuous in the presence of the suffering of others, but they had become morally color-blind. They had come to believe that for themselves a crooked line might at times be the shortest distance between two points. That was the very climax of tragedy. This is the case because sin is never so tragic as when it seems to triumph. It is never so deadly as when it seems to give life. It always brings disaster, but it is never quite so disastrous as when we seem to get by with it.

III

What did our Lord have to say to these men? He called them to repentance. This he did because they were sinners just as were those whom Pilate had slaughtered. They were sinners just as we are. There is no difference, said Paul, "for all have sinned." By this he does not mean that we have all sinned equally. There were two thorn trees that grew side by side on my father's farm. One of these had very few thorns while the other had thousands. But the one that was almost free of thorns could not for that reason say to its fellow: "You are a thorn tree, but I am a weeping willow." They were both thorn trees still. These needed to repent because they were sinners, even as you and I.

Now Jesus seems to regard repentance as the supreme antidote to suffering. What is it to repent? It is something more than being convinced that you are a sinner. It is something more than being sorry for sin. I am thinking of a man who used to turn from his slimy ways with his throat choked with sobs and his face wet with tears. Repentance is being so sorry for sin that we turn from it to God. The prodigal repented when he left the swinepen and kept going until he found the shelter of his father's arms. Repentance is the supreme antidote against suffering for two reasons.

First, repentance saves us from suffering because it prevents our wrong choices. We do not by repentance escape in the here and now the consequences of our wrongdoing. We must repent before we sin if we are to save

123

ourselves and others from the suffering that always follows in the wake of wrongdoing. After Esau had sold his birthright his tears over his tragic folly were vain tears, not because God refused to forgive, since God did forgive him fully and freely. But they were vain because his belated repentance could not put back into his hands the opportunities that he had thrown away in youth's bright morning long ago. If therefore you would spare yourself and others the penalty of pain, repent before you sin.

2. Then repentance, because it brings us within the will of God, helps to solve the problem of pain. This is the case because "All things work together for good to them that love God." If we co-operate with God by so loving him as to obey him, we make it possible for him to change all our losses into gains. As nature sometimes takes the wound of an oyster and changes it into a pearl, even so God can take our wounds, whatever their cause, and make them into jewels of priceless worth. Meet your suffering within his will and you too will be able to say: "We know that all things work together for good to them that love God."

XII

PERSISTENT PRAYER

"Shall not God?"

LUKE 18:7

"SHALL not God?" Through the story of which this question is a part Jesus is undertaking to teach us the importance and the reasonableness of a habit of prayer. He realized quite as well as we how easy it is for one to become discouraged in an effort to pray. He knows how prone we are to turn aside from this task that might be so rewarding to give ourselves to lesser tasks that seem to bring greater results. Knowing the tragedy of such failure he fairly taxes his vast abilities in an effort to teach us that we ought always to pray and not to faint.

I

Jesus taught us to pray by what he said about prayer.

His assertions regarding the privileges and possibilities of prayer often seem to our dim faith extravagant. He tells us, for instance, that prayer is not the privilege of the few but of the many. It is not simply for those who have climbed far up the hill toward God, but it is for ordinary plodders like ourselves. He asserts that everyone that asketh, receiveth; that he that seeketh, findeth; and that to him that knocketh, it shall be opened. The victories of prayer may be won by even the weakest.

Even so, failure may come to the strongest without it. One day Jesus came upon his disciples to find them hot and flustered. They had just made a terrible failure and were therefore filled with shame and confusion. A father had brought to them his afflicted lad. They had undertaken to cure him. But all their efforts had proved futile. They had succeeded only in winning the ridicule of the scoffers and in weakening the faith of this father who had come with such high confidence. But when Jesus came on the scene defeat was changed into victory. When therefore these disciples were alone with their Master they asked him this sane question: "Why could not we cast him out?"

What answer did our Lord give? He did not attribute their failure to their indifference. They were interested both in this father and in his son. Neither did he tell them that they had failed because of a lack of effort. They had done their serious and earnest best. No more did he tell them that their failure was due to the fact that they had undertaken a task that was too big for them, even when assisted by divine strength. He rather declared that they had failed in their efforts to help because they had failed to pray. If we refuse to pray, no amount of effort will atone for that failure when we go forth to battle.

But if what Jesus said about prayer was so impressive what he did about it was more impressive still. It was not

126

after a sermon on prayer that the disciples came saying: "Lord, teach us to pray," but it was after they had seen the Master on his knees. As they watched him at prayer they said: "Here is something real. Here is something far bigger and finer than we have ever done. Here is something that is supremely worth-while. We must learn the secret." Not only did they feel the reality and the worth of prayer when they saw the Master upon his knees, but they were heartened to believe that such praying was in some measure possible for themselves. Therefore they came with this wise prayer: "Lord, teach us to pray."

Our Lord is teaching us still. What place did he give to prayer in his own busy and triumphant life? The answer is that he gave prayer first place. Prayer was central in the life of Jesus. With us prayer is sometimes a preparation for the battle, but with Jesus prayer, in a very genuine sense, was the battle. That is, having prayed he went as an honor student might go to receive a medal or as a victor might go to receive the spoils of his conquest.

To be convinced of this it is only necessary to turn again to the Gospels. Here we see Jesus when he was obviously putting forth the utmost of his energy. Here we see him engaged in a conflict so strenuous that his sweat was as great drops of blood falling down to the ground. But there are other times when he walks with a serenity and poise that leave us amazed and wistful to this hour. When, let me ask you, were his seasons of conflict and of struggle, when his seasons of serenity and poise? Always his times of conflict were his prayer periods. If we are to judge by the New Testament the only work that ever really taxed the strength of Jesus was the work of prayer. Having prayed, I repeat, he went forth from the place of prayer as a victor to receive the spoils of his conquest.

Take Jesus' works of wonder, for instance. How easily they were performed! There was no sweat, no agony. When, for instance, a blind beggar asked to be led out of darkness into light, all Jesus had to do was to say: "Receive thy sight." When he stood by the grave of Lazarus there was no struggle, no desperate wringing of hands, only a simple prayer of thanksgiving: "Father, I thank thee that thou hast heard me." Then he called his friend from death to life. It all seems so easy.

Just as there was no agony, no bloody sweat in the doing of his works of wonder, no more was there in his dealing with the shrewd and hostile adversaries that dogged his steps toward the end of his ministry. These men would have given their very lives to have entrapped Jesus into uttering some unguarded word. They set their traps with consummate cunning. Yet he brushed these traps aside like so many cobwebs. Had a stenographer taken down his every word I daresay he would not have had to change his manuscript in the least. Having done well the work of prayer all else seemed to be easy.

It was so even to the end. Had I witnessed the struggle of Jesus in Gethsemane as "he offered up prayers and supplications with strong crying and tears," I should have been afraid for the future. I should have thought: "If he is so broken up now, how utterly will he go to pieces when he meets death eye to eye! Why does he not face the ordeal with the calm confidence of his three sleeping friends?" But when the final test came it was the three friends who went to pieces. It was before the kingly majesty of the man who had prayed that the soldiers staggered back and fell to the ground. Thus Jesus teaches us to pray both by what he said and by what he did.

II

What are some of the rewards of prayer?

1. The first and all-inclusive reward of prayer is that it lets God into our lives. To pray is to open the door to the Christ who is always knocking and waiting for us to invite him to enter. The eternal God becomes real to the one who truly prays. This, I repeat, is the all-inclusive good. There is absolutely nothing so much needed by all of us in these difficult days as a new sense of God. We can find this sense of God individually and as a group by prayer. When we enter a church where men and women pray we are constantly constrained to say: "Surely the Lord is in this place."

This, I repeat, is the all-inclusive blessing of prayer. If you are able to say with the psalmist: "I sought the Lord, and he heard me," if you have ever had an answer to prayer, the biggest thrill of that answer was not the gift that was put into your hands and into your heart. It was rather the new consciousness of God that came to you through that answer. This is the case because no gift can possibly be so great as the giver himself. The richest reward of prayer is a new awareness of the eternal God.

2. Because prayer brings a sense of God it also brings new courage and new power. That is only natural. How-

ever great our danger may be, however grim our foes, if God is real to us we can face them with steady eyes and quiet hearts. "I have set the Lord always before me: because he is at my right hand, I shall not be moved."

When the prophet said: "They that wait upon the Lord shall renew their strength," he was speaking out of his own experience as well as that of countless others. Some of you, I am sure, have found yourselves girded with a strength in the face of difficulty that was a thrill to your soul. Stanley declared that having found Livingstone in Africa, and then having found Livingstone's God, he came to be possessed of a stamina and a courage that his nonpraying companions did not possess. Beyond all doubt, prayer makes it possible for God to do in us and for us and through us what he simply cannot do if we fail to pray.

If you are finding yourself inadequate to the demands that life makes upon you, try prayer. What a fascinating story is that of the triumph of Daniel! When the politicians had secured the king's signature to a law that no man should pray to anybody for the next thirty days but the king himself, they were sure they had Daniel where they wanted him. But it so happened that Daniel was a praying man. Therefore when he knew that his death warrant had been signed he went up into his room and opened his window toward Jerusalem and prayed as he had done "aforetime." That is, prayer had been a habit of his life. That habit stood him in such good stead that he was able to see this trying hour through with honor. Babylon has been a ruin for long centuries. The one thing left standing

130

in it is the character of this man who knew how to pray. Prayer brings power.

3. Prayer is a means of helping others. This was the faith of Jesus. When he foresaw the sifting of Simon he prayed for him. On the night before he went away he prayed with and for his disciples. He also prayed for you and me on that fateful night. This he did when he made request not only for his present disciples, but for all who should believe on him through their word. Not only did Jesus pray for us when he walked among us, but he prays for us still. If we may believe our own Scriptures, prayer is one of the tasks that engages our glorified Christ to this hour. He is even now making intercession for us. Surely he believed in the efficacy of prayer for others.

Paul, who to a superlative degree shared the mind of Christ, shared his faith in prayer. He was constantly remembering his own converts, his friends—all men—in prayer. He was as constantly asking for the prayers of others. He never wrote but one letter, and that to the backslidden church of Galatia, without asking for the prayers of those backward and faulty believers. He was sure that the very weakest of them could so pray as to anoint his apostolic lips with grace and power.

Since prayer is a means of helping others it is more than a privilege, it is a solemn duty. "God forbid that I should sin against the Lord in ceasing to pray for you." If you find that the services in your church are wanting in warmth and power, try prayer. Pray for your minister that he may be able to bring to you and others a sense of God. Pray for your choir. Pray for the officers and teach-

131

ers in your church school. It is impossible to have a futile church or a futile service where members of the congregation really pray.

Since we can help by praying we ought to pray. Withholding prayer is a sin. The priest and the Levite who passed by on the other side have sat in the prisoner's dock along with the brigands for long centuries. But if we can pass by on the other side by failing to help by our gifts and by our efforts to bind another's wounds, we can also pass by on the other side by our failure to pray. "Ye also helping together by prayer," writes Paul. Therefore because we can help by prayer it is our duty to help. Withheld prayer is a sin.

Not only can we help by prayer, but there come times when it is the only way we can help. We can give of our money to the cause of missions if we have it. But even if we are too poor to give even a few pennies we can help by prayer. There come desperate hours in the life of those we love when we can help them in no other way. I have had occasion to think of what a terrible thing it would be to be unable to pray when there was nothing else that could be done for the one you love most dearly. There are times when it is the only means. Therefore let your voice rise like a fountain day and night both for yourself and for those who call you friend.

III

How then are we to pray? I am going to offer three suggestions:

1. If prayer is to accomplish its purpose we must pray

132

earnestly. God cannot give his best to the listless and the halfhearted. It is the earnest, energized prayer that is a mighty force. When John Knox prayed, "Give me Scotland or I die," God gave him Scotland because he could trust his people in the hands of one who was thus desperately in earnest to bring them spiritual health.

If therefore we are to find the best in prayer we must be in earnest about it. God cannot do much for us until we get to the end of ourselves. It is only when the heavy hands of a great need grip our shoulders and crush us to our knees that we really pray. Nothing worth-while is accomplished by the prayers of the halfhearted. Therefore if you would pray effectively you must be in earnest.

2. Pray expectantly. Remember that prayer is not a weird, strange experience. It is the very climax of sanity and common sense. Jesus reminds us that prayer is something with which we have to do in our relations with each other every day that we live. For instance, parents hear and answer prayer. "If a son shall ask bread of any of you that is a father, will he give him a stone?" No good father would be so heartless as to give his boy a stone on which to break his teeth when the boy needed bread. If we then with our imperfections answer the prayers of our children, how much more will God, the perfect father, "give good things to them that ask him."

The reasonableness and sanity of prayer is seen in the relation of friend with friend. When a certain villager was surprised at midnight by an unexpected guest, he was embarrassed by the fact that he had no bread to set before him. So what? He went out to knock on the door of the

133

house of a friend. This friend was in bed. It would seem that he had had trouble with the children and was afraid that this troublesome seeker after bread would disturb them. But in spite of all difficulties he got up and gave his friend as much as he needed.

As a climax Jesus declared that not only do fathers and friends answer prayer, but even heartless scoundrels. In proof of this he told the story of a judge with no regard for either God or man. Yet a widow, the very embodiment of helplessness, so prayed as to win a favorable answer from this cruel and crooked man. This she did in spite of the fact that he cared nothing for her nor for the rightness of her cause. He only hated being bothered. If such a judge will answer prayer, how confident we may be when we pray to a God who is at once a just judge, a loving friend, and a perfect father.

3. Finally, we must pray persistently. We are not to persist in order to make God hear us. We are to persist because we are sure that he will hear us. Once I went to a wedding rehearsal. The bride was thirty minutes late. I confess that I grew a bit restless, but the groom waited with calm confidence. I felt like saying: "Maybe she is not coming. Let us all give over and go home." But the groom was sure that she would come, therefore he waited. But his waiting was not in order to make her come; it was rather because he was sure that she would come. "And shall not God avenge his own elect, which cry day and night unto him, though he bear long with them? I tell you that he will avenge them speedily." Because this is true we ought always to pray and not to faint.

134

XIII

THE GREAT NECESSITY

"Ought not Christ to have suffered these things, and to enter into his glory?"

LUKE 24:26

IT was the first Easter Sunday. Jesus, our risen Lord, was abroad in his springtime world. In the richness of his love and mercy he has drawn near and entered into conversation with two of his grief-stricken friends who were on their way home from his funeral. Though the hearts of these two desolate friends burned within them as he talked with them by the way and opened to them the scriptures, they did not recognize them. This was the case, I dare say, partly because they were not expecting to see him, but more because their eyes were so fixed upon a cross on a skull-shaped hill and upon a tomb in Joseph's garden that they were blind to all else.

But in spite of their failure to recognize him their bleak winter was so thawed by his presence that they soon found themselves opening their hearts to him. Feeling that he would understand, they told him of their young and fear-

135

less prophet. They told of the daring hopes they had once cherished because of him. So daring had been these hopes that they had seen in this martyred prophet their own redeemer and the redeemer of Israel. But now that he was dead all hope had died with him; for what could a crucified Christ do for the redemption of a lost world?

Then it was that with great tenderness, and yet with pained disappointment, our Lord answered: "O fools, and slow of heart to believe all that the prophets have spoken: ought not Christ to have suffered these things, and to enter into his glory?" Of course "ought" is not used here in the sense that his suffering was deserved. This modern translation best brings out the meaning: "Was it not necessary that the Christ should suffer these things?" It is therefore evident from this passage that Jesus looked upon his cross not as a tragic misfortune, but as a necessity.

I

This was certainly the case as Jesus looked at the cross in prospect. It is evident to every candid reader of the Gospels that the cross did not take Jesus by surprise. Before he was called upon thus to suffer he had come to look upon that suffering as a necessity. As to the exact date when Jesus began thus to foresee the cross, we may differ. But as to the fact there can be no difference for those who take the New Testament seriously. Jesus himself spoke of his coming tragic death again and again and always he regarded it as a necessity.

When, for instance, he went for a retreat with his

disciples to Caesarea Philippi, he asked these friends as to the impression he had made upon them. When Simon had made his great confession Jesus concluded that they were far enough forward to face the cross. "From that time forth began Jesus to shew unto his disciples, how that he must go unto Jerusalem, and suffer many things of the elders and chief priests and scribes, and be killed, and be raised again the third day."

Later on, when the cross had come so near that he was being put under arrest, his friends were at once heart-broken and bewildered. They could not see how one so vital, one so like God, could allow himself to be done to death. Simon even struck a futile blow with his sword. But the Master spoke home to his bewilderment and despair with these words: "Thinkest thou that I cannot now pray to my Father, and he shall presently give me more than twelve legions of angels? But how then shall the Scriptures be fulfilled, that thus it must be?" It is as if the Master were saying: "I could escape, but only by failing to carry out the full purpose of God for my life."

Then came that lonely struggle in Gethsemane. Here it seems that for a moment Jesus hoped that there might be some way of avoiding the cross. Could not the God of infinite love find for him an avenue of escape? Listen to this prayer: "O my Father, if it be possible, let this cup pass from me: nevertheless not as I will, but as thou wilt." But his second prayer is not a prayer of petition but of acceptance: "O my Father, if this cup may not pass away from me, except I drink it, thy will be done." It is as if Jesus had said: "Inasmuch as this cup cannot pass from

137

me except I drink it, thy will be done." Here once more he accepted the cross as a necessity. Thus his tragic death as seen in prospect was constantly regarded by him as inevitable.

II

Now as Jesus regarded the cross as a necessity when seen in prospect, so he regarded it when seen in retrospect.

When, on the way to Emmaus, he talked with these two friends, the hard ordeal of the Crucifixion had become a fact of history. Its grim anguish was then only a memory. But having passed through death, having experienced the Resurrection, Jesus still regarded the cross not as a needless waste, but as an absolute necessity. Listen to him as he speaks to those who believed that his death had put an end to all their hopes: "O fools, and slow of heart to believe all that the prophets have spoken. Was it not necessary that the Christ should suffer these things?" It was as if he said: "You think that a crucified Christ can do nothing for the world, but the truth is that Christ crucified is the one hope of the world." It was just this conviction on the part of Jesus that his cross was a necessity that enabled him to see in that grim experience not a mere tragedy, but a triumph.

We can glimpse the reason for this when we realize that the degree of bitterness that is born of the tragedies we suffer depends largely upon whether they are needless or necessary. I once read of a father who drove into town with his five-year-old son. To this son he was devoted beyond the ordinary. It so happened that this father met some boon companions and drank more than was his custom. As he drove home he felt especially fit. Almost unconsciously he began to speed. By and by, in an effort to take a curve at high speed, he lost control and plunged down an embankment. He himself was only slightly injured, but his small boy was instantly killed. Of course the loss of his son would have been bitter under any circumstances, but its bitterness was brought to a climax by the fact that the father had to realize that his loss was the result of his own wicked folly.

Here's an exceedingly bitter cry: "O my son Absalom, my son, by son Absalom! would God I had died for thee, O Absalom, my son, my son!" David's heart is broken over the fact that his handsome and gifted boy now lies under a heap of stones in a traitor's grave. But the climax of his sorrow is born of the conviction that the tragedy was needless. Had he not passed his own responsibility onto the shoulders of others, had he only gone in person to look after his son he might have saved him. But this he failed to do. Therefore his loss is doubly bitter because he feels that it might have been avoided.

Now just as tragedy becomes more bitter because of its needlessness, even so it loses somewhat of its bitterness when we know it to be necessary. A few years ago a father was plowing in the field while his two small boys were playing near by. Suddenly he looked up from his work to see a huge dog coming toward the boys. He recognized at once that the dog was mad. Therefore he rushed to meet the oncoming beast, urging his boys to take refuge in a cotton bin. Thus the boys were saved, but the father was bitten from his face to his feet. So completely was he poisoned that medical skill could do nothing for him. But I am told that as the end drew near, in moments when he was free from delirium, he would smile into the face of his wife and say: "Don't you take it too hard. Remember that the boys are safe and that there was no other way." It was the faith of Jesus that through his cross he had accomplished something for us that he could not have accomplished in any other way.

III

If the cross was a necessity why was it so?

Let me begin with this testimony: Christ crucified is my one hope of salvation for time and for eternity. But having said this I make the further confession that I have found no fully satisfactory answer to this question. Of course I know something of what the theologians, past and present, have had to say. They throw light upon it, but I have yet to find an answer that I feel leaves nothing more to be said. It will possibly take much of eternity for the saints to fathom this question. But thank God we do not have to find a fully satisfactory answer to the mystery of the cross in order to reap its benefits.

There are certain answers, I think, that we may renounce altogether. There is, for instance, a superficial reading of the Gospels that has led some to believe that the cross was a necessity in order that the scriptures might be fulfilled. That the cross does fulfill the scriptures few Bible readers will deny. But it was not the scriptures that made the cross a necessity; it was the cross that

140

caused the scriptures thus to be written. I am quite sure that Jesus saw himself as the suffering servant of Jehovah in the fifty-third chapter of Isaiah. But it was not this great chapter that brought about the cross. It was the cross, rather, that gave birth to these words of deathless hope: "He was wounded for our transgressions, he was bruised for our iniquities: the chastisement of our peace was upon him; and with his stripes we are healed."

No more was Jesus crucified because the rulers among his own people and the powers of imperial Rome were too much for him. He died in weakness, but he did not die because of weakness. He makes us sure that life was not wrested from his clinging hands and gripping fingers. Jesus did not lose his life, he gave it. "No man taketh it from me, but I lay it down of myself."

Neither did our Lord die in order to appease the wrath of an angry God. Nothing can be further from the truth than this. It is a slander both against God and against the Son who came to reveal God. We must bear in mind always that the attitude of Jesus toward sinners was the attitude of God the Father. When Jesus prayed: "Father, forgive them; for they know not what they do," that prayer was the will of God. When Jesus was on the cross, God was on the cross. This was the conviction of Paul: "God was in Christ, reconciling the world unto himself." God the Father and God the Son were always at one. They were never more completely so than when Jesus hung by the nails.

Why then, I repeat, was the cross necessary? Of course my answer can be only partial.

1. To begin on the human side there came a time when Jesus so clashed with the authorities of his day that he had to go forward to his heroic death or compromise. He knew that it was not necessary for him to live, but that it was necessary that he be true to his own convictions and to the will of God. There was therefore that in his death that makes his suffering akin to that of other heroic souls who have died for conscience's sake. This is not to deny that there is that about the death of Christ that is unshared and unsharable. But there is also that which enables us with Paul to "fill up that which is behind of the afflictions of Christ."

2. Then the cross was a necessity because of who Christ is and who we are. It was impossible for one so sinless and tender of heart as our Lord to live among those so sinful and hard of heart as we are and not suffer the pangs of crucifixion. Further, that great word that he uttered, "Except a corn of wheat fall into the ground and die, it abideth alone" was true for him as for us.

3. But my conviction is that the supreme reason that the cross was a necessity is because God saw in that cross the best possible way of reconciling man to himself. In the light of the cross we see man at his wicked worst. But in this same light we also see man as a creature of infinite worth. At the cross we come face to face with a love that will not let us go. It is a tremendously arresting experience to have any creature love us well enough to be willing to suffer in our behalf. To know that God loves in that fashion is supremely compelling. There is nothing else that at once so wins and breaks our hearts as to be

able to say out of our own experiences: "He loved me and gave himself up for me." Herein his own words have been found true: "And I, if I be lifted up from the earth, will draw all men unto me."

IV

Now just as the cross of Jesus is a necessity, so is a proper response on our part a necessity if we are to realize the reconciliation that he died to bring. If you and I give ourselves to him as he gave himself for us, what will it mean to us personally?

1. First, if in response to his self-giving love we dedicate our lives to him, he will accept us and take us into his fellowship. The tragic quarrel between us and God will be ended. Being thus brought into fellowship with him we shall "have peace with God through our Lord Jesus Christ."

2. If we thus yield to God so as to be at peace with him, we shall come to possess inward peace. When we get right with God we get right with ourselves. "There is no peace, saith my God, to the wicked." "The kingdom of God . . . is righteousness, and peace, and joy in the Holy Ghost." There must be rightness with God before there can be peace within. But having thus yielded we can then claim the legacy that Jesus left to his friends: "Peace I leave with you, my peace I give unto you."

3. Finally, having yielded to our self-giving Lord, we not only have peace with God and peace within, but we have peace one with another. It is impossible to look with indifference or scorn or contempt upon any man when we

143

see in that man a "brother for whom Christ died." The saints of the early church went out to break down all barriers and to bridge all chasms between man and man and race and race. This they did because, having been reconciled themselves, they became ministers of reconciliation. They were ambassadors for Christ. They prayed men in Christ's stead to be reconciled to God. Thus they changed the world. Thus we may help to change it.

XIV

THE IGNORANT PROFESSOR

"Art thou a master of Israel, and knowest not these things?"

JOHN 3:10

IT is amazing how abysmal ignorance can often rub elbows with great learning in the same individual. The fact that one is an authority in a certain field does not make him an authority in another field. Here is a man who was, as another has suggested, at once the equivalent of a college professor, a judge of the supreme court, and a bishop in the church. He was a man of light and learning, yet he was strangely ignorant of the fact that life can be made over. He knew nothing of the new birth. Therefore Jesus asked him very tenderly, I think, and yet with real astonishment: "Art thou a master of Israel, and knowest not these things?"

I

The man of whom Jesus asked this question was named Nicodemus. He represents about the best in the life of his day. He was a man of position and prominence. He be-

145

longed to that cultivated class that gave to the world such scholars as Gamaliel and Paul. He was himself a scholar and a member of the court of the Sanhedrin. He was an honored and religious leader. All in all he was a very fascinating personality.

1. He was a man of open mind. In spite of the fact that he had arrived, so far as position was concerned, he was still intellectually curious. It was his curiosity in part, I think, that caused him to visit Jesus. The Master was just coming into prominence. He had recently cleansed the temple. Strange rumors were blowing about the streets of the city regarding him. Some claimed that he had powers beyond the human. Some declared that he had opened blind eyes and that he had cleansed lepers. Some were even hinting that he might be the long promised Messiah. These rumors excited the curiosity of Nicodemus. Thus curious he was eager for this interview.

Now I have heard curiosity condemned. Of course there is a wrong kind of curiosity. I dare say that not a few have taken their first drink or their first plunge into unclean living out of curiosity. But curiosity in the right direction is good.

"Twinkle, twinkle little star,
How I wonder what you are."

Because man wondered he made a telescope and looked at those stars and mapped the heavens. The name of that telescope was Curiosity. It is through the microscope of Curiosity that the scientist searches in his laboratory. It was on the good ship Curiosity that Columbus and Magel-

146

lan and Admiral Byrd and all the great explorers have sailed. Blessed is the man who is curious to know Jesus!

2. Not only was there curiosity in this visit but intellectual honesty as well. Nicodemus had heard that this new prophet was making strange and stupendous claims, or that at least such claims were being made for him. If these claims were true, this ruler of the Jews, being a religious leader, felt that he ought to know and act accordingly. If they were not true and this exciting man was only an imposter, he ought also to know that and act accordingly. Therefore this curious and honest man turned his feet toward the house where Jesus was stopping.

3. Not only was he curious and intellectually honest, he was also humble. He was willing to learn from anybody who was able to teach him. That is a fine characteristic. In the social scale Jesus and Nicodemus were a long way apart. This ruler of the Jews was an aristocrat; Jesus was a man of the people. Nicodemus had perhaps grown old in leadership, while Jesus was an unknown carpenter. Yet this distinguished man was not too proud to seek this young rabbi out and sit at his feet. It is as if a professor of Harvard University should go down on some mean street in Boston to learn from an obscure person.

4. Then it is evident that this ruler of the Jews, though earnestly religious, was genuinely dissatisfied with himself. Like so many in the church today he could not but realize that his religion had not met his deepest needs. With all his gettings he had not found the best. With all his achievings his heart was still hot and restless and hungry. I think more than all else it was his gnawing

147

hunger, it was his burning thirst, that sent him down to meet this rabbi from Nazareth.

5. Finally, this professor was possessed of a beautiful type of courage. Commentators differ widely regarding Nicodemus on this point. There are those who argue that he was fearless. They rate his courage at 100 per cent. Then there are others who give him credit for no courage at all. These call attention to the fact that he came to Jesus by night. That his coming by night has significance I think is beyond doubt. This is evidenced by the fact that whenever the author mentions the name of this ruler he reminds us that he came by night.

Why did he come by night? Some who argue that he was fearless affirm that he came by night because he was so desperately in earnest that he could not wait for the coming of the day. Others claim that he came by night because the night was the best time to come. It gave an opportunity for long and uninterrupted conversation. But taking a full view of this ruler I am driven to the conclusion that his timidity was at least a part of the reason for his coming by night. That he was a cautious and timid man I think is evidenced not simply by this scene, but by his next appearance on the stage.

When we next meet him the Pharisees have become thoroughly antagonistic to Jesus. They are out to destory him. They have already sent policemen to arrest him. When these officers return without the prisoner they ask: "Why did you not bring him?" With considerable embarrassment, I imagine, these officers replied: "Never man spoke like this man." At this the Pharisees are thoroughly

148

indignant. "Have any of the authorities or the Pharisees believed in him?" they asked. "But this crowd who do not know the law are accursed."

Then it was that Nicodemus spoke out in the Master's defense: "Does our law judge a man without first giving him a hearing, and learning what he does?" It is not a bold word such as Paul would have spoken. It is not so bold, I dare say, as Nicodemus felt he ought to speak. "Not all Pharisees have rejected him," he might have said, "I have seen him personally, and I am on the way to calling him Lord and Master." But instead of making a bold declaration he only asked a question. This, I think, indicates timidity.

Now the fact that Nicodemus came to Jesus and the further fact that he also spoke out in his defense indicate a high type of courage. For courage at its best is not freedom from fear. A bulldog has that type of courage. Courage at its best is that which leads us to defy our fears. Such was the courage of Nicodemus. He may have come timidly to Jesus. He may have spoken timidly in his defense. But this must not blind us to what really matters and that is that he did come and that he did speak out. The really courageous man is the one who follows the path of duty, even though his knees are shaking with terror.

II

Now suppose we join this cautious scholar as he goes to this interview. He begins the conversation in this fashion: "We know that thou art a teacher come from God." The reply of Jesus to this compliment seems entirely irrelevant.

149

But the Master is speaking home, not to the words of the professor's lips, but to the longing of his heart. Therefore he replies: "Except a man be born again, he cannot see the kingdom of God." He is saying to this professor: "You are not satisfied. In spite of a life of service to the church you have not found reality. You will never find it until you are born anew."

"How can these things be?" Nicodemus asks in amazement. Jesus is amazed at his amazement. He replies: "Are you a teacher of Israel, and yet you do not understand this?" (R.S.V.) Of course the possibility, the absolute necessity of the new birth is a fundamental truth of our holy religion. That a man can be born again is affirmed not only by the Scriptures, but by modern science as well. The psychologist is now as sure of the new birth as is the evangelist. Of course the psychologist usually calls this experience by a more high-sounding name. But religion and science agree in affirming that a man may be born anew.

To the testimony of the Scriptures and of the psychologists experience adds its voice. The new birth is a fact of experience. All about us are those who are being or have been born anew. There are those, for instance, who are born from beneath. I am thinking now of a lovely young woman I knew years ago. She was an eager worker in my church. To all appearances she was a beautiful Christian. But she became secretary to a man who was a scoundrel. For some years I lost sight of her. When I met her again she had undergone a radical change. Her facial expression was different. Her whole personality had altered. She had become coarse and loud in her talk. She gave me the impression that she had been born anew, born from beneath.

Now just as one may be born from beneath, even so he may be born from above. This new birth is a necessity if one is to see the Kingdom of God. A spiritual birth is just as necessary in order to enter the Kingdom of Heaven as a physical birth in order to enter this world. Therefore no amount of culture, no amount of decency, no amount of devotion, no amount of morality, nothing can take the place of the new birth. It is our greatest privilege. But it is far more than a privilege; it is an absolute necessity.

Having said this it is needful to remind you that we do not all enter this experience in the same fashion. This has been a source of perplexity to many earnest Christians. With some this experience is instantaneous and climactic. As I have dealt with seekers I have seen the light of the glory of God break over their faces as suddenly as a landscape is lighted when a cloud passes from the face of the sun. Many of the great saints have entered into this experience with the suddenness of the lightning's flash. Because this is true there are those who, lacking this climactic experience, fear they have never been converted.

But while many enter into this experience suddenly there are yet more who enter into it gradually. This some are prone to forget. An earnest man said to me some years ago: "I would not give the pop of my finger for any man's religion who cannot tell the day and the hour in which he was converted." How absurd! He might as well have said: "I would not give the pop of my finger for any

151

man's existence who cannot tell the day and the hour in which he was born physically." But it is not the how or the when of the new birth that counts, it is the fact. You might convince me that I am wrong as to the date of my birth, but you could never convince me that I am wrong about the fact of it. If you know the day and the hour in which you were converted, thank God for it. But remember there may be others who are more genuinely conscious of life through Christ than you are, and yet could not fix any birthday. These have blossomed into the knowledge of Christ as flowers bloom at the kiss of spring.

III

What did this interview do for Nicodemus? Does he go away from the presence of this young carpenter singing in his heart with Paul: "Old things have passed away; behold, all things are become new"? Is he conscious of a change within him so great that it can be adequately described only as a passing out of death into life? Has his night given place to glorious day? Has springtime come with life-giving beauty on the wintry hills of his heart? I think we must answer in the negative.

But while he is conscious of no radical change he has been deeply moved. The words of Jesus have thrilled him and have given him new hope. He feels in his soul the fundamental rightness of the man and of what he has said. Therefore when he hears the court, of which he himself is a member, condemn the Master without a hearing, he cannot but speak out in his defense. He does not speak so boldly, I repeat, as he or we should like for him to have spoken. But that timid defense cost him far more than a far bolder speech would have cost a man possessed of a greater natural courage.

Then followed an event so tragic and heartbreaking that it made all the former fears of this ruler seem utterly silly and sinful. Jesus has been done to death in a most ruthless and disgraceful fashion. Nicodemus realizes now that he can never tell him of the loyalty and friendship that through these months have really been in his heart. The help that he could have rendered is now forever impossible. But though he cannot now come "aforetime" as Mary did, he feels that he must do something. Therefore he makes an open confession of loyalty. This he does by assisting at the funeral. He brings a whole hundred-pound weight of myrrh and aloes. That was far too much, but it was his pathetic effort to express his unspoken love and thus atone for the past. I have been called upon to witness many a sorrow, but I have seen few deeper than that of some bereaved and broken heart who vainly seeks to say to the dead what he should have said to the living.

Nicodemus lost much by not coming sooner. But the supremely beautiful fact is that he did come. Thus coming he surely entered into that experience of which Jesus spoke that night when they listened together to the sighing of the night wind. We are sure of this because it was true then as it is true now that "we know, if we follow on to know the Lord." Is this your experience? What Jesus asked in the long ago he is asking today. As a member of the church, as a teacher in the church school, as a minister in the pulpit, do you understand this?

XV

ABSENT WITNESSES

"Woman, where are those thine accusers?
hath no man condemned thee?"

JOHN 8:10

THE scholars are uncertain as to where in the sacred record this story belongs. Some think that it does not belong at all. From certain of the ancient manuscripts it is omitted. However, speaking not as a scholar but merely as a Bible reader, I am sure that it does really belong. Here I feel is a true story. If it is not true it is one from which the truth itself might learn. Not only is this story true, but in my judgment it is factual. It is the record of an event that actually took place. It would have taken a superb genius indeed to have invented a story so true to life. Certainly it is consistent with what we know about the scribes and the Pharisees; it is yet more consistent with what we know about Jesus himself.

It is a sordid story, at least in its beginning. It shows something of the ugliness of human nature. But along with its sordidness it also has a rare beauty. Although

154

some faces in this drama are cruel and hard, there is another that is very strong and tender. If you love a story with a happy ending you would do well to memorize this. If it begins in a black night of storm it ends in the radiant glory of morning. Here a soiled rag of womanhood came to what looked like the end and found it really the "Land of Beginning Again."

I

Look first at the woman who is an unwilling actress in this drama. She is a nameless creature who is an adulteress. Of course there was a partner who shared her sin, but he is not mentioned. He is not even accused. In that day there was a double standard of morals. A man had rights that a woman did not have. Today that is largely changed. Probably the change will eventuate in higher standards for both man and woman. At present woman seems to have dropped nearer to the level of man rather than man climbing to the higher level once occupied by woman.

Not only was this woman guilty, but she had been caught in the act of shame. To be guilty is bad enough, but to be caught is, in the mind of many, worse still. All who knew her knew her guilt. Perhaps she was young. Perhaps she was one who had loved not wisely but too well. Perhaps she was more sinned against than sinning. Or it may be that she was cynical and hard, having walked long in the ways of evil. But whatever the case her sin was known. As her story opens there were eyewitnesses present who could testify against her.

155

Some of these witnesses had laid violent hands on her and had brought her into the presence of Jesus. Having thrust her forward into the limelight they told her story for all to hear. I have an idea that she resisted and resented this bitterly. She may have met Jesus before this humiliating experience. If so she probably dreaded facing him more than she dreaded facing the crowd and these hard men who had dragged her into his presence. Be that as it may, there she is surrounded by a gaping mob, a shamed creature for whom even the religious people of that day had neither care nor hope.

II

The next group of actors in this drama is made up of the witnesses for the prosecution. They are the men who have dragged the woman into the presence of Jesus. They are the scribes and the Pharisees. As a rule these two classes do not show up well on the pages of the New Testament. Yet because of this we are not to conclude that there was nothing good about them. There was much to be said in their favor. They were the upholders of the law. They were pillars in church and state. It was a part of their business to oppose such evil conduct as that of which this woman was guilty.

Along with much that was good in these scribes and Pharisees there was also much that was evil. In the first place, in this particular instance their motives were bad. They claimed to be acting out of zeal for the law; they wanted a clean individual and social life. But their real motive was their desire to involve Jesus in difficulty.

They were eager to discredit this young teacher whose popularity was causing them no end of trouble. In claiming to be concerned about the woman, while they were really bent only on embarrassing the Master, they were playing the hypocrite.

Not only were they hypocritical, but they were cold as icicles and hard as nails. In perpetrating this plot against Jesus they involved this woman in a very real and painful embarrassment. Yet they were totally indifferent to the woman herself. She was to them only "Exhibit A." They had involved her in this humiliating situation not because they were indignant at her sin; no more did they involve her because they were seeking by her punishment to build a cleaner community; least of all were they seeking by thus bringing her to Jesus to do her any real good. To her, I repeat, they were entirely indifferent. To them she was a creature beyond hope or help. Therefore her pain and shame in being thus exposed meant to them just nothing at all.

Now while they had not sinned as their victim had sinned they were still sinners. Theirs was the sin of disposition; hers was that of the flesh. These two kinds of sinners are always with us. We are accustomed to condemn those who sin after the flesh far more severely than those who sin by their indifference and coldness of heart. But this was not the case with Jesus. He seems to have hated and feared most the sins of the disposition. To his mind the decent and respectable elder son who had remained at home was far more hopeless than the prodigal who in penitence had come back after wasting his sub-

157

stance with riotous living. Jesus therefore had more hope for this woman than for her decent and respectable tormentors.

III

But the real center of the story is Jesus. When these men fling their victim at the feet of the Master they put to him a question: "The law of Moses," they declare, "commands that such creatures shall be stoned, but what do you say?" It is evident that these scribes and Pharisees know something about Jesus. They know enough to make them quite certain of the position he will take with regard to this woman. They are sure that he will be on the side of mercy. It is this conviction that accounts for their coming. They realized that if Jesus should agree with the law and say: "Yes, stone her by all means," then, by their scheme they would not embarrass him, but only add to his reputation. But they are certain that, in spite of what the law says, Jesus will not order her to be stoned.

In taking this position they were not mistaken. When they put their question, "Stone her or not stone her?" the Master gives no immediate answer. Instead he stoops down and writes on the ground. Why he does this we are not told. In my opinion he does it for two reasons. First, he is ashamed of these religious leaders. They are here as the representatives of God. Yet how terribly and tragically do they misrepresent him! Second, he is seeking to spare this woman. He sees how bitterly ashamed she is. Therefore he refuses to add to her embarrassment by looking at her. Those who enjoy another's shame are not like Jesus. He suffered in the shame of others, even that of this fallen woman.

When these scribes and Pharisees see Jesus thus writing on the ground and refusing to answer they are sure that they have gained their point. Therefore they begin to press him more urgently. "Shall we stone her or not stone her?" It is a yes or no question, as you can see. They are shrewd enough to know that if they can induce him to say either "Yes" or "No," they will have achieved their purpose. But he refuses to fall into their trap.

Nowhere does Jesus show his genius more convincingly than in the way in which he answered questions. Once his disciples asked: "Are there few that be saved?" They desired his yes or no, but Jesus did not so answer. He rather said: "Strive to enter in at the straight gate." He meant: "How many are saved or how few is not your business. Your business is to meet the conditions of salvation yourselves." Again they asked, "Is it lawful to give tribute to Caesar, or not?" Instead of answering "Yes" or "No" he requested a penny. When they handed him one he asked whose image was upon it. "Caesar's," they answered. "Right," he seemed to say, "therefore render to Caesar the things that are Caesar's, and to God the things that are God's."

Notice how Jesus answers the question of these scribes and Pharisees. He certainly is opposed to the stoning of this woman, yet he does not say so in so many words. Jesus never antagonized except when it was necessary. Had he forbidden them to stone her he would have alienated her tormentors, while leaving them utterly unconvinced of the rightness of his position. Bear in mind that he is just as eager to save these evil men as he is to save the woman.

Sometimes we congratulate ourselves for speaking our minds. That is all to the good if we have the right stuff in our minds and if we are convinced that our speaking will prove helpful. But there are times when speaking our minds does more harm than good.

With what sanity and tact Jesus meets this issue! "Stone her," he seems to say, "by all means, provided you yourselves are guiltless. Let him that is without sin cast the first stone. But of course if you are sinful you do not dare to throw a single stone." How utterly sane! What could be more absurd than for one sinner to stone another sinner? Of course we differ in the kinds of sin of which we are guilty and we differ in the degree of guilt, but all of us in some fashion are sinners. Therefore throwing stones either with our hands or with our tongues is never in order. It is neither sane nor Christian.

Then what? Convinced of the essential rightness of the position of Jesus, these witnesses against the accused slipped away one by one. Who is declaring now that the law of Moses ought to be enforced? Not the Master, but these scribes and Pharisees. By his wise answer Jesus not only cuts the ground from under them so far as bringing charges against himself is concerned, but he even brings them over to his side. By their own actions they are declaring that this unfortunate creature ought not to be stoned, at least not by themselves.

When the scribes and Pharisees are gone comes the big

moment for which the Master had waited. He now stands
erect and looks at the woman for the first time. Then he
asks: "Woman, where are those, thine accusers? hath no
man condemned thee?" I can hear her answer with a sob
in her throat: "No man, Lord." With none to testify
against her she has hope of winning her case.

IV

Why does Jesus ask about these absent witnesses? He
is certainly not seeking information. He is rather seeking
to bring to fruition the faith that has already been born
in the heart of this woman. What has been going on in her
mind during this trying ordeal? I think that she has come
to realize that the man into whose presence she has been
dragged so unwillingly, whose frown she has so greatly
feared, is really on her side—that he is not her enemy
but her friend. Here perhaps is what she is saying to herself: "These hard men have let me go. They have forgiven
me, thanks to the fact that Jesus has taken my part. Since
they have forgiven in their way, perhaps he will forgive
in his far fuller way." And that is just what he does. Here
are his own words: "Neither do I condemn thee: go, and
sin no more."

There are those who feel that the woman got off too
easily, that Jesus is here treating sin as a rather light
matter. It reminds one of Maeterlinck's picture of God
as lolling at his ease and watching the follies and even the
crimes of men as one might watch the playful antics of
puppies. But Jesus never made light of sin. Why then did
the Master let her off so easily? Because there was no

161

other way. Forgiveness is a gift. None of us, even the best, can ever earn it. What could this woman do toward turning back the leaves of the sordid book of her past and blotting out the ugly writing? Nothing at all.

"The Moving Finger writes; and, having writ,
Moves on: nor all your Piety nor Wit
Shall lure it back to cancel half a line,
Nor all your Tears wash out a Word of it."

What then are we to do about our sin? We are to do what this woman did. We are to accept the forgiveness of God and then turn our back upon that sin and forget it. When God forgives he forgets. This is his promise: "I will forgive their iniquity, and I will remember their sin no more." What God forgets you and I have a right to forget. This is in part what Paul meant when he said: "Forgetting those things which are behind, and reaching forth unto those things which are before, I press toward the mark for the prize."

Here then was a poor creature who had been dragged into the presence of Jesus, filled with shame and terror. She felt that she had reached the end of everything. There was not even a horizon in her life where she might hope for a dawn. But thanks to the forgiving love of Christ she found that it was not the closing in of night, but the dawning of a new day. Thus with boundless joy she planted her feet upon the borders of the "Land of Beginning Again." So may we if we dare to turn from the past, and in the fellowship of our Lord make a new start.

XVI

THE LUSTERLESS JEWEL

"Know ye what I have done to you?"

JOHN 13:12

WHAT had he done?

The story takes us back across the far spaces of the years to an upper room in the city of Jerusalem. Here Jesus has come with his disciples for the last Passover that they will ever celebrate together. There is about this scene the solemnity that goes naturally with dear last things. But there is far more. Here Jesus dares to displace the paschal lamb and to put himself in its place. This he does as he breaks the bread and puts a piece in the hand of each of his disciples saying in effect: "This is my body, my very self, my all, given for you." Thus this is a sacred and solemn meal, one that they share under the very shadow of the cross.

Since this is the case it is shocking to realize the spirit in which these disciples have come to this great hour. They have not come in humility; they have come rather with glowing cheeks and burning eyes. They have come hissing

163

hot words at each other. They have come arguing over who is to be the greatest, who is to be chairman of the committee, who is to head the delegation. Each one is pridefully contending for what he conceives to be his own rights.

Now this was probably a secret meeting, and there were no servants present to wash the feet of the guests. James and John might have volunteered for this menial task. Only recently, when they had sought first places for themselves, Jesus had told them that the one way to be first was to be servant of all. But they seem to have forgotten this. Therefore I would have been afraid to have suggested that they perform this task lest by so doing I should come to a better understanding of why the Master called them "sons of thunder." No more would I have dared make this suggestion to Simon, the natural leader of the group. Every man among them was too busy asserting his own rights, standing upon his dignity. Then it was that Jesus took the lowly task upon himself.

This he did not because he liked being a martyr. Jesus humbled himself here, as he humbled himself later by going to the cross, because there was no other way to put through a task that needed to be done. It is said that President Lincoln was walking one day with a friend along a path that was so narrow that the two had to walk single file. By and by they met another man. When this man kept the path Lincoln had to stand aside. The friend was indignant. "Mr. President," he said, "you should not have done that. You ought to have made him stand aside." "But," said the president, "had I not stood aside there

164

would have been a collision." Even so, Jesus saw that if he did not take this task upon himself it would simply be left undone.

"Know ye what I have done to you?" Jesus asks after he has resumed his place. What is the answer? He has rendered them a service that none other was big enough to render. By so doing he has taught them a lesson in humility. I am sorry I cannot find a more glamourous name for this fine jewel. Humility has such little glitter for most of us that it fails to thrill us. We tend to regard it as a pious church coin, worth perhaps a hundred cents in the dollar at prayer meeting, but far below par everywhere else. For this reason if one were to call us humble we would hardly know whether to feel complimented or insulted. If this virtue is a rare jewel it is one that for our eyes has largely lost its luster.

I

What do we mean by humility?

To begin negatively it is something that these disciples did not possess. Humility is certainly not a clamoring for first place. No more is it a prideful refusal to do a task just because it is menial. It is not a swaggering demand for position. It is not that spirit that often leads men to say: "If I can't be chairman of the committee I won't serve."

If humility is not self-glorification, no more is it self-contempt. There are those who think they are humble just because they say mean things about themselves. This is not humility. It is only an ugly caricature of humility. No man is in a better frame of mind to make a failure of life than the man who has no self-respect.

Look at the attitude of our Lord when he performed this task: "Jesus, knowing that the Father had given all things into his hands, and that he was come from God, and went to God; he riseth from supper, and laid aside his garments; and took a towel, and girded himself." Does that sound like self-contempt? At the very moment when he was most keenly conscious of his divine origin and of his divine destiny he stooped to do this slave's task. But he did not stoop in the spirit of a slave. Never was one girded with a higher self-respect. What then is humility?

1. Humility is the natural and inevitable result of facing the facts about ourselves. It has been suggested that while humility is based upon the truth, pride is founded on a lie. What are the facts about ourselves?

First, we are all the children of God. We are made in the divine image. Thus we are grand creatures. Listen how the psalmist puts it: "What is man, that thou art mindful of him? . . . Thou hast made him a little lower than the angels." Moffatt translates it "little less than divine." Not only are we grand creatures, made in the image of God, but we have been redeemed by the precious blood of Christ. Thus redeemed, we are to reproduce Christ. We are to say with Paul: "For to me to live is Christ."

But there is a second fact that we must face and that is that we have not lived up to our privileges. Though made for Christlikeness we have failed to realize our possibilities. In spite of the fact that it is the purpose of God that the beauty of the Lord should rest upon us as the sunshine rests upon the hills, we are far less winsome than we have any right to be. Paul declares that all of us have "come short." Most of us are not disposed to deny that. However much we may have attained we are yet only poor fractions of what we might be.

There is a story of a great artist who went one morning to a picture gallery where his own pictures were on display. He went early to avoid the crowd. But as he was going away a friend saw him. The artist sought to avoid this friend, but in vain. The friend understood the reason when he saw the artist's face wet with tears.

"What is the matter?" he asked.

"I have been looking at my own pictures," came the answer. "Those that I painted in my youth give a promise that I have failed to realize in my mature years. It is heartbreaking to face the fact that I have not become the artist that I might have become."

When we thus see ourselves in the light of what we might be, humility is a natural result.

2. Humility is childlikeness. First, a child is teachable. A child is willing to learn from anybody. A child is willing to lean upon a higher power. He is not self-sufficient. He realizes his weakness. I saw a little fellow run ahead of his mother on the street the other day, but when he came to a crossing he was not ashamed to reach his hand up to the hand of his mother. A child is willing to lean on a higher power.

Second, to be childlike is to be democratic. A child is free from snobbery. No normal child ever refuses to play with another child because that child is inferior in wealth or in social position. He does not stand aloof because he is of a different race or color. He is as much at home with the son of a pauper as the son of a king. Humility is child-likeness.

3. Humility is Christlikeness. Humility is the one virtue in himself to which our Lord calls our attention. "Learn of me; for I am meek and lowly in heart." So humble was he that he did this menial task of foot washing when nobody else would do it. So humble was he that "though he was divine by nature, he did not set store upon equality with God, but emptied himself by taking the nature of a servant; born in human guise and appearing in human form, he humbly stooped in his obedience even to die, and to die even upon the cross." (Moffatt.) To be humble is to be Christlike. It is to forget self in an effort to serve others.

II

Why is this virtue so priceless?

1. It is priceless because it is the very door into the kingdom of heaven. "Blessed are the poor in spirit: for theirs is the kingdom of heaven." The humble enter the Kingdom because they are capable of entering it, and no others are. Listen to this story: "Two men went up into the temple to pray; the one a Pharisee, and the other a publican. The Pharisee stood and prayed thus with himself, God, I thank thee, that I am not as other men are, extortioners, unjust, adulterers. . . . The publican, standing afar off, would not lift up so much as his eyes unto

heaven, but smote upon his breast, saying, God be merciful to me a sinner. I tell you, this man went down to his house justified rather than the other."

Why did the publican win while the Pharisee failed? It was certainly not because of any superiority on the part of this publican. The Pharisee was a far better man. He was upright and decent. He was a tither. But for him and men of his type there would have been no temple to which the publican could turn in his black hour. That which defeated him, in spite of much that was good, was his lack of humility. He asked for nothing because he needed nothing. Having already arrived he could not go any higher. This publican, on the other hand, entered the Kingdom in spite of his great sin because he was poor in spirit. It is only the humble who can enter and remain in the Kingdom. In the face of all others the door is shut.

There is nothing surprising about this. Humility conditions our entrance into all worth-while kingdoms. How do we enter the kingdom of knowledge? Only by the door of humility. I used to teach school. I am sure teachers will agree with me that the most difficult pupil is not the one who is a bit dull. The most difficult is the one who already knows, the one who was born educated. How did Huxley learn science? He tells us that he sat down before the facts as a little child.

Then humility is of value not only in the church and in the classroom, but in the world of business. I was reading recently of a man of ability who worked up from the ranks. He came to own a small railroad. He bought that road when it was bankrupt and made it a going concern. But he was so arrogant and overbearing that he could not get on with his employees. For this reason he sleeps today in an untimely grave. The man who gets on best is the man who is willing to learn, not only from his employer, but from his humblest employee as well.

Humility is as essential in making and keeping friends. If you are an egotist, if you play superior to those with whom you associate, you need not expect to have friends. This virtue is also necessary in the family circle. If either husband or wife is always right while the other is always wrong, if one has to sit at the feet of the other, there is tragedy present and greater tragedy ahead. Humility therefore is essential not only in prayer meeting but everywhere else. It is the door into all worth-while kingdoms and it is an essential for abiding in those kingdoms.

2. Humility is essential to our happiness. Sometimes we are proud of our pride. We look askance at the word of Jesus, "Blessed are the poor in spirit." But even if you question the happiness of those who are humble you cannot question the wretchedness of those who are proud. If you are forever standing on your dignity, if you are forever demanding recognition and appreciation, if you are bent on getting credit for everything you do, then you are headed for a stormy voyage. This is the case because however much honor and applause may come your way there will always be something to wound your pride.

3. Finally, humility is essential to our usefulness. This is true for a variety of reasons.

First, it is the humble who are most willing to serve.

170

Of course the proud will serve if the applause is sufficiently loud. They will serve if they gain proper recognition. They will serve if the task is not beneath them. But the humble will serve unconditionally. All they ask is for a task that needs to be done.

Second, the humble are most useful because their right attitude makes their service acceptable. We seldom help anybody by reaching down to him from superior heights. I had a friend in college who had deep wounds upon his soul because of an unhappy childhood. He had grown up in the midst of domestic conflict and heartache. While outwardly sunny, he told me in a hour of confidence that for years he had never gone to bed at night that he did not wish that he might not wake in the morning. With this battered soul I went to hear a brilliant minister preach. His sermon was eloquent but as we came away my friend declared that the minister reminded him of one standing at a safe distance on the shore and shouting to another who was drowning: "You fool, you had no business falling in." There could be no sharper criticism than that.

Finally, the humble are most helpful because of their right attitude toward God. The man who sets out on a mission of service, trusting only in his own sufficiency, must needs go alone. But the humble man goes in the strength of Almighty God. By his humility he enables our Lord to make good his promise: "Lo, I am with you alway even unto the end of the world."

171

XVII

CHANGING HEARSAY INTO EXPERIENCE

"Sayest thou this thing of thyself, or did others tell it thee of me?"

JOHN 18:34

THIS is a dramatic scene. Pilate is standing face to face with a prisoner who is none other than Jesus Christ. The moment therefore is one big with possibilities. Strange and disquieting rumors have been blowing about the streets of Jerusalem concerning this man. One report has it that some of his most enthusiastic followers, with more rashness than reason, had escorted him into the city with cries of "Hosanna to the son of David: blessed is he that cometh in the name of the Lord." Pilate, knowing the tempestuous temperament of the people under his authority, has found these rumors a bit disquieting. Yet he cannot feel that Rome has much to fear from a man just out of a carpenter shop, with only a handful of peasants at his back.

But now that Pilate stands face to face with Jesus he

finds him strangely disturbing. If this man is a pretender he is certainly not like any other that Pilate has met before. In spite of himself this Roman governor is impressed. Therefore with mingled awe and amazement he asks Jesus this question: "Art thou the King of the Jews?" In reply Jesus asks the governor this daring and searching question: "Sayest thou this thing of thyself, or did others tell it thee of me?" It is as if he says: "Pilate, are you speaking from hearsay or out of your own experience? Am I your king?"

That, I repeat, is a daring question. It is evident that Jesus had hope for Pilate. When our Lord was questioned by Herod he answered never a word. Jesus knew that Herod had stopped his ears to the truth so long that he had lost his capacity to hear, that he had shut his eyes to the light so long that he had gone blind. But the Master saw fine possibilities in Pilate. He believed that this Roman governor was yet capable of a high choice. Therefore he held open the door of his Kingdom to him with this question: "Sayest thou this thing of thyself, or did others tell it thee of me?" Thus Jesus invited Pilate to change hearsay into experience. Pilate was impressed, but he was not impressed enough to make the change.

Now there is a sense in which this story is entirely unique. Yet there is also that in it that comes very near to everyone. We, as avowed followers of this Christ, have united with his church, have acknowledged his kingship. But is that kingship a reality? In other words, is your religion a matter of hearsay or of experience? If it is only hearsay then you have missed the highest and the best.

173

This is not to say that hearsay is of no value. It is of vast value. But in the realm of religion it is not enough.

I

What is the good of hearsay?

We are indebted to hearsay for almost all the small knowledge we possess. How much, for instance, do you know about history? Very little at first hand. I am told that there was once a man named Julius Caesar who waged a campaign in Gaul. I am told further that this same Julius Caesar wrote commentaries about his campaign. These commentaries have been the plague of many a schoolboy. But whether Julius Caesar really wrote them or not is impossible for me to say. The one thing about them of which I can be sure is that somebody wrote them and that they gave me no end of trouble. I do not even know who discovered America except from hearsay. This is the case because whoever made the discovery beat me to it. I must depend on hearsay for this as for almost every other fact in history.

In like manner I take the little I know about astronomy from hearsay. I am told that the sun is 92,900,000 miles from the earth. I am told also that this sun has a temperature at its surface of about 12,000 degrees Fahrenheit. But I have never tested the truth of either of these statements. I never intend to. I am quite sure that even if the astronomers are a few feet off in their measurement one way or the other, life will go on for me practically the same. I am equally certain that if in estimating the temperature of the sun they have made a mistake of one or two

174

degrees, it will not greatly upset the noiseless tenor of my way. In matters of astronomy I take the word of the astronomers.

We have a saying that runs like this: "I am willing to take your word for that." So I am in a great many matters. For instance, I am told that if I hold my hand on a red-hot stove it will not only be very painful, but the hand will receive permanent injury. I will take your word for that. I do not intend to try it. There is a drink that, according to scientists, seems to stimulate while it really depresses. When a motorist takes it he thinks he is more fit to cope with an emergency, while in reality he becomes less fit because all his reactions have been slowed down. There are those who become victims to this drink. Such people it masters and enslaves, rots them down both in body and soul. But all this I take on hearsay. I never intend to put this drink to the test.

Naturally there are those who do not agree with me. They must find out for themselves. If a cocktail is offered in a social circle they take it. Sometimes they begin the custom from curiosity. Sometimes they begin because they feel that it would be a discourtesy to refuse. A young woman complained of how terribly embarrassing it is to have to make such refusals. But it seems to me that all the embarrassment should be on the other side. At least I believe that I have just as much right to my convictions as the other man has to his lack of convictions. Nor do I think it a matter of shame when I refuse to take a needless risk. If my hostess were to say to me: "Here is a sandwich; it is spread with a high-grade poison," I should not be tempted in the least to do other than take her word for it.

Even in matters of religion hearsay is priceless. It is such hearsay that makes this book we call the Bible the most precious in all the world. Listen to this: "I sought the Lord, and he heard me, and delivered me from all my fears." Just what fears were yapping at the heels of this frightened psalmist he does not see fit to tell us. He does tell us, however, that as he called on God the whole wolf pack took flight. That is only hearsay, but it is hearsay that warms my heart and gives me hope. We must all be unspeakably grateful for the hearsay that comes to us out of the Scriptures.

Priceless also is the testimony of the saints throughout the centuries. We all owe to them an unpayable debt. How greatly we are enriched by the testimonies of those whom we have known personally! I can never be sufficiently thankful for the God-possessed men and women whom I have known along the way. I am being constantly strengthened, gladdened, and encouraged by the faith of others. Certainly hearsay in the realm of religion is of vast importance. Rightly used it will lead to the supreme enrichment. Yet hearsay is not enough. To achieve its purpose it must be changed into experience.

II

Why is this the case?

1. This is the case, in the first place, because it is only experience that can satisfy the human soul. It is well to know about God. Theology is the queen of all sciences.

Yet no knowledge about God can take the place of knowing God himself. I may be an expert on bread. I may know all about its food value and how to prepare it, but not even the most perfect knowledge of bread can satisfy my hunger. However much I may know about water, my tongue will become swollen, my lips parched, my body tortured to the point of death unless I experience water by actually drinking it. It is fine to know about flowers. Botany is a lovely study. But no knowledge of botany can take the place of the perfume of the honeysuckle, nor the red of the rose. Even so, no knowledge about God can take the place of knowing God through Christ.

When therefore the psalmist sings: "As the hart panteth after the water brooks, so panteth my soul after thee, O God," he is voicing a universal longing. When Job wails: "Oh that I knew where I might find him!" he is uttering a cry that has sobbed its way through the centuries. When Philip prays: "Lord, shew us the Father," he is praying a prayer that is as old as man. It has been offered in some fashion by men of every age and of every kindred, tribe, and tongue.

What is the matter with our tired and restless world? If Isaiah were to appear on our streets today would he not search us with his question of long ago: "Wherefore do ye spend money for that which is not bread? and your labour for that which satisfieth not?" Our world is fretful and hungry for something or someone that it has not found. This is true even of many people in our churches. Some of you have not found in religion what you once hoped to find. You are absolutely certain that the Lord is a shepherd, but there is no song in your heart because you have not yet learned to sing "The Lord is my shepherd." You are certain that God loves all men, but you have not yet come to say out of your own experience that he "loved me, and gave himself for me." Hearsay is good, but unless we translate it into experience we never come to that spiritual certainty that alone can satisfy.

2. In the second place it is only those who change hearsay into experience who have an adequate passion for the sharing of their experience with others. To know any worth-while fact is to be possessed by an eagerness to share our knowledge. When Galileo was being tortured for saying that the earth moves around the sun he recanted. But as soon as the agony of his torture was eased he reaffirmed his original conviction. Being sure, he had to share.

If such eagerness to share the truth is characteristic of the scientist, it is even more so of one who has found reality in religion. Do you remember that leper of whom Mark tells? Life had dealt very harshly with him. It had dealt so harshly that though he still believed in power he no longer believed in love. So he came to the Master with this imperfect prayer: "If thou wilt, thou canst make me clean." Jesus responded to his imperfect faith and healed him. Having healed him the Master gave him this warning: "See thou say nothing to any man." So what? The healed man simply could not keep his secret. I have an idea that he fairly shouted to the first man he met: "Look at me! A little while ago I was a leper; now my flesh is like that of a little child. I am cured." So did he blaze his

178

story abroad that the Master could no longer openly enter the city.

It was this certainty that gave voice to the great prophets of the Old Testament. Some of them spoke with intense reluctance. Take Jeremiah, for instance. So little did his preaching seem to accomplish, except to make the preacher hated, that more than once he made up his mind to quit. "What is the use?" he said to himself. "Those to whom I preach do not repent; they only hate and persecute me. I will never preach again." But as often as he made that resolution he had to break it. This he did because the Word of God was as a fire shut up in his bones. The burning convictions of his heart made silence impossible.

This same passion for telling their story belongs emphatically to those whom we meet on the pages of the New Testament. Here are two of them before the same court that a few weeks ago had sentenced their Master to death. The court decides to give these two offenders a light sentence. They simply command them not to speak at all, nor teach in the name of Jesus. But Peter and John answer: "We cannot but speak the things which we have seen and heard." They are under the urge of a mighty assurance. They are in the grip of a compelling certainty. It is easy to keep silent about a religion of hearsay, but you can no more silence a religion of experience than you can dam up Niagara.

3. Not only do we need to change hearsay into experience to satisfy the longing of our own hearts and to give us an adequate passion for sharing our experiences, but we need to do this in order to have power for wit-

nessing. There is something compelling about a man who has made himself master of a subject, whatever that subject is. How gripping is the message of the man who brings fresh and authentic tidings of God! When the crowd turned away from hearing Jesus they said with awe: "He taught them as one having authority, and not as the scribes." What was wrong with the scribes? Their religion was largely a matter of hearsay. But Jesus could say always what he said to Nicodemus: "We speak that we do know, and testify that we have seen."

It was this same note of authority that enabled the early saints to turn the world upside down. Who would ever have chosen a Samaritan woman of such a soiled past for an evangelist? Yet when she left her water vessel and hurried into the village, she was so sure of Jesus that we read: "Many . . . believed on him for the saying of the woman." Thomas loved Jesus with all his big heart. But he would have been worth little as a witness had he not come to say to the risen Christ: "My Lord and my God." The power of Paul to convince men of his day and of all days was born not so much of his great ability as of his great certainty. The fact that he could say: "I know whom I have believed," made him a man of power. This same certainty is needed by us. We are not going to make any great dent on our hard world by the proclamation of a gospel that is only hearsay.

III

Is this certainty possible for us? If so, how can we find it?

It is my conviction that this certainty is possible for every one of us. This is not to say that all men have an equal capacity to realize God. There are some who see with clearer vision than others. But all men can realize him in some fashion. "If any man is willing to do his will, he shall know." This promise is not for certain elect souls who have a special aptitude for religion. It is for any man, for every man who is willing to do his will.

Not only does this word tell us that religious certainty is for everybody, but it also indicates the conditions upon which we may possess such certainty. In order to be sure of God it is not necessary to be perfect, it is only necessary to be willing wholeheartedly to do the will of God. If we are to realize God we must make a complete surrender to him. We must be willing to put ourselves and all we have into his hands. To all such God gives himself. "We are his witnesses of these things; and so is also the Holy Ghost, whom God hath given to them that obey him."

Sometimes this awareness of God comes instantly. Those who have been accustomed to dealing with seeking souls personally can testify that they have seen men pass instantly into a knowledge of God. But such instantaneous awareness does not always come. There are those who, having surrendered, become aware of God gradually. The light that breaks on them is more like the slow dawning day. But if any man surrenders, and persists in that surrender, he will come to certainty. He will realize the truth of those words from Hosea: "Then shall we know, if we follow on to know the Lord." Every one of us can thus change hearsay into experience.

BOOK 4

THE SEVEN WORDS

CONTENTS

I

THE FIRST WORD

"Father, forgive them; for they know not what they do."

LUKE 23:34

HAD YOU BEEN IN JERUSALEM ON THIS FATEFUL FRIDAY that changed the world, you would doubtless have been brought under the spell of the excitement of the hour. This excitement was born of the fact that three prisoners were about to pay the death penalty. One of them was a prophet from Nazareth. The other two were revolutionists. The crowd, with a natural love of the gruesome, was hideously eager for the show. This eagerness was doubtless heightened by the fact that all three of the doomed men were well known. This was certainly the case with the prophet. It was probably true of the two outlaws as well.

Not only were all three of these men well known, but they were all popular. The two revolutionists were ardent patriots. Having fought like men, like men they were determined to die. The crowd naturally looked upon them as heroes. The prophet had also been popular. He was so still. This was the case in spite of the fact

9

that most of those immediately surrounding the cross were intensely hostile. So bitter was their antagonism that, having nailed Jesus to the cross, they would not allow him to die in peace. Even the revolutionists, caught under the spell of their bitter antagonism, added their own insults to the senseless howls of the mob and to the cruel jibes of the churchmen. Then something took place that at first silenced one of these revolutionists, then changed his insults into prayers. What happened? The man on the central cross prayed this prayer, "Father, forgive them; for they know not what they do."

I

The fact that the first word that Jesus uttered upon his cross was a prayer does not surprise us. His had been a habit of prayer from his youth. Naturally, he would pray in this black and desperate hour. Even those who refuse to pray when the sea of life is smooth generally refuse no longer when their sea is being whipped by a tempest. There is a sense in which prayer is all but instinctive. When the ground gives way beneath our feet, when some dire tragedy wrenches every visible support from our clinging fingers, we reach for the Unseen almost as naturally as we shrink from a blow. But when we pray under such circumstances, it is almost invariably for ourselves. In our need we cry, "Lord, help me." Nor is there anything wrong in such prayers. We are invited to come boldly to the throne of grace that we may obtain mercy and find grace to help in every time of need. Had Jesus, therefore, thus prayed, it would have been only the natural and the expected.

But what does thrill us is that this first word of prayer that Jesus offered was not for himself. He did not ask for his own deliverance. He did not pray in that black hour for his loved ones, nor for his friends. He prayed for his enemies. He prayed for the soldiers and for the far more cruel churchmen who, having nailed him to the cross, were even then howling about him. It was around the bloody shoulders of these murderers that he flung the folds of this prayer, "Father, forgive them; for they know not what they do."

Once on a certain hill Jesus had preached in this fashion, "Ye have heard that it hath been said, Thou shalt love thy neighbour, and hate thine enemy. But I say unto you, Love your enemies, . . . and pray for them which despitefully use you." On another occasion he had commanded his followers to forgive, not once, but "until seventy times seven"—that is, without limit. Forgiveness was to flow from their hearts as constantly as waters from a gushing spring. What he had preached on the sunny hill of the Sermon on the Mount, he practiced on the grim hill of Calvary. Here he is offering unlimited forgiveness.

II

In asking forgiveness for his murderers Jesus was asking the best possible. This is the case because forgiveness means far more than being let off from a penalty. I am

11

thinking now of a man who committed murder. There was no possible doubt as to his guilt. He was tried and was sentenced to pay the penalty for his crime. But it so happened that he was a man of political influence. He had a heavy claim on the governor of his state. Therefore he was no sooner sentenced than he received a pardon. But in spite of his pardon he still had the stain of blood upon his hands. When God pardons, he does something for us that is far better than merely refusing to punish us as we deserve.

No more is forgiveness a way of escape from the consequences of our wrongdoing. If we sow tares, we are going to reap them, even though we find forgiveness. When David in hot blood had been guilty of adultery, when in cold blood he had committed murder, his faithful minister took his life in his hands and rebuked him for his sin. Then what? David might have come to hate his physician rather than his deadly disease. But he chose the wiser course. As Nathan spoke home to his heart, David's knees went weak, and with a voice choked by sobs he clutched at God's skirts and prayed, "Have mercy upon me." His prayer was not in vain. God heard and answered. He gave to the sinner abundant pardon. But though this forgiveness was full and complete, it did not save David from the terrible consequences of his sin. Instead, he suffered in brokenness of heart to the very end of his days.

A few years ago I went to see a woman who was dying of bichloride of mercury self-administered. She told me of the bitter experience through which she had passed. "At last," she declared, "I felt that I could not bear it any longer. But I am sorry now. I realize that I have done wrong. The reason I have sent for you is to ask you this question, Will God forgive me?"

With complete confidence I answered in the affirmative. I offered her salvation in the name of him who "was wounded for our transgressions." She claimed to accept that salvation, and I feel confident she went to meet her Lord in peace. But there was one something that this forgiveness did not do. It did not take the poison from her tortured body. In spite of the fact that she had been fully forgiven, she died.

What, then, is forgiveness? It is the restoration of a fellowship. When God forgives, he takes us back into his friendship and walks with us as if we had never sinned. He forgets all our ugly past. This is his own promise, "I will forgive their iniquity, and I will remember their sin no more." He treats us as Jesus treated his friends who failed him so miserably in Gethsemane. He had leaned heavily upon these friends. But the best they could do was to go to sleep. More than once he came to wake them, but in spite of all his efforts they threw their big chance away. So what? In spite of their failure we hear our Lord saying to them, "Rise up, let us go." He walked with failures as if they had never failed.

Now since forgiveness means the restoration of a fellowship, it issues in newness of life. As forgiven we

13

thus walk with our Lord, we come more and more to share his divine nature. When, therefore, Jesus prayed for the forgiveness of his enemies, he was asking for them the best possible. He was asking for their regeneration. He was praying that they might experience his fellowship. He was praying that even these murderers might be able to shout with one of the greatest of the saints, "Old things are passed away; behold, all things are become new."

It is significant also that Jesus offered this prayer for the forgiveness of his enemies with complete confidence. He was perfectly sure that full forgiveness was available for every one of them. When he prayed for himself in the garden, he prayed with a condition, an "if" upon his lips, "If it be possible, let this cup pass from me." But here he did not ask the Father to forgive, if forgiveness was possible. He knew that forgiveness was already in his own heart. He knew that what he was offering, God was offering also. Thus Jesus in perfect confidence asked for heaven's best even for his enemies.

III

Then the Master gave a reason why the Father should grant his request: "Forgive them; for they know not what they do." On the surface it seems that Jesus was pleading a palliating circumstance. It was as if he were saying, "These men are doing a terrible wrong, but since they are sinning in ignorance, they are not so guilty as they seem." But this is not what Jesus meant. He was not seeking to excuse their sin. The Bible is never eloquent in making excuses for sin. The individual who does so never wins his way into the presence of God. If you have an excuse for your sin, then you have a right to plead, "Not guilty." But if you dare make such plea, you will never be one inch closer to God than you are now. What, then, did Jesus mean by saying, "They know not what they do"?

He was not affirming that these who were doing him to death did not know that they were doing wrong. Such was not the case. They did know it, every man of them. Pilate, washing his soiled hands, did so in the realization that he had soiled his soul with the stain of a cowardly injustice. Judas, who hurried to empty his soiled hands of the thirty pieces of silver, in order to fill them with a hangman's rope, did so in the consciousness of his guilt. Annas, who had spun his web in the dark, knew that out of greed and envy he had helped to hound a good man to his death. There was not a man of them who with a clean conscience could plead, "Not guilty."

In what sense, then, were they ignorant? They were ignorant in that though they knew that they were doing wrong, they did not and could not realize just how great was their guilt. When Jesus said, "Father, forgive them; for they know not what they do," it was as if he had said, "Forgive them, for they need forgiveness so desperately. Forgive them, for they have committed a sin that is black beyond all their realization." That is doubtless true of

15

every sin we commit. We can never know what harvest we and others may have to reap because of one wrong decision or of one deed of disloyalty.

Thank God, this is also true on its brighter side. We can never know the high use that God can make of one right decision, of one word spoken in loyalty. A young physician called to see me a few years ago. "I became a physician," he declared, "because I knew that as such I would have the privilege of serving others, and as a Christian I was eager to do that." Then he asked, "Do you remember a walk we took together when I was in high school?"

"No," I answered with reluctance.

"Well, I remember it," he replied eagerly. "During that walk you spoke to me about becoming a Christian. As soon as we returned, I went to my room and surrendered to Christ."

What wonderful returns for so small an investment! We can never know, I repeat, the possible triumphant outcome of one right deed. No more can we know the possible tragedy of one wrong deed. Hence this prayer, "Forgive them," for their need was great beyond their knowing.

IV

If this prayer that our Lord offered in perfect confidence for God's best is to be answered for you and me, how are we to make that answer possible?

We must be willing to receive that forgiveness. That

we may be willing, we must realize our need. We must come confessing our sin. This is not a rigid rule passed by a narrow-minded God. It is the case in the nature of things. Only those who feel their need of forgiveness will give God a chance. Forgiveness is freely and eagerly offered to every man, but only those who know they have sinned and come short will be willing to accept this offer. Hence our gospel is a gospel for sinners, and for sinners only.

Our Lord enforced this truth by his most fascinating story. A father once prepared a feast to which both his sons were invited. One of these sons was a bit of a renegade, but the other was as decent as decency. While the younger had been a waster, the older had been a worker. When the younger son came home, his garments were stained with the filth of the swine pen. But the older son came with no stain upon him save the innocent soil of the fields. Naturally, this decent chap felt himself unmeasured leagues ahead of his prodigal brother. Not only so, but he had a right so to feel. Yet it was the prodigal who entered the banquet hall while his clean-living, hard-working brother shut the door in his own face.

Why was this the case? It was not because this father cared nothing for decency while he set a premium on profligacy. The door to the feast opened of its own accord to the prodigal because he came with this confession in heart and upon his lips, "I have sinned." That same door was shut in the face of his brother, shut by that

17

brother's own hand, because he came with this confession, "Lo, these many years do I serve thee, neither transgressed I at anytime thy commandment."

There you have it, two confessions: one, "I have *never* sinned"; the other, "I *have* sinned." Which is true? Which is yours? If the former, then you make this prayer of Jesus—this prayer that he offered both by his lips and by his cross—a sheer futility, so far as you are concerned. But if you come with this confession of sin upon your lips, if you come pleading

> Suffice it if—my good and ill unreckoned,
> And both forgiven thro' Thine abounding grace—

then a place at the feast of the fullness of life will be guaranteed to you.

II

THE SECOND WORD

"Verily I say unto thee, To day shalt thou be with me in paradise."

LUKE 23:43

THE FIRST WORD THAT JESUS UTTERED FROM HIS CROSS was a prayer for his enemies. This second word was an answer to prayer. It was an answer addressed to a single individual. Our Lord spoke to this man as if he were the only being in the world. What a satisfying answer he gave! What a strong staff he put into the hand of this dying man! What comfort this word must have brought! What comfort it has brought to countless needy souls since that far-off day! Of the seven words that Jesus spoke from his cross none, I think, is more appealing and satisfying to my own heart than this: "To day shalt thou be with me in paradise."

I

Who offered the prayer that brought this satisfying answer?

The man to whom Jesus spoke this word is one of the most striking personalities that we meet upon the pages of the New Testament. He was not a thief, in our sense of the word, but a revolutionist. He with his companion had belonged to the Jewish underground. Since they had not been able to organize armies and fight in the open, they had resorted to outlawry. They had organized guerrilla bands and had sought to prey upon Rome as ruthlessly as they felt that Rome had preyed upon them. Thus the man who offered the prayer that brought so rich an answer was a man of violence whose hands were deeply stained with human blood.

Nor was it by accident that our Lord was nailed to the central cross. That was a final malicious chuckle against Jesus on the part of his enemies. We can easily see the working of their minds. With a kind of fiendish glee they reminded themselves of the fact that throughout his ministry, Jesus had been a friend of sinners. They remembered how he had explained his having fellowship with Matthew and his brother renegades, by affirming that he had not come to call righteous people, but sinners. "All right," they sneered, "since he has made sinners his boon companions in life, we will give him the privilege of dying with them." Therefore they nailed him to the central cross.

One writer has suggested that this revolutionist had known Jesus before they met on the day of execution. One reason for believing this is that this outlaw addressed our Lord simply as Jesus. That is, he called him by the name that Mary called him when he was a boy in Nazareth. No other, so far as the record goes, ever addressed our Lord in that fashion. They called him Master; they called him Jesus Master, Jesus of Nazareth, Jesus, thou Son of David. But none other ever called him simply by the name of Jesus.

I am inclined to agree, yet I realize that this revolutionist might have addressed our Lord in this fashion, not because he knew so much about him, but because he knew so little. If we assume that these two had never met before, then about all that this outlaw knew of the man on the central cross was what he had learned from the crowd, from hearing Jesus' prayer for his enemies, and from seeing his name on the cross above his head. While no two of the evangelists agree on the exact wording of the charge against Jesus, Matthew's version seems reasonable: "This is Jesus the King of the Jews." Had this man never met the Master before, he might not have prayed to him at all. But if with such little knowledge he had trusted him enough to pray to him, he would have called him Jesus, for that would have been all that he knew.

But whether or not Jesus and this outlaw had met before, they had much in common. They were both ardent patriots. They were both men of courage and of action. In a sense they had struggled toward a common goal. Both had sought to help their people. Jesus had done so to the end. The outlaw had doubtless done so till his career of violence had caused him to degenerate. They were also akin in that they had been willing to give them-

21

selves for the cause that they held dear. In many respects, therefore, they saw eye to eye.

But if they had much in common, they were also vastly far apart. In seeking to save his nation Jesus had refused to resort to violence. He had no faith in physical force. He had said to those who listened to him, "Resist not evil." He had declared that the man who took the sword would perish by the sword. He had even reached such a climax of absurdity that he said, "Blessed are the meek: for they shall inherit the earth." Naturally, to this revolutionist such teaching seemed sentimental nonsense. Rome had inherited the earth, and Rome was not meek. The only way out was to meet force with force, violence with violence. Thus with much in common, Jesus and this revolutionist were yet very far apart.

As to which of the two was right, we are by no means agreed to this day. The vast majority, however, still side with the man of violence. Yet the verdict of history is on the side of Jesus. He was sure that violence does not have the final answer. "He beheld the city, and wept over it." The sound of his sobbing comes to us from across the centuries. Why is he weeping? Because his people are too blind to see the things that make for peace. They are bent on winning by force, and Jesus knew that that would end in disaster. "For the days shall come upon thee, that thine enemies shall cast a trench about thee . . . and shall lay thee even with the ground, and thy children within thee; and they shall not leave in thee one stone upon another." That prophecy was literally fulfilled in

22

less than fifty years. We are still by no means convinced that the meek will inherit the earth. But surely we have had to lose faith in the victory of the nonmeek. We have been forced to fear that if we do not cease to be violent, there will be no earth to inherit.

II

Why did this revolutionist pray?

He did not pray because he was frightened. He did not pray because he was seeking an easy way out of a hard situation. It was after this fashion that the lesser outlaw prayed. "If thou be Christ, save thyself and us." He did not suffer over being what he was; he suffered only in being where he was. But there is nothing of this mere seeking to escape in the prayer of this greater outlaw. Having taken the part of Jesus before he took his own, he asked not to be let off from suffering, but only to be remembered. His hell was in being what he was rather than in being where he was.

A recent writer for whom I have great respect affirms that we are wrong in calling this praying revolutionist penitent. He declares that the reason he prayed was he had had a vision of reality. Certainly he had had a vision of reality. But what had that vision done for him? What did a vision of reality do for youthful Isaiah? When he saw "the Lord . . . high and lifted up," he also saw himself. Having seen himself in the light of God, he did not like what he saw. Therefore he became penitent and cried: "Woe is me! . . . I am a man of unclean lips."

23

Against the white background of the innocence of Jesus this outlaw saw himself. Therefore he declared that though he was suffering the pangs of death, it was no more than he deserved. He was receiving the due reward of his deeds. A man who realizes that he deserves death knows that he has done something wrong. Had this man compared himself with the other revolutionist who was dying by his side, or had he compared himself with those howling churchmen who stood about the cross, he might have thought quite well of himself. But he could not feel that way once he had really seen Jesus.

Therefore I feel quite sure that his prayer was the prayer of a penitent. Whenever there is a sense of God, there is always a sense of sin. Not only so, but the more vivid the vision of God, the more poignant the sense of sin. To be convinced of this we need only to face the fact that the most tragic confessions of sin come, not from the lips of the greatest of sinners, but from those of the choicest of the saints. Throughout the centuries those men who have come closest to God are the ones who have poured forth confessions of sin that were most red with shame and wet with tears.

III

Look at the prayer of this repentant revolutionist.

His prayer was addressed to Jesus, in whom he saw, not simply a king, but the King. What marvelous insight he had! This kingship of Jesus was the central sarcasm of that black hour. It was by accusing him of being a pretender that Annas and his crowd had brought about his condemnation. Pilate knew that the charge was false. He was therefore eager to set Jesus free. At times it looked as if he were going to succeed. But finally one shouted: "If thou let this man go, thou art not Caesar's friend." At that Pilate went hot and cold. He had to stand well with Caesar, cost what it might. Therefore he was afraid to release a man accused of being a pretender, even though he knew the accusation false.

When the underlings had seen that Jesus was condemned as a pretender, they took up the charge. The soldiers in their glee told themselves that a king must be properly dressed, so they put a scarlet robe on him. A king must have a scepter, so they put a reed in his hand. A king must have a crown, so they made him a crown of thorns. As a climax to the joke Pilate had placed this above his head, "This is Jesus the King of the Jews."

But to one man this kingship was no joke. With matchless insight this outlaw saw in the man who was dying at his side a King who could grant favors beyond death. Therefore he prayed, "Jesus, remember me when thou comest in thy kingdom."

This prayer was personal. The dying man was praying for himself. I know it is possible for us to be self-centered in our prayers. I know there are those who warn against praying for oneself. Yet to be so unselfish as to refuse ever to pray for yourself is to surpass your Lord. Jesus prayed for himself again and again. Of course we must pray for others. But we often fail to have either the inclination or the faith to pray for others till we have prayed for ourselves. The man who has cried, "God be merciful to me a sinner," and has received an answer is then the more ready to pray for his needy fellows.

This was a prayer of faith. In fact I think a more daring faith is hardly to be found in the Bible or out of it. He did not pray, "Remember me *if* thou comest in thy kingdom," but, "Remember me *when* thou comest." Then his faith was further indicated by the seeming modesty of his request. In fact his humility as contrasted with that of James and John, who asked for first places, was my first thought on reading his story. But he was making no modest request. So grandly did he think of Jesus that he was convinced that to have a place in his heart, to be remembered by him, was the very best that could be his, either in time or in eternity. Thus he asked for no throne, no seat among the mighty, only to be remembered.

IV

This prayer received an answer. It was an answer of assurance.

"Verily I say unto thee." No honest man could have spoken such a word unless he had been certain of the truth of what he was saying. Our Lord gave to this dying outlaw certain assurances that are as precious to us as they were to the man to whom he first gave them in the long ago.

1. Jesus here gave assurance that life goes on. He said

26

to this outlaw, "To day shalt thou be with me in paradise. As death cannot stop me, no more can it stop you." "To day shalt thou be." That means the survival of personality. George Eliot's dream of being immortal through the immortality of the human race is utterly futile. Our race is not immortal. Even though it might continue for a billion years, it is still headed toward utter extinction. But we live individually. Jesus knew that this revolutionist would still be himself beyond death. Even so, I will always be I; you will always be you.

2. Jesus here gave assurance of an abiding fellowship with himself. "To day shalt thou be with me." How had these two come to be together in the here and now? This repentant revolutionist was not with Jesus simply because he was on a cross so near him that had their hands been free, they could almost have touched each other. The lesser outlaw was just as close as the one to whom Jesus was speaking. These two had come together when this greathearted outlaw had prayed and received forgiveness. For to be forgiven as we saw in the first sermon is more than the removal of a penalty. It is the restoration of a fellowship. Together then, they would go on being together through time and through eternity.

3. Jesus here gave assurance of the heavenly home. He called the place of meeting paradise. In his conversation with his friends a few hours before, he had called it the house of many mansions. The saints of yesterday were accused of being too otherworldly. That is, they thought too much about the life to come and too little

of the life that now is. Such a charge could not possibly be brought against us. I am afraid that instead we are too hitherworldly. We need to brace ourselves with the certainty of the homeland of the soul. Personally I rejoice in the assurance that when Jesus stepped into God's house he had a redeemed revolutionist by the hand.

4. Jesus here gave assurance of the immediacy of our heavenly home. The belief that at death we fall asleep to wake at some far-off resurrection was not the faith of Jesus. It is not the faith of the New Testament. This is the shout of its saints, "Blessed are the dead which die in the Lord." Such are blessed at once because to be "absent from the body" is to be "present with the Lord."

5. Finally Jesus here gave assurance that those who turn to him are saved instantly. We do not have to wait for his pardon. It may be ours at once, even now.

A few years ago I was talking to a rather cultivated woman who seemed to know little of what it means to be a Christian. "Did you know," I asked, "that God has set a definite date for your salvation?" She looked a bit surprised and answered in the negative. "Well," I replied, "he has. If I show you that he has, will you keep your engagement with him?" After a moment she answered seriously that she would. "All right," I said, "here it is. 'Now is the accepted time; behold, now is the day of salvation.' "

If you will turn to him, you will be with him today. Being with him in the here and now, you can continue with him forevermore.

III

THE THIRD WORD

"Now there stood by the cross of Jesus his mother. . . . When Jesus therefore saw his mother, and the disciple standing by, whom he loved, he saith unto his mother, Woman, behold thy son! Then saith he to the disciple, Behold thy mother!"

JOHN 19:25-27

THE FIRST WORD THAT JESUS SPOKE FROM THE CROSS was a prayer for his enemies. The second, spoken to a revolutionist who had become a friend, was an answer to prayer. This third was addressed to Mary and to his beloved disciple. Of all others, these were nearest to him in loyalty and in devotion. Here we have his final message to the two whom he loved best. To his mother he said, "Behold thy son!" To the disciple, "Behold thy mother!"

I

While this word has in it something of the expected, it has yet more of the unexpected.

In the light of the fact that Jesus shared the faith of his people we are not surprised that he spoke here as a

29

family man, as a devoted and dutiful son. We can understand this when we bear in mind that Jesus was a member of a people that magnified family life to a superlative degree. The Jews believed that the family was a divine institution. They believed that "God setteth the solitary in families." They recognized the fact that children were not so much born as made. Therefore they gave particular emphasis to the high and solemn responsibility of parents. They affirmed that what a child becomes depends mainly upon his parents. "Train up a child in the way he should go: and when he is old, he will not depart from it." Jesus himself gave further emphasis to this responsibility by walling the child about by a wall of millstone, saying, "Whoso shall offend one of these little ones . . . , it were better for him that a millstone were hanged about his neck, and that he were drowned in the depth of the sea."

But if the Jews gave particular emphasis to the obligations of parents to children, they also emphasized the duty of children to parents. Ours is a day that has put the accent upon rights rather than upon responsibilities, but the two belong together. In the state, to claim the rights of a citizen one should be willing to discharge the obligations of a citizen. Even so in claiming the privileges of sonship one should be willing to discharge its obligations. This is true even of those who dare to remind their parents that they did not ask to be born and for that reason have no obligations. Of course they did not ask to be born, nor would their parents ever have asked for them to have been if they had known they would become such moral nitwits. All rights involve obligations. This is true everywhere—in the state, in the church, in the home. Therefore the Jews strictly obeyed the command, "Honour thy father and thy mother."

That Jesus shared this faith is beyond doubt. This, fact is indicated by his hot indignation against those religious leaders who permitted a son to refuse to support his parents if he would only declare that the substance that should have gone into this withheld support was given to God. But it was the conviction of Jesus that no service to others could atone for the neglect of one's parents. Paul was speaking to the same purpose when he said, "If any provide not for his own, and specially for those of his own house, he hath denied the faith, and is worse than an infidel." Therefore in providing for Mary, Jesus was simply doing the duty that was closest to him. Even the burden of a world's redemption could not obscure for him his loving obligation to his bereaved and widowed mother.

But if this devotion of Jesus to his mother is to be expected, what he actually said to her and to his best friend is, to me at least, somewhat surprising. This is the case because of both what he said and what he failed to say. Bear in mind that Jesus was dying. Bear in mind also that these were his last words on this side of death to the two whom he loved best. Under these circumstances I should have expected something more than a mere, "Behold thy son! . . . Behold thy mother!"

For instance, I should expect this devoted son to have given some hint to his perplexed mother of the meaning of his mysterious suffering. It seems that he might have reminded her that by thus dying he was to become the supreme magnet of the ages. What is perhaps stranger still, he said nothing to Mary of life beyond death. She was now getting well into years. She was not very long for this world. Yet he did not remind her of the house of many mansions of which he had spoken to his disciples. He did not say to her anything akin to the word that he had just spoken to the dying revolutionist. He made no mention of the certainty of a glad reunion beyond this world with its crosses, griefs, and graves.

Instead of comforting Mary by disclosing the afterlife, Jesus spoke solely of the life that now is. He was concerned to provide for his mother, not simply in the beautiful by-and-by, but in the heartbreaking here and now. It is arresting to see how much of the earthly ministry of Jesus was devoted to providing for the physical needs of people. Even after he had risen from the dead, those hands that had throttled death were not above preparing breakfast for a few fishermen who had just come from a fruitless night of toil. Here on the cross he remembered that his mother must have bread and a place to live, not simply tomorrow, but today.

But in providing for Mary in the house of his beloved disciple, Jesus was doing more than merely seeing to it that she should have bread and shelter. He was providing her a home. Home is more than a place to live; it is a

32

place to love. Lacking this, home is just another name for hell. He knew that Mary would feel more at home in the house of this disciple than anywhere else; that this beloved friend would be able above all others to understand and to sympathize with her. Therefore he said, "Behold thy son! . . . Behold thy mother!"

Perhaps the most astonishing fact of all is that Jesus here told his mother to adopt another son when she already had four sons of her own. She also had at least two daughters. Since these sons and daughters had been trained by the same parents that had trained Jesus, they were no doubt loyal to the faith of their fathers. In all probability every one of them was a person of character and of standing in the community. Yet Jesus completely ignored them. He passed them by as if they were dead, and entrusted his mother to a friend.

II

Why did Jesus act in this strange fashion?

The fact that our Lord chose a friend to provide a home for his mother indicates a division in his own family. When Simeon took Jesus as a little child into his arms, he told Mary that a sword would one day pierce her heart because of that child. She found that saying tearfully true. Matthew tells us that Joseph, who is thought to have died when Jesus was in his early teens, was a just man. By this he does not mean that he was **fair,** but that he was an observer of the law. This zeal for the law was doubtless shared by Mary, and increasingly by her children. So true was this in the case of James that he could become the leader of the church in later years without having to suffer persecution at the hands of his fellow Jews. But Jesus did not see eye to eye with his family in this matter of the law, as in various other particulars. Hence when he declared that a prophet has no honor in his own home, he was speaking out of a painful personal experience. Even Mary, in spite of her love for him and pride in him, could never quite understand him.

We see the first indication of this lack of understanding when Jesus as a lad went up to the Passover with Joseph and Mary. They lost him, and it was only after they had gone a day's journey that they missed him. Then they turned back in great anxiety to seek for him. When they found him in the temple, Mary asked with a tenderness that perhaps had in it a touch of impatience, if not of anger, "Why have you treated us like this?"

"Did you not know," came the reply of Jesus, "that I must be in my Father's house? You should have known where to find me since my first and supreme loyalty is not to you, but to God." Mary pondered all this in her heart, but she did not fully understand. Though she found her son and was privileged to have him with her after this for almost a score of years, yet there was a sense in which she failed to find him. Therefore she could never feel that he was altogether hers.

This lack of understanding seems to have persisted with the passing of the years. It shows up again at the wedding at Cana. Mary and Jesus were both present, though as we read between the lines it would seem that they did not come together. When the wine gave out, Mary said to Jesus, "They have no wine." His answer seems downright shocking. According to Moffatt he said: "Woman, what have you to do with me?" This word is not as rude as it sounds. Yet Jesus was telling Mary as tenderly as he could that his orders came from above. "Henceforth," he seems to say, "the index finger that points to the hour at which I am to act will be that of no human hand, but of my Father."

I think that this chasm that divided Jesus from his own grew wider still when he preached his first sermon in his home church. The whole family were doubtless in the synagogue that morning, keenly eager for their kinsman to make a good impression. Both their family pride and their faith were involved. When, therefore, they heard "the gracious words" that Jesus spoke, their hearts fairly sang. But soon all this music was changed into discord. As if seeking to be offensive, the preacher told his congregation that in the long ago when God needed a boarding place for one of his greatest prophets he could not find one among the Jews, but had to go to a woman who lived in the land of Jezebel. He told them further that though God was able and eager to heal lepers, the only man in the days of Elisha who had faith to be healed was an outsider named Naaman. At this affront the congregation was changed into an angry mob and the preacher into a fugitive. How the faces of James and

35

Joseph, of Simon and Jude, must have burned! How the heart of Mary must have broken!

Of course after this his devout brothers were prepared to give ear to almost any wild rumor. Those rumors were plentiful enough. One that persisted and that they found quite credible was that Jesus was really crazy. Therefore there was nothing for them to do but to go and bring him home, and thus spare themselves further shame. They had no trouble in locating him. They came upon a great multitude and learned that he was at the center of it. Being unable to come at him because of the crowd, they sent word that they with their mother were waiting for him. But instead of coming and talking the situation over, he refused even to see them. That was the last straw. There was nothing they could do but go home without him. Mary went along with them because she was almost as much perplexed as they.

At last black shadows began to gather. Angry threats were blown on almost every breeze. It seemed that death might be drawing near. It was then that Mary could endure her position no longer. She left her other sons, who as John tells us did not believe in their brother, and hurried to stand by her first-born. She still did not understand him. Many things he did grieved and perplexed her. But in spite of all this she loved him with a love stronger than death. Therefore we read, "There stood by the cross of Jesus his mother." She took her stand by the cross, even though she had, in a sense, to break with her other children in order to be there.

36

Jesus therefore entrusted his mother to his friend because his own loved ones were *not* present. Then he entrusted his mother to this disciple because he *was* present. This beloved friend was standing by. He was near in person because he was near in love and loyalty. Being thus in the danger zone, in the zone of shame and suffering, he was also, for that very reason, in the zone of usefulness. Our Lord is shut up to using those who are nearest to him. He is shut up to using those who are near enough to be willing to hear and obey his voice. There was a sense in which Mary had to go to the home of this beloved disciple. There was simply nowhere else for her to go.

Yet it was an unspeakable honor for this friend to be so trusted and so used. He had the privilege of doing for Jesus what Jesus could not do for himself. He had the privilege of taking the place of his Lord in the service of one whom he loved. In one sense his privilege was unique. In a profounder sense it belongs to every one of us. There is never a day in which we cannot represent our Lord. There is never a day in which we cannot do something for him by doing something for one whom he loves. All that is necessary in order for us to enter into this high privilege is our own willingness.

III

Here, then, are the last words of Jesus to the two he loved the best: "Behold thy son! . . . Behold thy mother!" Then what?

Prompt obedience. These two loving hearts yielded to the will of Jesus without question. We read that from that hour this friend took Mary to his own home. "From that hour" might mean as soon as the crucifixion was over. It might also mean that he acted at once. I like to believe that this latter was the case. If I am right, it would mean that this beloved disciple lived not too far from Calvary. It would mean further that Mary in going at once from the cross was spared the agony of witnessing the final hour. It would be so like Jesus to desire to spare her this. Having thus found shelter in the home of her adopted son, she waited in the fellowship of those whose hearts broke with her own, till the black shadows of that Friday gave place to the radiance of Easter morning.

"Suppose ye that I am come to give peace on earth? I tell you, Nay; but rather division." The Master is here speaking out of his own experience. He created division among his own people and in his own family. But I love to remember that division is not his final word. He is the great uniter. He divided his family only to bring them together into a closer fellowship. When we see Mary after Easter on her way to Pentecost, she has with her not just one son, but five. Her adopted son is with her; so also are James and Joseph, Simon and Jude (Acts 1:14). These have come to accept Jesus, not only as a brother, but also as Saviour and Lord.

IV

THE FOURTH WORD

"My God, my God, why hast thou forsaken me?"

MATTHEW 27:46

THIS IS THE FOURTH WORD THAT JESUS UTTERED FROM his cross. It stands at the center of the seven. It seems to me altogether fitting that it should be so, for here the tragedy of the crucifixion reached its climax. We may be sure of the genuineness of these words. They carry their credentials in their own hands. No writer of fiction would have put such an utterance upon the lips of his hero. No one painting a face like that of Jesus would have marred his canvas by such a seeming blemish. "My God, my God, why hast thou forsaken me?" I wonder what impression these words made upon those who first heard them.

I

What impression did they make upon Annas and company? Here were hard men who through envy and political trickery had deliberately brought about the crucifixion of Jesus. Having accomplished their purpose,

39

they would not even suffer their victim to die in peace. They stood about the cross and jeered. They claimed that they would be willing to obey him if he would only vindicate his sonship to God by coming down from the cross. "He trusts in God," they flung at him. "Let God deliver him now, if he delights in him." But God did not deliver him. Not only so, but Jesus seemed to take their side by declaring himself forsaken.

I wonder what impression these words made upon the friends of Jesus. There were not many friends present, but there was at least one who had to be present. He was nailed to a cross beside that of Jesus. I am thinking of that new disciple who in the maddest possible adventure of faith had asked Jesus to remember him when he should come in his kingdom. Jesus had answered his prayer with the calm assurance of God himself: "To day shalt thou be with me in paradise." But where was that assurance now? He who a while ago had been so confident of his ability to win through and to take his friend with him must now have seemed little more than a blind man undertaking to lead the blind.

I remember a story that I read as a boy. I think it was in one of McGuffey's readers. It told of a gentleman who one day attended a country church where he heard a venerable minister preach an impressive sermon on the crucifixion. The minister contrasted the death of Jesus with that of Socrates. Over and over he rang the changes on this word: "Socrates died like a philosopher; Jesus Christ died like a God."

40

But is this wild outcry the outcry of a God? By no means. I am happy to say that the minister was wrong. Jesus Christ did not die like a God. He died like a man. That is the very center of our hope.

II

Why did Jesus utter this bitter cry?

I think the simplest explanation is the one that is true. He uttered it because he felt himself forsaken. There was nothing of the actor about Jesus. He was always perfectly sincere. He was not fighting a sham battle. If this was a sham battle, then it has no meaning for us because our battles are very real. Jesus was here speaking out of a sense of desolation. He felt that he was treading the wine press alone.

Not only so, but he felt that his forsakenness was utter and complete. He had been forsaken before this hour by the religious leaders among his own people. He had been forsaken by his family. At last he had been forsaken by his friends. But he had foreseen this last tragedy and had fortified himself against it by the assurance of the divine presence. "The hour . . . is now come, that ye shall be scattered, every man to his own, and shall leave me alone: and yet I am not alone, because the Father is with me." But now the Father's face was hidden. Thus he felt forsaken of God and man.

It was in this feeling of being forsaken that the horror of the cross reached its climax. Here was "the crucifixion within the crucifixion." Jesus found forsakenness hard to bear because he was the most sensitive of men. He had a deep dread of loneliness. "Ye shall be scattered, every man to his own, and shall leave me alone: and yet I am not alone, because the Father is with me." No one would have said that except one who had a genuine horror of being left alone.

This loneliness was hard to bear, not only because Jesus was finely sensitive, but because it was in such sharp contrast to all that he had known before. It was so new in the experience of Jesus. A man who goes into the night from a brilliantly lighted room finds the darkness more depressing than if he went from a room lighted but dimly. Even so, no man misses the presence of God so much as one who has been keenly conscious of that presence through the years. Always God had been real to Jesus. Always he had been closer "than breathing, and nearer than hands and feet." But now that his Father's face was no longer seen, his heartache was by contrast all the sharper. After a day so full of brightness the darkness of this hour was all the blacker.

But that which brought this sense of forsakenness to its climax of bitterness was that it appeared to be without rhyme or reason. His suffering seemed for the moment so meaningless, so purposeless. We call this "The Cry of Dereliction." The word suggests a derelict ship. A derelict ship is one that has been abandoned. It has no captain. It has no crew. It has no compass. It has no cargo. It is bound for no port. Thus it has no meaning. Even so, for

42

That minister was right who, questioned by a bewildered father as to why God had let his son die a tragic death, answered that God was engaged in the same task when this man's son died that engaged him at the death of his own Son. He was in the midst of its black ugliness, sharing it and bringing out of it all possible good. The explanation of our fathers that God was here venting his wrath against sinners upon the sinless head of our Lord is an explanation that for us simply does not explain.

We find a further assurance that God had not forsaken Jesus in light of the fact he never forsakes anyone. Often we forsake him, but he never forsakes one of us, even the most hopeless rebel. When that foolish sheep had left the flock and had strayed into the wilds, the shepherd could not let it alone. He had to go seeking the silly creature until he found it. "God is like that," said Jesus. He never can stop until he finds us. Even when in our rebellion we enter the house of our own selfishness and slam the door in his face, he does not turn away. With unspeakable humility he still stands at the door and knocks. He never forsakes us however far we may go from him and however utterly we may rebel against him.

Therefore if God never forsakes one of his children, even the very worst, we may be sure that he did not forsake Jesus, whose one purpose in life had been to do the will of his Father. For God to have done so would have been utterly impossible. God has a character to support, even as you and I. When that psalmist of deep spiritual insight wrote, "He leadeth me in the paths of righteousness," he gave God's reason for so leading. That reason is not the one that I should have expected. He did not say, "He leadeth me because I am blind and ignorant." No more did he say, "He leadeth me because he knows that if I should go astray I might lead others astray." But here is the reason he gave: "He leadeth me in the paths of righteousness for his name's sake." God's character demands that he lead those who trust him in right paths till they come victoriously to a right goal.

Furthermore, for God to forsake one who trusted him would be to give the lie to every promise that the saints of the centuries have heard from his lips. The one characteristic of God which those who have ventured upon him are most sure of is his faithfulness. They declare with one voice that he will never let us down. They are convinced with a conviction born of experience that he can be depended upon to the uttermost. "I will never, never leave thee, nor forsake thee," is with them not a mere theory, but a tested fact. Cast down they often are, but forsaken never. This assurance of God's trustworthiness has sung its way through all the troubled centuries. Therefore we may be perfectly sure that the sinless Jesus was not forsaken upon the cross.

If we are right, how can we explain this sense of forsakenness? That Jesus felt forsaken is beyond question. I think it came about in part through his physical torture. Let us not forget that Jesus was a man. Let us not forget that he was just as human as we are. Many in our day have discovered afresh the terrible effect that torture may have upon the very strongest. Russia has demonstrated again and again through her cruel persecutions how even men of integrity and strength may be made to confess wrongs of which they know nothing. Torture weakens the whole man. Jesus had had to suffer terribly. He had endured four mock trials. He had been tried before Annas, Caiaphas, Herod, and Pilate. He had been crowned with thorns. He had been scourged. He had been now upon the cross for almost six hours. It is not surprising that this physical suffering had told in some measure upon his vivid sense of God. Any man who for long hours has felt pain walk with fire-shod feet along every nerve of his body knows how easy it is to lose a sense of the divine presence.

But the full reason why Jesus came to feel himself forsaken is, I repeat, beyond our human understanding. But of this much the writers of the New Testament are certain. Here on the cross Jesus was made "to be sin for us, who knew no sin." I think there is no doubt that our Lord recognized himself as the suffering servant of Jehovah. Here he was being wounded for our transgressions and bruised for our iniquities. "He saved others," his enemies shouted at him, "himself he cannot save." One hell from which he could not save himself and be our Saviour was this sense of forsakenness.

If this fact perplexes us, if it is beyond our understanding, it also gives us hope.

There was the Door to which I found no Key;
There was the Veil through which I might not see.

We too come to doors to which we find no key and veils through which we cannot see. The facile comfort given by those who have lived all their lives on the sunny side of the street may help little. In fact it may be positively irritating. But when we find one who has deeply suffered and has come through with a vital faith and a tender heart, to such we listen gladly. Here is one secret of the spell that our Lord casts over men. "In that he himself hath suffered being tempted, he is able to succour them that are tempted."

IV

Now what did Jesus do when his black hour was upon him?

He did not fall down in self-pity and give over the fight. No more did he declare in stubborn bitterness that he would see the hard ordeal through in his own strength. Instead he did what had been the habit of his life. He turned to God in prayer.

I know that this grim word is a question. It is, so far as the record goes, the only question that Jesus ever addressed to God. But that fact did not prevent it from being a prayer. It was a prayer offered in faith. It was offered with the conviction that God was still his very own. "My God," he prayed. As long as we can claim God as our very own, we cannot be utterly desolate.

47

Not only did Jesus pray in the faith that God was still his very own, but he prayed in the faith that God knew the answer to his perplexing question and that in his love he would give him the answer. So what? The God in whom he trusted did not let him down. He did not disappoint him. Having thus prayed, Jesus received an answer that enabled him to see the remainder of this crucifixion journey through with a quiet heart and with a serene mind. Having thus prayed, he was able to reach the end, not with a wail of despair, but with a shout of victory.

Here, then, is a word for every one of us. It is especially dear to those who have found life bewilderingly hard. Our Lord helps us by every word that he uttered from his cross. We can thank God for every one of them. But I am sure that there are many fine and sensitive and tortured souls who thank God for this word above all else, "My God, my God, why hast thou forsaken me?"

V

THE FIFTH WORD

"After this, Jesus knowing that all things were now accomplished, that the scripture might be fulfilled, saith, I thirst."

JOHN 19:28

I THIRST. JESUS DID NOT UTTER THIS WORD, AS A SUPER-ficial reading of the text might suggest, in order to fulfill the scriptures. Had such been the case, our Lord would have been little better than an actor, and he never put on an act. The assertion "that the scripture might be fulfilled" is the affirmation of a result rather than of a purpose. If Jesus did not utter this word to fulfill the scriptures, still less did he utter it as an appeal for pity. Jesus hated being pitied, as strong souls ever do. It was because of this hatred that he rebuked those women who sobbed over him as he journeyed to his cross. No more was this a grim bulletin announcing how the sufferer was faring as he did his last mile. Least of all was it a half-crazed cry that agony surprised from his unwilling lips.

Jesus was fully conscious of saying this word, as he

was of saying every other word that he spoke upon his cross. Indeed we may be certain that the principal reason for his refusing the medicated wine that was offered him before his crucifixion was that he might meet his ordeal intellectually alert and alive. He was determined to keep his faculties unbeclouded to the very end. This he did. Therefore Jesus knew exactly what he was saying when he cried, "I thirst."

In my opinion he was here once more engaged in prayer. But this prayer he offered, not to his Father, but to men. What is stranger still, he offered it to men who, either in cruel indifference or in vindictive hate, were making his last moments as bitter as possible. If this is a prayer, what an amazing prayer this is! It is also as beautiful as it is amazing.

I

Let us look at the beauty of this prayer.

1. It is beautiful in that it breathes a spirit of forgiveness. Some of us do not like to ask favors of anybody. But if we do have to ask favors, we desire to ask them only of those who are our friends. We certainly do not like to ask favors of those who have wronged us or who are hostile to us. The other day a father said to his son, who had become very much offended: "If you ever need my help, I will be glad to give it."

That son answered bitterly, "I would rather die of starvation than ask help from you."

50

Jesus was not like that. He was so forgiving that he was willing to ask a favor from even an enemy.

2. This prayer is beautiful in its humility. The man who was thus asking his enemies for a drink of water had been taunted for hours by having the fact of his weakness, his inability to save himself, flung into his face. Had Jesus been as proud as he was courageous, he would have died rather than confess that his enemies were right in affirming his human frailties. But he was not proud. Therefore he virtually took the side of his foes by confessing his need and throwing himself upon their generosity.

This was not the first time that Jesus had asked a drink of water from one who was not friendly: "There cometh a woman of Samaria to draw water: Jesus saith unto her, Give me to drink." But she looked at him with hard eyes and questioned, "How is it that thou being a Jew asketh drink of me, which am a woman of Samaria? for the Jews have no dealings with the Samaritans." Jesus answered, "If thou knewest the gift of God, and who it is that saith to thee, Give me to drink; thou wouldest have asked of him, and he would have given thee living water."

This was too much for the woman to believe. Therefore she asked him in amazement, "Art thou greater than our father Jacob, which gave us the well, and drank thereof himself, and his children, and his cattle?" "Infinitely greater," Jesus seemed to reply. "Whosoever drinketh of this water shall thirst again: ... but the water

51

that I shall give him shall be in him a well of water springing up into everlasting life."

Yet this man who claimed the ability to give an inward and unfailing spring was not too proud to ask for water at the soiled hands of an outcast woman or from the bloody hands of his murderers.

3. This prayer is beautiful in its faith in man even at his worst. In fact it reminds me of that trustful prayer that Martha and Mary offered for Lazarus, their sick brother. When they realized that this illness might prove serious, they did the most natural thing possible; they turned to Jesus, their wise and understanding friend. But in so doing they did not give him a blueprint of what he was to do. They simply told him, "He whom thou lovest is sick." It was their way of saying, "We know that you love our brother; we know that you love us. Therefore we leave our case in your hands with the firm faith that you will do what is wisest and best."

It was in somewhat similar fashion that Jesus prayed. He did not make his appeal to some single friendly face that he saw in the crowd. He did not point out the sponge, the reed, and the wine, and tell his helper what to do. He simply stated his need and left it there. It was a prayer, I repeat, akin to that of Martha and Mary, yet there was this wide difference: the two sisters were praying to one who was a friend, while Jesus was praying to those most of whom were even then howling with glee over his torture. He had a faith in God that nothing could kill, not even the cross. What is stranger still, he also had a deathless faith in men.

Without this amazing faith Jesus could never have become the world's Redeemer. The author of the letter to the Hebrews tells us that Christ "for the joy that was set before him endured the cross." He rejoiced in that grim instrument of torture because he was sure that his suffering would not be in vain. Knowing the human heart as he knew it, he never doubted that, lifted up from the earth, he would draw all men unto himself.

As this faith in man sent Jesus courageously to his task, even so it assisted him in performing that task. Such a faith is as needful for us as it was for our Lord. If we conclude with the cynic that the crooked can never be made straight, that conviction will tend to kill all earnest effort to help. Not only so, but even if we seek to help, our efforts are not likely to prove victorious. Generally speaking, the measure of a man's power to help his brother is the measure of the love in the heart of him and of the faith that he has that at last the good will win. Often, therefore, the very finest service that we can render our friends and our loved ones—husband, wife, and child—is just to believe in them. Here, then, is a prayer that Jesus offered in a spirit of forgiveness in humility and with a fine faith in men.

II

When did Jesus offer this prayer?

We find the answer in this twenty-eighth verse: "After

this, Jesus knowing that all things were now accomplished, that the scripture might be fulfilled, saith, I thirst."

That is, Jesus offered this prayer when the worst of his hard ordeal was behind him. When he came close to the end of his crucifixion journey, he became mindful of his own needs. We have a similar word in the Gospel of Matthew: "When he had fasted forty days and forty nights, he was afterward an hungred." During the days of his conflict Jesus was so absorbed in his battle with the tempter that he was not conscious of his hunger. It was only when the battle was over that he felt its gnawing pain.

An athlete in the course of an exciting game may receive a painful wound and be for the moment unconscious of it. But when the game has been played to the finish, then that wound will announce its presence. Some time ago I witnessed an all but fatal automobile accident. The driver of the car received a cut on the head that made his face red with blood. His wife and small boy were both knocked unconscious. Yet this man remained as cool and self-possessed as if nothing had happened. He telephoned for an ambulance. When it came, he rode with his wife and boy to the hospital sixty miles away. There he continued to be utterly free from nervousness till his loved ones were in bed and under the care of a physician. Then, knowing that he had done all he could, he went home and to bed for some much needed rest. But instead of resting he found himself in the grip of such a rigor as he had never known before. Even so Jesus had been so absorbed in other matters that he had not had time to think upon his own pain and upon his own needs.

First he had been concerned for those immediately about him. He had been concerned for those enemies for whom he had prayed. He had been concerned for the outlaw who had made his appeal to be remembered. He had been concerned about his bereaved mother. Jesus was bearing the burdens not only of those immediately about him, but of the whole world. Thus thinking upon others he had no time to think of himself. Many of those who are suffering today would forget much of their agony if they were to become deeply interested in the needs of others. It is wonderful how an effort to dry the tears of a neighbor will cleanse our own cheeks of their painful rain.

This fact gives us some insight into the nature of the sufferings of Jesus. His pain was not so much physical as mental and spiritual. It also gives us some small appreciation of the intensity of that agony. Death by crucifixion was about the most painful mode of torture that the fiendish ingenuity of man could contrive. That which brought this anguish to its climax was the burning thirst that it engendered through bloodletting. Hunger may be painful, but it is as starlight to sunlight in comparison to the pangs of thirst. Yet so great was his anguish of spirit that it was not till he had realized that all things were now accomplished that he prayed for water. Even the hot hell of thirst could not claim the attention of our Lord till he had won through. But having gained the victory, he was then eager to receive whatever help human hands could give. Hence he cried, "I thirst."

III

What came of this prayer?

Had I been present, perhaps in my cynicism I should have expected nothing to come of it. Yet I have to face this fact: Across the years I have sometimes been surprised at the lack of kindness on the part of some from whom I felt I had a right to expect it. But far more often I have been surprised by the kindness of others from whom I felt I had the right to expect nothing at all. How many times have strangers whose faces I had never seen before warmed my heart and made me half shamed by their unexpected kindness!

On a train the other day I saw an embarrassed little mother who was having a terrible time with a big yearling of a boy. The two were attracting the attention of everybody in the coach. I think almost everybody was sympathetic with the harassed mother, but nobody dared do anything about it. Yes, there was one exception. A husky chap who looked as if he might just have come from a wheat threshing took a hand. He bought some fruit and approached the bawling brat and said, "Here, put this down your neck." It was not very delicate language, but the howling yearling understood. He took the fruit and proceeded to put it down his neck, and there was a great calm. But what warmed my heart most was not the resulting quietness, but the kindness of the chap who took the mother's burden upon himself.

After Jesus had uttered this prayer for water, things continued for the moment just about as they had been before. The rabble still howled; a few were interested and sympathetic, but they did nothing about it. They only said, "Wait, let's see. Maybe that chap Elijah will come and help." But there was one man who simply could not take it. His kindness drove him into action. His action was immediate. He said, "This man is suffering intensely now. Not only so, but if I do not help him now, I can never help him because the end is very near." So we read of him that he ran.

Who was this soldier who served Jesus so beautifully in his last moments? Frankly we do not know his name. He was so busy doing his act of kindness that he failed to leave us his autograph. Yet I am sure that there is one place where his name is not forgotten. I am certain that it is recorded in the Lamb's Book of Life. Jesus was able to say to him a little later, with bold literalness, "I was thirsty and you gave me drink."

Now, if any of you have it in your hearts to envy this nameless soldier, I have for you this encouraging word. Such an opportunity is also yours even now. This is the case because Jesus is still on the cross. This episode on Calvary represents the eternal heartache of our Lord for the suffering of his people. He is still being crucified through the agony of those about us. If we have the heart to minister to them, we shall in no case lose our re-ward. One day Jesus will say to us, "I was thirsty, and ye gave me drink. . . . Inasmuch as ye have done it unto one of the least of these my brethren, ye have done it unto me." Man, what a chance!

VI

THE SIXTH WORD

"It is finished."

JOHN 19:30

FINISHED. THIS WORD SPOKEN BY OUR LORD AS HE HUNG on the nails might have been the saddest that ever fell from human lips. He might thus have been putting a bloody period to a life whose dearest dreams and holiest hopes had ended in utter failure.

In the far north at the foot of Mount McKinley a skeleton was found seated on the root of a tree. Just above was a finger carved in the bark, pointing down to the skeleton. Beside the finger were these words: "The end of the trail." They told the tragic story of one who had set out to climb that lofty mountain, but his strength had failed. He had died with his purpose unrealized.

Even so, by this word "finished" Jesus might have meant simply that he himself had reached the end of his trail. He might have thus been saying, "I am through. I have gone my limit, having won nothing but shame and defeat and death." But this word is not in reality a wail of despair. On the contrary it is a shout of triumph. It was uttered in the thrill of an irrepressible joy.

59

I

What is the secret of the joy that caused Jesus to speak this word?

He was not here rejoicing, as some have hinted, merely because he had reached the end of his earthly journey. Jesus was a normal man. He was a healthy man. As such he enjoyed the life that now is. As such he had a normal man's clinging to life. He was not so constantly homesick for his Father's house that he found no gladness in this present world. Those who call the here and now a "vale of tears," those who make

> Earth is a desert drear,
> Heav'n is my home,

their theme song, certainly do not agree with Jesus. As God called this world good on the day of creation, so Jesus thought of life as good.

That our Lord found this present life joyous is evident to any candid reader of the New Testament. He had certain gladsome words upon his lips again and again. One of them was this: "Be of good cheer." How futile it would have been for Jesus to have spoken in this fashion to troubled and perplexed men had his own face been black with despair. Another word was "blessed." "Oh, the blessedness, the gladness of the merciful," he shouted. "Oh, the joy of the meek, the happiness of the pure in heart." Jesus lived these beatitudes before they became articulate upon his lips. He knew through his own experience the joy that they express. I am not forgetting that he was "a man of sorrows, and acquainted with grief." But that fact did not prevent his being anointed with the oil of gladness above his fellows. It is my conviction that his was the sunniest face that ever looked out on this world and his the gladdest heart that ever beat in a human's bosom.

We can believe this, not only because of the New Testament record, but because it makes excellent sense. Jesus lived a consecrated life. He lived a life completely dedicated to the will of God. If I were to become convinced that the more completely one gave himself to God, the more miserable one would become, it would be very difficult for me to believe in God at all. Since Jesus lived a perfectly dedicated life, it was only natural that he should be the most joyous of men. He was joyous, not only during the springtime of his ministry when it looked as if victory was going to be easy; he was joyous to the very end. When the clouds gathered and he bowed with his disciples for their last prayer together, that prayer had in it this petition: "That they might have my joy fulfilled in themselves."

Since Jesus found life so joyous, it is very natural that he was not eager to leave it. He shrank from the ordeal of death, even as you and I.

For who, to dumb forgetfulness a prey,
This pleasing anxious being e'er resign'd,

61

Left the warm precincts of the cheerful day,
Nor cast one longing, ling'ring look behind?

Jesus therefore was not rejoicing simply because he had reached the end of his earthly journey. He loved life, and lived it with a glad and gallant heart.

The joy of Jesus was the joy of a man who had completed a task of supreme worth. He had not merely brought this task to an end; he had finished it. His victory was not partial, as is always the case with ours. The picture that he had painted was one to which he would not have added a single stroke. It was a picture from which he would have erased nothing. Just as Jesus a few hours before had said to the Father, "I have finished the work which thou gavest me to do," even so he was now shouting that same triumphant word from his cross. He was rejoicing over the finishing of the greatest of all tasks.

II

What was this task that Jesus had finished? What had our Lord come to do? To this question the Gospels give more than one answer. Look at a few of them.

1. "The Son of man is come to seek and to save that which was lost." He claimed that as a good physician he had come to attend, not those who were well, but those who were ill. He had come to save all the lost of the whole world. He had come to fulfill the sermon of the

angelic minister: "For unto you is born this day . . . ,
a Saviour, which is Christ the Lord."

2. "I am come that they might have life, and that they
might have it more abundantly." As we turn the pages
of the New Testament, we cannot help seeing that Jesus
fairly cast a spell over the men of his day. One secret of
that spell was that they found him so vital. He was beautifully alive. Again and again they came to him to ask him
about life. One day a young aristocrat dared in the face
of the crowd to kneel at his feet to put his question:
"What shall I do that I may inherit eternal life?" "I want
a quality of life," he seems to say, "that will be good today and good tomorrow and good to the end of time and
good to the end of eternity. How can I find it?" Jesus
knew the answer and gave it. He came that we might
have life.

3. Jesus came in quest of a kingdom. He came to build
men into a brotherhood. He came that we might say of
men and nations what Luke said of the saints after Pentecost: "The multitude of them that believed were of one
heart and of one soul." He declared that this brotherliness
was the hallmark of vital Christianity. "By this shall all
men know that ye are my disciples, if ye have love one
to another." He came to build a kingdom of right relations. He came to bring about that high consummation,
the doing of the will of God on earth, even as it is done
in heaven.

4. The all-inclusive reason for which Jesus came was
to reveal God. "No man hath seen God at any time; the

only begotten Son, which is in the bosom of the Father, he hath declared him." It was to make God known that Jesus came. Therefore if we desire to know what God is like, we can find our answer in Jesus. Nor could we possibly imagine a more satisfying answer. When Paul sought to say the best that he could say about God, he said that he was the Father of our Lord Jesus Christ. That is, God is like Jesus. Jesus revealed God by what he did upon the cross. Here on Calvary we see God's supreme revelation of himself.

III

Certain of our fathers used to call this "the finished work of Christ." In what sense were they correct?

Our Lord's work was not finished in the sense that in suffering love he is no longer seeking to save that which is lost. This tragedy on Calvary is a historic event that took place at a certain date on the calendar. But it is far more. It is a revelation of the eternal heartache of God for his children. It is a picture of what our Lord has suffered and does suffer and will continue to suffer till he finds and brings to his fold the sheep that have gone astray. But Christ's work is finished in that here on this skull-shaped hill he has given a revelation of suffering love that is final and ultimate. Beyond this not even the Son of God can go.

It is also easy to treat this finished work in a trite and wooden fashion as it applies to us. "Jesus Paid It All" holds in its hands a great and comforting truth. It may voice the glad faith of those who, having freely received, are eager freely to give. But it may also be the song of those who are too grasping to give either of their substance or of themselves. This word, "the finished work of Christ," is not out of harmony with Paul's admonition, "Work out your own salvation with fear and trembling." No more does it contradict that strong boast, "I . . . fill up that which is behind of the afflictions of Christ in my flesh."

What did Paul mean by this latter word? He did not mean that this suffering of our Lord on Calvary was incomplete or inadequate. He was simply affirming that a sacrificial Saviour must have a sacrificial minister to proclaim him adequately. He was saying that a Christ who has given himself to the uttermost must have a disciple who will give himself to the uttermost if that disciple is to achieve his highest usefulness. He is asserting with a fellow apostle, "He laid down his life for us: and we ought to lay down our lives for the brethren."

> Love so amazing, so divine,
> Demands my soul, my life, my all.

IV

"Finished." Since God through Christ has made, and is making, perfect provision for the salvation of all men, what are we to do?

We must face the fact that the realization of that salvation waits upon our co-operation. My father was a farmer. He was a Christian farmer. But the fact that he was a Christian did not mean that when the springtime came he prayed God to turn the soil and to sow wheat in one field and to plant corn in another. He prayed me to do that. He was wise enough to know that in spite of God's provision, both he and his family would starve if he refused to do his part.

It is certainly the will of God that we should have a peaceful and brotherly world. God has made provision for such a world, but he cannot realize his holy purpose without our co-operation. He is eager for a church that shall indeed be a glorious church without spot or blemish, but he cannot have such a church without our help. He longs with the very passion of Calvary that you and I shall be Christlike, that the beauty of the Lord shall rest upon us as the sunshine rests upon the hills. He has made provision for such Christlikeness, but that provision will go for nothing if we fail to do our part.

What, then, I repeat, are we to do? We are to bear in mind that our Lord is saying to us what he said to his friends in the long ago, "This is my body; this is myself, given for you and to you." Since this is true, we are to receive him as a gift. We are to do this in the realization that by so doing we receive power to become sons of God. Having thus received power to become, we also receive power to serve.

Hudson Taylor tells us that one holiday when he was a youth in his teens he was left alone. Time hung rather heavily on his hands. Therefore he hunted for something to read. He found a tract in which he was interested only because he knew there would be a story in it. But as he read this tract, he came for the first time upon this word, "the finished work of Christ." It laid hold of his youthful heart. "Then there dawned upon me the conviction," he writes, "that there was nothing for me to do but fall upon my knees, accept the Savior, and praise him for evermore."

In so saying, Hudson Taylor spoke a great truth. But of course he was the furthest possible from affirming that having accepted Christ there was nothing else for him to do. The amazing work that he accomplished is sufficient answer to that. He was only declaring with the saints of the centuries that salvation is not something to be earned, but a gift to be received. "The wages of sin is death; but the gift of God is eternal life." This eternal life is nothing less than God through Christ giving himself. Our Lord does not save us and then give himself. He saves by the giving of himself. We can be saved in no other way. We might be able to find reformation in our own strength, but we can be transformed only by receiving Jesus Christ and permitting him to transform us from within.

Here, then, in this finished work of Christ is the answer to our supreme needs and to our deepest longings. For to receive him is to find satisfaction for the thirsts of the soul. Not only so, but it is also to find satisfaction for our longing to serve. Everybody wants to count. "The sense of uselessness is the greatest shock that can come to a living organism." But by receiving Christ we find our

67

highest usefulness. "He that believeth on me . . . out of his [inner life] shall flow rivers of living water." Therefore since our Lord is inviting us to come to him and to receive his best, we ought to answer with joyful confidence,

> Just as I am, without one plea,
> But that thy blood was shed for me,
> And that thou bidd'st me come to thee,
> O Lamb of God, I come, I come!

VII

THE SEVENTH WORD

"Father, into thy hands I commend my spirit."

LUKE 23:46

I

FATHER, INTO THY HANDS I COMMEND MY SPIRIT. THIS IS the final word that our Lord uttered from his cross. Not only does this word tell us how Jesus died, but it also tells us how he lived. Charles Lamb wrote of a friend: "Who parted this life on Wednesday evening; dying as he had lived, without much trouble." What Lamb said of his friend is true of mankind in general. As a rule men die as they live. There is nothing in the mere act of passing that makes a bad man good, or a good man bad. Generally we die as we live. So it was with Jesus.

I was reading some years ago of a man who made himself famous in the restaurant business. He established restaurants all the way across our continent. When at last he reached the end of his earthly journey, those nearest to him gathered about his bed to hear his final words. When they bent over him to catch his last whisper, it was this: "Slice the ham thin." There was nothing necessarily

69

wicked about such a final word. It means only that his ruling passion was strong in death.

Not so long ago I was called to see a man who was desperately ill. Though he had largely wasted his substance in riotous living, when he realized that he was coming close to the end, he called for a minister. I went and, in the language of John Wesley, "offered him Christ." Not only so, but I believe that despite the lateness of the hour that offer was accepted. He seemed to receive it with joy, and his loved ones who stood about the bed rejoiced with him. But when a little later he became unconscious and then slipped away, his last word was not a prayer, but an oath. Of course he did not know what he was saying. But so long had he schooled his tongue in the language of blasphemy that he swore spontaneously. Generally speaking, I repeat, we die as we live.

As this is true on the dark side, so it is on the bright. I heard Dr. Edwin McNeill Poteat tell this bit about the home-going of his saintly father, who was also an able minister of the gospel. When this good man realized that he was close to the sunset, he called Edwin McNeill to his bedside and told him of his coming exodus. Then he requested of his son that he conduct his funeral services. "I realize," he continued, "that I am giving you a rather difficult assignment. But," he added, "if you will conduct my services this time, I promise never to ask you to do it again." I like that. So long had this saintly man lived in the fellowship of his Lord that he could even face death with a twinkle in his eye. Thus he died as he lived, in joyful confidence.

II

"Father, into thy hands I commend my spirit." As this word sums up the death of Jesus, so, I repeat, it sums up his life. As his robe was woven of one piece, so also his life was of one piece. There was no break between his living and his home-going. To be convinced of this we need only to turn afresh to the pages of the New Testament. Here we see that what Jesus did in his final moments he had been doing throughout the years.

1. In this word, "Father, into thy hands I commend my spirit," Jesus is quoting from the thirty-first psalm. In his final hour he turned to the hymnbook of his people. But this turning to the scriptures was nothing new in the life of our Lord. This was not the first time since he had come to the cross that he made use of this book. His cry of dereliction, though so fully his own that we tend to forget that it was first uttered by lesser lips, is also a quotation from the Psalms. In fact our Lord had so saturated his mind and heart with the Bible that both its thought and its language became his own.

For instance, when people came to him with questions, he would often ask, "Have ye not read?" or, "How readest thou?" When a certain lawyer asked him to tell what was the supreme commandment, Jesus did not express an opinion of his own; he simply referred his questioner to the Old Testament. On another occasion the Sad-

71

ducees, who did not believe in the resurrection, and who accepted only the first five books of the Bible, came to him with this rather comical story: There were seven brothers who, from the oldest to the youngest, had consecutively married a certain woman. Now, since they all married her, this was the question: If there is a resurrection, whose wife is she going to be? Personally, I have never felt that there would be any great contest for her. But that is not the point. The point is that Jesus answered that part of their story that had to do with the resurrection with a quotation from the book of Exodus.

As Jesus used the Bible for the instruction of others, even so he made use of it in the living of his own life. When I visited Mount Vernon, I was interested in the sword with which Washington armed himself during the Revolutionary War. The Old Testament was the sword of the Spirit with which Jesus fought his battles. Every onslaught of the enemy during his struggle in the wilderness he repelled by a thrust of this keen blade. It was only natural, therefore, that Jesus in his last hour should turn afresh to the book that had been his constant companion through his entire life. There was about it a beautiful spontaneity.

2. This word is a prayer. Jesus did not use the exact words of the scriptures. He added one word of his own. That was "Father." As our Lord had made a habit of saturating his mind with the Bible, so he had made a habit of prayer. He had taught men to pray by what he said. He had taught them also by what he did. In fact if we

take the Gospels as our guide, we discover that the only work that ever really taxed the energies of Jesus was the work of prayer. After he prayed, everything else seemed to come as a matter of course. From the place of prayer he went as a victor to receive the spoils of his conquest. Having thus practiced prayer day by day, Jesus found it perfectly natural to pray as he reached the end of his journey.

3. This prayer was an act of dedication. It was a committal. Moffatt gives this translation: "I trust my spirit to thy hands." This committal of himself to God was also a habit of Jesus. His Bible reading and prayer helped to this end. "I consecrate myself," is a part of the last prayer that he prayed with his disciples. Always he could say, "The Father hath not left me alone because I do always the things that please him." After he had made the commitment of himself to his Father a fixed habit of his life, it was only natural for him to fall asleep with this prayer upon his lips, "Father, into thy hands I commend my spirit."

III

"Father, into thy hands I commend my spirit." As these words sum up what both life and death meant to Jesus, they also sum up what they ought to mean to us. If we make this committal to God the habit of our lives, then we may be sure that such habit will stand us in good stead, both when we are in the thick of the fight and when we come to the end of our earthly journey. "I trust my spirit to thy hands." This is the whole meaning of our Christian religion. This is the least we can do and be Christian at all. It is the most we can do, either in time or in eternity.

1. Committal is the doorway into the kingdom. How do we become Christians? Our experiences are varied since God is a God of variety. We do not all react in the same fashion. But there are characteristics of conversion that are common to all of us. They are obedience, surrender, dedication. We enter by the door of commitment because there is none other.

Take Paul, for instance. When we read these thrilling words: "I saw in the way a light from heaven, above the brightness of the sun, shining round about me and them which journeyed with me," we say, "Of course Paul was converted after an experience like that. If I were to see such splendor in my sky, I too would be converted." But this would not necessarily be the case.

Paul might have gone from the brightness of the light of this vision into a deeper darkness than he had ever known before. This vision no more saved Paul than the sight of a laughing spring would save a man who was dying of thirst. Before the thirsty man can be saved, he must kiss the spring on the lips. Before Paul could be saved, he had to obey. He sums up his secret in one single sentence: "I was not disobedient unto the heavenly vision." The great apostle therefore entered the kingdom through the door of committal.

There was another apostle whose conversion was just

as real as that of Paul. Yet how commonplace his story seems! "As Jesus passed . . . , he saw a man, named Matthew, sitting at the receipt of custom: and he saith unto him, Follow me." Then what? We read the answer in this simple sentence: "And he arose, and followed him." Did he pray? Did he laugh? Did he sob? Did he shout and sing? We are not told. We are told only that he obeyed. He made a committal of himself. Thus he entered the kingdom.

That is the door that we must enter, for there is none other. Here was a lovely young aristocrat who was a far finer man than Matthew. He had almost everything in his favor. He was clean, courageous, and religious. Yet when Jesus gave him the same invitation that he gave to Matthew, when he said, "Follow me," the young ruler did not make the same response. Instead we read of him this tragic word, "He went away." He missed entering the kingdom, not because he was bad, but because he refused to make a committal of himself.

2. Not only is obedience the door into the kingdom, but it is the life of the kingdom. When the author of the book of Genesis undertakes to tell us what life meant to Enoch, he puts it in a single sentence: "Enoch walked with God." One day Enoch stretched a groping hand into the encircling gloom, and that almighty hand that is always feeling for yours and mine in the daylight and dark found the hand of Enoch, and he thus became acquainted with God. After he met God, nothing else seemed quite so worth while as to walk with him. But

how did this acquaintance ripen into friendship? The writer to the Hebrews answers that question: "He had this testimony, that he pleased God." That is, he walked with God through daily obedience.

So it was with Paul. When he first met Jesus, he surrendered to him. He died to his own will and to his own way. But that one death was not enough. Paul affirms, "I die daily." Every day he died afresh. He died to his own plans and purposes that he might make his own the plans and purposes of his Lord. It was this daily dying that enabled him to pass from the "these things" of his conversion to the "those things" of an ever-growing Christian experience.

3. "Father, I trust my spirit to thy hands." This is what the Bible means by perfection. If it is the least I can do and be a Christian, it is also the most I can do either in time or in eternity. In fact, if I do this, nothing else is required. This puts us all on an equal footing. There are a thousand things that you can do that I cannot. I can do some things that you cannot. But we can all do God's best. We can give ourselves to him. That is not only good, in the mind of our Lord; it is perfection.

IV

"Father, I trust my spirit to thy hands." Since this is all God asks of us, what ought we to do about it?

1. We ought to make full committal of ourselves in the here and now. We are to make this committal not because it is a small and easy matter. When Paul beseeches us to

present our bodies, our very selves, to God, he does not encourage us to do this because it will cost us nothing. On the contrary, it will cost us everything. We are to give in the faith that what we give he will accept. Let us therefore give ourselves to God with the assurance that he will gladly accept us.

2. Let us dedicate ourselves to God in the faith that what he accepts he remakes. I read of a great artist who was spending a few days in a humble home. It so happened that while he was a guest the little girl of the family had a birthday. Among the presents she received was a silk fan. It was a fairly ordinary affair, but when she showed it to the artist he said, "If you will let me keep this for a little while, I will paint you a picture on it."

But she snatched it away, saying, "You shan't spoil my fan."

If she had only trusted him, he would have given it back with its beauty and worth increased a thousandfold. Give yourself to God, and more and more he will transform you into the image of his glory.

3. Give yourself to God, and he will use you. He may not always use you in the way of your own choosing. He may not always lead you in green pastures beside still waters. He will not always use you in a fashion to make you comfortable. In using his own Son in the finest possible fashion he could not permit him to by-pass Calvary. As he uses you, you may become increasingly acquainted with the Cross. But use you he will.

4. Finally, if you give yourself to God, not only will

77

he accept, transform, and use you, but he will walk with you to the very end. I am quite sure that the Good Shepherd who has been with his sheep during the sunny days will not leave them at nightfall when they need him most. I have no slightest envy of the man who is master of his fate and captain of his soul. I have no desire to venture into life alone, nor do I dare face eternity alone. But if I pray with my Lord this prayer, "I trust my spirit to thy hands," I can face both today and tomorrow without fear.

INDEX OF SCRIPTURE TEXTS

The first number in the page reference is the volume number:

The second is the page number in that volume. Thus a sermon on the text Matthew 5:3 may be found in book 1, *The Sermon on the Mount,* beginning on page 9.

INDEX